THE GREAT BETRAYAL

"Crimson Ties of Empire"
(DAVID LOW, *Evening Standard*, 26 January 1942)

David Day

THE GREAT BETRAYAL

Britain, Australia
& the Onset of the Pacific War
1939-42

W · W · NORTON & COMPANY
New York   London

Published simultaneously in Canada by Penguin Books Canada Ltd.,
2801 John Street, Markham, Ontario L3R 1B4
Printed in the United States of America.

First published by Angus & Robertson Publishers in Australia and in the
United Kingdom in 1988. This edition published by arrangement with
Angus & Robertson Publishers, Sydney, Australia.

Library of Congress Cataloging-in-Publication Data

Day, David, 1949-
The great betrayal: Britain, Australia & the onset of the
Pacific War, 1939-42/David Day.
p.   cm.
Bibliography: p.
Includes index.
1. World War, 1939-1945—Diplomatic history. 2. Australia—Foreign
relations—Great Britain. 3. Great Britain—Foreign relations—Australia.
I. Title.
D748.D38   1989
940.54'0994—dc19   88-37238

ISBN 0-393-02685-X

W. W. Norton & Company, Inc., 500 Fifth Avenue, New York, N.Y. 10110
W. W. Norton & Company Ltd., 37 Great Russell Street, London WC1B 3NU

1 2 3 4 5 6 7 8 9 0

CONTENTS

Acknowledgements

Many people and organisations assisted to make this work possible. The Master and Fellows of Churchill College provided a congenial working environment for myself and my family during the first three years of my research. In 1985, Clare College kindly took over this role, awarding me a research fellowship and supplying a stimulating atmosphere for historical research, for which I have much to thank the Master, Fellows and students. It was there that this book was written.

The Managers of the Smuts Fund were generous with their assistance, helping to finance research trips to London and Australia. Richard Walsh, then Publisher of Angus and Robertson Publishers, provided generous support at a crucial time. Professor David Fieldhouse was all that a supervisor should be and much more. My Ph.D. examiners, Professor Tom Millar of the Australian Studies Centre, London University, and Dr David Reynolds of Christ's College, Cambridge, provided many helpful comments on this book in its earlier form. My wife, Silvia, read through several drafts and was able to provide valuable comments on its style and content. Others who helped to shape this work include Professor Geoffrey Bolton and Dr John McCarthy. Norman Rowe and Jill Wayment of Angus and Robertson Publishers, along with my copy editor, Alex Gray, combined to point out various errors of fact and expression. Any that remain are my responsibility.

For permission to quote from their books and other published sources, thanks are due to the following publishers: Leo Cooper for Brian Bond (ed.), *Chief of Staff*, vol. 2; extracts from Martin Gilbert's *Finest Hour* and *Road to Victory* are reprinted by kind permission of Curtis Brown Ltd on behalf of C & T Publications Ltd, ©1983 C & T Publications, ©1986 C & T Publications; Hodder and Stoughton for Sir John Colville's *The Fringes of Power*; Century Hutchinson Ltd for Major General Sir John Kennedy's *The Business of War*; the

Department of Foreign Affairs for *Documents on Australian Foreign Policy*, vols. 2–5; Cassell Ltd for David Dilks (ed.), *The Diaries of Sir Alexander Cadogan*; Collins Publishers for Sir Harold Nicolson's *Diaries and Letters*, vol. 2; Sidgwick and Jackson for Cecil King's *With Malice Toward None*; Angus and Robertson Publishers for Sir Earle Page's *Truant Surgeon*; the Australian War Memorial for Paul Hasluck's *The Government and the People*; Constable Publishers for Lord Moran's *Winston Churchill: The Struggle for Survival* and R. G. Casey's *Personal Experience*; Longman Cheshire for R. G. Casey's *Double or Quit*; the *Herald*, Melbourne; and the *Daily Telegraph*, Sydney.

For permission to quote from private papers, I should like to thank the following individuals and organisations: the Record Office in the House of Lords for the Beaverbrook Papers; David Higham Associates Ltd for the diaries of Sir Alexander Cadogan held in Churchill Archives Centre; Mrs MacGowan for the papers of Lord Casey; the British Library of Political and Economic Science for the Dalton diaries; Admiral Sir William Davis for permission to quote from his memoirs; David Edwards for the diaries of his father, Admiral Sir Ralph Edwards; F. H. Eggleston for the papers of Sir Frederic Eggleston; quotations of Crown-copyright records in the India Office Records and elsewhere appear by permission of the Controller of Her Majesty's Stationery Office; the Trustees of the Liddell Hart Centre for Military Archives and the Ismay family for the Ismay and Brooke-Popham papers; Mrs Henderson for the papers of Sir Robert Menzies; the Public Archives of Canada for the diaries of W. L. Mackenzie King; Lady Page for the papers of Sir Earle Page; the Public Record Office at Kew for permission to quote from Crown-copyright material in its custody; the University of Melbourne Archives for the papers of W. S. Robinson; Lady Seymour for the papers of Sir Horace Seymour; Commander Somerville for the papers of Admiral Somerville; Sir Alan Watt for his papers in the National Library of Australia; Rupert Wilkinson for Gerald Wilkinson's war journal; and Lady Willis for the papers of Admiral Willis. Parts of Chapters 13 and 14 first appeared in *Historical Studies* and I thank that journal's editor, Dr Stuart Macintyre, for permission to reproduce them here. If there are any other copyright holders whom I have inadvertently overlooked or have been unable to contact, I trust they will accept this apology.

Lastly, I would like to record a more personal appreciation for my wife, Silvia, and children, Michael, Emily and Kelly, who all helped to keep me going during this long labour. Also, without the initial and continuing support and confidence of my parents, this work would not have been possible and it is to them that it is affectionately dedicated.

DAVID DAY

ABBREVIATIONS

AA	Australian Archives, Canberra
AIF	Australian Imperial Force
AIIA	Australian Institute of International Affairs
AMF	Australian Military Forces
ANIB	Australian News and Information Bureau
AWC	Advisory War Council
BBC	British Broadcasting Corporation
BL	British Library, London
CAS	Chief of the Air Staff
CC	Churchill College Archives Centre, Cambridge
CGS	Chief of the General Staff
CUL	Cambridge University Library
DAFP	*Documents on Australian Foreign Policy 1939–49,* R. G. Neal et al., vols 1–6, Canberra
EATS	Empire Air Training Scheme
FUL	Flinders University Library, Adelaide
HLRO	House of Lords Record Office, London
HMG	His Majesty's Government
IOL	India Office Library
IWM	Imperial War Museum, London
KC	Liddell Hart Centre for Military Archives, King's College, London
LSE	London School of Economics
Menzies Diary	1941 Trip Diary, MS4936/13/3, Menzies Papers: NLA
NEI	Netherlands East Indies
NLA	National Library of Australia, Canberra
NMM	National Maritime Museum, Greenwich
PRO	Public Record Office, London
RAAF	Royal Australian Air Force
RAN	Royal Australian Navy
RN	Royal Navy
UAP	United Australia Party
UMA	University of Melbourne Archives

THE GREAT BETRAYAL

1

Introduction

The Colonial Mentality of the 1930s

*I*n December 1941, the Japanese navy attacked British and American possessions throughout the Pacific, establishing a new order in Asia and the Pacific with a series of quick and masterful strokes. Britain was left floundering in their wake as the ships of the Japanese navy laid down a daring challenge to the most powerful nations of the world. Australia, one of Britain's Dominions in the Pacific, was practically defenceless in the path of the Japanese onslaught. At this most critical point, Britain chose to concentrate her resources in the struggle against Germany and Italy rather than fulfil her Imperial defence guarantees in the Far East. This book examines Anglo−Australian relations against the background of this developing strategic dilemma and its ultimate resolution under the impact of Japanese militarism.

During the 1930s Anglo−Australian relations were dominated by the twin issues of economic and military security. As Australia's traditional protector, Britain held herself out as providing the answer to both problems and, in her sense of heightened insecurity, Australia was all too ready to believe in a British solution. Australian options were severely circumscribed by her membership of the British Empire and such was the extent of her dependence on Britain that she slipped into a position of increasing peril in the Pacific.

By 1930, Australia, having been a self-governing unity for three decades and being geographically isolated from Britain, might have been expected to be less attached to her former colonial master. However, it was not as "master" but as "mother" country that Britain was regarded by Australia. And it was the very distance from Britain and its antithesis, the proximity to Asia, that ensured Australia's tenacious hold on the bonds of Empire.

From our distant post-war vantage point, it is easy to miss an essential fact about inter-war Australian society — that there was an underdeveloped sense of Australian nationality caused by the country's incorporation within a wider and very powerful Empire. Most Australians were probably far from clear whether their primary allegiance lay with Australia or Britain. Moreover, they would have denied any conflict between the two, believing that it was perfectly possible to be both British and Australian in the same way as modern-day Queenslanders or Victorians divide their allegiance between their State and their nation. This sense of dual allegiance was fostered by the continuing importance of British-born Australians as a proportion of the Australian population. Even though the great majority of Australians were native-born by the 1930s, many were brought up by British-born parents. The idea that Britain was "home" was a long time dying in the harsh climate of the distant Dominion.

A glance at the Commonwealth *Year Book* for 1939 provides confirmation of the British basis to the Australian population. Reporting the results of the 1933 census, the official statistician noted a rise in the proportion of native-born Australians in the population to 86.3 per cent (up from 84.5 per cent in 1921). Those born in the British Isles represented 10.7 per cent of the population (down from 12.4 per cent in 1921). If those born in Britain are added to those Australians whose parents were born in Britain, the total would become much greater, although no such breakdown was provided in the figures. What the statistician did do was to classify Australians by nationality or allegiance, dividing the population into "British" and "Foreign". The overwhelming proportion of the population were classified as "British", the statistician noting that Australians were "fundamentally British in race and nationality", that they had the "essential characteristics of their British ancestors, with perhaps some accentuation of the desire for freedom from restraint".[1]

While the great majority of British-born Australians could be counted upon to provide a solid counterweight to the gradual development of Australian nationalism, they were ably assisted in this endeavour by the many second, third and fourth generation Australians whose allegiance to Britain and her Empire remained undimmed by time, distance or immediate ancestry. The epitome of this was R. G. Menzies, Australia's most notable political figure of the twentieth century, the son of native-born Australians who nevertheless developed such an abiding attachment to Britain and her institutions that it provided the core of his existence throughout his long life.

The sense of racial identification was fundamental to the continuing Australian attachment to Britain. The White Australia Policy was one of the first pieces of legislation enacted by the newly federated colonies in 1901 and it continued to receive unquestioned and vigorous support from all Australian political parties. It effectively excluded non-white immigrants from Australia, retaining the vast and sparsely populated continent as a white-dominated country within the surrounding and much more populated Asian region. The British connection allowed Australians to surmount this sea of coloured faces that they found so threatening and to reach out for the maternal hand of the country from which they had originally sprung. This reassuring British hand ensured that the immigration barrier erected by the White Australia Policy would stay firmly in place.

In theory, the constitutional framework of the British Empire by 1931 allowed for the almost complete independence of the Dominions. Under the Statute of Westminster of that year, Dominion laws could no longer be rejected on the basis that they conflicted with those of Britain. Dominions were empowered to legislate with extra-territorial effect and were given full legislative power to deal with matters of Dominion concern. In effect, their status as independent countries was officially acknowledged. However, along with New Zealand and Newfoundland, Australia deferred the adoption of the enabling legislation, the Statute of Westminster, preferring to remain in a state of formal dependence. The Labor Prime Minister J. H. Scullin described the Statute as being of "little importance" and refused to introduce it.[2]

Scullin's astute rejection of the Statute was recognition that, unlike South Africa and Canada, the Australian electorate would not approve of politicians who argued for Australia's independence from Britain. In fact, any hint of loosening the British lifeline was anathema to the electorate of the sparsely populated and poorly defended Dominion. By not adopting the Statute, Australia was denying to herself certain practical benefits, particularly in the areas of shipping and trade. Even the arch-Imperialist R. G. Menzies was forced to acknowledge its value.

However, it faced strong opposition from MPs worried that it might "give some support to the idea of separatism from Great Britain".[3]

Though in hindsight the approach of war seems to have dominated the 1930s, economic problems also loomed large. The decade was marked by the usual Australian attempts to obtain guaranteed access to the British market for their primary products and by the equally usual British attempts both to retain and increase their share of the Australian market in manufactured goods. For Britain, the Empire was seen as a means of halting her post-war economic decline and of insulating herself from the effects of the Depression.

In Britain's scheme of things, the Empire was to operate as a self-sufficient organism with the Dominions and colonies in symbiotic relationship to the mother country.[4] Britain would exchange industrial goods for cheap primary products from her Empire. This required the Dominions to remain underdeveloped, concentrating on their role as suppliers of food and raw materials. Though there was no British master plan for the economic subordination of the Empire, British officials tended to have such a theory as an ideal and their policies usually had the practical effect of creating subordination.

The size of the British market inevitably helped to reduce the supposedly interdependent relationship of Empire to one of great dependence by the Dominions upon Britain. In the context of the 1930s, with closed trading blocs and high tariff barriers, the Dominions had little alternative to selling the bulk of their produce to Britain, thereby greatly reducing Dominion bargaining power, especially as Britain often had access to non-Imperial, and often cheaper, alternative sources of food and raw materials. Even in 1938, six years after Empire preference schemes were introduced on a large scale, Britain was drawing on non-Empire sources for sixty-one per cent of its imports. In addition, imports were decreasing as a proportion of British national expenditure, making them less important to the British economy as a whole.[5] However, the Dominions continued to face the situation that the British market was vital for many of their primary products.

British industrial production was almost guaranteed its place in the Australian market. In September 1936 the United States Consul in Sydney reported slight inroads by American goods despite "a large Ottawa preference, despite additional advantages in primage taxes . . . and despite an inherent predilection to 'buy British'".[6] British money dominated the capital market and British firms enjoyed a far stronger hold on the Australian economy than any foreign competitor. It was not until the 1960s that the United States, and in some cases Japan, toppled Britain as Australia's chief foreign trading partner.[7] Unlike Canada, there was no industrial giant on Australia's border offering strong competition to Britain. (By 1931 the United States was providing sixty-one per cent of Canada's foreign investment compared with thirty-five per cent from Britain.[8]) Also, the Australian consumer had an ingrained preference for British goods. So, while there was some scope for bargaining by Australia, and there was an acknowledgement by Britain of the Dominions' retaliatory power[9], it was not a power that could be easily or lightly used.

What tipped the scales irrevocably in Britain's favour was the might of the Royal Navy, which provided, so the theory went, protection on the high seas for Australia's lifeblood trade with Britain. In return for this protection, there was a widespread feeling that the Dominions should be prepared to make economic sacrifices in order to bolster Britain's economic and military power. This feeling lay behind Australia's trade diversion policy of 1936 that was to cost her so dearly.[10]

The Ottawa Conference of 1932 marked the high point for the concept of a self-contained Empire. It established a series of trade agreements giving preferential access to the markets of each member country. Australia undertook to give British manufacturers access to the Dominion market, but, after domestic pressure, simply raised the tariffs on non-British goods rather than lowering the tariffs on British goods. This left Britain only partially satisfied while at the same time it antagonised a host of foreign competitors who reacted in kind against Australian goods.

The pattern of Imperial preference set at Ottawa had the immediate effect of building fences between Australia and non-Empire countries where there should have been bridges. It revealed a blinkered view of the world by Australia, seemingly incapable of foreseeing the repercussions that were likely to flow from it. And the offence was compounded in 1936 with the trade diversion policy which sought to restrict the import of Japanese textiles and American automobile parts into Australia and substitute them with British goods. This policy revealed anew Australia's inability to face up to its situation — that it was a distant and expendable portion of an Empire that no longer held sway in the Pacific. The predominant Pacific powers had for several decades been Japan and the United States, and it was against them in particular that Australia's trade diversion policy was directed.

Australia's desire to placate British demands and maintain the spirit of Empire with its explicit strategic promise of protection against attack produced a policy with serious drawbacks. By offending trading nations outside the Empire, Australia cut herself off from countries important to her economic recovery. It was soon only too obvious that the British Empire alone was not sufficient to absorb Australian produce[11], and that the tariff system begun at Ottawa was the stumbling block to the necessary expansion of trade with non-British nations. Reliance on British manufacturers also stymied the growth of an Australian secondary industry sector which, in turn, hampered the quick development of defence industries during the war. The exhortation to "buy British" was a factor in the low level of preparedness of the Australian forces in 1939.

The Anglo–American trade agreement of 1938 signalled the end of efforts to find a purely Imperial solution to economic ills. The Empire was acknowledged as providing only a partial answer to Britain's quest for markets. Imperial preference was seriously compromised as foreign markets were sought for the produce that the Empire had shown itself unable to absorb. The new economic links between the British Empire and the United States were an admission by Britain of new economic realities — that despite having a large part of the world's population and area under its influence or control, she could not create a self-sufficient unit along the lines of her former Imperial vision. America's economic power and potential as a market could no longer be denied. Britain's economic rapprochement with the United States began the collapse of the "Imperial economic order" that was so soon to be followed by the collapse of the "Imperial military order". In both cases, Australia was overtaken by events and was left floundering without support.

In the formulation of Australia's foreign policy there was probably less dissension between Australia and Britain than between the various parts of the British Government. There was sufficient precedent provided by Canada and South Africa for Australia to develop an independent foreign service capable of developing an Australian view of the world and of projecting an Australian view onto the world. Australia resolutely chose not to exercise that right until her precarious wartime position made it unavoidable.

Until then, she only had a High Commissioner in London, the former Prime Minister, S. M. Bruce, and, from 1937, a Counsellor at the British Embassy in Washington. Bruce also represented Australia at the League of Nations. Elsewhere, Britain represented Australian interests and pursued policies that were at once both British and Australian. As Australia declared in 1940, her foreign policy would "be so woven into the pattern of British foreign policy that it can be said that we make our contribution, exercise our influence but do not duplicate, or contrast with British policy".[12]

The Australian Government was supplied by the British Dominions Office with most of the information on which its foreign policy was determined. The Australian representatives in London and Washington were similarly reliant on British sources for the bulk of their intelligence. This was buttressed by British control of communications, whereby world news was channelled through the British wire and radio services in London to a receptive Australian audience. Even the External Affairs Department relied on the BBC news to keep abreast of overseas developments. This virtual monopoly on information ensured that Australia looked at the world through British eyes, thereby hampering the development of an independent perception of national interests and helping to ensure a continuation of the Dominion's dependence.[13]

It is clear that Australian relations with Britain during the 1930s were characterised by dependency. Australia exerted little influence on British policy makers and was largely unable to determine the direction of British, and consequently Australian, foreign policy.[14] This was made quite clear when Britain unilaterally reversed Imperial foreign policy in March 1939, abandoning the agreed policy of appeasement and commencing on a course that would lead to war with Germany.[15]

That said, it must be acknowledged that successive Australian governments seemed content with their status *vis à vis* Britain. They exhibited an almost total lack of interest in foreign affairs, the only notable initiative during the decade being the suggestion by Prime Minister Lyons for a Pacific Pact linking Britain, the United States and Japan. Such a pact was never a viable option in the context of the 1930s and it was quietly abandoned in the face of British opposition. As John McCarthy concluded in his study of Australian involvement in Imperial defence during the inter-war years, the Dominion "did not possess an independent defence and foreign policy and the low politico-military status this fact implied was largely accepted without question by the Australian government".[16]

Just as Australia was averse to charting an independent course in foreign policy, so too did she fall in with British defence requirements at the cost of pursuing distinctively Australian interests. Following the Great War, the Pacific Ocean was acknowledged as the likely arena of future conflict. To prepare for this eventuality, the Singapore naval base was planned. From 1921, this base provided the cornerstone of Australian defence policy. Although not finally completed until 1938, the base was designed to harbour a fleet of sufficient size to frustrate Japanese ambitions. It was supposed to protect the array of British possessions and interests in the Pacific and Indian Oceans.

From an Australian vantage point, Singapore was centrally placed to provide British naval protection throughout the Pacific. However the view from Whitehall was rather different. Singapore lay at the limit, rather than the centre, of British power. Instead of being ideally located for launching British naval power into the Pacific, Singapore was athwart the gateway to the Indian Ocean with its rich panoply of British possessions topped by the richest prize of all — India. It was as a lock on this gateway that Singapore was attractive to Britain. Its presence effectively limited Japanese territorial expansion to the Pacific Ocean. So long as Singapore was in British hands, Britain's Indian Ocean empire was secure. Australia's security was another matter.

The credibility of Singapore's capacity to provide protection for Australia was called into question many years before its ignominious collapse in February 1942. In 1921 a British admiral had questioned whether its position so far from the Australian east coast could adequately provide for the Dominion's defence. Two years earlier, Britain's former First Sea Lord, Lord Jellicoe, had authoritatively assessed that a fleet would not be sent to Singapore to meet a Pacific threat if there was a concurrent conflict in Europe. In a report on Australian defence needs, Jellicoe recommended instead a large Far Eastern fleet based at Singapore and jointly financed by Britain, Australia and New Zealand. The British Admiralty disowned his proposals and they were quietly shelved. They would have been as unpalatable in Australia as they were in Britain, although they would have ensured the defence of the Far East.[17]

Over the following years, the worth of Singapore and the capacity of Britain to supply a fleet for the Far East during a war on two fronts were repeatedly questioned. Britain replied with varying degrees of assurance that were invariably accepted. At the 1923 Imperial Conference, the First Lord of the Admiralty, Leo Amery, provided one such assurance to the Australian Prime Minister, S. M. Bruce, who replied that, while he was "not quite as clear as I should like to be as to how the protection of Singapore is to be assured, I am clear on this point, that apparently it can be done".[18]

Similar exchanges were repeated many times in the years leading up to Singapore's fall. Britain revealed a readiness to give an assurance when none was warranted, while Australia accepted each assurance without much close scrutiny. Instead of questioning the efficacy of the Singapore base for Australia's defence, Australians were principally concerned during the inter-war years with ensuring that a British fleet would be there when required. Britain never failed to assure the Dominions that they could rely on the arrival of the fleet to repel attacks. No one seemed to have asked why they were so confident of dispatching a fleet in war when it had never proved possible in peace.

Though various British officials occasionally admitted that Britain would have problems in fulfilling her guarantee, there was no retreat from the unequivocal promise to ensure Australian security by naval action based at Singapore. As Michael Howard has noted, Britain's commitment in the 1930s to the defence of Australia was "absolute". Howard claimed that, in the minds of her military advisers, the "need to defend Britain's

Eastern Empire bulked at least as large as the need to redress the balance of force in Europe, and at times, one is tempted to believe, very much larger".[19]

Britain had her own good reasons for deceiving Australia about her capacity to fulfil her defence guarantee. Any failure to provide Australia with an assurance of protection would call into question British power worldwide and make plain the shrinking tentacles of British sea power. The British Empire was held together by a belief in the Royal Navy's ability to patrol and control the seven seas. Doubts concerning the sea power would inevitably weaken the bonds of Empire and could cause its dissolution. As the most distant and most threatened of the self-governing Dominions, Australia and New Zealand would have found it untenable to give continued allegiance to an Empire that was plainly not ruling the waves.

So Britain conspired to keep the full knowledge from them, accepting responsibility in November 1939 for Australian defence even after declaring war in Europe.[20] However, earlier that year, Britain had felt so insecure in Europe that she had asked the United States to transfer a fleet to the Pacific in order to quieten the Australian anxiety.[21] It was a game of poker in which the stakes were the Empire itself and the bluff could only be called by Japan declaring war concurrently with Germany. When that occurred, the emptiness of the Singapore deterrent would be seen for what it was — a means of securing allegiance to an Imperial system that was steadily collapsing.

Britain could console herself with the thought that her assurances to Australia would never be tested. Even if Japan did the unthinkable and declared war while Britain was occupied in Europe, the situation would not be one of total gloom. After all, both France and Holland had important possessions in the Pacific and substantial naval forces with which to protect them. Together with Britain they constituted a powerful foe for an expansionist Japan, at least potentially. British optimism was also fuelled by the apparent lack of military prowess shown by Japan in its costly war in China. British ignorance of the Japanese military build-up combined dangerously with a sense of Anglo-Saxon superiority to produce a feeling that Japan could easily be defeated in any war with Britain.

In addition, Russia posed a continuing check on Japanese expansion, making it unsound for Japan to commit itself to distant adventures. Then there was the might of the United States fleet at Pearl Harbor which posed the most potent threat, lying as it did on the flank of any southerly thrust by Japan. Lastly, there was probably a feeling that even if everything else failed, Australia simply was not worth the effort for Japan to invade. In the event, this proved to be Australia's most useful weapon.

For Australia's part, there were important political reasons for not examining British defence capability too closely. If she was to admit that British defence arrangements in the Pacific were inadequate, the responsibility would shift onto the Australian taxpayer and require a greater diversion of resources into defence. At a time of economic depression, Australia was extremely reluctant to accept an additional burden on the public purse. Far better to trust the succession of British statements than open a veritable Pandora's box by calling the entire Far Eastern strategy into question.

In his role as official war historian, Paul Hasluck showed that Australia's defence expenditure during the 1930s was woefully inadequate. In 1927–28, defence spending represented 1.04 per cent of national income. Over the next decade it shrank to 0.61 per cent in 1932–33 and had only risen to 1.09 per cent by 1936–37. Though this was more per head of population than the other Dominions, it was much less than that of Britain. In 1927–28, the figure for Australia was £1 5s 5d per head, Canada 5s 7d, New Zealand 14s 1d, South Africa 11s 4d (whites only), and Britain £2 12s 2d. Australia needed to spend much more than the other Dominions because of her greater size and distance from Britain. She was likely to be in the front line of any war with Japan. Not only that, but the rearmament program beginning in 1934–35 was less than the figures suggested. Much of the money was spent simply on making good the deterioration caused by a lack of maintenance in the preceding years. Though finance was approved for capital spending, much of it remained unspent. Of nearly £25 million voted in 1937 for a three-year program of capital spending, little more than a third was spent by July 1939. As

(*Overleaf*) False sense of security: an Australian-made Wirraway flying over Melbourne
(Australian War Memorial)

Hasluck noted, it was "a tiny proportion of the nation's re-sources" when "the dangers were so great and so immediate".[22]

The effect of this parsimony was seen dramatically in September 1939 when Australia entered the war with a defence force hardly worth the name. The permanent army was a skeleton force of several thousand with little modern equipment. There were no operational tanks or other major units of mechanised equipment. The voluntary militia was 80,000 strong but its members only spent twelve days training in military camp each year. The only modern aircraft in the air force were seven recently delivered Wirraways. In reality, these American-designed aircraft were trainers though they had been sold to the Dominion as multi-purpose, two-seater fighters. In that role in 1942 they were swatted from the sky like flies by the Japanese. As for the navy, of its six cruisers three were more than ten years old, while its five destroyers dated from the Great War. To this were added two modern, locally built sloops.

As Treasurer, Richard Casey was in charge of financing the increased defence spending prior to the war. He was a strong proponent of rearmament, mainly out of a feeling that Australia was not doing enough to share the burden of Imperial defence. In January 1938, he claimed that Defence was the only department that could "write its own ticket", that any money it wanted it would get. Later that year, following the Munich agreement by which Britain and France acceded to German demands over Czechoslovakia, Casey wrote of his apprehension regarding the international situation and of the need for Australians to "pawn our shirts to try to ensure our security". Since Britain had "already decided on the shirt pawning business", Casey claimed Australia also had to "take our cue from her and do the same — for the obvious reason that our security and our future go up and down with hers".[23] However, after the war Casey admitted that his campaign to boost rearmament had been almost totally unsuccessful. Looking back at the statistics, he was unable to provide "any arguments to support the belief that the Lyons Government went out, horse, foot and artillery, to improve and increase Australia's defensive equipment".[24]

Apart from the issue of cost, a critical examination by Australia of Britain's defence capability would have called into question a central tenet of Australian political life — that Australia owed allegiance to Britain because she in turn guaranteed Australian "independence". A large part of the continued Australian confidence in British power was based on a firm but unspoken conviction that Australia was as important in British minds as Britain was in Australian minds.

If Britain was the mother country to most Australians, the implicit corollary in most antipodean minds was that the Pacific Dominions stood as sturdy sons to most Britons. Countless cartoons of the period portrayed just such a relationship. Viewing international relationships in these idealistic, familial terms inevitably led to the conviction that the mother would protect her children. It was inconceivable that Britain could have extra-Imperial interests that would outrank in priority her responsibility for Australia and, within the Empire, that Britain would feel more protective of India than she did of Australia. It is probably true to say that Australia saw *herself* as the jewel in the British crown.

In the rush to rearm in the late 1930s Australia was hamstrung by the requirement to purchase only British equipment. As McCarthy revealed, Britain worked hard largely to bar American products and expertise from the Australian market. Australia's defence position was seriously compromised by this requirement since British factories often were unable to supply Australian orders and in some cases the material supplied was second-rate. Only when Australia became so vulnerable by inaction, the threat from Japan so palpable, and the Government so obviously culpable, did Prime Minister Lyons move to explore alternative sources of supply. But when a proposal for an aircraft factory with American participation was mooted, Lyons was faced with protracted and strenuous objections from a Britain fearful of losing its dominance of the Australian vehicle market.[25]

The outbreak of war in 1939 found Australia with an air force not worthy of the name, flying aircraft unsuitable for modern combat. The army had a core of several thousand regulars supplemented by 80,000 part-time militiamen. Despite the increasing risk of war during 1938 and 1939, the Dominion had resisted proposals to raise a proper standing army. In any event, it would have been a force mainly of riflemen equipped for combat in the style of the Great War. The army lacked the mechanised strength that would soon prove so decisive in Europe.

It was at sea that Australia had its most formidable force. However, its six cruisers were not sufficient by themselves to secure Australia from a serious invasion attempt. Anyway, according to the dogma of Imperial defence, this was not their assigned role. Instead, they were to protect against cruiser raids on Imperial shipping and to provide a useful supplement to the strength of the Royal Navy. Security against an invasion relied as it had always done on Britain's promise to reciprocate Australian cooperation in a European conflict with the dispatch of a fleet to the Far East.

Despite clear indications that Australia could no longer rely on Imperial defence, the Dominion could not make the imaginative leap necessary to surmount the century and a half of colonialism and to recognise the peril which surrounded it. Time and the fall of events would soon test the strength of Australia's colonial mentality and the worth of the British defence assurance.

NOTES

1 *Official Year Book of the Commonwealth of Australia*: *No. 32, 1939*, Canberra, 1940

2 J. ROBERTSON, *J. H. Scullin*, Perth, 1974, p. 276

3 N. MANSERGH (ED.), *Documents and Speeches on British Commonwealth Affairs 1931–1952*, i, London, 1953, p. 21

4 See L. S. AMERY, *The Forward View*, London, 1935

5 I. M. DRUMMOND, *British Economic Policy and the Empire*, London, 1972, p. 21

6 P. G. EDWARDS (ED.), *Australia through American Eyes 1935–1945*, Brisbane, 1979, pp. 41–2

7 J. O. N. PERKINS, "Changing Economic Relations", in A. F. Madden and W. H. Morris-Jones (eds), *Australia and Britain*, London, 1980, pp. 180–6.

8 R. F. HOLLAND, *Britain and the Commonwealth Alliance 1918–1939*, London, 1981, p. 129.

9 I. M. DRUMMOND, p. 231

10 AUSTRALIAN INSTITUTE OF INTERNATIONAL AFFAIRS, (hereafter AIIA), *Australia and the Pacific*, Princeton, 1944, p. 8

11 *IBID.*, p. 9

12 W. J. HUDSON ET AL. (EDS), *Documents on Australian Foreign Policy*, iv, Canberra, 1980, p. 117 (hereafter *DAFP*)

13 P. G. EDWARDS (ED.), p. 54

14 See AIIA, pp. 6–7; E. M. Andrews, *Isolationism and Appeasement in Australia*, Canberra, 1970, p. 211; R. F. Holland, p. 167

15 N. MANSERGH, *The Commonwealth Experience*, London, 1969, pp. 282–3. Bruce later recalled the difficulties he had faced in learning of British policies before they were beyond the reach of Dominion pressure, complaining that it was only after policies were "almost unalterable that one can find out anything". N. Mansergh (ed.), p. 599

16 J. MCCARTHY, *Australia and Imperial Defence 1918–39*, Brisbane, 1976, p. 148

17 *IBID.*, pp. 8–9, 46

18 *IBID.*, p. 47

19 M. HOWARD, *The Continental Commitment*, London, 1972, p. 100

20 *IBID.*, p. 146

21 C. HULL, *The Memoirs of Cordell Hull*, i, London, 1948, p. 630

22 P. HASLUCK, *The Government and the People 1939–1941*, chap. 2

23 P. HASLUCK, p. 104; Letter, Casey to Keith Officer, 5 December 1938, Officer Papers, MS 2629, 1/631: NLA; See also Note for Cabinet speech prior to 1937 Imperial Conference by Sir Samuel Hoare, undated, Templewood Papers, IX:2: Cambridge University Library (hereafter CUL).

24 LETTER, Casey to Earle Page, 19 July 1957, Page Papers, MS 1633, Folder 1773: NLA

25 J. MCCARTHY, ch. 5

2

The Outbreak of the Second European War

September to December 1939

On 1 September 1939 German troops crossed into Poland in the first act of the Second World War. Britain and France declared war on Germany after their ultimatum to Hitler to withdraw from Poland was ignored. Britain's distant Dominions, Australia and New Zealand, dutifully lined up alongside the mother country in the second European war of the twentieth century. Australia heard Neville Chamberlain's solemn announcement of war on the BBC World Service and rushed with indecent haste to join the fray. This apparent unanimity of view between Australia and Britain concealed a widening divergence of interest between these two countries at opposite ends of the Empire. Rather than drawing them closer, the war would exacerbate their differences and pitch them into a competitive struggle for national survival that would reach its climax in 1942.

Australia was unique among the Dominions in being precariously placed at the limit of British sea power while at the same time being in the frontline facing Japanese military and economic expansion. The outbreak of war therefore posed the question to Australia of how far she would go in supporting Britain against Germany in a European war, where the military threat to Australia was distant, while an imminent and very direct threat loomed large in the Pacific.

Menzies' hasty declaration of war provided more than an inkling of how the Government perceived the priorities facing the nation. Unlike Canada or South Africa, where the declaration of war was left to the respective parliaments to deliberate upon, Menzies felt sufficiently confident to proclaim war immediately and automatically on learning of Britain's stance. His role was most closely akin to that of the British Viceroy in India who similarly plunged his charge into the distant European struggle without reference to his subjects. When Menzies was subsequently criticised for abandoning Australia's independence, he replied that he had acted in accordance with popular sentiment, that the British people needed quick assurances of support and that the King's declaration of war automatically created a state of war between Australia and Germany. This last justification was the one that most determined Menzies' action. His legalistic background could not conceive of the possibility of the King being at war in Britain but not in Australia.[1] As it happened, the monarch was King of neutral Ireland throughout the war and, in South Africa and Canada, was not at war until after the parliaments of those Dominions had so decided.

When Australia joined Britain in war against Germany she could not know that two years later she would face a war with Japan that would threaten her very existence. Nevertheless, Japan had revealed an aggressive intent as early as 1931 and it had been widely forecast that war in Europe could open the way for further Japanese expansion in the western Pacific. In fact, it was with Japan in mind that Australia had repeatedly sought assurances from Britain regarding her security. So it is reasonable to question whether wholehearted involvement in a European war did not threaten the Australian national interest given the likelihood of a war in the Pacific. Not only was the national interest threatened by participation in another European war but the whole rationale behind such participation, Australia's Imperial connections, had left the country ill-prepared for war. When it came, the Imperial connection demanded an Australian response on the understanding that, in the event of a threat developing to Australia, the Imperial connection would work in the other direction and ensure Australian security.

To Australia the link with Britain was indissoluble and of paramount importance. There was an implicit faith in Britain and the Empire and a trust in her "goodness". Part racial, part religious, part military, the Imperial idea reached an almost metaphysical plane, replacing religion as the cloak of respectability for Australian conservatism. Menzies, with his *Boys' Own* outlook on the world, recalled his formative years when "the maps of the world were patterned with great areas of red" and "of all the ancient landmarks that might be moved the British Empire seemed to be the most unlikely".[2]

Menzies' attitude was common among Australians during the 1930s, with allegiance to Britain going deep into the Australian psyche. As one contemporary observer noted, "Australia took it for granted, as part of the natural order of things, that Britain would maintain her general security".[3] Even the Labor leader, John Curtin, could maintain that "no part of the British Commonwealth is more steadfast in its devotion to the British way of life and British institutions than Australia".[4] Curtin's declaration was a recognition that the Empire was such a central tenet of Australian political belief that it could be ignored by politicians only at their peril.

Though Australia immediately lined up alongside Britain in September 1939, she did not put aside her pre-war commitment to appeasement. Up to the last moment, Menzies had urged an attitude of compromise upon the British Government.[5] And when war was declared, Australian Government Ministers were as anxious as most of their British colleagues to limit its extent and, if possible, bring it to an early end. Nobody wanted a repetition of the slaughter of the Great War and there was a fear, held more by some than others, that an Australian commitment to Europe would leave her vulnerable to a Japanese attack.

The Labor Party had urged for some time that an Australian defence policy should have as its first priority the defence of Australia. Such defence was to be provided by greater reliance on the army and air force. It was argued that a strong air force could prevent any invasion force lodging on Australian shores. In reply, Menzies and his conservative colleagues argued for a continuing commitment to the concept of Imperial defence based heavily on contributing to the power of the Royal Navy in the confident belief that Britain's navy would be made available to intercept an invasion force before it even reached Australian shores. Curtin's concept may have ensured Australia's defence but would have limited any Australian contribution to the general Imperial effort. Menzies' concept did the opposite — it skimped on positive measures for Australia's home defence while making generous contributions to the Imperial effort in the belief that the Empire would be there when needed.

Menzies' ability to deliver Australian contributions to Imperial defence was limited to some extent by the political situation in which his United Australia Party (UAP) ruled as a minority government with the tacit support of the rural-based Country Party. Two days after the outbreak of war, he cabled to the Australian High Commissioner in London, S. M. Bruce, advising that the question of an expeditionary force would not be discussed until the "position of Japan has been cleared up". Even though personally he could envisage the possibility of "reinforcing Singapore at some stage or putting garrisons into places in [the] Middle East", Menzies felt unable, officially, even to consider the question since, he confided, "any suggestion at present of sending troops out of Australia would be widely condemned".[6]

The Australian military historian David Horner has suggested that Menzies was greatly troubled by the potential threat from Japan and that this made him averse to the concept of an expeditionary force. But, as Horner also shows, Menzies was equally troubled by the political threat that confronted him as a Prime Minister of just six months standing presiding over a minority government that was being hard-pressed by both the Labor and Country Parties.[7] As he explained his predicament to Bruce on 27 October, he was under criticism from sections of the press while the Country Party was conducting a "specially poisonous public campaign". Menzies anticipated a serious challenge in the House of Representatives in mid-November — just at the time his Cabinet would be deciding on the dispatch of an expeditionary force.[8]

The Labor Party was opposed to the dispatch of an expeditionary force, while the Country Party sought to minimise the possible losses for primary producers caused by the war and the consequent shortage of shipping. Among his Cabinet there also were men more inclined than Menzies to give Australian security a high priority, though not to place it above the sanctity of the Empire as a whole. The Labor Party and Menzies' sceptical colleagues would have to be appeased by British assurances about Japan while the Country Party would require more basic British undertakings regarding the purchase of Australian primary produce. So, as he had indicated to Bruce, Menzies' natural inclination was to provide an expeditionary force as had happened during the Great War. But first he would have to disarm his critics.

Another impediment to such a commitment was the absence of a permanent Australian army. Despite the clear signs of an impending war and the massive rearmament effort in Britain, Australia had resisted calls for a standing army. Now, before an expeditionary force could be dispatched, it would first have to be enlisted and trained. Eleven days after the outbreak of war the Australian Cabinet tentatively decided to form one army division for "general war purposes" and to call up the militia for a period of more intensive training.[9] When Menzies announced the decision, he gave a clear signal that he envisaged overseas service for the division. He claimed that, while the "prime necessity" was to defend Australia, it "might be used to garrison some Pacific islands, to co-operate with New Zealand, or to relieve British troops in Singapore and at other points round the Indian Ocean, or it might be practicable to send some forces to Europe". On the one hand, he promised not to "diminish the security of Australia", while on the other, he reminded Australians of their obligation to maintain the "security of the Empire as a whole".[10]

As yet there was no mention of an Australian Imperial Force (AIF) as such. Instead, it was called a "special" force. The Government was still trying to satisfy both sets of critics — those who wanted the immediate raising and dispatch of an expeditionary force and those who wanted the first priority to be that of home defence before any external obligations were accepted. In fact, by raising the special division, under whatever name, the Government was bowing to the wishes of the first set of critics, while paying lip-service to the second set. As the Government had been advised by the Military Board, the training and equipping of the division could only be undertaken at the expense of the militia and to the short-term detriment of home defence. It was with reluctance that the Board agreed to the Government plan and only on condition that the first priority remain that of training the militia for its home defence role.[11]

Although the Military Board advice was soundly based, it was not calculated to capture the popular imagination, nor would it satisfy those critics who judged the present war effort in the terms of 1914 when there was little threat to Australia in the Pacific and Japan was an ally rather than a potential foe. It was with such critics in mind that the Government hurriedly pressed ahead with the raising of a full-time infantry division even though it could not be equipped for action within Australia. In his announcement of the force, Menzies claimed that Australia was further advanced in its mobilisation than in the previous war and dismissed any suggestion that he had "an easy-going attitude" to defence. The division, he said, "completely disproves the ill-founded and damaging suggestion that Australia is hanging back; that her Government is not alive to its responsibilities; that the spirit of 1914 is lacking".[12]

Although Menzies was moving cautiously towards the formation of an expeditionary force, the infantry division did not satisfy those critics voicing a clear and urgent call for a second AIF. Within days of Menzies' announcement, the Melbourne Argus berated the Government for incompetence over the AIF, claiming that it was out of touch with popular feeling which, the paper asserted, wanted immediate action.[13] On 20 October the Argus returned to the attack, urging that the formation of the second AIF be made top priority and for the Government to abandon its "obstinate adherence to the discredited theory that the Militia is still the first line of defence". It wanted the militia returned to part-time training on a level sufficient to "meet the fading emergency of an invasion of Australia" while allowing "normal peace-time industry" to be "as little disturbed as possible".[14] The call by the Argus would be a common theme throughout the war as Australia sought to harness the economic opportunities of wartime in order to pull the nation more firmly into the industrial age.

While Menzies tried to satisfy all his domestic critics, harsh words were being uttered in London at Australia's niggardly effort. Winston Churchill urged that Australian troops "should be in France by the Spring" and complained that "Australia appeared to be forming only one division, and even that was remaining at home for the present". He thought Britain should "press them strongly to do more".[15] Churchill's complaint was not shared generally by his colleagues who were much less eager to rush into the total war effort than he. Though brought into the War Cabinet as First Lord of the Admiralty by Chamberlain, Churchill was still a lonely voice in a Cabinet room dominated by the so-called "men of Munich".

In order to clarify British needs, Menzies dispatched his Minister for Supply and Development, Richard Casey, to London for a meeting of Dominion Ministers with British officials. In preparation for Casey's arrival, the British Chiefs of Staff prepared a report on the strategical situation which suggested that Dominion troops, with the exception of those from Canada, would be employed best in the Middle East. However, this suggestion was struck out by the War Cabinet for fear that it might not be acceptable to the Dominions.[16] At least in Australia's case, this fear was unfounded.

Casey very quickly let it be known that Australia was keen to dispatch its forces overseas but wanted an assurance from the British Government about the threat from Japan. After an informal discussion with several Cabinet members, Casey agreed to put their arguments to the Australian Government in order to "pave the way" for the official British assurance. As the new Dominions Secretary, Anthony Eden, explained to Chamberlain, "if we can give Casey a measure of comfort in respect of Japan's political attitude, combined with an indication of our willingness and ability to send capital ships to Singapore, should the need arise, the Commonwealth Government will then at once decide that the division which they are now training can proceed overseas".[17]

Eden made it quite clear that Britain was in the possibly invidious position of deciding whether to provide a verbal assurance about something that could not definitely be known in order to secure Australian assistance for the Imperial effort. If the position was invidious, the British War Cabinet did not seem to notice it. Only Halifax cautioned his colleagues to wait for opinions from the British ambassadors in Washington and Tokyo before giving Australia and New Zealand a "strong lead to send troops overseas". Churchill's reaction is interesting to note in view of his later elevation to the Prime Ministership. He dismissed Halifax's objections out of hand with the claim that the most Australia had to fear from Japan was a "tip-and-run raid, to repel which land forces were not required".[18]

Despite Churchill's optimism, Casey spent more than a month in London seeking what Britain was unable to give — a guarantee that Australian security would not be imperilled by the dispatch of its troops. Initially, it seemed like plain sailing. Casey expressed a willingness to send the troops and suggested the Middle East as the best destination for them. He informed his colleagues in Australia that Britain regarded any danger from Japan as being "remote", that both Canada and India had already agreed to the dispatch of their troops and that it was important to counter German propaganda claiming "half-hearted Dominions co-operation".[19] British Ministers were heartened by the readiness of Casey to fall in with British needs. As one member of the War Cabinet confided to a friend, the Dominions "seem to be playing up well. They have sent over a good lot of representatives and, as far as I can judge, there are no difficult questions between us."[20] After visiting the Allied lines in France, Eden reported that the Dominion. Ministers had been "very forthcoming as to the extent of the forces which they hoped to make available".[21] Casey may have been forthcoming but he was also shocked at the inadequate preparations being made in France to meet a German attack. He returned to London concerned to obtain definite assurances about the Far East and determined that Australian troops should not go to France.

Casey wanted an assurance not just about Japan's military intentions, but also about Britain's reaction to a war in the Pacific. Specifically, in what circumstances would a British fleet be dispatched to the Far East. As First Lord of the Admiralty, it fell to Churchill to assure Casey on this point. Churchill was both dismissive of Japanese naval capability and keen to obtain a commitment from Australia. He also had convincing reasons for believing that a serious Japanese threat to Australia was an extremely remote possibility. These considerations made him remarkably ready to provide the kind of assurance Australia needed. Churchill firmly believed that it would never be put to the test.

The British War Cabinet did not share Churchill's bravado and took fright at his promise to abandon the Mediterranean if Australian security was threatened. Churchill explained that his commitment was not originally meant to be an official commitment to Australia but was merely to assure Casey that there was "nothing to prevent the dispatch of an Australian force to the Middle East". Chamberlain immediately demurred, pointing out that Britain had always managed to avoid such definite commitments to Australia and to escape with vague assurances. In particular, Britain had "not been prepared to decide, in advance of the event, whether the Mediterranean should be abandoned to allow of a Fleet to go to the Far East".[22] Britain had pre-existing commitments to France and

Turkey to maintain a naval presence in the Eastern Mediterranean which would be compromised by Churchill's apparent assurance to Australia.

Churchill did not see it as a problem. He pointed out that his guarantee to Australia was hedged with sufficient provisos to make it most unlikely to be tested. For one thing, a fleet would not be dispatched simply on the declaration of war by Japan. There would first have to be an "invasion in force" of Australia, a situation Churchill could not envisage. His guarantee also depended on the continued neutrality of Italy allowing the Mediterranean to be so abandoned by the British. But, of course, it was most unlikely that the Japanese would threaten Australia, unless Italy became a belligerent or some other occurrence tied the Royal Navy to the western hemisphere. As Churchill confided to his colleagues, the crucial thing was to "reassure the Dominions, so that they would consent to the dispatch of their forces". The War Cabinet accepted this provided it was made clear to the Dominions that the precise British reaction to a Japanese attack would depend on the circumstances.[23]

That same afternoon, Churchill met with Casey to pass on the decision of his colleagues. He found that his confidence about Casey's malleability was a trifle misplaced. Acting on instructions from Menzies,[24] Casey now required an assurance about the British reaction to a Japanese attack on the Netherlands East Indies (NEI). If Britain failed to respond to such an attack, the Japanese would be lodged on Australia's doorstep and able to launch lightning attacks or even an invasion of Australia before any decent defence could be mounted. Though Britain could justifiably refuse to make definite commitments in terms of ships in the case of unspecified Japanese aggression, it was a little harder to escape with a vague assurance in the case of a Japanese attack on the NEI. Either Britain would respond or it would not. But even here Britain managed to hedge her obligations by playing the American card, claiming that it could not commit itself beforehand to a war against Japan over the NEI without knowing the attitude of the United States to such a conflict. Round and round the arguments went as Casey sought what Britain would never provide. As the Permanent Secretary of the Foreign Office, Sir Alexander Cadogan, complained, Casey was "being tiresome, but he was more or less knocked on the head".[25]

The British may have found Casey tiresome at times, but the Australian Minister was doing what he could to further British interests. In his cables to Australia there was little indication that he was seeking to protect Australian interests or that he had any appreciation of Australia having defence interests separate from those of Britain. His efforts were directed towards incorporating Australia into the Imperial war effort and assurances were sought simply as the necessary precondition for such incorporation. Even before his discussion with Churchill, Casey had received the Foreign Office view of the Far Eastern situation and had accepted it totally. He immediately informed Menzies that it "reads very satisfactorily from the point of view of our security in the Far East". Perhaps more importantly, he warned that New Zealand had already sanctioned the dispatch of their expeditionary force before even receiving the Foreign Office view.[26] In its urge to satisfy its critics, the Australian Government was in danger of upsetting its supporters by hanging back from an Imperial commitment and being caught flat-footed by the New Zealanders.

The Admiralty backed up the optimism of the Foreign Office with a naval appreciation that almost totally discounted the possibility of serious Japanese aggression against Australia. As Casey confidently interpreted the message to Menzies, a Japanese invasion of Australia was not possible "as long as there is a well-armed Australian military force and a superior British fleet in being in any part of the world". Moreover, Casey assured Menzies that Britain would place the security of Australia above that of her interests in the Mediterranean and that a squadron of battleships "sufficient to act as [a] major deterrent on Japanese action" would be dispatched to the Far East "from the moment that danger to either Singapore or Australia developed in a manner which made their protection a real and practical war need". Britain, he claimed, accepted "full responsibility of defending Australia or Singapore from a Japanese attack on a large scale and have forces at their disposal for these essential purposes".[27]

The result of Casey's arguments was that Churchill's memorandum was revised and re-presented to the War Cabinet on 23 November. Churchill argued that it now should satisfy the Australians even though Bruce had tried to claim the existence of a "definite pledge to send 7 capital ships to Singapore in the event of Japan entering the war". Churchill said that he had made it plain to Bruce that such a pledge would be "out of the question" and that, fortunately, the New Zealand delegation had adopted a "much more realistic view of the situation". Churchill's argument was that a British pledge as suggested by Bruce would commit Britain to tie up a large part of her navy merely on the formal entry of Japan into the war and without Japan necessarily making any overtly aggressive moves in Australia's direction. As for the crucial question of priorities of the Middle East *vis à vis* the Far East, Churchill assured the War Cabinet that his memorandum went no further than the assurances given to the Dominions at the 1937 Imperial Conference and moreover that his memorandum was "more elastic than this previous assurance". Australia's importuning was ascribed to a "long campaign of propaganda by the General Staff of Australia to divert money from the naval forces of the Commonwealth to the land forces". Churchill's arguments were accepted by the War Cabinet and Chamberlain proceeded that afternoon to pass the assurances on to Casey and Bruce.[28]

Whatever the worth of the British assurances, they were the best that could be obtained in the circumstances and went further than those demanded by the other Dominions. But then Australia needed more than the others because of its vulnerability. Bruce and Casey pronounced themselves satisfied and Casey undertook to cable immediately to Canberra with his opinion that the "wise and proper course would be for them now to authorise the dispatch to Europe of the Australian Expeditionary Force". Eden informed the War Cabinet that Casey expected the Australian Government to make an early decision and that the Australian contingent could sail within a few weeks.[29]

In fact, the Australian Government had already instructed its military planners to prepare plans for the dispatch of the force though it withheld making any decision on whether the plans would actually be put into operation.[30] It is likely that Menzies remained personally committed to the expeditionary force but wanted to ensure that it would have positive political results. This required, among other things, that New Zealand did not act out of step with Australia and allow it to be said that the Menzies Government was insufficiently supportive of the Empire. So Menzies appealed to his counterpart across the Tasman not to commit their forces for several weeks. He argued that there was some uncertainty still regarding a possible German invasion of Holland and that such an invasion could cause Japan to strike at the Netherlands East Indies. Menzies also indicated some annoyance that Britain was able to find the shipping for Australian troops but not for Australian primary produce. But the New Zealand Government merely confirmed what Menzies already knew from Casey — their commitment of forces had already been made.[31]

By delaying his approval for the dispatch of the troops, Menzies apparently hoped to squeeze concessions from Britain regarding the purchase of primary produce and thereby gain the connivance of the Country Party in the decision on the expeditionary force. Before receiving a reply from New Zealand, Menzies suddenly disconcerted Casey by claiming that the situation in France did not seem "sufficiently urgent to justify us incurring risk with our own defensive position". Menzies implied that Australia would take such risks only if Britain agreed to take both men and wheat. As he informed Casey, "having regard to the shipping position, we must determine the relative priority of such things as wool and wheat, and the special Division".[32]

This was a fine sense of political timing by Menzies and he covered the blatancy of his bluff by claiming a concern with Australia's defence position. The bluff worked. Britain agreed to purchase a huge quantity of Australian wheat far beyond its needs or capacity to ship it across the world. The Country Party was satisfied; the Labor Party was kept at bay by the assurances Casey received from the British Government; and the Anglophiles were satisfied with the subordination of Australian interests to those of the Empire. Menzies' bluff worked because it suited Britain to obtain the commitment of troops. However, perhaps of even more importance, the Australian wheat was cheap at a time when Britain was being pressured by Canada, their usual principal supplier, to buy wheat above the ruling market price.[33]

On 28 November the Australian Cabinet approved the dispatch of the 6th Division, which was to leave for the Middle East after completing basic training in Australia. It was anticipated that the force would leave Australia in January 1940 and, after further training in the Middle East, join British forces in France in time for the German offensive expected to occur during the

European spring. Though Menzies emphasised to Casey that the training period in Australia would allow a "period for clarification of [the] international situation without prejudicing our strength here", this was a consideration probably of more moment to some of his colleagues than to Menzies himself. As Menzies indicated, it was the view of *the Government* and not necessarily his personal view that the extra period in Australia would be valuable.[34]

It has been claimed that the Australian barter of men for wheat sales was evidence that "the Australian Government had a clear appreciation of what it considered its own vital interests to be and was quite capable of looking after them".[35] This is given added force by Menzies' angry cable to Casey protesting at Britain's tendency to take Australian agreement for granted with regard to the timetable for the dispatch of the troops. According to Menzies, the "*general feeling of Cabinet*" resented the British tendency to "treat Australia as a Colony and to make insufficient allowance for the fact that it is for the Government of Australia to determine whether and when Australian Forces shall go out of Australia".[36]

The Australian anger, and their successful attempt to link wheat sales with the dispatch of the division, certainly gave the appearance of the Government being conscious of its interests. But the reality is not so stark. After all, Menzies continually stressed the concern of his Government with the situation in the Far East and that the dispatch of the troops would be dependent on the Government being satisfied that the possible threat from Japan could be disregarded. And yet their dispatch was authorised after learning of New Zealand's decision, rather than because of any guaranteed stability in the Pacific. Though Menzies protested his Government's annoyance about the timetable for the departure, Australia fell in with the British plans and dropped any stipulation that the departure of the troops would depend on the prevailing situation in the Pacific.

Britain would not stand or fall depending on the commitment of one Australian division. Australia, however, well might, especially as the division was the only body of even partially trained soldiers that Australia possessed. It was in Australia's national interest that her own security be assured before the dispatch of any troops from her shores. This the Government failed to do, though it did exhibit a clear appreciation of its own vital interests in terms of ensuring its political survival. Australia was treated like a colony because it acted like one.

The commitment of the 6th Division was based on the assurances received by Bruce and Casey that Australian security would not be imperilled by the absence of this partially trained fighting force. Though Bruce had serious doubts about the worth of the British assurance, he apparently decided not to jeopardise the Australian commitment by calling the assurance into question. After the meeting on 20 November between himself, Casey and several British Ministers, Bruce was left with important reservations that, in the course of time, were proved to be remarkably prescient. In particular, he acknowledged Britain's relative naval weakness and its inability to "deal with the situation in Home waters, in the Mediterranean and in the Pacific at the same time". Equally important, Bruce doubted the sincerity of Churchill's promise to protect Australia and judged that his "real" strategy was to "win in the European theatre with a full concentration of our forces and not dissipate them by trying to deal with the situation in the Far East at the same time".[37] Though Churchill was not yet Prime Minister, he was in control of naval dispositions. Bruce's misgivings, therefore, were potentially of great importance. But Canberra never heard them.

Instead, Australia committed its troops to a distant battle based on an assessment of probabilities that was known by at least one of its authors to be unrealistic. As Bruce confided to a colleague, the British assessments of the Far East "drew a somewhat over-optimistic picture" and were "obviously framed in order to reassure Australia and make certain that the Expeditionary Force should be dispatched at an early date".[38]

It was not only the 6th Division that Australia committed to the Imperial cause. The Royal Australian Navy (RAN) was taken over almost completely by Britain and set tasks in the British interest far from Australian shores. Though Australia now exercised more control over her navy than in 1914, she still accepted that the RAN would be ordered to commence hostilities on a signal from the Admiralty rather than the Navy Office in Melbourne.[39] Under Menzies, and according to the theory of Imperial defence, the RAN was expected to play the main role in the protection of Australia from invasion. It would do this as an integral part of the Royal Navy (RN), of which it became a minor and largely subservient part.

Just prior to the declaration of war, Britain advised Australia that the assistance of the RAN was required in the Mediterranean. At the same time an Australian cruiser, *Perth*, was in the process of being delivered from Britain but was intercepted en route by order of the Admiralty and detained for use by the RN in the West Indies, almost as far from Australia as it was possible to be. Britain was within her rights to do this, but it understandably caused considerable dissension within the Australian Cabinet, which was only placated by an assurance from Menzies that the arrangement was "merely a temporary one and that it could be reviewed at a subsequent date".[40] In fact the *Perth* was retained in the West Indies until March 1940. As for the British request for help in the Mediterranean, the Australian Government was advised by its Naval Board (dominated by RN officers on secondment) that it should comply with the request in order to ensure that Britain would provide the promised help in the case of Australia being threatened.[41] On the actual outbreak of the war, the British request was put to one side until the international situation, particularly the attitude of Japan and Italy, became clearer.

Within a week of war being declared, the British Government suggested that Australia provide one cruiser (in addition to the one already commandeered for the Atlantic) and five destroyers for use outside the Australian naval station, in Singapore. This suggestion was based on the assumption that Japan would remain neutral and the naval threat to Australia would consist of occasional attacks on shipping by armed raiders.[42] On 6 October, Australia agreed to the dispatch of the cruiser and five destroyers to Singapore with the proviso that they would return to Australia if Japan entered the war. Britain then requested that the destroyers be sent to the Mediterranean in return for two British cruisers being sent to Australia. The cruisers were considered to provide better protection against armed raiders while the destroyers would release British destroyers for anti-submarine work in the Atlantic.[43]

Australia's agreement to the British request was made in principle on 6 November. Eight days later, Britain requested that the ships be moved forthwith since the British ships had already been moved from the Mediterranean in anticipation of the Australian arrival. Australia was also informed that the two British cruisers would not arrive in November as promised but, in February 1940, at the earliest. In the event, the cruisers never arrived. But the Australian Government accepted the British explanation for their late arrival and authorised the dispatch of the destroyers to the Mediterranean. This decision was based, at least in part, on advice received from the chief of the Australian navy, Admiral Colvin. Colvin was a British officer on secondment from the Admiralty and his colleagues in London had used naval signals to brief him on the British arguments.[44]

By the end of November, Australia had more or less willingly agreed to denude itself of trained men and naval ships in the increasingly tenuous expectation that Britain would respond likewise in the case of Australia being attacked by Japan. By the middle of December, she had made a similar agreement with regard to the air force.

Before the war, the Labor Party had argued in favour of a strong air force as the most suitable and economical means with which to deter any invasion force. With the army and navy now committed to overseas theatres of operation, the development of the Royal Australian Air Force (RAAF) as a viable deterrent force should have been regarded as a matter of vital national interest. Instead, the Government agreed to support the Empire Air Training Scheme (EATS), a scheme proposed to Britain by Bruce, which had the effect of turning the RAAF into an organisation devoted to the recruitment and basic training of aircrew destined for operations in Europe.

Menzies announced the scheme on 11 October in terms designed to camouflage its real purpose. While acknowledging its importance for the defence of Britain, he also claimed that it provided a "powerful deterrent to aggression against Australia". This was nonsense and Menzies probably realised it. But it was essential to appease those Australians who wanted the first defence priority to be that of home defence. In a statement several months later, Menzies scaled new heights of absurdity when he justified the EATS effort with the claim that it put Australia "well on the way to becoming a Great Air Power". He conjured up a vision of the training aircraft and their partly trained pilots being able to be "organized at relatively short notice into an effective striking force against an aggressor" such that they would "render the Commonwealth secure against any serious attack".[45] Even allowing for the widely held low opinion of Japanese military abilities, Menzies' claim was a reckless exaggeration made for political purposes and in the expectation that it would never be tested. When it was put to the test in 1942, it produced the inevitable disaster when the RAAF's inadequate training aircraft were pitched against the superior Japanese fighters.

The Government's air defence priorities were further confirmed in February 1940 with the appointment from Britain of Air Chief Marshal Burnett to head the RAAF. As David Horner has observed, Burnett's "main purpose was to train aircrew for the RAF and he was little interested in the home defence of Australia".[46] With General Squires heading her army, Australia now had a triumvirate of British officers in charge of her defence.[47] But, more importantly, the political and diplomatic triumvirate of Casey, Bruce and Menzies ensured that the Australian Government was largely in accord with the Imperial imperatives that these officers had brought to their task.

Menzies' view was clear: Australia's continued "independence" could only be achieved by her continued dependence on Britain. He claimed that a self-reliant defence policy would force Australia to "mortgage itself for the next century". In an argument that survives to the present day, Menzies argued that Australia was only able to maintain her independent existence because she belonged to "a family of nations, the central nation of which is still ... the most powerful and the most resolute country in the world".[48] Menzies' failure to understand that Australia's continued survival, as with any country, rested primarily upon her own efforts was to place Australia in a position of great peril. The security of the distant Dominion was only one of many British interests and was, as would soon be plain, far from the most important.

NOTES

1 R. G. MENZIES, *Afternoon Light*, London, 1967, p. 16.
2 *IBID.*, p. 187

3 AIIA, p. 6
4 *IBID.*, p. 16
5 See CABLE, Menzies to Chamberlain, 1 September 1939, *DAFP*, ii, Doc. 174
6 CABLE, Menzies to Bruce, 5 September 1939, in *DAFP*, ii, Doc. 195
7 D. M. HORNER, *High Command*, Sydney, 1982, pp. 28–31
8 CABLE, Menzies to Bruce, 27 October 1939, *DAFP*, ii, Doc. 309
9 CABINET MINUTES, 14 September 1939, CRS A2697, Vol. 2: Australian Archives (hereafter AA)
10 *TIMES*, London, 16 September 1939, p. 8
11 "REPORT BY MILITARY BOARD on the Raising of a Special Force for Continuous Service either in Australia or Overseas", 13 September 1939, CRS A5954, Box 261: AA
12 TRANSCRIPT OF BROADCAST BY MENZIES, 15 September 1939, CRS A5954, Box 261: AA
13 *ARGUS*, Melbourne, 20 September 1939
14 *ARGUS*, Melbourne, 20 October 1939
15 WAR CABINET CONCLUSIONS, 19 October 1939, CAB 65/1, W.M. 53(39): Public Record Office (hereafter PRO)
16 WAR CABINET CONCLUSIONS, 30 October 1939, CAB 65/1, W.M. 65(39): PRO
17 LETTER, Eden to Chamberlain, 3 November 1939, *DAFP*, ii, Doc. 325
18 WAR CABINET CONCLUSIONS, 2 November 1939, CAB 65/2, W.M. 68(39): PRO
19 CABLES C4 AND C7, Casey to Menzies, 5 and 6 November 1939, *DAFP*, ii, Docs 327 and 332
20 LETTER, Sir Samuel Hoare to Lord Lothian, 12 November 1939, XI:5, Templewood Papers: CUL
21 WAR CABINET CONCLUSIONS, 18 November 1939, CAB 65/2, W.M. 87(39): PRO
22 WAR CABINET CONCLUSIONS, 20 November 1939, CAB 65/2, W.M. 89(39): PRO
23 *IBID.*
24 CABLE, Menzies to Casey, 14 November 1939, *DAFP*, ii, Doc. 361
25 CADOGAN DIARY, 20 November 1939, ACAD 1/8, Cadogan Papers: Churchill College (hereafter CC)
26 CABLE C24, Casey to Menzies, 16 November 1939, *DAFP*, ii, Doc. 368
27 CABLE C26, Casey to Menzies, 17 November 1939, *DAFP*, ii, Doc. 372
28 WAR CABINET CONCLUSIONS, 23 November 1939, CAB 65/2, W.M. 92(39): PRO
29 WAR CABINET CONCLUSIONS, 24 November 1939, CAB 65/2, W.M. 93(39): PRO
30 CABINET MINUTE, 20 November 1939, *DAFP*, ii, Doc. 374
31 CABLE, Menzies to Savage, 21 November 1939, *DAFP*, ii, Doc. 378
32 CABLE, Menzies to Casey, 21 November 1939, *DAFP*, ii, Doc. 379
33 R. J. HAMMOND, *Food*, iii, London, 1962, pp. 522–4; J. L. Granatstein, *Canada's War: The Politics of the Mackenzie King Government 1939–1945*, Toronto, 1975, pp. 63–4; S. J. Butlin, *War Economy 1939–1942*, Canberra, 1955, pp. 86–94; I. Hamill, "An Expeditionary Force Mentality?

The Despatch of Australian Troops to the Middle East, 1939–1940",
Australian Outlook, 1977, pp. 319–29

34 CABLE, Menzies to Casey, 28 November 1939, *DAFP*, ii, Doc. 392

35 I. HAMILL, pp. 319–29

36 CABLE, Menzies to Casey, 1 December 1939, *DAFP*, ii, Doc. 398 (author's emphasis)

37 "JOINT MEETING", 20 November 1939, CRS M100, "November 1939": AA

38 LETTER, Bruce to Officer, 12 December 1939, MS 2629, 1/879, Officer Papers: National Library of Australia (hereafter NLA)

39 G. H. GILL, *Royal Australian Navy, 1939–1942*, Canberra, 1957, pp. 61–4

40 CABINET MINUTES, 29 August 1939, CRS A2697, Vol. 2: AA

41 J. MCCARTHY, p. 146

42 CABLE NO. 191, Eden to Whiskard, 8 September 1939, *DAFP*, ii, Doc. 214

43 WAR CABINET MINUTES, 17 October 1939, CRS A2673, Vol. 1, Minute 32; Cabinet Minutes, 31 October 1939, CRS A2697, Vol. 3: AA

44 D. M. HORNER, p. 25

45 TRANSCRIPT OF BROADCAST BY MENZIES, 11 October 1939, CRS A5954, Box 235; "The Empire Air Scheme: What it Involves and How it Increases Australia's Security", press statement by Menzies, 29 February 1940, CRS A5954, Box 103: AA

46 D. M. HORNER, p. 28

47 As it happened, Squires had fagged for Colvin at Eton. See CRACE DIARY, 30 October 1939, 69/18/1, Crace Papers: Imperial War Museum (hereafter IWM)

48 HERALD, Melbourne, 17 October 1939

3

Sailing Off to War

January to June 1940

*A*ustralians welcomed in 1940 with all the gusto of peacetime. Shortages were still unknown and Menzies' prescription of "business as usual" proved to be popular medicine for most Australians. In Britain it was much the same, except for the blackout which cast a shadow over the New Year gaiety but was widely regarded as more nuisance than necessity. Only at sea was the war carried on in any real sense. In France, British and French soldiers manned the Maginot Line and hastily constructed additional defensive positions to cover its glaring inadequacies. Their enemy was the severe winter rather than the Germans who still declined to attack. There was no certainty that the so-called phoney war would ever be more than just that. In Downing Street, John Colville, a young private secretary in Chamberlain's office, thought that the chances were "fifty-fifty on peace or the real outbreak of war".[1] Although the possibility of peace remained on the British agenda, the war machine was beginning to build up such momentum that soon it would be impossible to stop.

Across the world, Sydney Harbour became crowded with the comfortable passenger liners that normally plied the route between Australia and Britain. But on this occasion they were there to collect part of the Dominion's manhood for the second European war. Australian men were not loath to leave the lingering atmosphere of the Depression behind and embark on the cruise of a lifetime, though for many it would prove to be their first and last. Australia was paying the dues on the Imperial

(*Overleaf*) The first convoy of Australian troops leaving for the
Middle East, January 1940
(AUSTRALIAN WAR MEMORIAL)

defence insurance policy. In this case the dues were 6500 men
of the 6th Division, the initial contingent of the second Australian
Imperial Force (AIF).

With their departure, Australia became firmly tied to the
British cause against Germany. Australian ships were operating
with their British counterparts in the Mediterranean; Australian
aircrew were training for roles in the RAF to be played out in
the distant and unfamiliar skies of the northern hemisphere;
Australian troops were taking up garrison duties in the Middle
East to release British troops for service in France where the
Australians would join them after a period of further training.
Australian security was dependent on two assumptions — that
the Pacific would remain aptly named and that, if not, Britain
would rush to her defence.

The first four months of 1940 provided Australia with a
quiet period in which to muster her resources and channel a
greater effort into her own defence. In view of the uncertain
outcome in Europe, Japan was holding back from any overt
moves southward. This gave Australia the opportunity to build
up her defences in case the European war went against Britain
and so prevent the long-promised dispatch of a fleet to the Far
East. If Australia recognised it as an opportunity, she made
little attempt to make use of it. Instead, the Government seemed
to succumb to the rather unreal atmosphere of a war without
fighting. In January it approved a proposal to appoint "someone
with a thorough knowledge of Palestine ... to organise trips,
so that parties of men could be taken during weekends and
other leave periods to some of the many interesting places that
abound in that country".[2]

At the same time, Menzies ordered a re-examination of
Australia's war effort. He was not trying to boost defence
measures in an attempt to cover the gross deficiencies in Australian security. Far from it. He was concerned that the rush of
measures introduced at the beginning of the war were already putting unreasonable strains on the Australian economy
and unduly disrupting civil production. To Menzies, the war
remained as an unfortunate interruption to his vision for the
industrialisation of Australia. Rather than focusing his attention
on mobilising the nation to win the war, Menzies preferred to
concentrate on preparing for the post-war period which, he

predicted, would "witness a great growth in Australia's importance as an industrial and manufacturing nation". As part of this
plan, Menzies tried to establish an Australian car industry,
albeit controlled by British capital, to combat the increasing
penetration of the local market by the American industry. The
plan came unstuck when the details were revealed of a secret
deal giving the local company a government-guaranteed monopoly of the market. When this was combined with suggestions
of corruption, the resulting furore forced Menzies to withdraw
the agreement.[3]

Those Australians who could foresee the potential scale of
the European conflict urged greater action upon the Government. From London, the Australian businessman Clive Baillieu
tried to galvanise his colleagues in Australia into recognising
that the phoney war would soon become a "supreme conflict
with Germany". He expressed puzzlement at the continued
importation of luxuries into Australia and feared that domestic
political factors were unduly influencing the Government to
delay taking action. Baillieu argued that it was "good politics
as well as sound patriotism to ... secure public endorsement
of a program of action which will enable the Government to
direct the resources of Australia without limit".[4] He might also
have added that such a program would be good business for
the mining and manufacturing industries that his family
controlled.

Baillieu's worries were as well-founded as his prediction of
total war. In the financial year 1939-40, Australian expenditure
on the war represented just 4.9 per cent of gross national
spending. Though this was more than three times the expenditure of the previous financial year, it remained a minuscule
amount compared to the proportion Britain spent on the war
and to the proportion Australia would spend later. As an
indication of the extent of economic mobilisation, in 1942-43
the comparable figure for Australia would be 36.8 per cent.[5]

Of course Australia was not in the frontline in 1940. But a
more fundamental reason for the Government's failure to mobilise resources for defence was Menzies' continuing faith in
the possibility of a peace settlement. In 1939 he had consistently
pressed Britain to accommodate German demands, some of
which he thought perfectly reasonable. Now the hiatus in the

war sustained his hopes for peace. On the one hand, Australia provided Britain with the resources of war while, on the other, she urged Britain to adopt measures that would avoid these resources ever being used.

Australian peace moves in early 1940 took three forms. The first was to press for the formulation of "peace aims" that could provide the basis for any negotiated settlement. The second approach was to resist strenuously any proposals that would extend the conflict in Europe and reduce the chances of peace. The third was to do all in their power to prevent the entry of Japan into the war against Britain.

On 2 January 1940, Bruce sent Menzies a long letter on the question of peace aims in order to enlist his support in a campaign to wean the French Government away from its idea of imposing a harsh peace on a defeated Germany. Engaged in the third Franco–German conflict within seventy years, France was understandably anxious to prevent a repetition by limiting Germany's ability to wage war. Unlike the French Government, Bruce visualized a post-war world in which "Germany would play an appropriate part as a great nation resulting from a peace settlement which had faced the vital problem of disarmament, territorial adjustments, Colonies and the economic needs of all nations".[6] According to Bruce, such a peace settlement could be achieved after Britain and France had won the war decisively. But he was not confident that such a clear-cut victory could be achieved.[7] His proposal for a "soft" peace was designed to weaken the German will and entice Germany to the peace table well before military means alone were able to achieve it.

Bruce's letter struck a sympathetic chord with Menzies who was anxious to act in the manner Bruce suggested but at the same time felt constrained by political imperatives not to reveal his views to either his colleagues or the Australian people. He released his frustration by means of his private correspondence with Bruce. Angrily, he denounced Churchill as a "menace" and "publicity seeker" who "stirs up hatreds in a world already seething with them" and who is "lacking in judgement". Like Bruce, Menzies foresaw a possible need for a "new alignment of nations in which not only Great Britain and France, but Germany and Italy, combined to resist Bolshevism". With this in mind, it was vital that the German nation be preserved as a possible future bulwark against Russia and that "soft" peace terms were formulated before the "heat of battle and the bitterness and privations of war . . . inevitably lead us to another Versailles".[8]

While Menzies and Bruce could confide their true fears about the war, they both were very circumspect about broadcasting them. The choice of private letter rather than cable as the means of correspondence was an indication of how carefully the two men felt they had to proceed in discussing this issue. The means of communication also imposed its own limitations on the speed of their discussion. It took Menzies more than seven weeks to receive and reply to Bruce's letter of 2 January. At this rate the events of the war would soon overtake this leisurely intercourse and render it academic.

According to Menzies, Bruce's proposal was already largely academic since political pressures in Australia would prevent him giving effect to the proposal. When he had raised the matter with his Ministers he found them, "with one or two exceptions, quite unresponsive" and committed to the "almost pathetic belief that the dismemberment of Germany would alter the German spirit and outlook". Though he undertook to "work upon their minds", Menzies felt considerably constrained by the likely reception to any attempt at diluting the ardour for war.[9] His public image was already tainted by his prewar support for appeasement and the supply of pig iron to Japan, and by various laudatory remarks during the 1930s about the fascist system in Italy and the Nazis in Germany. The political risks in giving effect to Bruce's suggestions were more than Menzies was prepared to bear.

An examination of the War Cabinet minutes confirms the reality of Menzies' limited political manoeuvrability on this issue. They record that "the views of the High Commissioner as to the nature of the Empire's peace aims and the proposed course of action did not meet with general approval". Unlike the British War Cabinet minutes, there is no record of the discussion but it is clear, as Menzies acknowledged to Bruce, that a majority of his colleagues would not countenance any softening of Allied war aims.[10] However, there were ways that he could act without exposing himself to the same degree of political risk.

As a corollary to Bruce's efforts to achieve an early peace, it was important that the war should not be widened and allowed to gather an independent momentum. Hence the horror of Bruce and Menzies when they learnt of proposals by Churchill to mine Norwegian waters in order to block the transport of Swedish iron ore to Germany. Between January and March 1940, the two Australians made strenuous efforts to delay and, if possible, to defeat what Bruce called Churchill's "ill-considered stunt".[11] At a crucial British War Cabinet meeting on 12 January, it was Menzies' objections that Chamberlain cited when successfully opposing Churchill's plan. Though the Australian opposition was not the only impediment barring the progress of Churchill's cherished project, it tipped the balance and caused Churchill to abandon his advocacy of it with an angry declaimer on the "evident necessity to carry the Dominions with us in any direction".[12]

Australian appeasement of Japan was the third strand of the Dominion's efforts at peace. With Australia devoid of basic defence materials and busily dispatching its trained troops overseas, it was a matter of obvious importance that Japan remain neutral. Still, Australia tended to pursue this objective with almost leisurely detachment. The Japanese were keen to see the appointment of an Australian Minister to Tokyo following the appointment of Richard Casey as Minister in Washington. But Menzies was far from hasty in obliging. He satisfied his Cabinet with a decision in principle to make such an appointment but then deferred to the opinion of Bruce and the British Foreign Office and allowed the matter to lapse.[13] It was only after the German invasion of the Low Countries, the fall of France, and the entry of Italy into the war in June 1940 that Australia took the matter up again and pressed it with any degree of urgency.[14]

On the question of wool and wheat sales to Japan, Australian views were more definite. This was a reflection of their importance to the Australian economy and of the importance of the Country Party to the political survival of conservative government in Australia. With this in mind, Menzies opposed the strengthening of any British trade embargo of Japan. Britain had undertaken to purchase Australia's wool clip for the duration of the war which meant that all wool exports from the Dominion had to be approved by London. Although Australia had suspended the sale of scrap iron to Japan, the suspension of wheat and wool sales had deeper economic and political ramifications. As Menzies advised Bruce, it would have a "disastrous effect on [the] Australian wool market".[15]

On 17 February, Bruce informed Menzies that British policy on wool for Japan was determined by their concern not to be "off side" with America and he suggested that Menzies "mark time and wait on events" since Australia also had a "paramount interest in the maintenance of the closest cooperation with the United States of America on all questions concerning the Far East".[16] But Menzies rejected this, confiding to Bruce that his "difficulties on all war matters are great and growing" and that his political demise was made more likely by his failure to achieve satisfaction on wool sales.[17]

February 1940 was a time of considerable political turmoil for Menzies. The appointment of Casey to Washington caused a by-election which was won by the Labor candidate. Menzies' political future looked increasingly threatened since a general election had to be called within six months. To bolster his position he readmitted the Country Party to his Cabinet, a move that increased his pressure on Britain for satisfaction regarding wool sales. Bruce was instructed to adopt a "stiff attitude" with British officialdom to get the matter resolved.[18]

With the appointment of the Country Party leader, Archie Cameron, as Minister for Commerce, the pressure became even more intense. In a memorandum for the Australian Cabinet at the end of March, Cameron warned of likely difficulties with Britain over a wide range of primary products and complained of Britain's "growing tendency" to emphasise her "own particular requirements and display indifference to the fate of Australia's other exports". Cameron's immediate complaint was a decision by Britain to take less dried fruit from Australia and more from Turkey with whom she had recently concluded a diplomatic agreement and whom she was anxious to keep out of the German camp. Cameron successfully enlisted Cabinet support for a strong protest to Britain over the issue, which threatened the livelihood of some of his supporters. It was a pity that Cameron's strident economic nationalism went little further than sultanas or he might have realised the deeper significance of Britain's willingness to overthrow her Imperial source of dried fruit in favour of Turkey with its large army and its strategic situation in the Middle East.[19]

More than indifference to the fate of Australia's export industries, the dispute over the Japanese embargo revealed increasing evidence of British indifference to Australia's fate *per se*. As Bruce had indicated, Britain was adopting a tougher line with Japan on the sale of primary produce at the behest of the United States. Though the British War Cabinet was ambivalent about the American stand, they recognised the desirability to "keep in step with the United States Administration", which was increasingly underwriting the British war effort.[20] Churchill was prominent in his support for the tougher American policy, claiming that it was "very much to our interest that the United States should bring increasing pressure to bear on Japan, as this would not only help China but embarrass Japan, without causing any blame to rest upon us".[21] This argument had little appeal to the Australian Government, which was less cavalier about disturbing the stability of the Pacific and less interested in helping China than in seeing Japan bogged down in an Asian land war.

These differences between Australia and Britain in their approach towards Japan would become more marked with the passage of time. But it was already apparent which ways they both were heading. Britain's dominant and ever-increasing interest was to retain American support for her war effort and even enlist her as an ally. This British interest made the entry of Japan into the war of lesser concern in Whitehall than what it might bring in its train. What particularly concerned defence planners was the possibility of Japan attacking either Malaya or the Netherlands East Indies (NEI), and leaving America on the sidelines. Britain had to achieve the closer involvement of America in Britain's war in Europe but faced the considerable obstacle of the American public's distaste for another European land war.

A possible way around this obstacle was for Britain to bring America into the war via the back door. Americans were less antipathetic to a war against Japan which, by its expected nature, would be mainly naval and therefore not involve the huge casualties of a European land war. It would suit Britain to have Japan in the war if it brought America in as well. Since British planners did not have a high regard for Japanese military ability, they did not expect to have to pay too high a price for American entry. The seeds of this policy were planted in January 1940 with the tougher American attitude towards Japan; Churchill was its foremost advocate in London.

The drift of British policy was not realised in Australia. According to the prevailing Imperial dogma, Australia and Britain could not have divergent foreign policies. The concept of Britain having opposing interests to Australia was not readily understood in Canberra. Thus any Australian criticism of British foreign policy in the Far East blamed the blinkered view of the British Foreign Office rather than accept the reality that Britain was pursuing narrow national interests in the Far East at Australia's possible expense. According to Menzies, British policy makers simply did not have a "practical and realistic view of the Far-Eastern position". He argued that a British offer to Japan of a "real gesture of friendship with some real assistance in the settlement of the Chinese question, accompanied by a proper recognition of Japanese trading ambitions, might very easily produce peace in the Far East".[22]

As a Pacific country, it was also in Australia's interest that the closest links be developed with America. The United States Pacific fleet provided a real deterrent to Japanese expansion and, in the absence of the British fleet, could be crucial to Australia's defence. Yet Australia continued to hold America at arm's length. Australian cable communications with America continued to be routed through Canada in order to protect the business of the British Empire cable system. Despite pressure from American companies, backed by the US State Department, Australia refused to allow direct wireless communication between the two countries although a radiotelephone link had been permitted. In the view of John McEwen, Australia's Minister for External Affairs, "the fact that the Empire is at war makes it particularly desirable that the Empire cable system should be protected from a form of competition which would militate against its preservation".[23] One practical effect was to limit severely the amount of Australian material in American newspapers and thereby hamper the development of those close relations that Menzies claimed to want.

In the case of civil aviation, Australia resisted American attempts to establish a direct aerial route across the Pacific to Sydney despite the obvious advantages for Australian–American

links. Such a route was rejected by Australia until America first
agreed to allow a British route across the Pacific via the established staging post of Hawaii. Although Britain had no intention of developing such a route during the war, Australia stuck
firm to its demand, allowing the possible post-war economic
benefit to Britain to outweigh her own defence interests. When,
in October 1939, Australia decided to send an industrialist to
examine the possibility of purchasing defence equipment from
America, they had to dispatch him by the first available ship.[24]
Not only did Australia refuse to permit an American air route,
but she also refused to break the impasse by herself developing
an alternative air route across the Pacific that would have
avoided Hawaii and provided an extra aerial lifeline connecting
Australia to Britain and North America.[25]

Much of the limited Australian effort to foster better relations
with America was designed as much to benefit Britain as Australia. The Dominion allowed itself to be used as a stalking
horse, posing as an extra and independent voice pushing the
British case in order to overcome the American suspicion of
foreign propaganda.[26] This was especially the case when the
phoney war came to its sudden end following the German
invasion of Norway and Denmark.

On 8 April, German troops landed at several points along
the Norwegian coast while others marched across the border
into Denmark. Their invasion pre-empted similar action that
Britain had been planning with the encouragement of Churchill.
When the German invasion of Norway was contested by ill-
prepared British troops, the British force was quickly routed
after suffering severe punishment from German aircraft without any protection from the RAF. It emphasised the difficulties
faced by infantry when their forces lack control of the air.
It was a lesson that Churchill was slow to learn, as many
Australian troops would find to their cost in Greece and
Singapore.

Even though the Norwegian fiasco was largely Churchill's
responsibility, it was Chamberlain who had to pay the political
cost for it. On 10 May he resigned in favour of a national
coalition government led by Churchill. Though Churchill became Prime Minister, he had not been the only contender for
Downing Street. Both the Foreign Secretary, Lord Halifax, and
David Lloyd George, Britain's Prime Minister during the

Great War, were backed by factions within the Commons. Only Churchill wanted an all-out war with Germany and his accession would have profound significance for the security of Australia. His commitment to total war required the gathering together of all Imperial resources for the titanic struggle in Europe. There could be no diversion to the Far East to meet possible threats or even, as it turned out, actual ones. Also central to Churchill's strategy was the need to draw the Americans into the war. If the entry of the Japanese was required to achieve this, then in Churchill's view that was a price worth paying.

As it happened, the war initially widened out to Hitler's design rather than Churchill's. On the day of his elevation to Downing Street, German forces crossed into Holland and Belgium in a lightning drive towards France. While Churchill battled to control the situation in Europe, the stability of the Pacific was a shambles. The Dutch colonies in the Far East were cut off from the succour of their metropolis like so much windblown fruit. The fall of France on 17 June added Indo-China and the French Pacific islands to the territories ripe for gathering by the Japanese.

Australia reacted to events in Europe with much alarm but still little action directed towards her own protection. Earlier, the Government had adopted a policy of producing aircraft locally as a way of overcoming difficulties in purchasing aircraft from Britain. This policy would also avoid the costly accumulation of aircraft reserves that might never have to be used and would create manufacturing skills and capacity that could easily be switched to civil purposes in the post-war period. The initial plan was to manufacture 180 Beaufort aircraft, the first ninety for purchase by Britain, after which Australia would take delivery of her allocation, in late 1941 at the earliest. The planes were designed for sea reconnaissance in line with the British opinion that the threat to Australia would be posed by occasional cruiser raids.

Following the German attack on Denmark and Norway it no longer seemed wise to rely solely on the production of the Beauforts. But a proposal to purchase forty-nine Hudson aircraft from America caused serious dissension within the Government with fears that the Hudsons would make the Beauforts, when eventually produced, appear outdated by comparison

and fit only for training purposes. The Treasury remained cost
conscious despite the deteriorating war situation and proposed
that Australia make do with the training aircraft supplied under
the Empire Air Training Scheme during the eighteen months or
so before either Beauforts or Hudsons could be delivered.
Though Menzies was opposed to the Hudson proposal, the
combined weight of the Chiefs of Staff forced him to give way.
The head of the Defence Department, Frederick Shedden, warned
that "it would be risky to take the responsibility of not adopting their decision, unless financial considerations absolutely
preclude such a course", particularly since the worsening situation "may focus local public opinion on the adequacy of our
local Defence measures even more than on our Empire contribution".[27]

On 30 April, in the expectation that Italy might enter the
war, the Dominions Office suggested that the second and third
convoys of the AIF en route to the Middle East be diverted
to Britain. For a time Australia overruled the advice of the
Dominions Office and its own Chiefs of Staff and halted one
convoy at Colombo and the other at Fremantle until they had
assurances about the repercussions on the Pacific of events in
Europe. Until March 1940 the three Australian Chiefs of Staff
had actually been British officers on secondment from London.
After the death of General Squires in March, an Australian
general, Sir Brudenell White, was hauled from retirement and
appointed Chief of the General Staff (CGS). White had served
in the Boer War and the Great War, had trained at the British
Army Staff College, and had spent three years at the British
War Office. He was sixty-four when appointed CGS. With
White now in attendance, the Chiefs recommended that the
advice of the Dominions Office should be "conformed to un-
reservedly". To its credit, the Australian War Cabinet demurred
at accepting this advice, but only so as to await advice from the
British Chiefs of Staff, which was hardly likely to differ from
that of their subordinates in the Antipodes.[28]

In the event, Italy held its hand and the Dominions Office
withdrew its advice for the diversion of the convoys. Instead,
Britain requested the power to divert the convoys without
reference to Australia if Italy again seemed likely to enter the
war and so threaten the passage of the convoys through the
Red Sea. The War Cabinet agreed to the British request on

the understanding that "immediate action may be a vital factor in the safety of a convoy", but expressed the desire that "any such decision should be communicated forthwith for the information and concurrence of the Commonwealth Government". In the event, Australia's concurrence would be largely a matter of form.[29]

The episode highlighted how little consideration the Government was giving to Australia's own position. Britain's difficulties in Norway and the possibility of Italy entering the war were precisely the sort of events that had been predicted to create a more aggressive policy by Japan. Yet this aspect of the new strategical situation received little immediate consideration in Canberra.

Menzies as Prime Minister ensured that the Anglophile advice of Bruce and the "Australian" Chiefs of Staff received a good hearing in Cabinet. After seven months of war, his political survival remained at the top of his personal agenda. He could not acknowledge that Australia's survival and his own could be pursued at one and the same time — that by energetically working for Australia's survival, he would be ensuring his own. On 2 May, in the midst of the political and military crisis in London, Menzies cabled to Chamberlain setting out the problems preventing him from attending a proposed Prime Ministers' conference in London. It would depend, Menzies advised, on the political position in Australia at the time and when the forthcoming general election was to be held. An added reason was the "necessity of continual watchfulness over [the] Australian war effort" though, as he observed, this too had "political implications".[30]

If anything should have rushed Australia to action stations, it was the German invasion of the Low Countries, not only because of its European implications but because of the instability it caused in the Pacific. Instead, Menzies blithely announced to his War Cabinet on 13 May the advice of his Chiefs of Staff that "no military action was necessary at present in addition to that already in hand". This bland pronouncement apparently caused consternation among some of his colleagues who rejected his advice and agreed to accelerate the war measures already approved and even to examine the possibility of increasing them. It was not a full-blooded roar of disapproval for Menzies' complacency, but it was close to being one. In fact, the concern of the War Cabinet remained divided between boosting Australian help for Britain and boosting Australia's own defence. On 14 May it decided to dispatch to Britain a large proportion of Australia's stock of small arms ammunition and to examine the "practicability of accelerating deliveries [of other munitions] to the United Kingdom and the effect this would have on the requirements of the Australian Defence Services".[31]

By 21 May the German tank columns had struck deep into France and the outlook was becoming increasingly gloomy for the French army and the British Expeditionary Force fighting alongside them. Churchill's mind was already turning towards the dogged defence of Britain itself.[32] While Britain anxiously counted its meagre stock of rifles, the Australian Government was beginning to accelerate its own war effort, though much of it was destined for the defence of Britain.

At the War Cabinet on 21 May, the Australian industrialist Essington Lewis was appointed Director General of Munitions Supply with direct access to Menzies and the "greatest possible degree of freedom from ordinary rules and regulations". Sir Keith Murdoch was appointed Director General of Information and given similarly wide-ranging powers and responsibilities. Approval was given for a dry dock to be constructed in Sydney capable of taking capital ships — that is, battleships and aircraft carriers. Moreover, nearly six months after the outbreak of war, a Director General of Recruiting was appointed.[33] These were dramatic responses to a critical situation, but they also were largely cosmetic, especially with regard to the vital defence of Australia.

On 22 May, Australia allowed the Admiralty to withdraw the two RN cruisers it had offered her in 1939 and which were en route to Australia. It also agreed to recruit and train nearly 2000 sailors for various duties outside the Australian naval station. Approval was given to the raising of a third army division for use overseas. Although the Government balked at the recommendation of General White that Australia concentrate her "further efforts on the raising of forces for service abroad rather than on provision for home defence", it noted the possibility that training for the militia, Australia's home defence force, might have to be postponed until 1941. As for the acceleration of munitions production, the War Cabinet approved the expenditure of £425,000 to establish extra production capacity for ammunition and explosives while simultaneously approving the diversion to Britain of substantial quantities of mortar and other shells.[34]

Six days later, in the midst of the Dunkirk evacuation, Australia agreed to release to Britain the forty-nine Hudson aircraft that it had on order in the United States and to dispatch a squadron of Hudson aircraft to Singapore in order to release a British squadron for use elsewhere "in accordance with the principles of Empire Defence". All these decisions were predicated on the assumption and the promise that they would be reciprocated by Britain if Australia experienced a similar level of threat. Although Australia was not yet making the all-out war effort that the situation demanded, she was making real sacrifices in her own defence position in order to shore up the British position. As the Chiefs of Staff indicated to the War Cabinet, the measures adopted would "naturally reduce the scale of Australian defence ultimately aimed at" although they would "not reduce the scale that has been existing up to now". Cold comfort indeed. But the War Cabinet concurred with the advice, apparently agreeing with the Chiefs on "the vital and immediate necessity for reinforcing the United Kingdom".[35]

The German *Blitzkrieg* attack into France had confirmed the worst fears of Menzies and Bruce. They had always doubted the Allied ability to secure victory against Germany and they now began to foresee the unthinkable, that Britain instead might succumb to the Germans. Australia was kept ignorant by Britain regarding the seriousness of the position in France. The British Government refused to answer Menzies' requests for detailed information and did not inform him of the evacuation from Dunkirk until it was almost over and had been made public by the BBC. In the absence of information, Menzies relied heavily on the pessimistic opinions of Bruce and quickly and correctly assumed, to the consternation of the British War Cabinet, that France was in danger of imminent collapse.[36]

The third convoy of the AIF was on its way towards the Middle East and the question again arose regarding its possible diversion to Britain. The War Cabinet expressed misgivings about this because it would cause the splitting of the AIF between Britain and the Middle East. Instead, they suggested that the troops be sent either to India or South Africa for the completion of their training before being dispatched to a suitable operational theatre along with the troops from the previous convoys.[37] As he later confided to Bruce, Menzies did not share the misgivings of some of his colleagues. He requested his High Commissioner to assure Britain that the questioning of their destination was not of his doing and that he would be "strongly advising" his Cabinet to accept Britain as the destination for the troops.[38]

On 25 May, Bruce met with the new First Lord of the Admiralty, A. V. Alexander, to explain the Australian disquiet and to satisfy himself about the measures being planned by the RN to deal with a German invasion of Britain. Alexander can only have added to Bruce's gloom, providing no evidence of detailed plans and simply fielding each question with generalities and platitudes. He assured Bruce that the Royal Navy would do their best and that the Admirals of the fleet were "full of beans".[39]

Britain already was preparing plans to meet the eventuality of a French collapse. In fact, on the day of Bruce's meeting with Alexander, the Chiefs of Staff presented a report to the War Cabinet considering all the implications of such a collapse, including the possible effect on Singapore, a base still judged to be "very important for economic control, particularly of rubber and tin". The Chiefs now made the awful admission that a French defeat would make it "most improbable that we could send any naval forces there, and reliance would have to be placed upon the United States to safeguard our interests".[40] This was a view that destroyed Australia's whole understanding of Imperial defence and should have immediately called into question any further Australian contributions overseas. But Bruce did not think to question Alexander on this aspect of the changed situation.

Britain also was slow to enlighten Australia about the crisis facing her defence planners. On 30 May, the Dominions Secretary assured Menzies that, even with a collapse of France and the entry of Italy into the war, Britain had "every intention of maintaining the security of our vital interests in the Near East and of course in the Far East".[41]

On 13 June, three days after Italy did declare war and as the collapse of France seemed certain, Menzies was provided by Britain with a revised outlook for his "most secret and personal information". This outlook revealed for the first time the British determination to hold onto its interests in the Mediterranean at the possible cost of those in the Far East. He was informed that their intention was to "hold Egypt and to this end we will retain a Capital ship fleet based at Alexandria as long as possible", which would also "exercise a restraining influence on Turkey and the Middle East". In the event of Japan also declaring war, it was admitted that it would be "most unlikely that we could send adequate reinforcements to the Far East" and would "therefore have to rely on the USA to safeguard our interests there". But this gloomy prognosis was balanced by an over-optimistic forecast of British efforts against Germany which held out the hope that by naval blockade, bombing, and the incitement to revolt, Germany could be brought virtually to her knees in 1941.[42]

Menzies presumably comforted himself with this optimism and reminded himself that the pessimistic side of it was, as yet, hypothetical. There is little indication that he passed on the import of the message to his colleagues or the defence chiefs. Instead, his immediate reaction to the new military situation was to pledge Australia's full support to Churchill in his decision to fight on and to promise to follow Britain into "whatever sacrifice victory may demand".[43]

On 28 June, Britain reiterated its message about the difficulty of dispatching a fleet to the Far East, this time in the form of a cable from the Dominions Secretary to the Australian Government setting out the Allied naval weakness consequent on the fall of France. It claimed that Britain had formerly been prepared to "abandon the Eastern Mediterranean and dispatch a fleet to the Far East relying on the French Fleet in the Western Mediterranean to contain the Italian Fleet" but that now she had to "retain in European waters sufficient naval forces to watch both the German and Italian Fleets and we cannot do this and send a fleet to the Far East". This should have been the introduction to a cable urging Australia to greater self-reliance in the absence of the fleet. But it was neither used as such by Britain nor read that way by Australia. Instead, London used it as an argument for Australia to denude herself still further of men and equipment. Britain asked that Australia supply a division of troops and two squadrons of aircraft for the defence of Malaya.[44]

In the absence of ships at Singapore, there was little sense for Australia in protecting an empty naval base but there was much sense for Britain in denying to Japan and the Axis powers the rubber and tin resources of Malaya. With the collapse of France, British hopes for victory against Germany rested more than ever on a successful naval blockade stopping the flow of essential commodities. Rubber and tin were high on this list of commodities and the defence of Malayan rubber trees assumed a higher importance in British plans than the defence of a naval base at Singapore that had never seen a British fleet and now probably never would.[45] But Australia remained transfixed by the thought of ships steaming to her rescue and her reaction to the British request was predicated on the assumption that the troops were protecting the base at Singapore rather than the bowls of latex attached to the bases of countless rubber trees in the Malayan hinterland.

Both Britain and Australia were in positions that they had always sought to avoid. Britain was at war with a combination of European powers but with no European allies of her own capable of providing a numerically strong army. Australia was caught up in a European war that had removed the protective cover traditionally provided by the RN. Though their predicaments were similar, their reactions were not. Under Churchill, Britain battened down its island fortress and prepared to withstand whatever Hitler cared to throw at it. The war effort became total as Britain drew on her inner resources while trying to attract the support of other countries to her cause.

Under Menzies, Australia accelerated her lacklustre war effort but with much of the benefit being destined for Britain. There was a realisation that the Dominion was insufficiently defended and a determination that this should be concealed from the public. The press found it increasingly difficult to reconcile the military disaster in Europe and its implications for local defence with the lack of vigorous government response in Australia. The Sydney *Daily Telegraph* called on Menzies to clean up his administration and go to the United States to buy aircraft and other war supplies. "Be honest, Mr. Menzies," it said, "and admit that we are as unprepared, muddled, and confused as Britain was 18 months ago".[46] But Menzies had already agreed to hand over to Britain the aircraft it had on order in the United States.

On 12 June, Menzies called together his leading defence

officials to meet with Sir Keith Murdoch in an attempt to allay public concern. The Chief of the General Staff, Sir Brudenell White, informed Murdoch that Australia would need 202,000 men for a limited mobilisation but could not even contemplate such a figure since it lacked the equipment to arm them. With the limited equipment on hand, he believed Australia could aim at a home defence force of 130,000. These men would be trained for four months and returned to their civilian employment from where they could be called upon in an emergency. After nearly twelve months of war, White soon expected to have 75,000 men with four months training behind them.[47]

White assured Murdoch that distance from Japan was Australia's safeguard, that "no bolt from the blue could descend upon you, and until the British Navy is defeated you cannot have anything of strength descend upon you very suddenly". By only calling up one-third of militia forces at any one time, he would not "disturb the civilian population more than can be helped" and would economise on "equipment, accommodation and clothing, as well as meeting civil needs as far as possible". Even if he could train and equip 130,000 men, White readily admitted that it would only be sufficient to defend against raids and not an invasion. In the case of an invasion, the guns and ammunition on hand in Australia would not last more than a month. As Murdoch observed, "that is what you cannot tell the public".[48]

White did take solace from the conviction that a Japanese invasion would only be mounted after the unthinkable had happened — that is, if the Royal Navy was "wiped off and Japan had complete control". In such an eventuality, he claimed, no amount of self-defence would be enough to withstand a Japanese attack for more than six months. Under further questioning from Murdoch, White admitted that financial constraints limited the militia numbers, that he could "enlarge our camps very considerably at a considerable expense. There are money limits. The amounts spent on these hutted quarters horrify me, knowing that at the end of the war they will be debris." In addition, there was a serious shortage of instructors, while the reserve of ammunition was considerably depleted after supplying fifty million rounds to Britain. A survey of strategic raw materials revealed a similarly sorry story with, in some cases, no government stocks on hand at all.[49]

One participant at this meeting suggested that Australia could overcome the equipment shortage by mass production of a simpler standard of equipment more commensurate with the capacity of the country's industrial base. This would have allowed for a large, lightly armed and mobile army very much on the scale that Japan would use so effectively in 1942. Though the idea was thought to be interesting, it was not taken up. Quite the reverse. On the spur of the moment, Menzies gave Essington Lewis authority to investigate the local manufacture of tanks after having been assured by Murdoch that the "public would love to know you are making tanks". This decision eventually led on to a full-scale production program that absorbed much money and manpower without producing one operational tank before the whole program was finally scrapped in 1943. As for manpower for munition production, Menzies rejected the idea of industrial conscription which, he claimed, would only cause disputation with the trade unions, most of which were led by "simply impossible people", many of them communists. So Australia remained as dependent as ever on the promised ability of the Royal Navy to intercept and defeat an invasion force before it reached her relatively defenceless shores. This dependence continued despite the obviously increasing burdens being placed on the Royal Navy in the northern hemisphere.[50]

Instead of cultivating new allies for a possible defence against Japan, Australia made efforts to enlist the more active support of America in Britain's defence. At Bruce's suggestion, Menzies tried to organise a joint appeal by the Dominions to Roosevelt to provide aircraft and volunteer pilots for Britain. The appeal was designed to buttress a similar one made by Churchill for American aircraft. Though the idea for a public appeal for volunteer pilots was rejected as alarmist, Churchill encouraged Menzies to make a personal and private request to Roosevelt.[51]

As British troops retreated to the beaches of Dunkirk and again as France was set to fall to the Germans, Menzies made appeals to Roosevelt calling on him to do his utmost for Britain. He held out the spectre of a British defeat and warned of the implications for America if the Royal Navy fell into German hands.[52] It has been claimed that these appeals "represent a noteworthy stage in the development of Australian foreign policy",[53] a thesis that is hardly sustainable by the facts. After all, Menzies was acting on the advice of his Anglophile High Commissioner and with the encouragement of Churchill to enlist the support of America for Britain's cause in Europe. In Washington, Casey was acting in perfect tandem with the British Ambassador, Lord Lothian, who claimed their relationship to be "as close as one blade of a pair of scissors to the other".[54] There was little attempt by Menzies or Casey to replace Britain with America as the guarantor of Australian security in the Pacific. Yet that was what Australia desperately needed. Instead, she adopted an ostrich-like stance, afraid to make energetic arrangements for her own defence for fear of antagonising the Japanese.

Of more immediate security interest to Australia was the position in New Caledonia, a French island lying off the populous eastern coast of Australia less than 800 kilometres by bomber or battleship from Brisbane. The sovereignty of this island with its valuable nickel deposits became a matter for dispute after the French collapse. There were suggestions that Australia should declare the island a protectorate in order to dissuade any Japanese ambitions in that direction. The island could provide an essential staging post in a Japanese attack on Australia while its position astride sea and air communication routes with North America made it a matter of vital concern to the Dominion.

At a meeting of the Australian War Cabinet on 18 June, the Chiefs of Staff were in attendance for a discussion on the implications of a possible Japanese occupation of New Caledonia. Australian weakness was starkly revealed when the Chiefs counselled against taking over New Caledonia. They advised that Australia would be unable to hold the island if Japan used her superior sea power to wrest it from them. They also cautioned that such action could provoke Japan to take similar action against the Netherlands East Indies, thereby isolating Australia from Singapore. The discussion quickly degenerated into an anxious questioning of Australian defence preparedness during which it was admitted that the newly appointed Director General of Munitions was producing munitions only to meet a minor attack. Menzies stepped in to allay the consequent alarm with an assurance that this was an initial objective and that the Director General had "a mandate for the production of the greatest possible quantity in the shortest possible time".[55] This seemed to satisfy his colleagues about munitions, while on New Caledonia, Menzies cabled to London for the advice of the British Government.[56]

London warned of difficulties with Japan if any attempt was made by Australia to occupy French territories in the Pacific. Instead, in an effort to deter the Japanese, Britain was attempting to extract a declaration from the United States that it would not tolerate any change in the status of Pacific territories.[57] In the interim, and following a lead from the New Zealand Government, Australia sent a message to French officials in New Caledonia and Tahiti offering "practical cooperation". What Australia had in mind was a strengthening of commercial relations to take up the slack created by the interruption of trade with metropolitan France and to prevent Japan obtaining a larger economic stake in the territories. At the same time Australia was careful not to prejudice Japan's present volume of trade. Australia's sudden realisation of her own vulnerability prompted such an ultra-cautious policy towards New Caledonia that the External Affairs Department argued that Australia's interests would be served best by New Caledonia coming under Vichy jurisdiction, and thereby becoming the de facto defence responsibility of Italy and Germany, rather than invite possible Japanese intervention by encouraging a Free French administration.[58]

Australia had been caught flat-footed by the Allied collapse in Europe but persisted with its adherence to Imperial defence. Although there was some acceleration in defence spending, the main change to Australia's defence armoury was the adoption of an even more craven policy of appeasement towards Japan. Canberra had always been averse to implementing Britain's black list of Japanese firms that diverted trade to Germany, especially if it affected Australian sales of primary produce.[59] Canberra now came under increasing Japanese pressure to lift the embargo on the export of iron ore to Japan. Though this was refused, Menzies did continue the export of scrap iron while ordering that the news was not to be published.[60] Also, on 19 June, the War Cabinet agreed to take immediate action to establish an Australian legation in Tokyo "before the international situation deteriorated further to the disadvantage of the British Empire".[61]

On 27 June, the Australian Cabinet set the tone for the

Australian policy towards Japan when it decided that, without a general settlement in the Pacific, it was in Australia's interest for Japan to continue in her conquest of China. London was informed that Australia "could not contemplate being at war with the Japanese" and Britain was requested to "persuade the United States to allow their Fleet to remain in the Pacific".[62] However, any move of the United States Pacific fleet to the Atlantic was counted by Churchill as a positive move towards war with Germany and therefore to be applauded.

Menzies' cautionary cable was received in London at about the same time that Britain received a list of Japanese demands designed to test British will in Asia in the wake of the disasters in Europe. Japan demanded that Britain withdraw her garrison at Shanghai and close the Hong Kong frontier and the Burma Road, both being important Chinese lifelines to the outside world. The demands put Britain in an invidious position. If she acceded to them she would reduce the resistance of the Chinese in their war against Japan and thereby offend the Americans. However, if she rejected the demands, there was no way that she could prevent Japan from exerting her will by force of arms.

On 29 June, Lord Halifax confirmed to the British War Cabinet the dire nature of their position in the Pacific and, as a consequence, of Australia's. He reported the opinion of Lord Lothian, Britain's Ambassador in Washington, that America was "unlikely to use force in defence of British or French interests in the Far East" and that Britain would "have to rely on their own resources".[63] Britain was therefore forced into a policy of self-reliance that Australia would have done well to emulate. Instead, Australia continued to allow her own interests to be subordinated to those of Britain.

NOTES

1 COLVILLE DIARY, 31 December 1939, in J. Colville, *The Fringes of Power*, London, 1985, p. 62

2 WAR CABINET MINUTES, 18 January 1940, CRS A2673, Vol. 1: AA

3 LETTER, Fairbairn to Menzies, 16 January 1940, CRS A5954, Box 235: AA; "Motor Car Industry", statement by Menzies, 31 January 1940, CRS A5954, Box 103: AA; Article by Menzies, *Herald*, Melbourne, 7 February 1940

4 LETTER (COPY), Sir Clive Baillieu to M. H. Baillieu, 11 March 1940, AA 1970/559, Bundle 2, High Commissioner Bruce — Miscellaneous Papers — 1939–1945: AA; Baillieu suggested that the letter be circulated among other prominent Australian businessmen.

5 S. J. BUTLIN, *War Economy 1939–1942*, Canberra, 1955, p. 489

6 LETTER, Bruce to Menzies, 2 January 1940, CRS M103, "January–June 1940": AA

7 LETTER, Bruce to Menzies, 6 February 1940, CRS M103, "January–June 1940": AA

8 LETTER Menzies to Bruce, 22 February 1940, CRS M103, "January–June 1940": AA

9 *IBID.*

10 WAR CABINET MINUTES, 5 February 1940, CRS A2673, Vol. 1: AA

11 CABLE NO. 72, Bruce to Menzies, 26 January 1940, *DAFP*, iii, Doc. 34; See also Docs 11–14, 25–26, 33, 49, 76, 79–81, 83

12 M. GILBERT, *Finest Hour*, London, 1983, pp. 130–1

13 See *DAFP*, iii, Docs 27, 42, 89, 111; P. G. Edwards, *Prime Ministers and Diplomats*, Melbourne, 1983, p. 124

14 See: *DAFP*, iii, Docs 405, 418, 441

15 CABLE, Prime Minister's Department to Bruce, 5 February 1940, *DAFP*, iii, Doc. 41

16 CABLE NO. 127, Bruce to Menzies, 17 February 1940, CRS M100, "February 1940": AA

17 CABLE, Menzies to Bruce, 21 February 1940, *DAFP*, iii, Doc. 70

18 CABLE, Prime Minister's Department to Bruce, 9 April 1940, *DAFP*, iii, Doc. 128

19 CABINET MINUTES, 29 March 1940, and Memorandum by Cameron, "Economic Relations with United Kingdom Government", CRS A2697, Vol. 3: AA

20 WAR CABINET CONCLUSIONS, 23 January 1940, CAB 65/5, W.M. 21(40): PRO

21 WAR CABINET CONCLUSIONS, 10 February 1940, CAB 65/5, W.M. 38(40): PRO

22 LETTER, Menzies to Bruce, 22 February 1940, CRS M103, "January–June 1940": AA

23 LETTER, McEwen to Casey, 27 May 1940, CRS A3300, Item 91: AA

24 See CORRESPONDENCE FILE CONCERNING TRANS-PACIFIC AIR SERVICE, CRS A461, I 314/1/4, Part 2: AA; War Cabinet Minutes, 5 October 1939, CRS A2673, Vol. 1: AA

25 WAR CABINET MINUTES, 4 and 29 April 1940, CRS A2673, Vol. 2: AA

26 See CRS A3300, Item 93: AA

27 TELEPRINTER MESSAGES M.1663 AND M.1672, Shedden to Menzies, 16 and 17 April 1940; Defence Committee Minute, 17 April 1940; Report by Treasury Finance Committee, 17 April 1940; all in CRS A5954, Box 232: AA

28 WAR CABINET MINUTES, 1 May 1940, CRS A2673, Vol. 2: AA
29 WAR CABINET MINUTES, 8 May 1940, CRS A2673, Vol. 2: AA
30 CABLE NO. 197, Menzies to Chamberlain, 2 May 1940, PREM 4/43A/11: PRO
31 WAR CABINET MINUTES, 13, 14 May 1940, CRS A2673, Vol. 2: AA
32 M. GILBERT, p. 376
33 WAR CABINET MINUTES, 21 May 1940, CRS A2673, Vol. 2: AA
34 WAR CABINET MINUTES, 22 May 1940, CRS A2673, Vol. 2: AA
35 WAR CABINET MINUTES, 28 May 1940, CRS A2673, Vol. 2: AA
36 WAR CABINET MINUTES, 16 May 1940, CRS A2673, Vol. 2: AA
37 See WAR CABINET CONCLUSIONS, 26 and 29 May, 5, 13 and 16 June 1940, CAB 65/7, W.M. (40)139, 146, 155, 165 and 168: PRO
38 CABLE, Menzies to Bruce, 18 May 1940, *DAFP*, iii, Doc. 253
39 NOTE OF INTERVIEW BETWEEN THE FIRST LORD AND BRUCE, 25 May 1940, Alexander Papers, AVAR, 5/4/12(a): CC
40 "BRITISH STRATEGY IN A CERTAIN EVENTUALITY", Report by Chiefs of Staff, 25 May 1940, CAB 66/7, W.P. (40)168: PRO
41 CABLE, Caldecote to Commonwealth Government, 30 May 1940, *DAFP*, iii, Doc. 317
42 CABLE Z106, Caldecote to Whiskard for Menzies, 13 June 1940, *DAFP*, iii, Doc. 376
43 CABLE, Menzies to Bruce for Churchill, 17 June 1940, *DAFP*, iii, Doc. 392
44 CABLE NO. 228, Caldecote to Commonwealth Government, 28 June 1940, *DAFP*, iii, Doc. 459
45 REPORT BY THE CHIEFS OF STAFF, 25 June 1940, CAB 66/9, W.P. (40)222: PRO
46 *DAILY TELEGRAPH*, Sydney, 7 June 1940
47 "NOTES OF DISCUSSION IN WAR CABINET ROOM", 12 June 1940, CRS A5954, Box 468: AA
48 *IBID.*
49 *IBID.*
50 *IBID.*; "Production Orders for Armoured Fighting Vehicles", War Cabinet Agendum No. 150/1940, by Brigadier Street, 26 June 1940, CRS A5954, Box 262: AA
51 J. L. GRANATSTEIN, p. 120; War Cabinet Conclusions, 23 May 1940, CAB 65/7, W.M.139(40): PRO
52 CABLES, Menzies to Casey, 26 May and 14 June 1940, *DAFP*, iii, Docs 280 and 380
53 P. G. EDWARDS, "R. G. Menzies Appeals to the United States, May – June 1940", *Australian Outlook*, April 1974, p. 70
54 R. G. CASEY, *Personal Experience 1939–46*, London, 1962, p. 43
55 WAR CABINET MINUTE, 18 June 1940, *DAFP*, iii, Doc. 399
56 CABLE, Menzies to Caldecote, 18 June 1940, *DAFP*, iii, Doc. 400
57 CABLES, Z134 AND NO. 187, Caldecote to Whiskard, 20 and 21 June 1940, *DAFP*, iii, Docs 413 and 415
58 CABLE, Menzies to Governor of New Caledonia, 24 June 1940; War Cabinet Minute, 25 June 1940; Departmental Memorandum for Mr J. McEwen, Minister for External Affairs; *DAFP*, iii, Docs 427, 435 and 440
59 WAR CABINET MINUTES, 16 May 1940, CRS A2673, Vol. 2: AA

60 CABINET MINUTES, 17 June 1940, CRS A2697, Vol. 4: AA
61 WAR CABINET MINUTE, 19 June 1940, *DAFP*, iii, Doc. 405
62 CABINET MINUTES, 27 June 1940, CRS A2697, Vol. 4; Cable, Menzies to Dominions Office, 27 June 1940, AA CP 290/9, Bundle 1[16]SC: AA
63 "POLICY IN THE FAR EAST", Memorandum by Halifax, 29 June 1940, CAB 66/9, W.P. (40)234: PRO

4

The Battle for Britain
Is Fought

July to October 1940

*A*fter the fall of France, it was widely expected that the German army would rush on to invade Britain. From July to October 1940, the British Government was preoccupied with fending off this threat. Many people in Britain predicted defeat for their country. At the Foreign Office, Sir Alexander Cadogan privately predicted at the end of June that Germany would probably attempt an invasion within the next fortnight for which Britain was "completely unprepared. We have simply got to die at our posts — a far better fate than capitulating to Hitler as these damned Frogs have done. But uncomfortable."[1] Under Churchill's determined leadership this characteristic British pluck would be transformed into optimistic bravado. With this, and the considerable benefits provided by the English Channel, Britain would try and hold off the German challenge.

Australia was also considering the possibility of a British defeat and the consequences for the Dominions. The Chief Justice, Sir John Latham, wrote to Menzies on 20 June to canvass the prospects for Australia and the other Dominions attaching themselves to the United States in the case of Britain being ruled by a puppet government. Though he did not want to over-emphasise the possibility of such an event, he counselled Menzies to be "prepared for events which may possibly take place with very little warning and which we are unable by our own efforts to prevent". Menzies thought this prediction was "undoubtedly a realistic one" and undertook to involve Latham and the Governor General in any such decision.[2]

Apart from the threat to Britain, two other areas occupied

the minds of British defence planners. The first was the Mediterranean where the French fleet had been neutralised, while the Italian fleet was now hostile. With British naval bases at Gibraltar and Alexandria, Britain could effectively seal up the Italians in the Mediterranean, prevent them from linking up with the German navy in the Atlantic, and deploy the British Mediterranean fleet in other areas. Though this option was urged upon Britain from various quarters[3], it was never adopted. Two reasons were paramount in the rejection. One was the effect that such a move might have on British influence in the Middle East with its important oil supplies. Another was the fixation with creating an anti-German coalition among the countries of the Balkans and Turkey that could strike at what Churchill called Germany's soft underbelly. It was a notion that he carried over from the disastrous Gallipoli campaign of the Great War, and much effort and many lives would again be lost in unsuccessfully trying to implement this vision.[4]

The other area of concern to British defence planners in mid-1940 was the Far East where Britain faced Japanese demands to close the supply routes to China, particularly the Burma Road. The United States offered "diplomatic but not armed support" in the event of Britain choosing to resist the Japanese demands.[5] Once Britain had chosen to concentrate her naval forces in Home waters and in the Mediterranean, her ability to manoeuvre in the Far East was severely circumscribed. Despite this weakness and the lack of support from America, Halifax recommended that Britain resist most of the Japanese demands. He urged the War Cabinet to ignore Menzies' warning for Britain to be "very careful to avoid any action which would cause Japan to become involved in the war". Though his colleagues supported his recommendations, they added the proviso that Australia and New Zealand be consulted before a definite reply was sent to Tokyo.[6]

Halifax's victory was short-lived. Without American support and in the absence of the Far East fleet, the British resistance to the Japanese was primarily composed of bluff. The possibility that the bluff might be called became a matter of serious concern in Whitehall with the Chiefs of Staff and Churchill combining to reverse the War Cabinet decision. The Chiefs warned the War Cabinet that, if Britain adopted "a policy in the Far East which may lead us to war with Japan, having at the same time informed our Dominions that we are unable to render the assistance which we promised them, it seems to us extremely unlikely that Australia and New Zealand will release any further forces for service overseas".[7] When the War Cabinet came to discuss their report on 5 July, it was pointed out that British trade in the Far East, as well as Australia and New Zealand, "would be put in peril" by war with Japan.[8] For once, at least, British policy and Australia's expressed interest seemed to coincide rather than collide. In fact the differences were as deep as ever.

Though Australia was brought into the discussion as being opposed to risking war with Japan, the feeling of Bruce and Menzies was directed towards achieving an overall Far Eastern settlement with Japan that would satisfy Japanese economic and territorial ambitions within certain defined limits. The British decision to accede to the Japanese demands would buy temporary peace but, in Australia's view, would begin a process of retreat with no limit on the extent of Japanese expansion. The Dominion made a determined effort once again to change British policy.

On the day of the War Cabinet meeting, Bruce met with two senior officials of the Foreign Office to set out his ideas for a "broad settlement" in the Far East. Under Bruce's plan, Britain would help to force China to a peace table at which Japan would be given "economic opportunity" in China, while America and Britain would tackle China's restoration. What Bruce had in mind was for the Chinese market to be divided between Japan, which would supply consumer goods, and Britain and America, which would supply the capital goods such as industrial machinery. British colonies also would be opened to Japanese goods and there would be increased opportunities for Japan in self-governing parts of the Empire. Since this last provision would affect Australia, it was only to be done after discussion with the government concerned. As well, Britain would discuss with other European countries the means for "establishing [the] territorial position in [the] Far East".[9] Presumably, some of these countries would be prevailed upon to cede part of their Far Eastern possessions to the Japanese.

The cost of Bruce's plan for a broad settlement would be borne by the Chinese, who would lose their economic independence; the British, who would lose commercial advantages within their colonies and perhaps some of their colonies; other European powers and America, who would cede part of their possessions to Japan. Australia would be a major beneficiary from any settlement that removed the threat of war with Japan. Bruce also intended that Australia would gain an increased share of the Japanese market for her iron ore and wool. There was much to gain and little to lose for Australia in such a settlement.[10]

Menzies backed Bruce completely in trying to foist his plan upon the British. He dismissed the Burma Road as a "trifle" which should not be "allowed to stand in the way of a Japanese settlement". He correctly pointed out that Australia was "vitally affected" by the question and that they "would not relish having to defend ourselves against even a minor attack from Japan in less than a year from now". Not that Menzies expected such an attack but, as he warned Bruce, the "inability of Great Britain to send Naval forces to Singapore has occasioned a degree of anxiety among the Members of the Cabinet which can only be increased by any approach to Japan which stops short of being realistic and comprehensive".[11] An immediate effect of the anxiety within the Cabinet was its deferment of any decision on the British request for Australian troops and aircraft to be sent to Malaya. The view of the Australian Chiefs of Staff was that it would be better for Australia to dispatch troops to India to relieve British troops there for use elsewhere. But the War Cabinet left it in abeyance until the expected receipt of a further military report from the British Chiefs of Staff.[12]

To Australia, war with Japan was anathema *per se* and especially so after the British decision to withdraw its assurance to dispatch a Far East fleet on the outbreak of such a war. To Britain, and particularly to Churchill, war with Japan was anathema only in so far as it detracted from the war in Europe. In the context of mid-1940, with America unwilling to back Britain against Japan, a Pacific war could have spelt the end for Britain's war against Germany. Churchill's inclination therefore was directed towards giving way to the Japanese with a view to retrieving the British position once the war in Europe was settled. A broad settlement was not part of Churchill's scheme as it would solidify the Japanese expansion and make it difficult to reverse. However, talks about a settlement were permissible as they bought time and kept Japan out of the war.

In the event, Britain managed to satisfy practically everyone. She decided to accede to the Japanese demand on the Burma Road for a period of three months over the wet season when traffic would anyway be difficult. During that period, talks would be held with Japan to explore the prospects for a wider settlement. So Australia was consoled but, as Halifax confided to a former colleague, Britain's main intention was to buy time rather than achieve a settlement along the lines suggested by Australia. In three months the Battle of Britain would be decided and the threat of a German invasion would recede during the winter.[13]

Despite the worsening situation in the Pacific, Australia continued to hold America at arm's length. During the anxious days of the Burma Road debate in early July, Pan American Airways was inaugurating its trans-Pacific service to New Zealand after five years of negotiation and requested that it be given landing rights at Sydney as well. Pan American wanted to fly its Australian-bound passengers direct from New Caledonia to Sydney without having to connect with a Qantas Empire Airways flight in New Zealand. As it had done previously, the Australian War Cabinet refused until government-to-government discussions could be held with the object of securing British landing rights at Hawaii.[14]

Pan American tried to activate sympathetic Australian pressure groups by an inspired public relations plan designed to ridicule the Australian decision. They announced that Australia-bound passengers would be off-loaded in New Caledonia and put on board a yacht for their onward passage to Sydney. Even then the Government refused to budge, opting instead to connect the Qantas trans-Tasman service with the Pan American flight in Auckland so that passengers would be unlikely to take up the yacht option. If this did not work, then a Qantas flight would be sent from Sydney to New Caledonia to bring on any passengers wanting to go by yacht. This resolute reaction thwarted Pan American's plans and kept American–Australian links to a minimum.[15] This was despite the obvious defence advantages for such an air link being established and in the knowledge that the United States navy had been "quietly slipping funds to Pan American Airways for the development of civil air bases".[16]

The pressure from Pan American did not disappear after the rebuff from the Australian Government. In Washington,

Casey became the object of attention when the airline warned him that it might cancel its operations to New Zealand if Australia continued to refuse landing rights. But Casey dismissed this as being "typical of this company's tactics" which he described as "unsavoury" and "notably lacking in frankness and honesty". He recommended that Australian landing rights should not be granted without "prior discussion with [the] British Government who may ask that you make your agreement conditional [upon] certain matters connected [with the] Atlantic service".[17] So Australian security again took second place to the possible commercial advantage of Britain. It was not done consciously. Though Casey and Menzies expressed a great need for closer ties with America, their refusal of this practical and important proposal was done without any apparent thought to the possible implications for Australia's defence interest.

At the same time as the Australian Government was rejecting Pan American's request, they were confronted with another suggestion designed to achieve added security for Australia in the Pacific. This suggestion came from the pioneer Australian aviator P. G. Taylor, who requested permission to take delivery of one of the flying boats on order from America and use it to survey an alternative trans-Pacific air route across the central Pacific, avoiding Hawaii and America and linking up with the British West Indies and thence to Canada or Britain. He also urged the purchase of three additional flying boats to operate as a reconnaissance patrol across areas of the Pacific to the north and east of Australia. The War Cabinet referred Taylor's proposal for investigation. When it finally resurfaced at the War Cabinet three months later, it was rejected.[18] Australia remained in self-imposed, semi-isolation at a most critical time in its history.

Britain also was going through a critical time as it prepared to withstand the might of the German air force. In mid-July, Hitler ordered preparations to be organised for a possible future German invasion of Britain while German bombers were already making nightly raids over British cities, though still on a small scale. August and September 1940 saw these raids escalate into the terrible German bombing blitz that laid waste many urban areas of Britain and killed thousands of civilians. Churchill inspired and directed the national will into a struggle for survival for which no sacrifice seemed too great. It was a titanic struggle that Britain threw herself into once the option of a peaceful conclusion had been firmly rejected by Churchill. But the talk of peace persisted, albeit in private or in convoluted forms.

Menzies and Bruce did not share Churchill's confidence in a British victory. Though they had to be circumspect in expressing and promoting their views, they both made efforts to oppose Churchill's policy of total victory against Germany. Their opportunity came during July when Hitler made peace overtures towards Britain in order to consolidate his territorial gains in Europe without also having to subdue Britain. In the aftermath of the incredible German victory against France, it seemed to some people that Britain had little choice but to accept whatever Hitler offered. Lloyd George argued that at some point Britain would have to negotiate peace with Germany. He described Churchill's policy as a very dubious gamble and freely predicted his downfall once the country lost its hysterical infatuation with him.[19] For their part, Menzies and Bruce tried to prepare the ground for a possible negotiated peace by again pressing Britain to formulate definite war aims to counter Hitler's peace proposals.[20] With clear negotiating positions established on both sides, the chances for mediation were stronger, or so the Australians seemed to surmise.

Churchill dismissed Bruce's suggestion to formulate war aims more specific than the overriding aim of total military victory. Despite Churchill's opposition, Bruce remained determined to "hammer at other members of the Government".[21] However, once the battle was joined with Germany in the skies over Britain, the talk of mediation would be even more fruitless. This only served to intensify Australian anxiety in the Far East where British and Australian interests increasingly stood in sharp contrast to each other.

On a commercial level, Australia was concerned that British actions against Japan would disturb Australia's trading relationship with her Pacific neighbour.[22] Then a threatening change of government in Tokyo focused Australian concern on the more immediate matter of national security and cast considerable doubt on the Australian support for a general settlement with Japan. At Bruce's prompting, Menzies set out the Australian position in the light of the political changes in Tokyo. It was also

apparent that the United States would resent any general settlement concluded at China's expense. It was Menzies' view that
the three months' closure of the Burma Road would no longer
provide an opportunity to reach a general settlement and that
until the situation in Europe was clarified no meaningful discussions could be held. Instead, Menzies now urged a policy
of "playing for time in discussions for a general settlement
while ... working in as close co-operation as obtainable with
the U.S.A., giving way only under force majeure on questions
which are not absolutely vital".[23]

In contrast, the New Zealand Government absolutely rejected
the notion of a general settlement, arguing that an appeasement
policy was "no more likely to be successful in the Far East
than it was in Europe". Though New Zealand felt an appeasement policy would put her in more peril than a policy of
firmness and resistance to Japanese demands, this diminutive
Dominion imitated Australia in subsuming her perceived national
interest to that of Britain. As the New Zealand Prime Minister
Peter Fraser put it,

> while we neither understand nor sympathize with the policy
> that has been adopted vis-a-vis Japan, we are nevertheless
> unwilling by stressing this view to add unnecessarily and perhaps
> uselessly to the difficulties of His Majesty's Government in the
> United Kingdom whose decision on this difficult and delicate
> matter we have accepted in the past and will no doubt accept in
> the future.[24]

So the two Dominions with the most to lose accepted, albeit
with misgivings, the British lead on the Far East on the assumption that Britain had their interests at heart as much as her
own. But Britain was preparing to fight for her own survival in
the Battle of Britain and the interests of the Dominions were
far from the centre of her present concern.

Under the new administration in Tokyo, Japan was adopting
a more aggressive attitude towards Britain, arresting fourteen
British citizens in Japan and Korea. At the same time, America
was adopting a stiffer attitude towards Japan by placing an
embargo on the export of aviation spirit, a move that increased
the chances of Japan striking out for the oil reserves of the
Netherlands East Indies. This scenario concerned the British
Government at the end of July as the Chiefs of Staff tried to

agree on an appreciation of the Far East for the Australian Government. It was on the strength of this report that the future dispatch of Australian troops would depend.

The British attitude to a Japanese attack on the Netherlands East Indies (NEI) was a matter of vital concern to Australia. Churchill's reaction was to argue that such a Japanese move would have to mean war with Britain since Australia and New Zealand would "regard our acquiescence as desertion".[25] However, it was the Chiefs of Staff who had to provide for such an eventuality and they did not find it easy to make such a pledge. They turned to the War Cabinet for instructions while warning that "Australia has indicated that it is in the light of this appreciation that the decision will be taken as to whether they can spare an additional division for Malaya".[26]

The matter came before the War Cabinet on 29 July. Churchill, whose time and mind were concentrated on safeguarding the security of Britain, failed to see any urgency in the question but again agreed that it should be a *casus belli*, that Britain would declare war automatically in the event of a Japanese attack on the NEI. Lord Caldecote pointed out that the urgency was not caused as much by the likelihood of a Japanese attack as by the necessity to provide reassurance to Australia. He confided to his colleagues that "certain important convoys were shortly due to leave Australia. He thought that Australia and New Zealand would only be prepared to agree to the convoys sailing if they knew that we had reached a decision to resist by force Japanese aggression in the Dutch East Indies." Only then did Churchill seem to treat the matter seriously, observing that a pledge to resist an attack on the NEI could involve a commitment to withdraw the British fleet from the Mediterranean.[27] Nevertheless the Chiefs were requested to prepare a report based on British resistance to a Japanese attack on the NEI. However, Halifax was also instructed to inform the Dutch that Britain's capacity to assist would depend on the United States and that the Dutch should be "encouraged to sound the United States Government as to what their attitude would be".[28] In fact, the British attitude was summed up by Churchill's comment on "the importance of playing for time" in the hope that within several months Britain's position "might well be much stronger".[29]

The discussion of a possible guarantee to the NEI clearly

illustrated Britain's inability to cope with a war in the Far East without sacrificing interests closer to home, particularly in the Mediterranean. It also illustrated Britain's reluctance to make such a sacrifice, but not to make such a guarantee. The object clearly was to secure not the NEI but the continued commitment of Australian troops to the British war effort.

When the Chiefs of Staff had completed their report on the Far East, the Secretary to the War Cabinet, Sir Edward Bridges, asked the War Cabinet for a quick decision as Australia and New Zealand were becoming "somewhat restive" and were "reluctant to dispatch further troops until they have received the military appreciation of the situation in the Far East". He assured the War Cabinet that the report did not commit Britain in advance to any particular policy if the NEI was attacked. In fact, the report downplayed any threat to Australia while emphasising the importance of Australian reinforcements for Malaya.[30]

In an additional report by the Chiefs dealing with possible assistance to the Dutch to meet a Japanese attack on the NEI, it was admitted that British forces in the Far East were not sufficient to "give any appreciable assistance to the Dutch". More importantly, it argued that "any attempt to produce an adequate naval concentration at Singapore in the present world situation would be unsound". Without military support from the United States, the Chiefs considered the maximum British effort would be to "send one battle-cruiser and one aircraft carrier to the Indian Ocean to be based at Ceylon for the purpose of protecting our vital communications and those round the Cape to the Middle East".[31] This was an admission of British priorities that would see their reinforcements concentrated in the Indian Ocean, leaving Australia devoid of the promised naval cover. However realistic, such a report could never be revealed to Australia.

When the War Cabinet considered the reports on 8 August, Churchill intervened to offer a way out of the predicament by glossing the pessimism of the Chiefs with his own optimistic appreciation.[32] Instead of discouraging the Dominions with the Chiefs' baldly pessimistic appreciation, Britain's weakness in the Far East and her switch in priorities from the Far East to the Mediterranean would be concealed by a reassuring cable from Churchill to Menzies. This cable brimmed with an optimism that the Chiefs were unwilling to communicate. Churchill considered that war with Japan would not occur unless Germany had successfully invaded Britain and that once this danger had abated, he expected "easier times in the Pacific". He claimed that, in adopting a yielding policy towards Japan, Britain had "always in mind [Australia's] interests and safety". Though he knew the United States would not react to a Japanese attack on the NEI, Churchill pointed to the United States Pacific fleet as comprising "a grave preoccupation to the Japanese Admiralty". In the event of such an attack, Churchill claimed that Britain would "of course defend Singapore which, if attacked, which is unlikely, ought to stand a long siege". He also undertook to "base on Ceylon a battle cruiser and a fast aircraft carrier which ... would exercise a very powerful deterrent upon hostile raiding cruisers". He did not indicate that the Ceylon force was meant for the protection of the Middle East and the sea routes approaching it rather than for the protection of distant Australia.[33]

As for the question of a fleet for the Far East, Churchill held out the tantalising prospect of a strengthened fleet in the Eastern Mediterranean that "could of course at any time be sent through the Canal into the Indian Ocean or to relieve Singapore", though he admitted that he would not do this "even if Japan declares war until it is found to be vital to your safety". As for the possibility of a serious Japanese invasion of Australia, Churchill considered this "very unlikely", but made the solemn promise that, if "Japan set about invading Australia or New Zealand on a large scale I have explicit authority of Cabinet to assure you that we should then cut our losses in the Mediterranean and proceed to your aid sacrificing every interest except only [the] defence position of this island on which all else depends".[34] This was a rash promise made on the eve of the Battle of Britain and in the confident but misplaced expectation that it would never be called upon. However, it had the effect that Churchill intended. For more than a year, his promise provided a touchstone to reassure the Australian Government whenever it considered the further commitment of its forces to the British cause.

Churchill's grand promise was long on generalities and short on specifics. For instance, at what point in a Japanese invasion would Britain move to assist Australia? Churchill implied that it would be only after a substantial Japanese force had actually landed on Australian soil. However, given the organisational problems of moving ships and troops, it would take several months for a British force to reach Australia in sufficient strength to dent an invasion, by which time all could well be lost. After all, as Sir Brudenell White had acknowledged in June, Australia only had enough stocks of guns and ammunition to last one month of heavy fighting. Additionally, there was no indication of what level of assistance Australia could expect from Britain in such a dire event. The only limit Churchill put on his promise was the defence position of Britain. But that had previously included the need to contain the Italian fleet in the Mediterranean to prevent its entry into the Atlantic. Even if the British fleet in the Eastern Mediterranean was removed, much of it would presumably be kept at Gibraltar and in the Red Sea to prevent the passage of the Italian fleet onto the world's oceans. If so, the promised Far East fleet would not amount to much. As well, the Australian commitment to the Middle East was now considerable. These troops would be put at risk in any hasty abandonment of the Mediterranean, a factor that had probably occurred to Churchill.

In early August, Bruce had informed Menzies of British military weakness in the Middle East, a fact that only confirmed Menzies' worst fears. He replied that he had already recognised the "grave danger" to the British position and that Britain's expulsion from the area would "give spectacular and far-reaching results, involving not only our elimination from a vital sphere but endangering our interests in Iraq, Iran and India, as well as giving encouragement to Japan for acts of further aggression".[35] This was a good understanding of the impact on Britain of defeat in the Middle East but it addressed the issue from Australia's viewpoint hardly at all. It was the last time when the British commitment to the Middle East could still be questioned. Before long it would assume such a scale that a strategic withdrawal from the area would be unthinkable, at least to Churchill. By failing to question the continuing rationale of the commitment from Australia's view, Menzies helped to ensure its continuance and killed any remaining possibility that a British force could be found to resist a Japanese attack in the Pacific.

As the Battle of Britain intensified, men and munitions

Australian High Commissioner to Britain, Stanley Bruce, with
Australian troops in England, August 1940
(AUSTRALIAN WAR MEMORIAL)

were concentrated overwhelmingly in repelling the attacks of
Goering's Luftwaffe, with the Middle East forces coming a
relatively poor second in Britain's priorities. This was especially
true with regard to aircraft which were needed desperately at
home. Though Australia was devoid of any modern fighter
aircraft of her own, Bruce did not request such aircraft for
Australia, appealing instead for Britain to reinforce the Middle
East. On 4 September, Bruce urged Menzies to impress on
Britain "our vital interest in [the] Middle East" and to advocate the "maximum effort there compatible with [the] safety of
[the] United Kingdom".[36] Menzies supported this appeal with
a cable calling for a greater British effort to secure the Mediterranean and the Middle East and implying that Britain was
over-protected at home. If Britain was over-protected, Australia
was grossly under-protected, but that was not Menzies' top
priority. Though he recognised that a British defeat in the
Middle East would probably lead to the withdrawal of the
fleet from the Eastern Mediterranean, he did not seem to recognise that this might allow for a Far East fleet and therefore
be very much in Australia's interest.[37]

Meanwhile, Menzies found himself at odds with Bruce in
London and Casey in Washington over Australia's policy towards Japan. Menzies had set out the latest Australian view as
being temporarily in accord with that of Britain — that a
general settlement in the Pacific could not be finalised until the
situation in Europe was clarified and that, in the interim, war
must be avoided with a judicious mixture of firmness on vital
matters and flexibility on others. The United States was to be
informed of, and hopefully involved in, all British moves.[38]
However, the question of when to be firm was not easy to
determine.

After the Japanese arrest of fourteen British citizens, London retaliated with the arrest of Japanese citizens in Britain.
Though Bruce had supported this action, the Australian Government was not directly consulted by Britain but merely informed after the event.[39] Menzies was very alarmed at the
danger of this petty provocation escalating into war and urged
the British Government to eschew such tactics of bluff and
pursue a policy that was "firm but such as will, if possible,
avoid war". How such a policy was to be implemented, Menzies
would leave to the judgement of the British Government.[40]

On 6 August, the same day that Menzies was urging one policy on the British Government, Bruce was pursuing activities in the opposite direction and in contradiction to Australia's expressed policy. At a private lunch with the Japanese Ambassador to Britain, Bruce set out his ideas for a general settlement in the Far East along the lines he had previously discussed with Menzies but which Menzies now believed to be inappropriate.[41] He also pressed his views on British Cabinet Ministers known to be amenable to such a settlement and encouraged British businessmen with interests in Japan to add their weight to the pressure on the British Government.[42]

Meanwhile, Casey seemed to come under the spell of the anti-Japanese lobby in the United States and, on his own initiative, urged Halifax to adopt a firm policy towards Japan. Though Bruce kept his activities concealed from Menzies, the Australian Prime Minister did learn of Casey's and quickly moved to stop him in his tracks. He described Casey's proposal as being a "policy of maximum irritation to Japan by [the] Empire single handed". With no prospect of United States support, Menzies argued that Britain must adopt a middle course, playing for time until events in Europe made her stronger in the Far East.[43] For a time during August 1940, Menzies, Bruce and Casey were pursuing three conflicting policies towards Japan though, in the final event and despite particular misgivings, Australia fell in with whatever Britain decided.

So it was with regard to the dispatch of troops to Malaya. Australia had deferred reaching a decision on this issue pending a report from the British Chiefs of Staff on the Far Eastern situation. Australia now grabbed with relief and little scrutiny Churchill's assurance regarding the abandonment of the Middle East. Though the Australian War Cabinet would have preferred to send the troops to India rather than Malaya and to have Britain equip them with artillery and machine guns rather than denude the Australian militia of such weapons, the dutiful Dominion complied with British wishes.[44] Ironically, the less likely it became that a Far East fleet would materialise at Singapore, the more Australia committed men and equipment to the protection of the empty naval base.

Australia's commitment of troops to Malaya was linked with a reversal of Australian policy regarding the appropriate

British response to a Japanese attack on the NEI. After trying for so long to obtain a British commitment to treat such an attack as a *casus belli*, Australia now sought to dilute any such commitment. The Government was conscious that an automatic commitment would produce war with Japan but not necessarily produce the means from Britain with which to fight such a war. Though Australia realised that Japanese occupation of the NEI would neutralise the Singapore naval base and seriously affect Australia's strategic position, the Government counselled that "our policy should be to take a realistic view of such an act of aggression in the light of our military position at the time".[45] So much for Australia's policy of firmness towards Japan on vital matters. If the NEI was not considered vital, it is difficult to conceive of anything short of direct invasion of Australia being so considered. Perhaps, even then, it would have been argued that, provided Sydney and Melbourne were not attacked, Australia could live with a partial Japanese occupation. Such were the straits to which Australia was reduced by its Imperial commitment to the Middle East.

Though Australia did demur at the British suggestion to dispatch further Australian air force squadrons to Singapore, this was as much in Britain's interest as Australia's. As Menzies pointed out, any further commitment of service squadrons outside of Australia would endanger the training program of personnel needed for Australian air defence needs as well as for the five squadrons overseas and the Empire Air Training Scheme. Australia had made substantial contributions towards the air defence of Britain in the wake of the fall of France and she became increasingly anxious to recover the aircraft contributed to Britain's defence and to continue with the expansion of the RAAF which was still devoid of modern aircraft.

In early July, Casey had organised a meeting in New York between Dominion representatives and an official of the British Ministry of Aircraft Production to press for the release to the Dominion of aircraft engines ordered from the United States. They were persuaded to channel their request through the Dominions Office in London where it was promptly filed and forgotten. On 21 August, the Dominions Secretary, Lord Caldecote, was urged by the Minister for Aircraft Production, Lord Beaverbrook, to give the Dominions' representatives some satisfaction, at least by acknowledging their cable and letting them know that their request was under consideration.

Rather candidly, Caldecote replied that the problem of "how best to tell the Dominion Governments that we cannot give them what they want has presented some difficulty".[46] His problem was solved by Bruce who absolved Britain from any immediate need to respond to the Dominion requirements.

Bruce had been given the task of expediting the delivery to Australia of aircraft and of the tools with which to manufacture them. On 27 August, he had separate meetings with Britain's Secretary of State for Air, Sir Archibald Sinclair, and Lord Beaverbrook. Beaverbrook in particular was opposed to the export of aircraft and machine tools from Britain and continually bombarded Churchill with notes to this effect. As he informed the British War Cabinet in September, the "Battle of Britain was the only battle that counted".[47] The problem for Australia was that Bruce was inclined to agree with this view and moderated his arguments accordingly. Thus, when arguing Australia's case with Beaverbrook, Bruce was careful to assure him of the Dominion's "preparedness to fit in with the United Kingdom requirements". Although Bruce suspected that Beaverbrook was concealing the extent of British aircraft production, he did not press hard for Australia's requirements to be fulfilled.[48]

Apart from his concern for the Battle of Britain, Bruce was also hamstrung by the pressure he had been applying for the dispatch of aircraft to the Middle East. Bruce did not want the immediate delivery of the 571 aircraft Australia needed for the planned expansion of the RAAF. He simply wanted an agreed program for the delivery of these aircraft no matter how extended the program or how much it was hedged about with provisos regarding the state of the Battle of Britain.[49] Bruce was doing his utmost to protect British interests while appeasing Australian anxieties with a conditional British undertaking of doubtful value. As Beaverbrook acknowledged when proposing that Britain should give such an undertaking, "the Dominions are completely sympathetic to the urgent, over-riding considerations which prevent our meeting their aircraft requirements just now".[50] After a further discussion with Aircraft Production and Air Ministry officials, Bruce was assured that a program of deliveries would be drawn up in a month's time, once the position in Britain was clearer. Bruce responded gratefully, promising to "try and induce Australia to allow the matter to remain in abeyance until the beginning of October".[51]

It now would take that much longer for discussions to begin and for Australia to realise that Britain would not be supplying her with aircraft.

While Whitehall continually delayed any decision on the supply of aircraft to Australia, the Air Ministry was busily shipping aircraft to other countries. As Beaverbrook triumphantly announced to Churchill on 2 September, the RAF strength had increased by some 1000 aircraft since mid-May 1940 while 720 aircraft had been shipped abroad, mostly to the Middle East.[52]

At the same time that Bruce was temporising on aircraft and the Battle of Britain was raging, the question arose of reopening the Burma Road once the three months closure was completed. No progress had been made in Anglo–Japanese talks, since the course of such talks was determined by the battle raging in Britain's skies. The outcome of that battle remained unclear until October. Nevertheless, the British Ambassador in Tokyo, Sir Robert Craigie, planned in early September to raise the question of a general settlement with Japan. Though such a settlement was favoured by Bruce, he was concerned that Britain was seeking discussions without first determining the details of what she was prepared to concede to the Japanese and of what she was seeking in return, and without the involvement of the United States. Accordingly, he tried to pressure Britain to formulate clear proposals for such a settlement.[53]

While Bruce had some success with Halifax, Churchill's strategy in the Far East remained one of delay. As Churchill now admitted to the War Cabinet, Britain's victory in the Battle of Britain would not change her position of weakness in the Far East which was caused by the commitment to the Middle East. And the possibility of war with Japan was to be deplored because it would "fundamentally affect our strategy in the Middle East". In Churchill's view, British strategy in the Far East was determined by the greater priority accorded to the Middle East. As such, the policy of delay would not end with a successful conclusion to the Battle of Britain, but would continue until she had successfully fought the European war to a conclusion. British policy therefore had to continue to "go some way in offering inducements to Japan, and possibly also to go some way in using threats, but not to commit ourselves irrevocably to forcible action".[54]

Menzies tended to support Churchill on this policy of delay, except that he hoped the end of the Battle of Britain would allow London more easily to reach a general settlement in the Far East. In the interim, Australia fell in with British policy believing their aims to be identical. In fact, the Australian War Cabinet seemed to be quite embarrassed when their opinion regarding a Far East settlement was sought by Britain. They took almost two weeks to agree on a reply which supported British policy. They left the details of its implementation to London since the British Government could "best judge the danger of war with Japan". Implicit in this was an understanding that British policy would have the security of Australia as a top priority.[55] With *carte blanche* from Australia and with the most token prior consultation with the Dominions, Britain announced in early October its intention to reopen the Burma Road.[56]

On 4 September, the British Chiefs of Staff submitted to the War Cabinet their view of future strategy. According to this, Singapore's value had shrunk to being a "potential base" for a British fleet though the Chiefs claimed that, even when empty, Singapore would "restrict Japan's naval action". Much of its value now lay in the "exercise of economic pressure and for the control of commodities essential to our own economic structure". As an indication of how the Chiefs viewed developments in the Far East, they also cited the importance of Malaya as a "footing from which, eventually, we can retrieve the damage to our interests when stronger forces become available".[57]

As for the Pacific, the Chiefs did not contemplate providing any forces and reflected Churchill's confidence that a "full-scale invasion" of Australia and New Zealand would not be mounted by Japan, "at least until Japan had seized Singapore and consolidated her position in the Far East". They also repeated his assurance regarding the abandonment of the Far East.[58] Australia desperately wanted to believe in it and took it at face value, handing over men and equipment in exchange for a blank cheque of doubtful value that could only be banked after the bailiffs had already broken down the front door.

Australia's reliance on Britain to keep her out of war with Japan also was misplaced. Britain was anxious to avoid a single-handed war against Japan but Churchill quickly quashed an argument from the Foreign Office that "it was not in our interests that the United States should be involved in war in the Pacific".[59] He was so concerned at the effect of this argument that he immediately instructed that Britain's ambassadors be clearly informed that "nothing . . . can compare with the importance of the British Empire and the United States being cobelligerent".[60] For Australia, there was the awful prospect that her own security would be sacrificed to the Japanese in order to satisfy the paramount British interest of drawing the Americans into Europe. But the Dominion remained blind to her dilemma.

NOTES

1 CADOGAN DIARY, 29 June 1940, in D. Dilks (ed.), *The Diaries of Sir Alexander Cadogan O.M. 1938–1945*, London, 1971, p. 308

2 LETTERS, Latham to Menzies, 20 June 1940, Menzies to Latham, 22 June 1940, Latham Papers, MS 1009/1/5459: NLA

3 See W. K. HANCOCK, *Smuts*, ii, Cambridge, 1968, p. 354; R. A. Callahan, *Churchill: Retreat from Empire*, Tunbridge Wells, 1984, pp. 102–3

4 See A. J. P. TAYLOR, "The Statesman", in A. J. P. Taylor (ed.), *Churchill: Four Faces and the Man*, London, 1969, pp. 42–3

5 "POLICY IN THE FAR EAST," Memorandum by Halifax, 29 June 1940, CAB 66/9, W.P. (40)234: PRO

6 WAR CABINET CONCLUSIONS, 1 July 1940, CAB 65/8, W.M. 189(40): PRO

7 "POLICY IN THE FAR EAST", Report by the Chiefs of Staff, 4 July 1940, CAB 66/9, W.P. (40)249: PRO

8 WAR CABINET CONCLUSIONS, 5 July 1940, CAB 65/8, W.M. 194(40): PRO

9 TALK WITH SIR HORACE SEYMOUR AND MR ASHLEY CLARKE, 5 July 1940, CRS M100, "July 1940"; Cable No. 520, Bruce to Menzies, 6 July 1940, CP 290/7, Bundle 2, Item 12: AA

10 *IBID*.

11 CABLE, Menzies to Bruce, 9 July 1940, CP 290/9, Bundle 1[16]SC: AA

12 WAR CABINET MINUTES, 9 July 1940, CRS A2673, Vol. 3, Minute 398: AA

13 LETTER, Halifax to Sir Samuel Hoare, 17 July 1940, Templewood Papers, XIII: 20: CUL; War Cabinet Conclusions, 10 and 11 July 1940, CAB 65/8, W.M. 199 and 200(40): PRO

14 WAR CABINET MINUTES, 11 July 1940, CRS A2673, Vol. 3: AA. See also Letter (copy), Fairbairn to Massey-Greene, 13 July 1940, and given to Casey in Washington by another businessman, W.S. Robinson, 21 August 1940, CRS A3300, Item 89: AA

15 See CRS A461, I314/1/4, Part 3: AA

16 LETTERS, Casey to Group Captain Pirie, Air Attaché at the British Embassy, 26 April 1940, Pirie to Casey, 8 May 1940, CRS A3300, Item 87: AA

17 CABLE NO. 201, Casey to Minister for Air, 18 August 1940, CRS A3300, Item 89: AA

18 WAR CABINET MINUTES, 10 July 1940, CRS A2673, Vol. 3: AA; P.G. Taylor, *The Sky Beyond*, Melbourne, 1963, p. 132; War Cabinet Minutes, 3 September 1940, CRS A2673, Vol. 3: AA; War Cabinet Minutes, 1 October 1940, CRS A2673, Vol. 4: AA; David Day, "P.G. Taylor and the Alternative Pacific Air Route 1939–45", *Australian Journal of Politics and History*, Vol. 32, No. 1 (1986)

19 See TALK WITH LLOYD GEORGE, 23 July 1940, 11/1940/74, Liddell Hart Papers: King's College (hereafter KC). See also Channon Diary, 24 July 1940, in R.R. James (ed.), *Chips: The Diaries of Sir Henry Channon*, London, 1967, p. 262

20 LETTER AND MEMORANDUM, Bruce to Halifax, 21 July 1940, CRS M103, "July–December, 1940": AA; Cable, Menzies to Bruce, 22 July 1940, *DAFP*, iv, Doc. 30

21 CABLE NO. 602, Bruce to Menzies, 26 July 1940, *DAFP*, iv, Doc. 36

22 CABLE, Prime Minister's Department to High Commissioner's Office, 23 July 1940, *DAFP*, iv, Doc. 34

23 CABLE, Menzies to Bruce, 25 July 1940, *DAFP*, iv, Doc. 34

24 CABLE, Fraser to Commonwealth Government, 30 July 1940, *DAFP*, iv, Doc. 42

25 MINUTE, Churchill to Ismay, 25 July 1940, quoted in M. Gilbert, p. 679

26 "FAR EASTERN POLICY", Report by the Chiefs of Staff, 27 July 1940, CAB 66/10, W.P. (40)289: PRO

27 WAR CABINET CONCLUSIONS/CONFIDENTIAL ANNEX, 29 July 1940, CAB 65/14, W.M. (40)214: PRO

28 WAR CABINET CONCLUSIONS, 29 July 1940, CAB 65/8, W.M. 214(40): PRO

29 M. GILBERT, p. 686

30 "THE FAR EAST. APPRECIATION BY THE CHIEFS OF STAFF", 5 August 1940, with covering note by Bridges, CAB 66/10, W.P. (40)302: PRO

31 "ASSISTANCE TO THE DUTCH in the Event of Japanese Aggression in Netherlands East Indies", Report by Chiefs of Staff, 7 August 1940, CAB 66/10, W.P. (40)308: PRO

32 WAR CABINET CONCLUSIONS/CONFIDENTIAL ANNEX, 8 August 1940, CAB 65/14, W.M. (40)222: PRO

33 CABLE NO.262, Caldecote to Whiskard, 11 August 1940, *DAFP*, iv, Doc. 64

34 *IBID.*

35 CABLE, Menzies to Bruce, 8 August 1940, *DAFP*, iv, Doc. 54

36 CABLE NO. 766, Bruce to Menzies, 4 September 1940, *DAFP*, iv, Doc. 101

37 CABLE NO. 471, Commonwealth Government to Caldecote, 7 September 1940, *DAFP*, iv, Doc. 106; See also Doc. 136

38 WAR CABINET MINUTES, 2 August 1940, CRS A2673, Vol. 3: AA

39 WAR CABINET CONCLUSIONS, 1 August 1940, CAB 65/8, W.M. 217(40): PRO

40 CABLE, Menzies to Bruce, 6 August 1940, CRS A3300, Item 9: AA

41 TALK WITH JAPANESE AMBASSADOR, 6 August 1940, CRS M100, "August 1940": AA

42 LETTER, Sempill to Bruce, 19 August 1940, AA1970/559/2: AA
43 CABLE NO. 120, Menzies to Casey, 12 August 1940, CRS A3300, Item 9: AA
44 CABLE NO. 457, Menzies to Caldecote, 29 August 1940, *DAFP*, iv, Doc. 84
45 *IBID.*
46 See LETTER, Beaverbrook to Caldecote, 21 August 1940, and Letters, Caldecote to Beaverbrook, 24 and 29 August 1940, BBK D/333, Beaverbrook Papers: House of Lords Record Office (hereafter HLRO)
47 PREM 3/33: PRO; See also War Cabinet Conclusions, 27 September 1940, CAB 65/9, W.M. 260(40): PRO; Dalton Diary, 27 September 1940, Dalton Papers: London School of Economics (hereafter LSE)
48 TALK WITH SINCLAIR AND TALK WITH BEAVERBROOK, both 27 August 1940, CRS M100, "August 1940": AA
49 TALK WITH BEAVERBROOK, 28 August 1940, CRS M100, "August 1940": AA
50 LETTER, Beaverbrook to Caldecote, 1 September 1940, BBK D/333, Beaverbrook Papers: HLRO
51 TALK WITH SIR CHRISTOPHER COURTNEY, 31 August 1940, CRS M100, "August 1940", and Talk with Air Commodore Slessor (Air Ministry) and Major Buchanan (Aircraft Production), 2 September 1940, CRS M100, "September 1940": AA
52 MINUTE TO CHURCHILL, 2 September 1940, BBK D/414, Beaverbrook Papers: HLRO
53 CABLES NO. 761 AND NO. 772, Bruce to Menzies, 3 and 5 September 1940, *DAFP*, iv, Docs 97 and 103; Talk with Major Morton, 6 September 1940, CRS M100, "September 1940": AA
54 WAR CABINET CONCLUSIONS, 4 September 1940, CAB 65/9, W.M. 241(40): PRO
55 CABLE NO. 133, Menzies to Bruce, 10 September 1940, and Cable No. 483, Menzies to Caldecote, 17 September 1940, *DAFP*, iv, Docs 116 and 121; War Cabinet Minutes, 10 and 16 September 1940, CRS A2673, Vol. 3: AA
56 WAR CABINET CONCLUSIONS, 3 October 1940, CAB 65/9, W.M. 265(40): PRO
57 "FUTURE STRATEGY", Appreciation by the Chiefs of Staff, 4 September 1940, CAB 66/11, W.P. (40)362: PRO
58 *IBID.*
59 WAR CABINET CONCLUSIONS, 2 October 1940, CAB 65/9, W.M. 264(40): PRO
60 MINUTE, Churchill to Eden, 4 October 1940, PREM 3/476/10: PRO

5

Japan Begins to Move

October to December 1940

*D*uring September 1940, the Battle of Britain had raged without interruption as German bombers thundered across the light-blue English skies, leaving death and destruction to mark their passing. Australia watched with trepidation as the fate of the mother country was decided afresh day by day. Though the RAF fighter aircraft exacted a heavy toll from the German airmen and forestalled the threat of invasion, events elsewhere cast a shadow over this success, at least as far as Australia was concerned. While Britain could rest secure from invasion during the coming winter months, Australia's predicament in the Pacific worsened.

As Churchill had acknowledged, Britain's *prestige* in the Far East would be enhanced by her victory in the air war over England. But British *strength* in the Far East would not change. Ships and aircraft could alter the Far Eastern balance in Britain's favour but their prior commitment to the Middle East made this impossible. In fact, the balance changed even more in Japan's favour as Britain's attention was focused on the battle at home. During September, Japanese forces marched into northern French Indo-China in a move that continued their encirclement of China but also had potentially serious implications for the Singapore naval base. In addition, Japan, Germany, and Italy on 27 September signed the Tripartite Pact which recognised their separate territorial ambitions and their agreement to combine against the United States if it entered the war.

The conquest of Australia was acknowledged by the Japanese as one of her ultimate ambitions in the Pacific. As Paul Hasluck wrote later, the pact "made it more probable than ever that sooner or later, at a moment when the British Commonwealth was most distressed, Japan would strike".[1] The formalisation of the relationship between the Axis Powers was seen in a similar light in London with one official going so far as to "welcome it because it clears up the Far Eastern situation".[2] While British officials could welcome the fact that far-off Japan had painted herself with the colours of the Axis, Australia should not have been so sanguine. But that was the Australian reaction, the Government paying the pact scant regard and keeping to its commitment to embark the 7th Division for duty overseas.[3]

In the Middle East, British forces were on the defensive as Italian troops moved along the coastal plain towards the important naval base at Alexandria. Outnumbered five to one by the Italians, Britain faced the prospect of losing her hold on the Eastern Mediterranean and perhaps being expelled from the Middle East altogether. Australian troops and ships were committed to hold the region for Britain and their numbers swelled to meet the threat from the Italians. The 7th Division, which Australia had agreed to dispatch to Malaya, was sent instead to the Middle East to complete the build up of some 50,000 Australian troops committed to that theatre, with another 60,000 in AIF training camps in Australia. The Australian troops diverted to Britain during the battle for France were sent on to the Middle East to form the basis of the 9th Division, so that by early 1941 three divisions of the AIF were in the Middle East.

Australia was as resolved as Britain that the Middle East must be held and the presence of her troops helped to ensure that her will did not weaken. The problem was that the commitment to the Eastern Mediterranean not only denuded Australia of fighting men and equipment but negated Britain's ability to dispatch a fleet to the Far East for the naval protection of Australia. The struggle in the Middle East also soaked up the aircraft, tanks, and other equipment surplus to Britain's requirements at home, but of which Australia was particularly deficient. This effectively limited the extent to which Australia could appeal for such equipment for her own defence since it would be at the expense of her troops fighting real battles in the Middle East.

September also saw the first major offensive by British

forces since their expulsion three months earlier from the beaches of Dunkirk. Britain tried to capture for General de Gaulle the Vichy French port of Dakar on the West African coast. However, the plan went awry when the Vichy Government sent cruisers to defend the port against the attacking British naval force which included the RAN flagship, the cruiser *Australia*. The loyal Dominion was not informed of the failure of the operation before it first appeared on the pages of Australian newspapers. Though Australia had never succeeded in throwing off its colonial mentality, she still rankled at being treated in a colonial manner. So the Dakar fiasco produced the first major dispute of the war between Australia and Britain.

It was ironic that Australia should become so disturbed over a matter of form rather than substance. There were good reasons for having a serious set-to with London over its refusal to fulfil Australian requirements of aircraft and the effective negation of their traditional commitment to dispatch a fleet to the Far East. But it was over a matter of appearances that Menzies was urged by Bruce to make a stand. In a strongly worded message to Churchill on 29 September, Menzies questioned the decision to attack Dakar without "overwhelming chances of success" and berated the British Prime Minister for not keeping the Australian Government informed which, he claimed, had "frequently proved humiliating". As a final dig, Menzies told Churchill of the Australian Government's anxiety that the difficulties in the Middle East, where "clear cut victory is essential", may have been underestimated.[4]

Menzies' message caused considerable annoyance in Whitehall. With the unanimous approval of his War Cabinet, Churchill immediately replied with a stinging rebuttal of the Australian criticisms. Dismissing the Dakar attack as just a minor operation, Churchill chided Menzies for not extending a "broad and generous measure of indulgence" towards Britain for the "great exertions we have made" in the general war effort. As for the particular criticisms of the attack, he refused to accept that an operation must have an overwhelming chance of success or that the Dakar operation was a "half-hearted attack". It was galling for Churchill to receive any criticism of his strategic prowess and particularly so at a time when the greatest achievement of his life, the Battle of Britain, was being fought to a successful conclusion. He had outmanoeuvred those people in Britain prepared to accept a compromise peace with Germany only to find his distant Dominion demanding overwhelming chances of success and questioning Britain's ability to hold the Middle East. Churchill had incurred the displeasure of some of his own colleagues in reinforcing the Middle East at the expense of Britain's own defence and now Menzies implied that he had put it at risk. Churchill rounded on his Australian counterpart over this, supplying Menzies with details of the British reinforcements and strenuously denying that the "Mother Country has shirked her share of perils and sacrifice".[5]

Menzies' critical cable had been sent to Churchill in the immediate wake of the Australian general election on 21 September in which the Labor Party had come close to ousting him from office. His continued tenure in the Prime Ministerial Lodge depended on the support of two independent MPs. As one sympathetic observer noted, Menzies' position was "extremely difficult" as he had "made so many enemies in politics and has so few real friends".[6] Menzies was well aware of his vulnerability but he was equally determined to shore up his position and retain his grip on power.[7] This may have been responsible for his reaction to Churchill's angry cable.

While Menzies' survival was threatened by humiliating incidents like Dakar, the support for his party rested on an identification with Britain and Churchill in their titanic struggle against Germany. A vote for Menzies was a vote for Churchill, or so Menzies had implied during the election campaign. As such, any public breach between the two men could have devastating political results. So Menzies was as alarmed by Churchill's cable as Churchill had been angered by Menzies'. In a humiliating climb-down, Menzies admitted that his cable had been "crudely expressed" and denied "even the faintest suggestion that you or the British Government are half-hearted in policy, spirit or achievement". He pointed to the political problems that might soon see him removed from office and gushingly proclaimed his pride to be associated "with the efforts of Winston Churchill and the British people". Menzies denied any imputation that Britain had "shirked her share of the perils or sacrifice" in the Middle East but equally rejected any such imputation about Australia. He proudly proclaimed that his Government had overruled "much public doubt caused by a real fear of what Japan may do" and had raised naval, air, and military forces for Britain's use overseas.[8]

In order to ensure continued Japanese passivity, Australia was careful not to antagonise her by any provocative actions. In particular, the Australian Government resisted attempts by residents of New Caledonia to break with the Vichy Government of France. During August 1940, the Vichy Government took advantage of the Australian anxiety to strengthen its own forces in the colony by dispatching a naval ship from Tahiti. Australia still held back from taking any action, hoping that an accommodation could be reached with the Vichy officials on the island. Britain now wanted action to remove Vichy and install an administration sympathetic to de Gaulle. Accordingly, the War Cabinet urged the Australian Government to dispatch the RAN cruiser, *Adelaide*, to the island, ostensibly to restore the *status quo ante*, but in the hope that its arrival would inspire the Free French elements to mount a *coup d'état*.[9] Though Australia was opposed to any change in the political status of New Caledonia, the Government acceded to the British request by agreeing to send the *Adelaide* as far as the New Hebrides where it would await events before possibly proceeding to New Caledonia. The Dominion resisted British attempts to provoke a "de Gaulle revolution" since, they claimed, it would be just playing into Japanese hands without benefiting the Allied cause.[10]

In the event, Australia allowed the *Adelaide* to go on to New Caledonia where, as London had anticipated, the force of its presence eventually overcame the resistance of the Vichy officials.[11] Though Australia claimed to recognise the Pacific as an area where she had a predominant interest, she buckled under British pressure to pursue a policy that she felt was bristling with potentially dangerous implications for Australian security. It was not, as one writer claimed, a situation where "Australian and Imperial interests more or less coincided".[12] Quite the opposite as far as Canberra was concerned. As Australia feared, though probably not as a direct consequence, the dispatch of the Australian cruiser to New Caledonia was followed within days by Japanese troops marching into Saigon thereby pre-empting any pro-de Gaulle coup in that colony and bringing Japanese forces that much closer to Singapore.

One of the consequences of Australia's close election contest in September was a renewal of calls for the establishment of a national government. Sections of the press had been increasingly critical of the Menzies administration but they were practically united in calling for the political parties to set aside their differences for the common cause.[13] But there were insuperable obstacles blocking such an achievement. The Labor Party was racked by divisions, especially in New South Wales, and was barely held together by the force of John Curtin's leadership. He was not sufficiently safe from attack to adopt the idea of a national government even if he accepted it as a dire national need. The election result had left the Parliament so evenly divided that some Labor tacticians preferred to bide their time in the expectation that they might soon form a government in their own right. As well, bitter experience of previous "national" administrations acted as a cautionary reminder for advocates of political unity. During the Great War, the formation of Billy Hughes' national government had split the Labor Party and robbed it of the opportunity to implement its policies. In the 1930s a similar administration under the former Labor Treasurer, Joe Lyons, had kept Labor out of power for almost a decade.[14]

Though Australian politicians could not agree on the formation of a national government, they did implement the next best thing. On 28 October, Menzies established an Advisory War Council comprised of four Government Ministers together with four Labor members. Though this move helped to stabilise the political situation, there was a price to be paid. The Labor members had to be taken into the Government's confidence and made privy to decisions on defence. In the privacy of the Council room, the Labor members could question the rationale of Government defence policy and exploit the potential differences among the Government ranks on the relative priority of home defence. They also had the opportunity to interrogate the Chiefs of Staff about the Government's defence effort and to question the continued relegation in priority of home defence.

At the first meeting of the Council on 29 October, Curtin requested information on the "present disposition of the ships of the R.A.N. and the possibility of disposing them for the defence of the waters to the north of Australia" as well as "information regarding naval mines and the possibility of arranging for a battleship to be located near Singapore". Two weeks later, Labor's deputy leader, Frank Forde, followed up his leader's question by asking for the time it would take RAN units to return in the case of an attack against Australia. He also asked the new Chief of the General Staff (CGS) Lieutenant General Sturdee, whether Australia was "in a position to defend herself today" and, if not, "when it is expected that Australia will be in such a position".[15] These were questions that were not usually posed since it had been a basic presumption that Australia never would be in such a position. While Menzies and his military advisers were facing these questions, military representatives from Britain, Australia, and New Zealand were meeting in Singapore for a conference on Far Eastern defence. The deficiencies in the defence of Singapore exposed by this conference added to the political pressure on Menzies to provide a greater effort for the defence of Australia.

The dearth of British naval ships in Far Eastern waters was becoming an increasing worry and was matched by a growing realisation that the forces deployed in Malaya and Singapore would be unable to prevent a Japanese takeover. The newly appointed British Commander in Chief at Singapore, Air Chief Marshal Sir Robert Brooke-Popham, set out the parlous position of his new command. In a letter to General Ismay, Churchill's Chief of Staff, he acknowledged that the "requirements of Singapore must come a bad third to those of the British Isles and of the Middle East". Nevertheless, he pressed for the deficiencies at Singapore to be made good now and not after a war had begun with Japan. He complained that his frontline air strength was fourteen per cent of the level recommended by the Chiefs of Staff and that there were no modern fighters or long-range bombers. He was also "very short" of field artillery and had less than half the recommended level of anti-aircraft guns.[16]

The weaknesses of Singapore still did not prompt the Australian Government to increase its own defences now that the much vaunted naval base was shown to be a paper fortress. In fact, the Singapore conference had reaffirmed Australia's strategic touchstone — that the defence of Australia hinged on the defence of Singapore. The conference therefore increased the British pressure on Australia to dispatch yet more troops from its own shores to build up the defences of Singapore. The 7th Division, originally destined for Malaya, was then on its way to the Middle East. So a brigade of the still-forming 8th Division was dispatched for garrison duties in Malaya on the understanding that eventually they would be replaced by Indian troops, with the Australians being sent on to join their comrades in the Middle East.[17]

Following the revelations of the Singapore conference, it was more important than ever that Australia build up her own defences, particularly in the air. But the expansion of the air force depended on the supply of suitable aircraft from Britain and these were not being made available. Bruce had fulfilled his undertaking not to press Britain on this subject during September while the Air Ministry in London was supposedly preparing its planned program of deliveries to Australia. Nine, not four, valuable weeks elapsed before Bruce took the matter up once again only to find that Britain still refused to give any written undertaking as to how she proposed to supply Australia's aircraft requirements. According to the Air Ministry, Churchill was being pressed by Beaverbrook to keep tight control over aircraft distribution.[18]

Bruce complained to British officials that he was faced with having to admit to Canberra that "there were no plans and that no indication could be given as to how and when Australia's requirements could be met". He confided that this would create a "most deplorable impression upon the Australian Government" and pleaded to be able to "send at least a reasonable reply to Australia". He pointed out that Britain would be "committing itself to very little if it agreed a tentative programme but by doing so they would avoid what looked like ... degenerating into a first class brawl".[19] Bruce failed to realise that Britain could not draw up such a program because she had no intention of sending operational aircraft to nonactive theatres such as Australia, whatever the risk might be of future hostilities with Japan.

It was a further week before Bruce reported his difficulties to Australia. In a cable on 14 November, he claimed that he had refused to accept a blank refusal from Whitehall and had demanded from the Ministry of Aircraft Production "reasonable information" about "how and when it is contemplated your requirements will be met". Failing satisfaction, Bruce proposed to take the matter up with Churchill as the "continuance of the present position is quite intolerable".[20] It was nearly three months since Bruce first had raised the matter with British officials in August. He had not only failed to secure the delivery of even one aircraft to Australia during that time but had failed even in his limited aim of securing a tentative program of deliveries. He also had deliberately failed to inform Australia on the progress of his efforts for fear of causing a dispute between the two countries. In truth, Bruce sympathised with Britain's predicament in Europe and was not prepared to accord a high priority to Australia's potential peril in the Pacific. His apparent apathy was matched by an almost similar lack of concern from Australia.

Though Bruce was informed in September of Australia's vital aircraft needs for the expansion of the RAAF, the Australian Government did not provide him with the constant pressure that such a problem demanded. This was partly due to Bruce who delayed informing Australia of the resistance he was meeting in London. But it was also due to the political problems in Australia, both before and after the September election. For too long political survival outranked national survival in the priorities of Australian leaders.

Only at the end of November, in the wake of the defence conference at Singapore, did Australia increase the pressure on Britain for the supply of aircraft on order. The War Cabinet was then informed of plans to achieve a minimum strength for the RAAF of 320 modern aircraft. Even this strength for the whole of Australia was less than that recommended by Britain for Singapore and Malaya. More important was the admission that Australia had at the end of November only forty-two modern aircraft, and none of these were fighter planes. The RAAF needed 278 more aircraft just to provide the planned thirty-two squadrons with their initial allocation and without making any allowance for wastage. Of the thirty-two squadrons, only two were to be equipped with fighter aircraft since it was considered that the Royal Navy would prevent the possibility of high performance, land-based planes gaining a base close enough to attack Australia. Thus, even if the RAAF had been supplied with the aircraft it requested, it would not have been much better equipped to face the threat that eventually developed in 1942.[21]

While Bruce was in London deferring consideration of Australia's perceived needs, Menzies seemed to be more concerned with turning the war to the advantage of Australia's post-war industrial development. Instead of bending his efforts to obtaining modern fighter aircraft, Menzies sought to increase the production of aircraft within Australia as part of an integrated Empire scheme whereby Australia would supply planes for that part of the British Empire east of Egypt. Such a scheme had certain long-term defence advantages for Australia but it would require some years to reach fruition and defence advantages were not the ones Menzies had uppermost in his mind. Rather, he hoped to use the establishment of such an industry in wartime as the basis for a British-controlled automobile manufacturing industry in peacetime that would quash American pre-war moves to dominate the Australian automobile industry. However, before such an industry could be established, trained men, machine tools and other essential equipment would have to come from Britain. It thus would face the same problems as Bruce was experiencing in trying to extract promises of aircraft. As well, it was predicated on the assumption that Australia would specialise in the production of certain types of aircraft for general use, with other types coming from Britain.[22] Menzies also entertained similar hopes about the establishment, with British assistance, of a shipbuilding industry in Australia.[23]

Despite the increasing evidence that Imperial defence would not work in Australia's favour, the Dominion did not make any great effort to ensure her security by other methods, though there was some extension of Australian representation abroad with the appointment of Sir John Latham as Australian Minister to Japan. This appointment was a reflection of Australia's anxiety to ensure peace in the Pacific and an implicit recognition that she could hold different views from Britain on how to achieve it. Under pressure from Whitehall and Bruce, Menzies had delayed sending a Minister to Tokyo for over a year. It was perhaps more than coincidence that Latham's appointment was announced in August shortly before the Federal election, though he did not present his credentials in Tokyo until Christmas Eve 1940. Part of Latham's delay in arriving in Japan was caused by the apparent obligation to travel by a British ship and thereby take thirty-eight days to do what could be done in fourteen days by a Japanese ship. But he was also delayed by having to await the outcome of the Australian election and consult with the incoming government. His brief from Menzies' re-elected Government was to foster friendship with Japan, though on important issues "his aim would be to temporise and gain time to allow for the development of the growing strength of our defences". The concept of a general settlement in the Far East remained to one side.[24]

As for Australian relations with the United States, there was a growing conviction that Australian security hinged on the power of the United States Pacific fleet at Pearl Harbor to deter Japan from any adventures southward. But this conviction was still not reflected in any rush by Australia to develop closer relations with Washington. Casey, as the Australian Minister to the United States, had carved out a position of some influence in the American capital but his role remained one of acting in close consultation and co-ordination with the British Ambassador, Lord Lothian. They talked together practically every day and would often visit the State Department or Roosevelt in tandem, as if there was no distinction between the interests they were representing. As Casey later proclaimed, the first priority was "close integration of the British countries" followed by the "closest possible British–American relations".[25]

However, even Casey seemed to sense that there was potential for conflict between Australia and Britain in their relations with Washington. This was true with regard to competing demands for American aircraft and also with regard to occasional proposals that arose for the transfer of part of the United States Pacific fleet to the Atlantic. It is possible that Casey's close relationship with Lord Lothian served Australia well in this respect at least. They shared a conviction in the deterrent power of the United States fleet and opposed any proposals for its transfer from the Pacific.[26]

Much of Casey's activity in Washington during 1940 was devoted to publicising the British cause with a view to moving America closer to involvement in the war. Only part of the effort involved creating a sense of American responsibility for Australian security. In backing Casey's proposals for publicising Australia in the United States, the Australian Department of Information acknowledged Britain's naval "embarrassment" in the Far East and proclaimed America's Pacific policy as the "vital element in present Australian security".[27] In December 1940 an Australian News and Information Bureau (ANIB) was established in New York. Menzies justified it to the Labor members of the Advisory War Council in terms that would appeal to their inclinations, even going so far as to suggest that Britain "might be defeated in the war and a re-grouping of English-speaking countries might arise".[28] But economic reasons also played their part. As the report on its establishment indicated, the ANIB after the war would play a "very great part in assisting us to find markets throughout the Pacific".[29] At the same time, the Australian Government remained reluctant to forge any closer defence links that could imply any diminution of her links with Britain.

At the beginning of September, Casey foresaw the possibility of the United States obtaining base facilities in the south-west Pacific along lines recently granted to them by Churchill in the British West Indies. Though he advised Canberra that a United States request was unlikely at present, he suggested that he be provided with the "most telling arguments that I could have up my sleeve for use on appropriate opportunities".[30] After three weeks without a reply from Canberra, Casey again asked for the Australian view which, he assured them, would not commit Australia to any action but he urgently needed "talking points as to broad avenues of possible cooperation in [the] Southwestern Pacific".[31] From his Washington vantage point, Casey seems to have had a clearer view of Australia's dangerously exposed position than the Government in Canberra. His call for possible American bases was a switch in thinking from his previous opposition to allowing Pan American Airways landing rights in Australia. But Canberra remained unrepentant.

The War Cabinet was advised that Casey's proposals necessarily involved consultation with the British Government in relation to her Pacific colonies such as Fiji. The War Cabinet agreed to seek a "considered appreciation" from London. There was no sense of urgency in the Australian response nor any apparent eagerness to place Australian facilities at the disposal of the United States.[32] Casey later used his own initiative to urge Lothian to "seek authority to offer free joint use to [the] United States for any defence purpose of any of [the] Pacific Islands regarding which [the] United States have claimed sovereignty from Britain".[33]

Casey made more attempts on his own initiative to strengthen defence ties between Australia and the United States than the Australian Government ever sought to make during 1940.[34]

It was not that Casey wanted the United States permanently to replace Britain as Australia's traditional protector. His starting point for all his dealings in Washington was that Australia was a British country. Without interfering with this rigid relationship, Casey tried to make Washington recognise the defence of Britain's Empire, including Australia, as being an American interest. According to Casey, it was important that Americans were not urged to defend the British Empire but that they be allowed to "continue to act on the assumption that American defence policy should be based on American interests".[35] Despite Casey's efforts, the Australian Government continued to hold America at arm's length, made some concession to Japan with the appointment of Latham, and bowed to British pressure not to appoint a Minister to China. But it was her relations with the neighbouring Dominion of New Zealand that provided a graphic illustration of Australia's continuing *non possumus* attitude towards her own defence in the Pacific.

In mid-August, the Minister for External Affairs, John Mc-Ewen, submitted a proposal to the Australian Cabinet for the exchange of liaison officials with the New Zealand Department of External Affairs. He pointed to the close identity of interest between the two countries and argued that an exchange would allow for "consultation before the formulation of policy" without the expense of establishing a High Commissioner's office in Wellington. McEwen was careful to assure his colleagues of just how economical his proposal would be. At a time when the two Dominions might soon find themselves standing alone in the Pacific, McEwen's measure was an obvious move in Australia's interest. In 1939, the lack of such consultation had led to political embarrassment for the Australian Government over the New Zealand decision to dispatch an expeditionary force. Despite the obvious advantages, it was approved but never implemented, perhaps because Australia did not want to appear to be co-ordinating policies separate from those of London.[36]

Similarly, Australia now fell in with London and Washington and stepped up the economic pressure on Japan despite Australian fears that it might push Tokyo towards war. On the emotive issue of scrap iron for Japan, Australia had resisted public pressure to place an embargo on its export, partly for economic reasons but also for fear of causing resentment in

Japan.[37] However, in early November, Australia submitted to British pressure to impose an embargo on scrap iron and other "strategic war materials" in an effort to prevent Japan accumulating stockpiles of such materials with which to wage war.[38] The corollary of this argument, which Australia implicitly ignored, was that the decline in Japanese stockpiles produced by such an embargo would eventually reach a critical level at which point Japan would face the alternative of either being impelled into war or submitting to the will of the de facto Anglo–American alliance. By this logic, the embargo would limit Japan's freedom of diplomatic manoeuvre and perhaps hasten her entry into the war rather than prevent it.

The invasion and defeat of Britain was made unlikely by early October. With the RAF very much intact, on 17 September Hitler had postponed his invasion plans. On 2 October 1940, the Royal Navy's Director of Naval Intelligence, Admiral Godfrey, advised that the threat of invasion was steadily diminishing, an opinion shared by Churchill a week later when he confided to Beaverbrook that the "Invasion danger is easier". On 12 October, Hitler ordered the postponement of the invasion until the spring of 1941. By late October, British authorities had conclusive evidence that German attention had switched towards an attack on the Balkans.[39]

According to the official history of British intelligence operations, Whitehall saw the planned Balkan offensive as being aimed at threatening their hold on the Middle East and diverting resources from the defence of Britain; that Whitehall "failed to discern that the strategic purpose underlying these attacks was to safeguard the southern flank of Germany's invasion of Russia". In other words, despite the successful Battle of Britain, British authorities still regarded an eventual German invasion of Britain as being the main aim of Berlin. As such, they were justified in retaining the maximum strength in the British Isles with which to beat off such an invasion. In fact, on 16 October, just four days after Hitler had called off the invasion, Britain's Minister for Economic Warfare, Hugh Dalton, confided in his diary of growing rumours "through various telegrams and other agencies, that the Germans may attack the Russians in the spring". Militarily, Britain was not yet out of the woods but at least the German wolf was no longer breathing down her neck.[40]

Meanwhile, Australia was steadily drifting into a position

of great peril. As a naval officer in the RN's Plans Division recalled, British naval opinion was convinced by late 1940 that Japan would enter the war "as soon as she could swallow up the British Far Eastern Empire — Australia included, without undue hazard to herself".[41] Britain was planning on the basis of these assumptions and allocating the Pacific as a sphere of American control while retaining control of the Indian Ocean for herself in any joint war with Japan. Australia complied with this arrangement, although as we have seen, she made little effort to encourage closer collaboration with the United States. This was partly but not wholly due to America's own reluctance to be seen publicly edging towards war during a Presidential election year.[42]

Britain's policy for any Far Eastern war was established by Churchill to be one of strict defence until the war in Europe was won. In late October, Churchill supported the restoration of Britain's battleship construction program because, he argued, "at the end of the war we should be faced with the formidable task of clearing up the situation in the Far East, and we should be unequal to that task if we fell behind Japan in capital ship construction".[43] This implied a definite commitment to wrest back from Japan any gains she might make during the war. But Britain did not envisage having to make any great commitment in the interim to prevent Japanese gains becoming too extensive. According to Churchill, British policy called for a "strict defensive in the Far East and the acceptance of its consequences".[44] Churchill and the Chiefs of Staff relied on an optimistic perception of Japan's military ability that was partly based on Japanese difficulties in the Chinese war and partly based on racist notions of Japanese inferiority.[45]

While establishing a strictly defensive policy in the Far East, Churchill continued to maintain for Australia's benefit the fiction that the Dominion's security remained guaranteed by Britain. Even as he announced to Menzies his plans to build up a "very large army representing the whole Empire and ample sea power in the Middle East", he was careful to add that such a build up also would allow for a "move eastward in your direction if need be".[46] There was no provision in this blasé assurance for the possibility of simultaneous attacks by Germany in the Middle East and Japan in the Far East. Australia preferred to accept the assurance at face value rather than question it and have to adopt an expensive policy of greater defence self-reliance. After decades of dependence and in the depths of a war when items of defence equipment were almost impossible to obtain, such a switch in defence policy would have been fraught with difficulties. Not least would have been the political difficulty of explaining to an anxious electorate that the conservative touchstone of Imperial defence had ceased to operate.

Meanwhile, Britain continued her policy of "tightening the screw" on Japan, though not without some misgivings by the Foreign Office that the policy of increasing firmness not backed by the ultimate sanction of armed force was liable to come unstuck at an inconvenient moment. This was the clear implication of a memorandum by "Rab" Butler, Parliamentary Under Secretary at the Foreign Office and Chairman of the War Cabinet's Far Eastern Committee. In mid-December, he reported to the War Cabinet that the "cumulative effect" of the increasing economic embargo against Japan "may be considerable" and warned that "diplomatic persuasion and economic pressure depend for their ultimate effectiveness upon a backing of potential force".[47] In the wake of the Tripartite Pact and following the lead provided by the United States, Churchill seems to have ignored this advice and to have been emboldened in his policy of increasing the economic pressure on Japan.

In Churchill's view, Britain had little to lose. According to his calculation the Japanese would not move in great force against the British Empire in the Far East, except for Hong Kong, so long as the United States fleet remained at Honolulu where it provided a potential threat on the flank of any deep move to the south by the Japanese. If Anglo–American pressure provoked Japan into declaring war on the English-speaking world, then Churchill would be well content. That is, provided America adopted Britain's view of responding to a Japanese attack with a defensive strategy in the Pacific while concentrating her main effort against Germany. This America agreed to do after talks in November 1940 between Roosevelt and his defence chiefs. Churchill exulted on learning of the American decision which he described as "strategically sound and also most highly adapted to our interests".[48]

The possible implications for Australia of Churchill's strategy were shattering but the loyal Dominion remained, at best, dimly aware of her predicament. She continued with her commitment to the Middle East and maintained pressure on Britain to build up her forces in that region. As for Singapore, that was meant to be protected by land and air forces until relieved by the arrival of a fleet. After the Singapore defence conference, the weakness of the air forces at Singapore became painfully apparent. Australia's reaction was to agree to the dispatch of poorly equipped Australian troops whose task was to defend, without adequate air cover, a naval base with no ships.[49]

Though the Australian Government tended to be apathetic towards the home defence of the Australian continent, they were well aware of the deep public anxiety, with its long-established racial overtones, regarding the possibility of a Japanese invasion. While Menzies dismissed the likelihood of such an invasion, he realised that it was of vital political importance that the Australian public continued to place its faith in the system of Imperial defence and that it not become aware of the deficiencies at Singapore.

This was Menzies' argument when reporting to London on the Australian Government's reaction to the Singapore defence conference. On 1 December, he warned Whitehall that the "extent of Australian co-operation in overseas theatres is dependent on the Australian public's *impression of the degree of local security that exists*". Accepting the inadequacy of British naval forces at Singapore, Menzies pressed for "immediate action to remedy deficiencies in Army and Air Forces both in numbers and equipment", but then undercut this plea by agreeing to dispatch to Singapore a brigade of the 8th Division together with various items of military equipment. Thus Australia became further denuded of trained troops for the sake of maintaining the myth of Singapore in the Australian consciousness.[50]

The following day, Menzies disclosed this cable to the Labor members of the Advisory War Council. They were more concerned with the reality of Australian security rather than the public's impression of it. The depth of their concern was revealed when they recommended that "further enquiries should be made as to the possibility of obtaining immediate delivery of fighter types of aircraft, and the importance of the continuance of the negotiations was emphasized". But it was not London that they had in mind for supplying aircraft but Tokyo. They had adopted enthusiastically a suggestion by the newly appointed Minister to Japan that Australia should look to Tokyo for the supply of their aircraft requirements. It really was a terribly naive idea but it provided a dramatic illustration of Australia's desperate search for some accommodation with Japan and of its frustration at the British failure to supply her urgent defence requirements. Though Tokyo replied that it was "anxious to supply both service and training types", the Japanese regretted they were unable to deliver until the end of 1941. Then they delivered with a vengeance![51]

A more fruitful suggestion was made by the Labor members when they argued that recent British successes in the Middle East should allow Britain to divert from the Mediterranean three or four battleships for basing at Singapore. Menzies' reaction was to seek Churchill's view informally on the matter from Bruce before making any formal request.[52] There is no indication that Bruce or Menzies bothered to follow up this request. They did not support the depletion of naval strength in the Mediterranean and were aware that it probably would not be acceptable to Whitehall.[53] Instead, the Advisory War Council was informed by Menzies of the return of two RAN vessels to the Australian naval station.[54] Menzies also gave them the substance of a cable from Churchill on the pretext that it constituted a reply to their request when in fact it was a response to Menzies' cable of 1 December. He apparently omitted from his report to the AWC, Churchill's acceptance in the cable of the Australian brigade for Singapore.[55]

This cable from Churchill was a further effort to reassure Australian anxiety about the Far East while simultaneously drawing off Australian forces for the Middle East. He rejected any immediate possibility of dispatching the Mediterranean fleet to Singapore and counselled Australia to "bear our Eastern anxieties patiently and doggedly" on the express understanding that "if Australia is seriously threatened by invasion we should not hesitate to compromise or sacrifice the Mediterranean position for the sake of our kith and kin". He confided that the danger of war with Japan was "definitely less" than six months previously and, even if Japan did enter the war, he was "persuaded" that the United States would "come in on our side, which will put the naval boot very much on the other leg, and be deliverance from many perils".[56] It would be deliverance for Britain certainly, but possibly quite the opposite for Australia.

In order to continue the Australian commitment to the Middle East, Churchill again argued forcefully, but tenuously, that Britain's policy was to build up a huge Middle Eastern force that would be kept in a "fluid condition" to prosecute the war in the Eastern Mediterranean or to reinforce Singapore. He observed that "great objects are at stake and risks must be run in every quarter of the globe".[57] In fact, Australia was being asked to run great risks in its quarter of the globe in order to shore up British interests in another quarter. However, Churchill's assurances had the effect he desired. Australia went ahead with the proposal to send a brigade of its troops to Malaya, kept to its Middle East commitment and accepted Britain's refusal to send the fleet to Singapore. Australian concern over the British bastion became overshadowed by political storms in Canberra and by Menzies' decision to visit London.

The ostensible reason for Menzies' visit to London was to discuss the defence of Singapore in the light of the alarming conclusions of the Singapore defence conference. However, such a visit had been on Menzies' private agenda almost from the beginning of the war. The conference conclusions simply provided a pressing and dramatic rationale that would overwhelm any opposition to the visit.[58] The close election result had confirmed his position at the top of a political framework verging on collapse and had made Menzies more amenable to take political risks that would either shore up his position in Canberra or even lead to greater heights in London. At just forty-six years of age he had reached the peak of Australian politics only to find the view from the top disappointing. Despite his unanimous re-election to the party leadership he remained ensconced in the Lodge on sufferance from MPs who hated him for his arrogance and from a country unable to decide on an alternative because of the divided Labor Party.

The criticism of Menzies' leadership intensified after the election. His political troubles were caused as much by his attempts to introduce limited war measures, such as petrol rationing, as they were by his failure to institute measures consistent with total war. He was not satisfying either group and the contrast between his strong words and vacillating action only served to create an impression of weakness. Following a speech by Menzies criticising public apathy towards the war, the Sydney *Sun* replied with a blistering editorial blaming Menzies for creating the apathy and claiming that it was "not apathy that is the trouble, but the lack of confidence in leaders who fail to lead".[59]

Under the pressure of this mounting criticism, Menzies made a private approach to Churchill through the British High Commissioner in Canberra urging that there be a conference of Dominion Prime Ministers in London. This suggestion was made in late October before the results of the Singapore conference had been relayed to Australia. He also requested that the idea for such a conference in London should be seen to come from Downing Street and not from the Dominions. His political opponents would be unable to deny him the trip to London if Churchill issued general invitations to the Dominion leaders, but they could well prevent Menzies taking the initiative to organise such a conference.[60]

Churchill was not about to play Menzies' game. The idea of Dominion Prime Ministers meeting together and perhaps interfering in the strategy of the war did not have any appeal for him. Instead, Menzies was invited to visit the Imperial capital by himself.[61] This was not what Menzies wanted but he overcame possible political opposition to a lone visit by seizing on the conclusions of the Singapore conference as justification for urgent talks with Churchill. On 25 November, he informed the Advisory War Council of the "alarming position in regard to the defence of Singapore, as revealed by the report of the recent Singapore Conference, and the probability that a request would be made to Australia for the dispatch of a Brigade Group, together with certain essential supplies of munitions". He claimed that "this and other matters which he had in mind indicated the necessity for the Head of the Government to visit London for a discussion with the Prime Minister of the United Kingdom". This had the effect Menzies desired, though problems in Parliament during early December prevented him from making firm plans for the visit.[62]

Despite the urgency Menzies claimed for the trip, it was not until 17 December that he advised Bruce that he would "accept [the] outstanding invitation to visit London to discuss matters of mutual war importance". Even then, he did not propose leaving until mid-January, after the Christmas holidays and during Australia's parliamentary recess when he could not be ousted in his absence.[63] As the Melbourne *Age* observed, it was the best time for Menzies to leave since the political situation was "as placid as can be expected at any period during this Parliament, and that, while it may deteriorate within a year, it is hardly likely to improve".[64] En route to London, Menzies proposed visiting Australian troops in the Middle East. His program would land him in London in February 1941, some three months after he had informed the Advisory War Council of the pressing need for consultations with Churchill.

Menzies had complained long and often about the lack of consultation by Britain about policies affecting Australia's national interest. His visit to London would give him the opportunity to put Australia's view at the highest level and in the most direct manner. There was much that needed to be said if Australian security was to be safeguarded in the Pacific. Events would reveal that Menzies was not the man to say it.

NOTES

1 P. HASLUCK, p. 294
2 HARVEY DIARY, 29 September 1940, ADD. MS. 56397, Harvey Papers: British Library (hereafter BL)
3 P. HASLUCK, p. 229
4 CABLE, Menzies to Bruce, 29 September 1940, *DAFP*, iv, Doc. 144
5 CABLE, Churchill to Menzies, 2 October 1940, *DAFP*, iv, Doc. 152; See also War Cabinet Conclusions, 1 October 1940, CAB 65/9, W.M. 263(40): PRO; See also Talk with Churchill, 2 October 1940, *DAFP*, iv, Doc. 153
6 LETTER, Sir Frederick Eggleston to R. Mackay, 8 October 1940, MS 423/1/143, Eggleston Papers: NLA
7 CABLE, Menzies to Bruce, 4 October 1940, CRS M100, "October 1940": AA
8 CABLE, Menzies to Churchill, 4 October 1940, *DAFP*, iv, Doc. 158
9 WAR CABINET CONCLUSIONS, 30 August 1940, CAB 65/8, W.M. 238(40): PRO
10 See *DAFP*, iv, Docs 83, 88, 89, 92, 93, 102, 105 and 109
11 See *DAFP*, iv, Docs 110−14, 124, 126, 130−3 and 138
12 M. SIMINGTON, "Australia and the New Caledonia Coup D'Etat of 1940", *Australian Outlook*, 1976, p. 91
13 See *SUN*, *Sydney Morning Herald*, Sydney, *Advertiser*, Adelaide, 14 October 1940; *Sun*, *Herald*, Melbourne, *Courier-Mail*, *Telegraph*, Brisbane, 15 October 1940
14 See P. HASLUCK, pp. 247−71
15 ADVISORY WAR COUNCIL MINUTES, 29 October 1940, CRS A2682, Vol. 1, Minute 7; Letter, Forde to Shedden, 12 November 1940, CRS A5954, Box 495: AA

16 LETTER, Brooke-Popham to Ismay, 26 October 1940, V/1/1, Brooke-Popham Papers: KC

17 See P. HASLUCK, pp. 294–7; D. M. Horner, pp. 51–2

18 TALK WITH CAPTAIN BALFOUR (AIR MINISTRY), 5 November 1940, CRS M100, "November 1940": AA

19 TALK WITH SIR CHARLES GARDNER, 6 November 1940, CRS M100, "November 1940": AA

20 CABLE NO. 1006, Bruce to Menzies, 14 November 1940, CRS M100, "November 1940": AA

21 WAR CABINET MINUTES, 26 November 1940, CRS A2673, Vol. 4, Minute 632: AA

22 CABLE NO. 122, Menzies to Bruce, 9 September 1940, CRS A5954, Box 223; "Production of Aircraft in Australia", War Cabinet Agendum No. 229/1940 by Fadden, 14 October 1940, CRS A5954, Box 223; War Cabinet Minutes, 31 October 1940, CRS A2673, Vol. 4, Minute 598: AA

23 CABLE NO. 987, Menzies to Bruce, 5 November 1940, and Bruce to Menzies, 28 November 1940, CRS A1608, H61/2/1: AA

24 ADVISORY WAR COUNCIL MINUTES, 29 October 1940, CRS A2682, Vol. 1, Minute 4: AA

25 LETTER, Casey to Norman Makin, 6 June 1946, MS 4663, Makin Papers: NLA

26 See R. G. CASEY, *Personal Experience, 1939–46*, London, 1962, p. 40; Cable, Casey to Department of External Affairs, 3 October 1940, CRS A3300, Item 10: AA

27 LETTER, Keith Murdoch to Casey, 9 September 1940, enclosing report by R. J. F. Boyer, head of the American section at the Department of Information, CRS A3300, Item 66: AA

28 ADVISORY WAR COUNCIL MINUTES, 25 November 1940, CRS A2682, Vol. 1, Minute 41: AA

29 CABLE NO. 52, Menzies to Casey, 28 December 1940, CRS A3300, Item 66: AA

30 CABLE NO. 240, Casey to External Affairs Department, 3 September 1940, CRS A3300, Item 38: AA

31 CABLE NO. 280, Casey to External Affairs Department, 24 September 1940, CRS A3300, Item 38: AA

32 WAR CABINET MINUTES, 24 September 1940, CRS A2673, Vol. 4, Minute 526: AA

33 CABLE NO. 292, Casey to Menzies, 1 October 1940, *DAFP*, iv, Doc. 151

34 See R. G. CASEY, *Personal Experience*, pp. 36–7, p. 50; see also, for example, *DAFP*, iv, Docs 99, 151, 168, 173, 177

35 CABLE NO. 279, Casey to Department of External Affairs, 24 September 1940, *DAFP*, iv, Doc. 137

36 SUBMISSION BY MCEWEN, 13 August 1940, *DAFP*, iv, Doc. 71

37 DRAFT CABINET SUBMISSION BY DEPARTMENT OF EXTERNAL AFFAIRS, 7 October 1940, *DAFP*, iv, Doc. 161

38 CABINET SUBMISSION by E. J. Harrison, Minister for Trade and Customs, 1 November 1940, *DAFP*, iv, Doc. 186

39 See "THE NAVAL MEMOIRS OF ADMIRAL J. H. GODFREY", Vol. 5, pp. 161–2, GDFY 1/6, Godfrey Papers: CC; Minute, Churchill to Beaverbrook, 9

October 1940, BBK D/414: HLRO. See also Harvey Diary, 24 November 1940, ADD. MS. 56397, Harvey Papers: BL; Cadogan Diary, 31 December 1940, in D. Dilks (ed.), p. 346

40 DALTON DIARY, 16 October 1940, Dalton Papers: LSE; F. H. Hinsley, *British Intelligence in the Second World War*, i, London, 1979, pp. 259–60

41 "MY LIFE", Memoirs of Admiral Davis, p. 203, WDVS 1/3, Davis Papers: CC

42 See CRS CP 290/7, Bundle 1, Items 2 and 4: AA

43 WAR CABINET CONCLUSIONS, 25 October 1940, CAB 65/9, W.M. 277(40): PRO

44 MINUTE M.333, Churchill to First Lord of the Admiralty and First Sea Lord, 22 November 1940, PREM 3/489/4: PRO

45 See C. THORNE, *Allies of a Kind*, London, 1978, pp. 3–7

46 CABLE (DRAFT), Churchill to Menzies, 12 December 1940 (sent 13 December), PREM 4/43B/1: PRO

47 REPORT BY THE FAR EASTERN COMMITTEE, 17 December 1940, CAB 66/14, W.P. (40)484: PRO

48 See fn. 44

49 WAR CABINET MINUTES, 26 November 1940, CRS A2673, Vol. 4, Minute 632: AA

50 CABLE NO. 627, Commonwealth Government to Cranborne, 1 December 1940, *DAFP*, iv, Doc. 212

51 ADVISORY WAR COUNCIL MINUTES, 2 December 1940, CRS A2682, Vol. 1, Minute 50: AA; See also Letters, McEwen to Menzies, 14 November and 12 December 1940, CRS A5954, Box 230: AA

52 CABLE NO. 1464, Menzies to Bruce, 3 December 1940, *DAFP*, iv, Doc. 214

53 CABLE Z.408, Dominions Secretary to Menzies, 12 December 1940, CRS CP 290/7, Bundle 1, Item 3: AA

54 ADVISORY WAR COUNCIL MINUTES, 2 and 12 December 1940, CRS A2682, Vol. 1, Minutes 48 and 53: AA

55 ADVISORY WAR COUNCIL MINUTES, 8 January 1940, CRS A2682, Vol. 1, Minute 80: AA

56 CABLE NO. 510, Cranborne to Commonwealth Government, 23 December 1940, *DAFP*, iv, Doc. 236

57 *IBID.*

58 See DAVID DAY, *Menzies and Churchill at War*, Sydney, 1986, chs 1–3

59 *SUN*, Sydney, 12 November 1940

60 CABLE NO. 377, UK High Commissioner to Dominions Office, 23 October 1940, PREM 4/43A/13: PRO

61 WAR CABINET CONCLUSIONS, 4 November 1940, CAB 65/10, W.M. 282(40): PRO

62 ADVISORY WAR COUNCIL MINUTES, 25 November 1940, CRS A2682, Vol. 1, Minute 39: AA

63 CABLE NO. 1701, Menzies to Bruce, 17 December 1940, CRS M100, "December 1940": AA

64 *AGE*, Melbourne, 27 December 1940

6

Menzies in London

January to April 1941

When Menzies left Sydney for London on 15 January 1941, the war was going much better than anyone had expected six months previously. A series of spectacular victories against the Italians in the Middle East had transformed the outlook for the British hold on that region. Italian forces that had pushed into Egypt were either captured or fleeing far back into Libya. Australian troops had played an important part in the British victories. Britain's implicit faith in ultimate victory against Germany looked more tenable though it remained an article of faith rather than of logic.

On 10 January, Hitler finally cancelled preparations for an invasion of Britain and directed German efforts towards an attack on Russia in the coming spring. For the purposes of deception, Germany maintained the appearance of a threat across the narrow waters of the English Channel and succeeded in convincing Britain that an invasion remained the principal German preoccupation.[1] From now on, it would become increasingly difficult for Britain to refuse the dispatch of defence matériel because of any overwhelming threat to its own survival. To a considerable extent, both Australia and Britain were competing for resources to meet potential rather than actual threats.

While Britain's potential threat from Germany lay just across the nation's narrow moat, the Japanese threat to Australia was still far distant. But then, Britain retained a much greater capacity to meet the threat posed by Germany than Australia had at its disposal in the Far East. The RN remained in home waters or nearby; the RAF remained largely tied to Britain's skies; the British army remained rooted to the protection of its homeland. Of thirty-six British army divisions formed or forming, only four were overseas. One was in Iceland to pre-empt a German invasion, while three were in Egypt. Nearly 2,000,000 men of the British army remained in Britain's island garrison.[2]

Australia also had three divisions in the Middle East but they represented almost the whole of her trained troops. At home, the local defence forces remained at a "Dad's Army" level. The enthusiasm of the troops could not compensate for the lack of modern equipment. Seven months after Menzies authorised the local production of tanks, the first wooden mock-up was nearing completion. Without the finished article, there was no hope of repelling an invasion force from Australia's shores. Naval forces in Australian waters were only sufficient to provide a small measure of protection against armed raiders stalking the trade routes of the Indian and Pacific oceans. They had no way of preventing Japanese naval forces from mounting an invasion of Australia. In the air, Australia had nothing that could match the Japanese fighter planes. So, while Australia's threat was further distant than Britain's, the risks she was running were very much greater as she had no real defence against attack. That did not prevent the first echelons of the third Australian division committed to the Middle East from arriving there in January at the same time as Menzies left Australia on a four-month trip that would take him round the world.

The defence of Australia certainly figured among Menzies' priorities in planning his visit to London, but it was not his first priority. Basically he was a peacetime Prime Minister trying to use peacetime methods and assumptions to plan for war. Moreover, in war planning, Menzies' mind was continually torn between the necessities for war and the needs of post-war reconstruction. On 3 January, Menzies cabled to Bruce with the main objects of his London visit, confiding that a "clear definition of where we stand in [the] Far East, and [a] reasonably long range policy [in the] Middle East, would enable me to plan Australia's effort on [the] man-power side more soundly". He also wanted to "give [the] United Kingdom Government a clear picture of [the] amazing munitions potential developed and developing here, and to see how far greater joint use of it could be arranged". There was no mention here of Australia's serious defence deficiencies or those of Singapore. Menzies' concern was to be assured of continued peace in the Pacific so that Australia could quietly transform itself into an Imperial workshop that was, unlike Britain, safe from the nightly depredations of German bombers.[3]

Menzies' precarious position in the Australian Parliament remained his dominant concern. He confided to Bruce that he was "a good deal exercised" about making the visit since the "political position here [is] precarious and [my] principal lieutenants in cabinet [are] not very experienced". He asked for an assurance that his trip would prove fruitful and that he would get "prompt and sufficient opportunity for consultation" with Churchill and the British Cabinet.[4] Though Bruce had already received Churchill's blessing for the trip, he now cautioned Menzies against coming, claiming that there was little that he could achieve in London. Even though Bruce had spent the previous four months vainly seeking a program of aircraft deliveries for Australia, he obviously did not feel that this was a matter that Menzies could pursue. In fact, he assured Menzies that "developments over [the] past few months have removed all the major issues on which you would have had to take a strong line". Although he admitted that Britain's reduced purchases of Australian primary produce were urgent subjects for discussion, he noted that they were also "difficult politically" for Menzies to handle. Bruce warned that Menzies could only achieve something of substance from Britain if he was prepared to confront Churchill, but that this might damage their relationship and prove counter-productive.[5]

Despite Bruce's warning, Menzies was quick to decide in favour of his trip. In justifying it to the Advisory War Council, he pointed to many reasons that necessitated his absence from Australia. Singapore was one of them but not the most important. The whole situation in the Far East and the Empire's position towards Japan was first in his proclaimed priorities. The actual situation at Singapore was listed simply as a "matter for frank discussion". After the Far East came the Middle East. This partly concerned his worries about the tenuous nature of the British position in that region, but there were also such matters as the release of news and the standard of equipment for the AIF. Recent victories should have removed the immediate worry about British strength in the Middle East while the other concerns were hardly matters to propel a Prime Minister round the world. The third matter concerned the possibility of winning the Vichy Government to the Allied side and gaining the assistance of their fleet in the Mediterranean. This would increase Britain's ability to dispatch a fleet to the Far East. However, with German troops in Paris, Menzies left unsaid how the allegiance of the Vichy Government could be achieved. It was an amazing proposal that never again saw the light of day and was presumably introduced for the sole reason of gaining a political commitment from his Labor opponents not to move against him while in London.[6]

Two final matters — obtaining the transfer to Australia of aircraft and shipbuilding productive capacity — also had much appeal to the Labor members though they were of prime concern to Menzies in his vision of an industrialised Australia. This vision had little immediate application for Australia's defence but much long-term application for her post-war development.[7] However, Britain was already ordering merchant ships from yards in the United States and ordering aircraft on a large scale from both Canada and the United States. On this occasion, distance was Australia's downfall. It was nothing personal. It was simply cheaper, quicker and easier to purchase ships from pre-existing yards in America and aircraft from North America where a well-developed industry already existed. As for the wholesale transfer of British industries to Australia, it was clearly easier, and better for morale, to repair bomb-damaged factories than to ship them to the other side of the world. But Menzies remained optimistic, with his vision of an industrialised Australia having the additional desired effect of exciting the imagination of the Labor members who agreed not to use their parliamentary numbers to embarrass him in his absence.[8]

Though Singapore had slipped in Menzies' priorities, its security was being further imperilled at the very time that Menzies was packing his bags for London. The British Chiefs of Staff had acknowledged that the number of aircraft needed for the defence of Singapore was 582 but now refused to supply such a number. On 10 January, they informed Brooke-Popham that just "336 should give [a] very fair degree of security". Brooke-Popham observed privately that the Chiefs apparently now had included Burma within the area that the 336 planes were meant to defend thereby reducing the effective level still further. However, he was not prepared to fight over

numbers, accepting that he would be limited to 336 for 1941.[9]
Churchill soon quashed even these limited hopes.

Despite the fact that the Chiefs had made their commitment to supply the 336 aircraft "subject to [the] general
situation and supply of aircraft", Churchill immediately countermanded it. He claimed that he had not approved these "very
large diversions of Force" and that his instructions to the
Chiefs had "an opposite tendency". He maintained that the
"political situation in the Far East does not seem to require,
and the strength of our Air Force by no means warrants, the
maintenance of such large forces in the Far East at this time".[10]
The Chiefs soon assured Churchill that his fears were ground-
less, that the figure of 336 aircraft was a "long-term target"
and that they did not intend to make "any appreciable diversion
of our war effort to the Far East at the present time". However, they did argue for a start on their long-term program
with a "very small increase". They pointed out that there were
no fighter planes at all in the Far East and that they proposed to
start forming two fighter squadrons at Singapore. Churchill
even balked at this, asking what exactly it would entail.[11] He
only relented on learning that it would mean a loss of just
eight pilots from Britain with the remainder coming fresh
from flying schools in Australia and New Zealand. The aircraft
would be forty-eight Brewster Buffaloes from America, an
out-moded type that proved to be no match for the Japanese
aircraft in 1942.[12]

So Menzies was defeated on Singapore even before he left
Australia. Churchill obviously was determined not to make the
scale of diversion that Menzies and Australia desired. As for
Menzies' vision of transferring industrial capacity to Australia,
this battle also was lost before it began. At the same time that
Churchill was placing strict limits on aircraft for Singapore, the
British War Cabinet was placing similar limits on any transfer
of industrial capacity. In discussing a plan to set up an Eastern
Group Supply Council that would co-ordinate the production
of munitions within the Eastern Empire, the British War
Cabinet opposed any transfer of productive resources from
Britain that would "conflict with our vital requirements in the
near future". The British chairman of the proposed Council
was also to be "informally warned not to lose sight of the effect
of new production on future [British] trade".[13]

Though Menzies flew out of Sydney unaware of the resistance he would face in London, he had been advised by Bruce of a fresh problem on the horizon. It concerned the question of British assistance for Greece which unexpectedly had mounted a stiff resistance over some months to an Italian invasion. Now a German attack was anticipated and Churchill was keen to send troops into Greece before it began, even though he anticipated the eventual defeat of any such force.[14] The problem was that they would have to come from Egypt where British forces were currently pursuing the Italian army far back into Libya. This pursuit would have to be suspended if assistance was sent to Greece and the opportunity of totally expelling the Italians from North Africa would be lost. Though Bruce could not decide between the two options, he gave Menzies forewarning of the problem, which was causing him "grave anxiety", not least because of his feeling that London had not "thought it out in all its implications".[15] With his forthcoming visit to the Middle East, Menzies had the perfect opportunity to settle his own mind on a strategic question that would later dominate his visit to London.

When he finally left Sydney on 24 January, Menzies was still in two minds about the wisdom of his trip. He was taking political risks by his absence from Australia in order to amass the political credits that would ensure his continued tenure at the Lodge. Perhaps at the back of his mind even then was the possibility of transferring his considerable talents to Westminster. This possibility would soon dominate his thinking and ultimately lead to his downfall. As he recognised on his departure, the London trip could either make or break his political future. He confided in his diary that, "for once in my life I am off upon a chancy undertaking".[16]

In his absence, Menzies appointed the Country Party leader, "Artie" Fadden, as Acting Prime Minister. He may well have considered that such an appointment from outside his own party would prevent the creation of a de facto successor for his position. Fadden was a former Queensland accountant who had only been in the Federal Parliament since 1936 and had only been party leader since October 1940 when he was chosen as a compromise candidate to end a deadlock between two evenly divided factions. As Paul Hasluck observed, Fadden was "not the cleverest, the most experienced, or the wisest man

in the Country Party, but he was the best colleague and probably the staunchest character". In a similar vein, the British
High Commissioner assessed Fadden as the "arch-mixer", claiming that "you couldn't meet a better chap in a bar. Streams of
rollicking smut ... Good-natured, shrewd, likeable, has hardly
any real thought of his own, means well."[17] But Fadden's
obvious limitations proved to be strengths in the circumstances
of 1941. His natural amiability and readiness to co-operate
with his Labor opponents were the very attributes that Menzies
lacked.

Even Menzies was prepared to put greater emphasis on
defence, albeit that of the Far East as a whole, after stopping at
Singapore on his way to the Middle East. With the bare facts of
Singapore before him, his comfortable beliefs about Imperial
defence proved more difficult to sustain. After talking with
British commanders, Menzies noted the grievous deficiencies in
aircraft and military equipment and observed that the "absence
of naval craft must encourage the Japanese".[18] The Australian
Government had been alerted to these deficiencies by the report
of the Singapore defence conference but only now did Menzies
seem to treat them seriously. Previously, Menzies had also
been aware of, and even supported, Britain's decision not to
dispatch a fleet from the Mediterranean to the Far East prior to
Japan's entry into the war. On leaving Singapore, he expressed
a determination to see that the "Far Eastern problem must be
taken seriously and urgently". In his diary, he wrote of being
resolved to "make a great effort in London to clarify this
position. Why cannot *one* squadron of fighters be sent out
from N. Africa? Why cannot some positive commitment be
entered into regarding naval reinforcement of Singapore? At
this stage, misty generalizations will please and sustain the
Japanese, and nobody else."[19] This was the first and last time
that Menzies would reveal such a fervid concern about Far
Eastern defence. As his plane flew him on from Singapore, so
the problem receded in his consciousness.

Meanwhile, in his absence, the Australian Government was
being pressed by the Labor Opposition to take a more forthright
attitude towards the defence of Australia and to pay less attention to its Imperial defence commitments. There was not much
resentment at Britain's failure to fulfil her part of the defence
pact, but there was a growing realisation that Australia would

be thrown onto her own resources, at least in the initial phase of any war with Japan. At a meeting of the Advisory War Council on 5 February, Curtin warned that Australia had to prepare for the possibility of a partial occupation by Japan and that the country must "put their best efforts forward to maintain both Australian and Empire integrity". With considerable pre-science, he predicted that Japan might make a "bold move contrary to strategy" and called for the enlargement of the Australian defence program to "ensure that all steps possible are being taken for effective defence".[20]

The Chief of the Air Staff (CAS) intervened at this point to allay Curtin's fears, reminding him of the long lines of communication that would be involved in any invasion of Australia and that "Japan must take into consideration the British stronghold at Singapore and the possible assistance that would be rendered by the Netherlands East Indies". What was not admitted was that Japan's lines of communication to Aus-tralia would be very much shorter than Britain's if Whitehall was faced with expelling such an invasion from her distant Dominion. Both the CAS and the naval chief denied that the Dominion's commitment to Imperial defence was detracting from the local defence effort. These assurances seem to have worked.[21]

Rather than calling for the Government to make a greater effort, the Labor members agreed that the problem lay with the Australian public who were in ignorance of their country's "alarming situation". They recommended the issue of a press statement by the Advisory War Council "so that the position might be brought nearer home to the general public". Then, in a discussion on Britain's response to the Singapore defence conference, the Council accepted the British assurance that "everything possible was being done to remedy the situation, having regard to the demands of theatres which are the scenes of war", namely the Middle East and Britain itself. This effectively concurred with the re-ordering of British priorities, placing the Middle East above that of the Far East.[22]

Within days the international situation gave serious cause for concern when it appeared that Japan was preparing to strike at Britain's possessions in the Far East. Churchill's re-action was to appeal to the United States to "inspire the Japan-ese with the fear of a double war". Britain had been fighting

America's war by proxy in Europe. Churchill held out the spectre to Roosevelt of military disaster in the Mediterranean if Britain was forced to dispatch a fleet to the Far East to protect Australia from invasion. He acknowledged Australia's parlous position after sending "all their best-trained fighting men to the Middle East" and warned Roosevelt that "any threat of a major invasion of Australia of New Zealand would, of course, force us to withdraw our Fleet from the Eastern Mediterranean with disastrous military possibilities there".[23] Of course, when such a threat did develop in 1942, Churchill refused to stand by this apparent pledge, maintaining that Britain would only denude the Mediterranean of the fleet in the case of a major invasion force actually landing in Australia.

When Australia learned of the increased threat of war, the Labor Party was able to use its influence under Fadden's administration to have a statement issued by the Advisory War Council calling for the "greatest effort of preparedness this country has ever made". However, the practical measures were slow to come. Curtin's suggestion for a test mobilisation was refused because of "its effect on industry" while his draft statement was toned down for fear of creating panic.[24]

Despite the amendments to Curtin's statement, there were panic headlines when it appeared in the Australian press on 14 February. These prompted the War Cabinet to rebuke Fadden for issuing a joint statement. They instructed that any future statements should be made by him alone and that all such statements, whether by members of the Government or Opposition, should be subject to press censorship.[25] Their instructions were buttressed by a report from Bruce in London of British Government alarm that an "over excited press" might "increase an already high tension and even precipitate war".[26] Apparently Australians were meant to be kept in ignorance of the hostile forces welling up around them.

That same day, Brooke-Popham met the Australian War Cabinet to settle their minds about Singapore while simultaneously seeking the commitment of more Australian forces and munitions for its defence. The Dominion would have to shoulder Britain's Imperial burden in the Far East as well as the Middle East, while the usual assurances about Australia's defence were made and accepted. The War Cabinet was told that Singapore was designed to withstand an attack for six months but could probably last for nine months and that a landward attack was unlikely because of the unsuitable terrain. When the Army Minister, Percy Spender, questioned the strength of Britain's commitment to the defence of Singapore in view of her refusal to base a fleet there, Brooke-Popham informed the War Cabinet of Churchill's instruction to him on his departure from London. This was to "hold Singapore until capital ships could be sent" and that Churchill had assured him that "We will not let Singapore fall". Brooke-Popham then announced Britain's dispatch of Brewster Buffalo aircraft and blithely maintained that British pilots and aircraft in Malaya were "considerably superior" to the Japanese who were not "air-minded".[27]

Brooke-Popham's confident demeanour impressed the War Cabinet sufficiently for him to achieve his aim of gaining Australia's continuing commitment to Imperial defence. Despite doubts by Spender and the Navy Minister, Billy Hughes, Brooke-Popham was relieved to report to London that the Australian Government was "definitely out to help and fully realised that the defence of the whole area from Burma to New Zealand was essentially one problem". He was not so happy with the Labor members of the Advisory War Council, which he also addressed that day, though he considered that Curtin was "reasonably good".[28] Nevertheless, as a result of Brooke-Popham's visit, the Advisory War Council concurred with recommendations of the Chiefs of Staff maintaining Australia's emphasis on raising and equipping troops for the AIF rather than for the Australian Military Force (AMF) which was directed towards local defence. Curtin acknowledged that Britain was doing her utmost to strengthen Singapore and pledged that he would intervene to stop industrial disputes threatening the production of munitions in Australia.[29]

Brooke-Popham's success in Sydney was achieved mainly through the fortuitous circumstance of being able to announce the dispatch of the Buffalo aircraft. This announcement seemed to confirm to the Australians his assurances regarding Britain's commitment to the defence of her interests in the Far East. With considerable relief, Brooke-Popham confided to the British Air Ministry that when Labor members of the Advisory War Council had cross-examined him, he was "very glad" that he was "able to rub in the fact of those 67 Brewster Buffaloes being on the way to Singapore" and that, before receiving news of the

Buffaloes, he had "sent a signal to the Air Ministry emphasizing the attitude·that Australia might take if I went there empty-handed".[30]

Although Australia accepted Britain's good intentions in regard to her defence, she was anxious about the level of naval assistance that she now could count on in the event of war with Japan. The only indication from London had been the declared intention to base a battle cruiser and an aircraft carrier in the Indian Ocean that could form the nucleus of a Far East fleet in the case of hostilities. No indication was provided of when such a fleet would be formed or of its planned strength. Australia could not contemplate the fact that no fleet was planned and Fadden pressed London for a full statement of naval forces in the Indian Ocean and of "any action proposed to augment it in [the] event of hostilities with Japan".[31] Fadden also asked Menzies to try and winkle out this information from Whitehall.[32]

It was at this time in February 1941, while Menzies was in the Middle East, that the British proposal for assisting Greece assumed a concrete form. Anthony Eden was dispatched to Cairo by Churchill with clear instructions to send "speedy succour to Greece", that it was Britain's "duty to fight, and, if need be, suffer with Greece".[33] The concept of an expeditionary force to pre-empt a German invasion of Greece had important strategic implications for Australia. Not least was the consideration that Australian troops would form a substantial part of any such force. Apart from concern for their safety in this risky enterprise, their deeper involvement in the European struggle would make it that much harder for them to be extricated in the event of them being required back in Australia for the defence of their homeland. The naval implications were even more serious. It would add substantially to the tasks of the Mediterranean fleet and create a line of communication across the Mediterranean that would have to be defended by British ships. The possibility of transforming the Mediterranean fleet into a force for the protection of Australia might be lost for ever.

Britain's Middle East commanders were divided about the wisdom of the proposed Greek expedition, while Australia's commander of the AIF, General Blamey, had serious misgivings about it. Menzies had been warned by Bruce that the expedition posed serious and fundamental strategic problems.

Australian Prime Minister, Robert Menzies, filming the destruction in
Tobruk Harbour in February 1941 while *en route* to London
(AUSTRALIAN WAR MEMORIAL)

It constituted a gross dereliction of duty when Menzies ignored
these warnings and failed to avail himself of the military coun-
sel on hand in the Middle East to reach a considered judgement
on the expedition. Had he done so, military opinion could
have solidified sufficiently to obstruct Eden when he arrived in
Cairo to give effect to Churchill's instructions. Instead, Menzies
played the politician, patting his troops on the back, taking
movie film of their exploits and generally building up political
credits.[34] By the time he arrived in London, the groundwork
had been laid by Eden for the expedition and it had become
that much harder for Menzies to oppose it, even if he had been
so inclined.

While the Greek decision proved to be a calamity for Australia, decisions were also being made in Washington that carried worse portents for the Dominion. Staff conversations between British and American military officers confirmed their

pre-existing but separate decisions to fight a defensive holding war against Japan in the Pacific while concentrating the bulk of their resources on the European war. In his instructions for the British delegation, Churchill made clear that the United States navy would be "in charge in the Pacific" and that the delegation must not request their American counterparts to "come and protect Singapore, Australia and India against the Japanese". Above all, "nothing should stand in the way of the main principle, which was that all efforts should be directed to the defeat of Germany — the minimum force being left to hold Japan in check".[35] The subsequent Anglo–American agreement along these lines was a simple recognition of their national interests — that no calamity in the Pacific could compare with defeat in Europe. Only after Germany had been subdued would they turn their attention to Japan and retrieve what they had lost in the interim. Australia obviously could not be so complacent. Her national interest could not encompass the possibility of invasion by Japan and her possible "retrieval" by Britain at some later date. The problem was that Australia's leaders had no clear conception of a national interest separate from that of Britain.

On 7 February, Australia's naval attaché in Washington cabled news of the staff talks to Australia. This secret information lay behind much of the anxiety that surfaced during the Advisory War Council discussions on 13 and 14 February. Australia was on notice as to the risks she must run in the Pacific. In the circumstances, her alarm was muted. This was partly due to her continued acceptance of British assurances, which this time claimed Australian security as "essential to our defence" and reaffirmed the necessity to retain control of Singapore.[36] The possible contradiction in the strategy of retaining Singapore while concentrating on Germany seemed not to concern Australian minds. The implications really were too terrible to contemplate. Instead, they took solace from Britain's commitment on paper and tried not to wonder why it never seemed possible to transform it into real men and real ships in the Far East. After all, had not Brooke-Popham come with positive proof, in the form of sixty-seven Buffalo planes, of Britain's good intentions and will to resist Japan?

As for America, Washington argued that an invasion of Australia was "beyond the present resources of Japan" and that anyway, the Australian contribution to the war effort could be replaced by "further supplies from the Western hemisphere". If Britain insisted on an Allied naval force for Singapore, the United States declared that she would have to send it herself as it was "preferable for armed forces of each nation to operate in areas in which its own interests are primarily involved". She warned Britain not to count on American help when making her strategic calculations for the Far East.[37] Australia received notice of the American attitude on 24 February. It was more important than ever that Britain be pressed to fulfil her role as the traditional guarantor of Australia's security.

Menzies arrived in London from the Middle East on 20 February. One week later he met with the Chiefs of Staff and Britain's Service Ministers for a discussion on Britain's military strategy. Again the assurance was wheeled out that Britain would cut her losses in the Mediterranean and go to Australia's assistance if her security was imperilled by Japan. Although this had underpinned Australian strategic decisions for over six months, it was only now that Menzies sought to invest it with greater precision. After having visited the huge military establishment, much of it Australian, that was being created in the Middle East he realised that a sudden naval withdrawal from the region would be no easy task and might be at the cost of the Australian troops. He questioned how Britain could dispatch a fleet to the Far East from the Mediterranean when there were "land forces which cannot be deserted?" Though the implicit contradictions within it should have suggested that it was an assurance never meant to be implemented, this was a conclusion that Menzies was unable to reach. Instead he resorted to blaming it on muddle-headed British planners.[38]

Menzies had been instructed by his colleagues to clarify the British naval reaction to war with Japan. It was of vital importance for Australia to know with some precision the extent of naval help she could expect from London to withstand a Japanese attack. It was a question that London was equally anxious not to answer. Their reluctance arose partly from the practical difficulties of predicting with any accuracy the course of such hypothetical events. But it also arose from the desire to conceal from Australia the extent of its vulnerability in order to divert her energies away from local defence and towards Imperial defence. This diversion had been so successful that Menzies

now absolved Britain from her traditional guarantee to provide
naval forces for the Far East out of concern for the protection
of Australia's continuing contribution to Imperial defence.

At a meeting on 8 March with the First Lord of the Admiralty, A. V. Alexander, and the Vice Chief of the Naval Staff,
Admiral Phillips, Menzies officially released Britain from her
undertaking to desert the Mediterranean, informing them
that Australia was "no longer satisfied with the general round
statement that in the event of the outbreak of hostilities with
Japan ... [Britain] would, if necessary abandon the Mediterranean and come to the assistance of the Dominions with
capital ships". He reminded them that the "Dominions had
very large forces on land in the Middle East, and public opinion
would not stand for those forces being left improperly protected by a complete withdrawal of Naval Forces from the
Mediterranean".[39]

Menzies' solution was to press for Britain to dispatch fighter
aircraft to Singapore in place of the ships. He latched onto
Churchill's revelation of Britain's considerable fighter strength
and pressed for some squadrons to be sent to the Far East.
These would have a political as well as a military value. Thus
Menzies requested that the aircraft be Hurricanes with their
high public profile following their successful sorties during the
Battle of Britain. Australian survival required more than public
relations, but Menzies' political survival might hinge on some
concrete achievement of this nature. Certainly he could not
return with a simple re-statement of assurances already given.
As he informed the Admiralty meeting, he would "rather take
back with him the certainty that some definite help would be
given to the Dominions in the case of a war with Japan, even if
it were less than they had perhaps, in the past, been led to
suppose". What would not suffice were "rhetorical phrases
such as 'cutting our losses in the Mediterranean and proceeding
to your assistance'".[40]

Menzies' willingness to absolve Britain of her traditional
undertaking reflected his personal commitment to the priorities
of Empire. He justified the consequent effect on Australian
security by taking comfort from British assertions about Japanese
military inferiority. Accepting these assertions, Menzies argued
that air rather than naval reinforcement of the Far East was the
"great deterrent". Had Menzies' call for Hurricanes for Singapore been successful, it could have tipped the balance in the

subsequent defence of that city in 1942. However, before leaving London, Menzies would retract his call and satisfy himself with a British promise to reinforce Singapore only after it had been attacked. The Hurricanes were sent to Singapore in January 1942 in fulfilment of this promise. But there were only fifty-one of them and they arrived unassembled in crates. They were too little and too late to affect the battle.[41]

Though Menzies seems to have realised that the traditional British promise of a Far East fleet was no longer a naval possibility in the circumstances of 1941, it was a conclusion carefully kept from the Australian people. On 12 March, four days after Menzies effectively released Britain from her naval promise, Fadden reported to a joint meeting of both Houses of Parliament on the results of his talks with Brooke-Popham. Acknowledging the "importance to Australia of the defence of Singapore", Fadden confidently proclaimed that the "assurances we have received from the British Government ... enable me to tell you that the defence of Singapore will be an Empire defence. Australia will not be alone." Accepting Churchill's argument that it would be "folly to have too many units *idly standing by* to meet the *possibility* of a threat to Singapore", Fadden nevertheless announced to Australia's assembled representatives that "in the event of Japan entering the war against us we are assured by the United Kingdom Government that an immediate redistribution of the Naval Forces would be made should the threat to our communications in the Pacific and Indian Oceans be relatively greater than that in the Atlantic".[42]

This was not much of a promise on which to base Australia's defence but it was deemed sufficient to allow the Dominion to continue its industrial transformation without the disruptive effects entailed by a policy of defence self-reliance and total mobilisation. Thus, in concluding his parliamentary address, Fadden stressed the export orders for defence equipment won by Australian manufacturers and left to "the imagination of honourable members the future results of the industrial and manufacturing revolution which is now taking shape in our midst".[43]

With his acceptance of British naval priorities, Menzies renewed his search for a general settlement with Japan. Such a settlement would ensure Australian security and allow for her contributions to Imperial defence free of any substantial diversion to local defence. Though Menzies did not foresee Japan entering the war of her own volition, he did fear that British policy could impel Japan to act against her self-interest, perhaps to protect national honour in the face of British provocation. His fears were aroused after a visit to the Foreign Office during which he described the present British policy as one of "drift" and warned against the "mental condition of thinking that all was lost and making up our minds that there must be war". Menzies proposed that talks be held "with a view to finding a basis on which the Far East could be settled". His entreaties fell on deaf ears. Britain could not contemplate any settlement in the Far East. As the British officials pointed out to Menzies, the Japanese wanted territorial concessions in the Far East, not simply economic ones. But more fundamentally, any settlement would "involve our throwing over China ... a thing to which the United States would never agree".[44] Britain risked war with Japan in order to retain United States support against Germany. As Menzies recognised, Australia could be the loser from such a policy.

Menzies pinned his hope on Eden, Britain's absent Foreign Secretary who was then in the Middle East co-ordinating policy towards Greece.[45] In order to pressure the Foreign Office, Menzies made a forceful speech in London deprecating its policy and maintaining that peace with Japan was not impossible. When news of the speech reached Australia, a political storm broke out, with allegations from Labor MPs of appeasement by Menzies. It was made worse by arriving in the wake of the warnings by the Advisory War Council of the dire threat Australia faced in the Pacific. The Council had congratulated itself that these warnings, together with the "dispatch of a brigade of Australian troops for service in Malaya, had been effective in staying the hand of Japan in regard to any southward penetration she may have had in mind". Now Menzies' optimistic forecast of the prospects for peace undercut the effect of the warnings and promoted apathy among the Australian public.[46] When Menzies learnt of the furore in Australia, he immediately denied any suggestion of appeasement and any conflict between his views and those of the Council. But the controversy did affect Menzies' search for a peaceful settlement in the Pacific. Once again, he was on notice from his colleagues about the political risks involved in such a search and trod much more warily as a result.[47]

Menzies' troubles were increased by the deteriorating position in Greece. He had agreed to Australian participation in the expedition during an after-dinner discussion with Churchill at Chequers. Without seeking the opinion of Blamey, Menzies asked the Australian War Cabinet also to approve the expedition. Despite several serious reservations, the War Cabinet agreed with Menzies but did not seek approval from, or even inform, the Advisory War Council until after the Cabinet's consent had reached London.[48]

Menzies had been infected with Churchill's enthusiasm for the Greek expedition and was bitter in his denunciation in mid-April when it all fell apart. On 14 April, he described the War Cabinet as

> *deplorable — dumb men most of whom disagree with Winston but none of whom dare to say so ... The Chiefs of Staff are without exception Yes-men, and a politician runs the Services. Winston is a dictator ... The people have set him up as something little less than God, and his power is therefore terrific. Today I decide to remain for a couple of weeks, for grave decisions will have to be taken about M. E., chiefly Australian forces, and I am not content to have them solved by [Churchill's] "unilateral rhetoric".*[49]

Not only was the British expedition to Greece summarily expelled by the German invaders and evacuated off the beaches at great cost by the ships of the Royal Navy, but the weakened British forces in Libya were faced with General Rommel who had arrived with the first elements of his future *Afrika Korps*. During April, disaster loomed on both fronts and the whole Middle East region seemed set to see a hasty British withdrawal under the impact of the two-pronged German assault through Greece and Libya.

If Britain was not going to dispatch a fleet to the Far East, Australia would have to defeat any Japanese invasion through a combination of air and land forces. Australia actually asked Britain for one modern fighter plane in early 1941. It was intended to perform aerobatics for public relations and fund raising purposes. On 20 February, the day of Menzies' arrival in London, Beaverbrook reluctantly agreed to the proposal.[50] The RAAF pilots now would have an opportunity to fly, one at a time, a modern fighter aircraft, albeit without guns. Ten months later, when the Japanese struck at Pearl Harbor and Malaya, this unarmed Hurricane would be the only modern fighter aircraft in the Australian arsenal. And it only arrived after the failure of an attempt by the Australian Government to have it diverted to the Middle East.[51]

When Menzies arrived in London, he therefore had one Hurricane in the Australian bag and a commitment of Buffalo aircraft for Singapore. Despite two and a half months in London, he would leave with little more to take back to Australia. His efforts were directed towards obtaining the delivery program for the Australian aircraft on order from Britain itself and, through Britain, from the United States. All Empire orders for aircraft from the United States were pooled in one British account and only released after agreement from London. New Zealand was in a similar plight with regard to aircraft. Like Australia, she had released to Britain in mid-1940 the Hudson aircraft she had on order in the United States. In April 1941, the Air Minister, Sir Archibald Sinclair, proposed that New Zealand be given back its Hudsons over the following eight months. This was refused point-blank by Beaverbrook who angrily instructed his staff to "file away Sinclair's demand ... I will not take any notice of it at all".[52] Australia's requests received similarly short shrift, though Menzies was too pre-occupied to notice.

On 9 April, after Menzies had been in London for seven weeks, the Defence Committee of the British War Cabinet finally approved a program of aircraft deliveries for Australia. The program had been drawn up after consultations between Beaverbrook and Sinclair and was designed to satisfy Australian demands with the absolute minimum number of mostly un-wanted aircraft. Sinclair informed the committee of his intention to offer Menzies twelve Beaufighters in December 1941 but, "if pressed", he might increase this to twenty. These would only be delivered to Australia after twenty-two British squadrons had been equipped with them and when production of the planes was running at 150 planes per month. The main aircraft to be supplied were Brewster Bermudas, a "type of aircraft in which the Royal Air Force was not particularly interested" and which was not even off the drawing board. Sinclair envisaged supplying Australia with 243 of these by mid-1942 as well as ninety-four Hudsons by December 1941.[53]

Although Sinclair's proposed offer to Menzies was far from generous, Churchill argued against it on the grounds that it would be "most unwise to fritter away aircraft to Australia, where they would not come into action against the Germans". His objections were not accepted. The Chief of the Air Staff, Sir Charles Portal, argued that it was in Britain's interest for Australia to get the aircraft as it would deter a Japanese attack and spare Britain from any diversion of naval forces. He also pointed out that Australia would "probably be ready to spare some of their squadrons for use elsewhere" and that, anyway, Britain did not have the aircrew to man them herself. The Dominions Secretary, Lord Cranborne, joined in from another direction, arguing the wisdom of satisfying Menzies on this point as Britain would "not be satisfying many of his other demands". With misgivings, Churchill eventually relented, provided that Sinclair not "promise more than was absolutely necessary".[54]

Sinclair fulfilled Churchill's entreaty and more so. When he and Beaverbrook met Menzies on the following day, they managed to secure Menzies' agreement to a delivery program that was even looser than that outlined to the Defence Committee. Menzies accepted twelve Beaufighters by December 1941 even though Sinclair was prepared to concede twenty. Beaverbrook undertook to expedite delivery of fifty-two Hudsons from the United States and the Bermudas were set at 243 to be delivered by mid-1942. It was another case of promises, promises. As Sinclair had assured Beaverbrook, "I shall be very careful to make it clear to him [Menzies] that my promises to him are not firm and that delivery must be governed by the war situation. Yes, we must see that these Dominions do not strip us of everything . . ." In fact, there was no fear of that. As Beaverbrook had informed Churchill just five days before the former's meeting with Menzies, the total British aircraft production during March 1941 was 1853 aircraft, twice that of the previous year, while fighter aircraft production was three times that of the previous year. Such was the expansion in production that Beaverbrook claimed he now was producing "more aircraft than the Air Ministry can use", a claim that he did not repeat to Menzies.[55]

Although Menzies accepted the aircraft delivery program proposed by Britain, he realised that it did not satisfy Australia's needs. However, he assured Fadden that Britain's needs at home and in the Middle East must take priority. He claimed that Britain was "sincerely desirous of helping us to the greatest extent possible" but she "cannot be pressed unduly, particularly in view of the pressure I have recently been exercising for the provision of adequate air strength in the Middle East".[56]

It was left to Bruce to fill the unaccustomed role of arguing Australia's case with a force that Menzies was not inclined to do. Bruce apparently feared for the political reaction in Australia if Menzies returned with such a meagre achievement. He remarked to Beaverbrook and Sinclair that it would be "a little difficult to convince the Government and people of Australia that the whole of the requirements of the United Kingdom must be satisfied before any of the Australian aircraft were released".[57] This was not a view with which Menzies could sympathise. He could not accept that the distant Dominion was running comparable risks in the Pacific to Britain. Britain, he maintained, was "treating us fairly".[58] In any event, Menzies argued, this extended program of deliveries had been supplemented by a "categorical assurance that should war occur in the Far East there will be an immediate review of air resources with a view to their re-disposition to meet the dangers on all fronts".[59] This was just the sort of general assurance that he had deemed unacceptable with regard to the dispatch of the Far East fleet.

As for Menzies' attempts to achieve a transfer of British productive capacity to Australia, they also were deflected and ultimately refused by British Ministers anxious to maintain an appearance of co-operation while at the same time erecting obstacles at every turn. Beaverbrook, in particular, proved to be very adept at this tactic, expressing support in principle for Menzies' proposal but ensuring that it would not be approved by the War Cabinet. Menzies reacted angrily at one stage when he wrongly believed that the Australian War Cabinet had undercut his efforts by reaching an agreement with an American company to establish an aircraft engine factory. To Menzies, it was not a question of producing aircraft in the shortest time for Australia's survival. It was a question of maintaining the economic interdependence of the Empire, shutting out American capital and furthering Australia's peacetime development. It all came to nothing when Beaverbrook and Churchill vetoed any transfer of British resources.[60]

Menzies' pressure on Britain to dispatch Hurricanes to Singapore also came to nothing. The Chiefs of Staff argued that the demands of the Middle East must take priority and that the Buffalo aircraft would "probably prove more than a match for any Japanese aircraft".[61] As for Menzies' request to be given a more precise undertaking as to the British naval reaction to Japanese entry into the war, he again was disappointed. Though he had been led to believe that such an undertaking would be provided, London waited almost until the last day before his departure and then refused his request. Menzies' request, buttressed by anxious queries from Canberra, had placed Whitehall in a quandary, having to state with more definition what Churchill's Chief of Staff, General Ismay, termed the "conflicting claims of the Middle East and the Far East".[62] When it was referred to the Defence Committee for a decision, Churchill ensured that Menzies' requests for the immediate reinforcement of Singapore would be refused and that London would continue to avoid any precise definition of her priorities.

The First Sea Lord, Admiral Pound, reminded the Committee of Britain's general assurance regarding the abandonment of the Middle East. He argued against providing Menzies with a precise timetable of naval reinforcements as there were "far too many unknown factors" and that it would be "wrong to abandon the whole of our interests in the Middle East until it became absolutely necessary to do so". Churchill immediately concurred, dismissing the likelihood of Japan entering the war and arguing for Menzies to be given a repeat of the assurance already provided, though with the provision that it "did not mean that we would give up our great interests in the Middle East on account of a few raids by Japanese cruisers". As for giving Menzies something to appease his domestic critics, Churchill refused to surrender "sound strategical ideas in order to satisfy the ignorance of the Australian Opposition". He requested that Australia form a fifth division of the AIF for Britain's use overseas.[63]

Britain's blunt refusal to spell out the fine print on its traditional guarantee to provide for Australia's security should have left Australia with few illusions about the urgent need for defence self-reliance. The reaction of Frederick Shedden, Secretary of Australia's Defence Department and a member of Menzies' group in London, was almost one of relief. He advised Menzies on 14 April that Australia now certainly knew where she stood, "the degree to which we must rely on our own efforts, and the necessity for expanding them to the utmost extent". He criticised the British Chiefs of Staff for exhibiting a "degree of complacency which we have come to expect about the defence of the Pacific region" and concluded that it is "evident that, for too long, we readily accepted the general assurances about the defence of this area". Now that their visit had revealed the "real situation in regard to a fleet for the Far East", Shedden urged that Australia must concentrate on providing for its local defence by aircraft and that "all possible efforts and resources should be directed to producing as much as we are able to do, as quickly as we can".[64]

Shedden's recommendation was buttressed by similar advice from Bruce who stressed the political necessity for Menzies to return with specific defence gains amongst his baggage. If necessary, he urged that Menzies should confront Churchill with the threat of Australia withdrawing her contribution from the British war effort unless she was given adequate assurances about her own defence.[65]

Shedden was proposing that Menzies adopt the policy of the Labor Party and admit, at least implicitly, that the conservative reliance on the Empire was worthless. This was not politically tenable for Menzies nor something he was personally able to do. Though he realised that London's blank cheque was liable to bounce if called upon, he did not anticipate having to call upon it. Like Churchill, he did not rate highly the possibility of a Japanese invasion of Australia. At the same time, he was beset with other concerns. He was increasingly convinced that the British position in the Middle East would have to be abandoned. This caused him to mute his calls for Australian defence. The political implications of the troops' peril were of great concern to him. On 16 April, Menzies confided to General Dill, Chief of the Imperial General Staff, that he was so worried about Tobruk and Greece that "he would hardly dare go home, and that he might as well go for a trip to the North Pole".[66] He also was being drawn into a political intrigue that had as its eventual aim the unseating of Churchill from the British Prime Ministership. Menzies' eyes were drawn to the tantalising prospect of forging a political future in London and perhaps even being the man to replace Churchill.[67]

For these reasons, Menzies accepted Britain's refusal to give precision to her traditional guarantee to provide for Australia's security. On 29 April, he attended a meeting of the Defence Committee at which his principal concern was British strategy in the Middle East and the need to plan for a possible evacuation from the whole region. This did not endear him to Churchill who was adamantly opposed to the suggestion of such a possibility and who had, the previous day, ordered that Egypt be held to the death. With access to Rommel's coded wireless communications, Churchill was aware of the German General's supply problems and foresaw how a stiff defence could send the Desert Fox scurrying back into Libya. Not being privy to this secret intelligence information, Menzies could only foresee defeat for the troops he had so recently reviewed in the Middle East. As for the Far East, he apparently accepted Churchill's assessment that Japan would not enter the war unless Britain had been invaded by Germany. The previous day, 28 April, Churchill had directed his Chiefs of Staff not to "make any further dispositions for the defence of Malaya and Singapore, beyond those modest arrangements which are in progress . . ."[68]

After more than two months in London, supposedly on a mission seeking urgent supplies for Singapore, Menzies had achieved nothing for the defence of the Far Eastern bastion. He was left clinging to the support provided by verbal assurances and the confident prediction by Churchill that, "if the Japanese did come in, he felt sure the United States would declare war".[69] Such a prospect might comfort Churchill who was keen above everything else to draw the Americans into the European war on the British side, but it should not have provided much comfort to an Australian Prime Minister, especially in view of the agreed Allied strategy to concentrate their resources on Germany.

Menzies not only accepted the British view on the Far East, he also concurred in a decision that would place Australia in even greater peril. Just two days before his departure from London on 2 May, an American proposal arose to transfer part of the US Pacific fleet to the Atlantic Ocean. Without bothering to seek Menzies' opinion, Churchill immediately supported this proposal. Menzies was furious, but only because he had not been consulted. He managed to have Australia consulted before the decision was confirmed to Washington and acted to ensure that Australian support would be forthcoming. Despite advice from Casey in Washington that the naval move would "leave British countries and interests in the Pacific in considerable peril", Menzies accepted the British argument that the "entry of the United States of America into the war transcends in importance every other present issue". Though it could be inimical to Australian interests, Menzies successfully pressed his War Cabinet to approve the measure. His main justification for the naval move was the favourable effect it would have on the European war. He also argued that the evidence of increasing American belligerence would probably deter Japan, while the assistance thereby provided to the Royal Navy in the Atlantic might make the formation of a Far Eastern fleet a practical proposition. It is questionable whether he really believed these arguments. In the event, they proved disastrously wrong. Japan was not deterred and the Far Eastern fleet was never formed.[70]

On 2 May, Menzies finally left London on his journey back to Australia. Before leaving he had two important meetings. The first was with Churchill on whom Menzies tried unsuccessfully to press the case for a reorganised War Cabinet over which Churchill would have less sway. The second meeting was with Beaverbrook who, despite refusing Menzies' requests for aircraft production equipment, was keen to enlist the Australian in his own campaign to limit Churchill's unbridled power over policy. He told Menzies that it was "absurd" that he should go back to Australia and promptly began a relentless press campaign in his *Daily Express* newspaper calling for Menzies' return to London as an Imperial representative in the British War Cabinet. With Churchill's determined pursuit of total victory and the sorry consequences of this in Greece, Menzies' mind was filled with gloom. In his diary, he wrote of being "desperately afraid of the future in Great Britain".[71]

Churchill's view could not have been more different. The United States Congress had approved the Lend-Lease Bill, thereby assuring Britain of a continuing flow of war supplies from America despite British dollar reserves becoming exhausted. The shift of United States navy ships to the Atlantic lightened the load of the Royal Navy and helped to tip the balance in the vital Battle of the Atlantic on which Germany was now concentrating most of her naval power. Although the Middle East situation looked bad on the surface, Churchill knew of Rommel's supply problems and the slender thread on which his run of victories was hanging. While Greece was a military disaster, Churchill knew that it had disrupted Germany's planned attack on Russia. The seal on Churchill's optimism came with the confirmation that in the spring Germany would direct its military might against Russia rather than Britain. The threat of invasion had receded, at least for 1941, and possibly for ever. Britain was very much stronger than she had been in 1940 when she had repelled the weight of the Luftwaffe. By 1942 she would be practically invincible against invasion, although far from strong enough to mount her own invasion of German-occupied Europe.[72]

The stark contrast in the outlooks of Menzies and Churchill was to cause a series of increasingly bitter disputes between Britain and her distant Dominion. It was regrettable that Churchill felt unable to share with Menzies the secret information on which his confidence was so soundly based. Instead, Menzies returned to Australia as a determined opponent of the British leader and with a gloomy view of the European war and the prospects for Britain. Unfortunately for Australia, Menzies largely shared Churchill's optimism about the Far East and the inability of Japan to mount a serious challenge to Australian security.

This relative optimism about the Far East, together with his abiding attachment to Empire, caused Menzies to continue holding America at arm's length. For this he had the support of most of his Cabinet. In March, the Australian Cabinet rejected a proposal to allow a direct radio-telegraph link between Australia and the United States despite strong pressure from the new External Affairs Minister, Sir Frederick Stewart, who, unlike McEwen in 1940, pointed to the "great political importance of rapid and convenient channels of communication between [Australia] and the United States at the present time". Cabinet was not impressed, again preferring to protect the British cable monopoly from competition.[73]

Stewart also urged that Australia re-examine the Pan American proposal for a direct air link between the two countries. He warned that continued refusal could jeopardise relations with America and noted that Britain had allowed Pan American flights via Hong Kong to Singapore without demanding reciprocal concessions from Washington. Fadden referred the matter to Menzies who consulted with British officials before agreeing on condition that America initiate the discussions and offer reciprocal rights to Britain. This effectively killed the proposal and left Australia without a direct air link in the months prior to Pearl Harbor. By May 1941, the indirect air link via New Zealand was reduced to a once-weekly service that caused costly delays in vital mail and passenger deliveries. As for defence industry links, Menzies unashamedly put Australian security at a disadvantage out of his concern to ensure that the "lines of industrial communication" would be "between Australia and Britain, not Australia and America".[74]

Menzies had left for London in January with his political security vying for his attention with Australia's military security. In his absence, his political position worsened. Fadden proved to be a popular, energetic leader willing to accord his ministers greater initiative than under Menzies.[75] The Labor Party had been invigorated by the sealing of the split within its New South Wales branch, and there was an immediate leap in its popular support. As an indirect consequence, Dr H. V. Evatt, the ambitious Labor MP, was brought into the Advisory War Council where he curbed Curtin's more accommodating position. Evatt was keen to take on the responsibility of government, either under Curtin or in a national administration, perhaps with himself as leader.[76] Menzies' agreement to the Greek expedition and his failure to obtain any real improvement in Australia's defence position eroded his fragile political leadership even further. In vain, he had tried from London to draw Curtin into a national government, though his efforts were not helped by newspaper speculation that he wanted such an administration as a means of allowing his own retention in Britain.[77] With all these worries and little to show for his absence, it is not surprising that Menzies, as his aircraft approached Sydney, confided to his diary the "sick feeling of repugnance and apprehension [that] grows in me as I near Australia".[78]

By the end of May 1941, after five wasted months, Australia was sliding into a position of great peril in the Pacific. She remained enmeshed in the system of Imperial defence and was making little effort to get untangled. Menzies returned from his long absence overseas after achieving virtually nothing to ensure the security of Australia. He had absolved Britain of her empty pledge to abandon the Mediterranean and dispatch a Far East fleet and had received in return a similarly empty pledge regarding the dispatch of aircraft. He had approved the transfer of part of the United States Pacific fleet to the Atlantic, an act that left Australia more unprotected than before.

Menzies had failed in his expressed purpose to obtain aircraft for the defence of Singapore while simultaneously approving the dispatch of Australian troops to Malaya, where they lacked proper protection from the sea and air. He had not obtained the transfer of aircraft factories from Britain and had vetoed his Cabinet's attempt to explore the American alternatives. He had left London with his relations with Churchill embittered, and this flowed over into the relationship between the two governments. His main achievement was a program of aircraft deliveries that provided little immediate succour for the Dominion. Moreover, the aircraft were unsuitable for use against the Japanese. The Dominion was no longer so blind to her predicament, but the Imperial relationship made her blind to any solutions. And time was no longer on her side.

NOTES

1 F. H. HINSLEY, *British Intelligence in the Second World War*, i, London, 1979, p. 261

2 "ARMY SCALES", Directive by Churchill, 6 March 1941, CAB 66/15, W.P. (41)69: PRO

3 CABLE, Menzies to Bruce, 3 January 1941, CRS CP 290/9, Bundle 1, Folder 5: AA

4 *IBID*.

5 CABLE NO. 14, Bruce to Menzies, 5 January 1941, CRS M100, "January 1941": AA

6 ADVISORY WAR COUNCIL MINUTES: 8 January 1941, CRS A2682, Vol. 1, Minute 79: AA; See also R. G. Menzies, *The Measure of the Years*, London, 1970, p. 45. Menzies claimed in this volume of his memoirs that the "whole reason" for his London visit was to "discuss what my Government believed to be a serious menace from Japan ... and to urge the strengthening of the defences of Singapore".

7 *IBID*.

8 *IBID*.; Advisory War Council Minutes, 9 January 1941, CRS A2682, Vol. 1, Minute 82: AA

9 CABLE NO. 39, Chiefs of Staff to Brooke-Popham, 10 January 1941, with attached note, V/4/6−7, Brooke-Popham Papers: KC

10 MINUTE D15/1, Churchill to Ismay, 13 January 1941, PREM 3/156/3: PRO

11 "AIR REINFORCEMENTS, FAR EAST", Note by Chiefs of Staff, 24 January 1941, with note by Churchill, 25 January 1941, PREM 3/156/3: PRO

12 MINUTE, Hollis to Churchill, 27 January 1941, PREM 3/156/3: PRO

13 MEMORANDUM by Secretary of State for India and Minister of Supply, 6 January 1941, CAB 66/14, W.P. (41)4; War Cabinet Conclusions, 9 January 1941, CAB 65/17, W.M. 4(41): PRO

14 See R. SHERWOOD, *The White House Papers of Harry L. Hopkins*, i, London, 1948, p. 240

15 CABLE NO. 38, Bruce to Menzies, 14 January 1941, CRS M100, "January 1941": AA

16 MENZIES DIARY, 24 January 1941, MS 4936, Series 13, Folder 3, Menzies Papers: NLA (hereafter listed as Menzies Diary)

17 P. HASLUCK, p. 266; Letter, Sir Ronald Cross to Cranborne, 20 January 1942, ADD. MS. 58240, Emrys-Evans Papers: BL

18 MENZIES DIARY, 29 January 1941

19 IBID.

20 ADVISORY WAR COUNCIL MINUTES, 5 February 1941, CRS A2682, Vol. 1, Minute 119: AA

21 IBID.

22 ADVISORY WAR COUNCIL MINUTES, 5 February 1941, CRS A2682, Vol. 1, Minutes 119 and 135: AA

23 CABLE, Churchill to Roosevelt, 15 February 1941, "The Prime Minister's Personal Telegrams", VI/1, Ismay Papers: KC

24 ADVISORY WAR COUNCIL MINUTES, 13 February 1941, CRS A2682, Vol. 1, Minute 145: AA

25 WAR CABINET MINUTES, 14 February 1941, CRS A2673, Vol. 5, Minute 801: AA

26 CABLE NO. 125, Bruce to Fadden, 14 February 1941, CRS M100, "February 1941": AA

27 WAR CABINET MINUTES, 14 February 1941, CRS A2673, Vol. 5, Minute 802: AA

28 LETTER, Brooke-Popham to Ismay, 28 February 1941, V/1/7, Brooke-Popham Papers: KC

29 ADVISORY WAR COUNCIL MINUTES, 14 February 1941, CRS A2682, Vol. 1, Minute 149A: AA

30 LETTER, Brooke-Popham to Sir Arthur Street, Under Secretary of State for Air, 22 February 1941, V/2/4, Brooke-Popham Papers: KC

31 CABLE NO. 87, Fadden to Cranborne, 12 February 1941, *DAFP*, iv, Doc. 285

32 CABLE NO. 57, Fadden to Menzies (in Cairo), 12 February 1941, *DAFP*, iv. Doc. 287

33 NOTE, Churchill to Eden, 12 February 1941, PREM 3/294/2: PRO

34 See DAVID DAY, *Menzies and Churchill at War*, ch. 3

35 DEFENCE COMMITTEE (OPERATIONS) MINUTES, 17 December 1940, CAB 69/1, D.O. (40)51: PRO

36 CABLE NO. 98, Burrell to Colvin, 7 February 1941, *DAFP*, iv, Doc. 278

37 CABLE NO. 159, Burrell to Colvin, 24 February 1941, *DAFP*, iv, Doc. 318

38 MENZIES DIARY, 27 February 1941; Cable No. 166, Menzies to Fadden, 1 March 1941, *DAFP*, iv, Doc. 328

39 NOTE OF CONVERSATION, Menzies, Shedden and Bruce with Alexander and Phillips, 8 March 1941, AVAR 5/5/13, Alexander Papers: CC

40 *IBID.*; Cable M1, Menzies to Fadden, 4 March 1941, *DAFP*, iv, Doc. 330; Note of Conversations at UK Admiralty, 8 March 1941, *DAFP*, iv, Doc. 343; Menzies Diary, 8 March 1941

41 MENZIES DIARY, 8 March 1941; S. Roskill, *The War at Sea*, London, 1956, ii, p. 8; Two later deliveries of fifty and forty Hurricanes arrived in late January and early February respectively, as Singapore was set to fall. Most were retained for use in the NEI.

42 ADDRESS by Fadden to Joint Meeting of both Houses of Parliament, 12 March 1941, CRS A5954, Box 308: AA

43 *IBID.*

44 RECORD OF MEETING AT UK FOREIGN OFFICE, 26 February 1941, *DAFP*, iv, Doc. 324; See also J. Kennedy, *The Business of War*, London, 1957, p. 190; Letter, Sir H. Seymour to his wife, 27 February 1941, SEYR 2/4, Seymour Papers: CC; Cadogan Diary, 26 February 1941, in D. Dilks (ed.), p. 358

45 MENZIES DIARY, 26 February 1941; See also J. Kennedy, p. 190

46 ADVISORY WAR COUNCIL MINUTES, 28 February 1941, CRS A2682, Vol. 2, Minute 174: AA; See also David Day, chs 4–5; War Cabinet Minutes, 5 March 1941, CRS A2673, Vol. 6, Minute 894; Cable No. 98, Fadden to Menzies, 5 March 1941, CRS CP 290/9, Bundle 1[11]SC: AA

47 CABLE NO. 17, Menzies to Fadden, 6 March 1941, CRS M100, "March 1941": AA

48 MENZIES DIARY, 23 February 1941; Cable No. 82, Fadden to Menzies, 26 February 1941, CRS CP 290/9, Bundle 1[11]SC; Advisory War Council Minutes, 28 February 1941, CRS A2682, Vol. 2, Minute 223: AA

49 MENZIES DIARY, 14 April 1941; See Cadogan Diary, 7 April 1941, in D. Dilks (ed.), p. 370

50 LETTERS, Sinclair to Beaverbrook, 19 February 1941, and Beaverbrook to Sinclair, 20 February 1941, BBK D/32, Beaverbrook Papers: HLRO

51 In May, Australia's Air Minister, John McEwen, urged that the Hurricane be diverted to Libya. He argued that Australia was not using single-seater fighters, that the planes had little operational or training value and that maintenance and spares would be a big problem. Two months later, he asked Menzies why there had been no reply to his suggestion. In a draft reply, Menzies agreed with McEwen that the plane should go to Libya and asked him for its present whereabouts. This draft was not sent when it was realised that the plane was about to arrive by ship in Australia. On 21 August, Menzies announced its arrival and that it would be used for exhibition flights. See CRS A1608, N.55/1/3: AA.

52 See BBK D/32, Beaverbrook Papers: HLRO

53 DEFENCE COMMITTEE (OPERATIONS) MINUTES, 9 April 1941, CAB 69/2, D.O. (41)12: PRO

54 *IBID.*

55 MINUTE (COPY), Beaverbrook to Churchill, 5 April 1941, BBK D416; Letters, Beaverbrook to Sinclair, and Sinclair to Beaverbrook, both 16 March 1941, BBK D/32; Letter, Beaverbrook to Sir Charles Wilson, 19 April 1941, BBK D/141, Beaverbrook Papers: HLRO

56 CABLE M57, Menzies to Fadden, 10 April 1941, CRS A5954, Box 617, "Prime Minister's Visit to United Kingdom 1941. Paper No. 19": AA

57 MINUTES OF MEETING AT MINISTRY OF AIRCRAFT PRODUCTION, 10 April 1941, CRS A5954, Box 617, "Prime Minister's Visit to United Kingdom 1941. Paper No. 19": AA

58 MENZIES DIARY, 10 April 1941

59 See fn. 56

60 See DAVID DAY, *passim*

61 DRAFT REPLY by Chiefs of Staff to Memorandum by Menzies, 9 April 1941, PREM 3/156/4: PRO

62 MINUTE, Ismay to Churchill, 4 April 1941, PREM 3/156/4: PRO; For the cables between Menzies and Fadden on the subject of Far Eastern reinforcement, see AA CP 290/9, Bundles 1[11, 12 and 13]SC: AA

63 DEFENCE COMMITTEE (OPERATIONS) MINUTES, 9 April 1941, CAB 69/2, D.O. (41)12: PRO

64 MEMORANDUM, Shedden to Menzies, 14 April 1941, CRS A5954, Box 625, "Prime Minister's Visit to U.K., 1941. Paper 7A": AA

65 LETTER, drafted by Bruce apparently intended for submission by Menzies to Churchill, 7 April 1941, CRS M103, "1941": AA.

66 J. KENNEDY, p. 97

67 See DAVID DAY, chs 10−11

68 DIRECTIVE BY CHURCHILL, 28 April 1941, PREM 3/156/6: PRO; Defence Committee (Operations) Minutes, 29 April 1941, CAB 69/2, D.O. (41)20: PRO

69 DEFENCE COMMITTEE (OPERATIONS) MINUTES, 29 April 1941, CAB 69/2, D.O. (41)20: PRO

70 DEFENCE COMMITTEE (OPERATIONS) MINUTES, 30 April and 1 May 1941, CAB 69/2, D.O. (41)21 and 22: PRO; Cable M97, Menzies to Fadden, 2 May 1941, and Cable No. 328, Casey to Department of External Affairs, 2 May 1941, *DAFP*, iv, Docs 443 and 445

71 MENZIES DIARY, 1 and 2 May 1941

72 For the effect of the Greek campaign on Germany's planned attack on Russia, see CABLE, Churchill to Eden, 30 March 1941, ISMAY VI/1, Ismay Papers: KC; On 27 April, Britain's Joint Intelligence Committee finally conceded that an invasion of Britain was no longer Germany's immediate priority. The Dominions were kept ignorant of this change in Britain's fortunes. On 31 May, Australia was advised that an "invasion of the United Kingdom probably remains Germany's 1941 objective". See F. H. Hinsley, p. 264; Cable Z196, Cranborne to Menzies, 31 May 1941, AA CP 290/7, Folder 1, Item 5: AA

73 CABINET MINUTES, 12 March 1941, and Letter, Stewart to Senator McLeay, 6 January 1941, CRS A2697, Vol. 6: AA

74 LETTER, Stewart to McEwen, 25 March 1941, Cable No. 164, Fadden to Menzies, 16 March 1941, and Cable M81, Menzies to Fadden, 25 April 1941, CRS A461, I 314/1/4, Part 3: AA; Cable No. 165, Fadden to New Zealand Government, 7 May 1941, CRS A5954, Box 343: AA; Letter, Menzies to Churchill, 29 March 1941, CRS A5954, Box 617: AA

75 LETTER, Hughes to Menzies, 21 February 1941, CRS A5954, Box 630: AA

76 LETTER, Evatt to Menzies, 24 May 1941, Evatt Papers, "War — ALP Government, Formation of, 1941": FUL

77 CABLE M72, Menzies to Curtin, and Cable, Menzies to Fadden, both 22 April 1941, CRS A5954, Box 630: AA; *Sun*, Sydney, 23 April 1941

78 MENZIES DIARY, 23 May 1941

7

Menzies' Total War

May to August 1941

*M*ay 1941 was one of the blackest times of the war for Britain. After being bundled out of Greece by the German army and Luftwaffe, Britain was thrown onto the defensive as it fought desperately to retain its hold on the Middle East. Many of the evacuated troops from Greece were sent to Crete which was set upon in its turn by the overwhelming force of the Luftwaffe which dominated the skies of the Eastern Mediterranean. In Libya, Rommel had outflanked the weakened British forces and sent them scurrying far back into Egypt. Australia's 9th Division retreated to Tobruk where it dug in for one of the longest sieges of the war, while in Cairo contingency plans were prepared for the complete evacuation of British forces from Egypt.

On 3 May, Menzies had flown out of Bristol bound for Washington, deeply depressed about the possible future course of the war. While in London, Menzies had become disenchanted with Churchill's leadership and had been made aware of the wide-spread opposition among military and political figures to Churchill's control of strategy. He allowed himself to be enticed by siren calls from these figures which suggested he might topple Churchill himself. He decided that Churchill's untrammelled hold over strategy had to be broken by the combined pressure of the Dominions and saw himself playing a leading part in the political changes that he believed were necessary in London. Australia was saddled with a Prime Minister who had become more concerned with political intrigue against Churchill than with the security of the country in his charge.[1]

In Menzies' absence, and partly freed from his influence, the Australian Government adopted a slightly more resolute attitude towards local defence. The political position in Australia remained precarious for the coalition Cabinet and the Labor Party was increasingly pressing their opponents to accord Australia's own defence a priority at least equal with that accorded to the Middle East. On 8 May, Curtin used his platform within the Advisory War Council to oppose any further reinforcement of Egypt and to suggest that Britain's Mediterranean fleet be withdrawn before it became trapped there by the possible German capture of Gibraltar and Suez. He claimed that a timely withdrawal would allow the Italian fleet to be bottled up instead and would improve the "prospects of a British Fleet based on Singapore, immediately relieving Australia and the Empire of the danger of Japanese entry into the war". Although Curtin accepted that the defence of Britain was of "paramount importance", he questioned whether "this should be wholly accepted from the point of view of the requirements of Australian defence".[2]

There was much to recommend Curtin's suggestions. Britain had successfully encouraged Australia to think of her defence as beginning at Suez but there was little basis to the belief. Although Australian trade with Britain travelled via the Suez Canal and the Mediterranean, it was a lifeline that had an obvious alternative around the Cape of Good Hope. In fact, for much of the war the Mediterranean was closed to Allied shipping. Suez was important for British trade with India since the route round the Cape was a proportionally much greater distance on the India route than the Australia route. Churchill admitted as much himself in 1952. He claimed then that, following the granting of independence to India, "the Canal means very little to us. Australia? We could go around the Cape."[3] Apart from its importance to the India trade, the Suez Canal occupied a strategic position in the Middle East, a region of vital British interest.

Though Curtin's suggestions may have made sense for Australia, they received scant regard from the Government members of the Council. Spender argued that any British withdrawal from the Mediterranean would discourage the entry into the war of the United States, while Hughes dismissed Curtin's ideas completely, claiming that the Mediterranean position was not desperate and "must be resolutely faced". At this, Curtin backed down, undertaking that he would only raise the possibility of such a withdrawal in the event of the United States coming into the war.[4]

Curtin's colleagues were more resolute in their recommendations. The ambitious Dr Evatt, who was secretly planning to join a national government with Menzies, reminded the Council that Britain had not yet supplied the military appreciation of the Middle East requested by Australia two weeks previously. He urged that more pressure be applied to obtain this and that "no further A.I.F. troops should be sent abroad, as every trained and equipped man in Australia was an additional protection against Japanese intervention". He was supported to some extent by Norman Makin, the Labor MP, who observed the "tendency to commit Australia to greater obligations overseas than originally contemplated". In particular, he referred to the surreptitious way in which the 9th Division was formed from troops originally sent overseas as reinforcements for the 6th Division. The Government's immediate inclination was to disparage these suggestions. In fact, it was only after the extended discussion about the Mediterranean that Fadden informed the Labor members of his Government's agreement to the transfer to the Atlantic of much of the United States Pacific fleet. Like the commitment to Greece, the Council was presented with a *fait accompli*.[5]

Apart from the fact that a timely withdrawal from the Mediterranean would have enhanced Australia's defence position, there were many who questioned whether it would prove a disaster for Britain. Certainly, when the prospect of a withdrawal seemed imminent it was treated with relative equanimity in some British quarters. On 29 April, Britain's Minister for Economic Warfare, Hugh Dalton, wrote in his diary of being "mentally prepared to lose Egypt, Syria and Palestine, in addition to North Africa, Spain and Portugal and also a part of the fleet while we are trying to get it out. This would lengthen the war though not alter its end."[6] According to the planners at the War Office, the importance of the Middle East was of the first magnitude, but not vital.[7]

Two days before Curtin made his suggestion for a withdrawal from the Mediterranean, the Chief of the Imperial General Staff, General Dill, had proposed a similar move to Churchill, urging that Britain abandon the Middle East and concentrate all armoured forces in England to guard against a possible invasion. Though Dill was rebuffed at this attempt he did succeed at the end of June in blocking a move by Churchill to dispatch an extra supply of tanks through the hazards of the Mediterranean to the embattled forces in Egypt. Dill's view was that Britain could not afford to "run any more risks in home defence, where disaster would lose the war — disaster in the Middle East would not".[8]

From his post at the Admiralty, Admiral Sir Gerald Dickens tried to reassure Admiral Cunningham at Alexandria that a naval withdrawal would not be a "mortal blow". He reminded Cunningham that the British fleet had "evacuated the Mediterranean before and we survived" and that, in the long view, "one could watch a series of withdrawals on our part in the Near and Middle East with a good deal of resignation".[9] Dickens' view was not one that Cunningham could share from his vantage point at Alexandria. Nor was it generally accepted within the Admiralty.[10] But, as another naval colleague later observed, Cunningham's insistence that British battleships were essential for the war in the Mediterranean was not borne out by events. Towards the end of 1941, Britain lost the use of its three battleships in the Mediterranean with "no effect whatsoever on the Med'n Campaign!"[11]

Though the Mediterranean was top of the strategic agenda in May, Australia's political agenda had other pressing matters for consideration. In February 1941, the breach in the Labor Party had been healed when the breakaway branch in New South Wales reunited behind Curtin's leadership. The political gains were immediate, with the New South Wales election in May putting the Labor Party back into power in that State. Later that month, a Federal by-election in South Australia confirmed the trend away from the conservatives. Though a Federal election was not necessary until 1943, the Government could not ignore the loss in its public support. It only needed a switch in allegiance by the two independent MPs for Menzies to be evicted from the Lodge. This fact concentrated the minds of the Australian politicians as they welcomed Menzies back to the helm.

Fadden had warned Menzies that the Australian public was waiting for a decisive lead from the Government for a "fuller war effort" and that the New South Wales election result could precipitate a "frontal attack" by the Labor Party. Though he resented the criticism, Menzies reassured Fadden that he was returning "impressed with [the] gravity and urgency of our position and, so far as Australia's war effort [was] concerned, the sky will be the limit". He promised to make public statements which would call for everything to be put on a complete war basis.[12] Australia needed more than statements. The press were already renewing their clamour for a national government able to produce an intensified war effort.

Evatt greeted Menzies on his arrival in Sydney with an offer to join a "national" administration.[13] Menzies' colleagues demonstrated a similar lack of political loyalty, with many actively conspiring to bring him down.[14] But they could not strike until Menzies first had a chance to draw on his London experience to provide the leadership that Australia demanded. As the residual goodwill and esteem earned during his trip disappeared, alternative leaders were not slow to appear.

From the ranks of Menzies' increasingly restive colleagues, the Army Minister, Percy Spender, had already put the case for a greater war effort. In a forceful memorandum to Fadden on 21 April he predicted the possibility of Australia's three divisions in the Middle East being lost to the Germans and warned of the open invitation this would provide to the Japanese. More importantly, he confided that, after eighteen months of wartime preparation, the army remained unable to "face an enemy powerful enough to reach these shores in any substantial force". Stressing the "extreme gravity of the present situation", Spender cited the case of anti-tank units sent overseas "without having even seen an anti-tank gun". He called for the introduction of a "sensible, balanced, and realistic" manpower policy so that Australia could "make the switch-over of plant and manpower to a full war footing a gradual, and largely voluntary process". He warned that the Government's laissez-faire policy would "produce far graver consequences than any positive action we take" and claimed there was a "stream of men for military and other national services who are still being dammed back". This was a harsh indictment of Menzies' war leadership and an eloquent and soundly based plea for a switch in emphasis from Empire to local defence.[15]

Most of Spender's sensible proposals were not implemented. Ironically, the situation in the Middle East had the effect of concentrating Australian energies on ensuring that the Middle East did not fall to the Germans rather than making Australia look to its own defences. In addition, Admiral Colvin had returned from another conference of defence representatives in Singapore with assurances about Australia's defence that conflicted markedly with Spender's allegations. Colvin passed on a claim by Brooke-Pophan: that the reinforcement of Malaya since October had "so materially strengthened their position that he was most optimistic as to the ability of Singapore to hold out, and to continue to operate as a Fleet Base". According to Brooke-Popham's account, the British delegates at the conference had been "very anxious to bring home to the Americans the necessity for their Pacific Fleet taking a more active part in a Far East War than it appears to be their intention at present". However, Colvin failed to impress this on the Australian Government as a cause for anxiety. In any case, the British delegates were acting at variance with Churchill's expressed policy not to press the Americans as to their appropriate role in the case of a Far East war. Though Colvin's report was unjustifiably optimistic, it semed to be what Australia wanted to hear and it helped to ensure an even greater Australian contribution to the defence of the empty British naval base. But the conflict between Imperial defence and local defence would not disappear.[16]

Menzies was not the man to resolve the conflict. Speeches were his forte and his homecoming speech went down well with its call for unity and a greater effort. When it had to be translated into action, Menzies faltered. Instead, his efforts were directed towards obtaining his early return to Britain where he had been led to believe a promising political future beckoned. His ambition was so clear and his efforts to achieve it so clumsy that the press in Britain and Australia soon filled with rumours regarding his intentions. It did not assist the promotion of an all-out war effort in Australia.[17]

On 28 May, Menzies reported to the Advisory War Council on his London visit in terms that revealed his intentions. Rather than listing his achievements for Australia in the Imperial capital, he regaled the Council with a litany of complaints about Churchill and the British War Cabinet in order to establish the rationale for another trip. He argued strongly for the inclusion of a Dominion representative in the British War Cabinet, a post that privately he saw himself filling.[18] Certainly a list of his failures in London would have occupied more time than his achievements, but Menzies kept the Council in the dark on both, only gradually revealing at later meetings the sorry story of his efforts.

At the War Cabinet the following day, discussion centred on the military situation in the Middle East where a German attack on Syria was feared imminent. This raised the prospect of British forces in Egypt being caught in a pincer movement from the east and west. Australia's original commitment to the region was dragging her deeper into the defence of a British interest far removed from her own shores. Faced with the situation in Syria, Australia pressed Churchill to dispatch more fighter aircraft from Britain to ensure the defence of both Libya and Syria.[19] Britain took this as a green light to use Australian troops in a pre-emptive strike into Syria without proper consultation with Canberra.[20] It also provided the perfect foil for any Australian requests for the dispatch of fighter aircraft to either Singapore or Australia.

The Australian concern with the Middle East increased after the fall of Crete at the end of May when thousands of British, Australian and New Zealand troops were captured by German parachute troops. Following hard on the Greek de-bacle and with the 9th Division trapped in Tobruk, Australia found it difficult to focus clearly on its own defence. Since Singapore was less likely to obtain either ships or aircraft, on 11 June Australia agreed to the dispatch of another infantry brigade to Malaya, making two-thirds of the 8th Division committed to that theatre.[21] The parlous position at Singapore was known in Canberra but Australia still sent troops to defend the undefendable while encouraging America to switch her naval concentration to the Atlantic. At the same time, her Chiefs of Staff admitted that they had no joint plans to meet specific forms of attack on Australia.[22]

The Australian attitude was typified by Billy Hughes. As Australian Prime Minister during the Great War, he had served on the Imperial War Cabinet in London and earned a reputation for upholding Australian national interests. Now he was Navy Minister and used his position to quash Labor Party proposals for concentrating greater attention on local defence. However, he remained alert to the possible political implications of the Government's neglect. During the course of a meeting in April 1941, he scribbled an anxious note to the acting Chief of the Naval Staff confiding his concern that "if it were known that we have *no* mines after *18* months of war — for Port Stephens or any other port — there would be trouble".[23] This suggested that political rather than military implications dominated Hughes' thinking and that of the Government.

The question of naval mines provided an insight into the state of the continuing debate on local defence versus Imperial defence. Though plans were laid before the war to commence production of naval mines, the first order was for only 500 mines and was not completed until mid-1941. This was despite advice in September 1940 that Australia would need 4000 mines to cope with a Pacific war. The Government was also advised then that Australia could no longer rely on a British fleet being provided at Singapore on the outbreak of such a war and that the Dominion must therefore prepare itself for a defensive naval strategy, with "one of the cheapest and best means of defence" being naval mines. On receipt of this advice, the government increased its order by an extra 1000 mines, still far short of the number needed for a Pacific war. At the same time, it accepted orders from Britain, New Zealand and Noumea for another 1400 mines.[24]

In June 1941, Menzies was informed of additional British orders for Australian-produced mines and that the first Australian minefield would be laid near Port Moresby. He was apparently unaware that completed mines were even being produced and he questioned whether defensive minefields should be laid prior to the outbreak of hostilities. Port Stephens, the gateway to the vital industrial area of Newcastle, was still without mines and the RAN simply did not have a sufficient number to protect the north and east coasts of Australia. It was not until the Labor Government assumed office in October that an order for an extra 2000 mines was proposed to protect the Australian east coast.[25] Despite Menzies' call for an "all-in" war effort, the Government was still guided by financial stringency, the quest for export orders and the overriding priority of Britain and the Middle East. It was in the Middle East that the Australian Government felt most at risk. As for local defence, it was imperative that Australians be made to *feel* secure rather than actually *be* secure in order for the Middle East commitment to continue.

As for Menzies, he placed his personal faith in the Japanese not entering the war. If they did so, he confidently expected that the United States would come in on the British side and prevent any serious threat to Australia. After finishing his trip across the United States, Menzies claimed in his diary to have been "left in no doubt (without words) that America will not stand by and see Australia attacked".[26] As he admitted, this was more a feeling than something for which he had hard evidence. In fact, the evidence was pointing in a different direction. America had explicitly disavowed any responsibility for Australia's naval defence and Menzies had been advised that it would be "quite impossible" for Australia to obtain American medium tanks "in any reasonable time". That left Australia with just ten light tanks that she used for training an armoured division for dispatch to the Middle East. Any supplies of light tanks that Australia had on order in America also would depend on British requirements in the Middle East.[27] Menzies' reliance on the Americans was tenuous indeed.

The other strand of his belief in the improbability of a Pacific war was based on his assessment of the objective Japanese interest being against such a move. While in London, Menzies had met with British businessmen seeking friendly relations with Japan and apparently had even dallied with the idea of making a Munich-type trip to Tokyo himself.[28] Back in Australia, Menzies continued to argue for a "realistic approach" towards Japan.[29] He still felt that Japan could be stopped by a chalk line on a map that would set an agreed limit to her expansion. Although Menzies had been berated by the Labor Party for his London speech on peace in the Pacific, Curtin now joined him in trying to reach an agreement with Japan. The Labor leader had cultivated private contacts with the Japanese Minister in Australia and, on 5 June, received the Advisory War Council's permission for these contacts to continue.[30]

Despite Menzies' criticism of the Foreign Office policy toward Japan, it was the Foreign Secretary, Anthony Eden, who made prolonged efforts to promote the sort of joint declaration advocated by Menzies, though, unlike Menzies, he did not envisage it as part of a general Pacific settlement. In November 1940, the exiled Dutch Government had asked Britain for an assurance of military assistance in the event of a Japanese attack on the NEI. Throughout 1941, Eden urged such an assurance on the War Cabinet.[31] In mid-May, following Menzies' departure, Eden seemed to achieve his objective when the matter came before the Defence Committee where he argued that British support for the NEI would be inevitable whatever the United States attitude and that it was better to make such a declaration now and possibly deter a Japanese attack.[32]

The First Sea Lord, Admiral Pound, was appalled by the practical implications of a unilateral commitment and reminded the committee that Britain's navy in the Far East was "very weak" and that it would be foolish to declare war automatically when "such action might lead to a damaging attack on our trade". Instead, he proposed that it would be better for Britain to "keep an open mind and to decide at the time whether it was to our advantage to declare war or not". In a remarkable switch of position, the Committee overruled Pound and threw its support behind Eden. Churchill, who was politically vulnerable at the time because of the sorry state of the war in the Mediterranean, bowed to the wishes of his colleagues and allowed the decision to stand, at least for the time being. At the same time, he emphasised that "there could be no redistribution of naval forces to strengthen the Far East". Churchill had a second line of defence with the Committee's instruction for Eden to consult with the Dominions and obtain their agreement to the declaration as well as to inform the United States.[33] These instructions, and the passage of time, allowed scope for the decision to be reversed.

Australia assisted by opposing a public declaration that did not include the United States. Acting on advice from Casey, Menzies argued that any unilateral declaration by the British Empire could emphasise the disunity with the United States and thereby have the opposite effect on Tokyo to that intended. Instead, Menzies proposed a private assurance to the Dutch authorities and urged that America join in such a message. Whatever happened, Menzies advised, Australia could not allow a Japanese invasion of the NEI to go unanswered.[34]

As time went on, all manner of conflicting messages came back to Whitehall. Australia and America opposed a public declaration, as did the British Ambassador to Tokyo. Then the American Ambassador in Tokyo was instructed to give a private warning to the Japanese, if and when a suitable opportunity arose, that the Americans had an interest in Britain's Far Eastern interests not being attacked.[35] These all combined to make Britain hesitate while the United States made its position clearer. When Eden brought the matter back before the War Cabinet at the end of July, he found that his previous support had withered away. Churchill's political position had strengthened in the interim and he succeeded twice in having the matter deferred. The British Prime Minister refused to believe that Japan had designs on Singapore and he argued against any commitment to defend the NEI while being unable to dispatch an adequate fleet. He advised the War Cabinet to await the stiffening of American opinion.[36] Churchill's determination to avoid a single-handed war against Japan left Menzies' chalk line undrawn. Australian efforts to pre-empt a Japanese attack on the NEI by stationing Australian forces there were successfully opposed by Britain as being provocative.[37]

The saga of the NEI declaration was overshadowed by much more momentous events in Europe. On 22 June 1941, Hitler unleashed the full might of his armed forces across the long border with the Soviet Union. This was the turning point in the war. Like Napoleon before him, Hitler's strength would be absorbed by the resilience of the Russian people and the size and harshness of their land. Although rumours of such an attack had been received in London from 1940 onwards, Britain was remarkably slow to give them credence and, when the attack occurred, few in London expected Russia to resist for more than a few months.

The implications for both Britain and Australia of the German attack were considerable. The pressure on Britain in the Middle East was relieved, at least for a time, while the prospect of a German invasion of Britain could be disregarded until at least the spring of 1942. Any development that ensured British security and brought ultimate victory closer should have brought comfort to Australia. But the German onslaught on Russia had darker portents for Australia as it created a new theatre of active operations against Germany that would eat greedily away at the mountain of munitions now being produced in Britain and America.

Putting his anti-Bolshevism to one side for the duration of the war, Churchill immediately undertook to supply Stalin with the wherewithal of war. As General Ismay later explained it, Britain faced a choice between reinforcing Russia or the Far East and decided that "the Russians must have priority and that a grave risk must be accepted in the Far east ... the collapse of Russia would mean Hitler's hegemony in Europe, while the collapse of Singapore could be retrieved after Hitler had been dealt with".[38] This commitment also placed an added burden on the Royal Navy which had to patrol the icy wastes of the Arctic Ocean to protect the sea route to Russia, while the naval commitment in the Mediterranean continued as usual.

As a side-effect, the German attack diverted attention in London from Churchill's leadership and defused the mounting criticism that had been accumulating after the defeat and partial evacuation from Crete.[39] It also relieved some of the pressure that had been building in Australia for their Middle East commitment to be brought to an end. Following the Crete defeat, the Australian Government had watched anxiously as the tiny garrison on Cyprus seemed destined to share the same fate. Half of this garrison was made up of some 800 Australian troops and they had been ordered to resist a German attack, though no reinforcements would be sent in the event of such an attack. Menzies stressed to Churchill the possible political repercussions in Australia that could result from a vain defence and a further defeat involving Australian forces.[40] This cable was not well received by Churchill who saw it as revealing a lack of fortitude by Australia.[41] Over the succeeding months, this feeling would be confirmed and intensified as the Australian Government began an incessant campaign for the relief of its troops in Tobruk where military disaster was expected on an even larger scale.[42]

Menzies had visited Tobruk during his tour of the Middle East and had seen how easily its Italian defenders had been overcome. It did not take much for him to envisage a similar outcome for the Australian defenders.[43] The Labor Party also was stepping up the political pressure on Menzies. Curtin, who seemed less than anxious to assume Menzies' mantle in wartime, was himself under pressure from Evatt who was keen to become part of the Government, either by pushing the conservatives to one side or by joining with them. Meanwhile, Menzies remained transfixed by the political future beckoning from Westminster which depended on his retaining the post of Prime Minister until he could make the switch. In the midst of these swirling political currents, and dragged down by the weight of Imperial ties, it is not surprising that Australia's national interest only came to the surface intermittently.

As the details of the defeats in Greece and Crete filtered

back to Australia, there was considerable bitterness engendered at the cavalier manner in which the Dominion troops had been committed to battle bereft of proper equipment and lacking the all-important element of air support. Ever since the defeat in Norway a year before it had been a cardinal principle of modern battle that infantry could not operate effectively without control of the skies above them. Menzies joined the howl of outrage following Crete with a political barb aimed straight at Churchill, the architect of the Norwegian campaign, commenting that it was "tragic to think that our forces in Crete suffered so much through the lack of proper equipment, and a full and adequate Air Force". Menzies warned pointedly and publicly that "this must be the final lesson".[44] However, in Menzies' mind the lesson was not one for Australia to learn. It had not shaken his faith in Imperial defence, just in its leaders. The Labor Party saw it differently, but it was principally a difference of emphasis.

Greece and Crete did affect, though not destroy, the willingness of the Labor Party to continue Australia's involvement in Imperial defence. At an Advisory War Council meeting on 12 June, Curtin urged that Australia, like Britain, must have its own defence as the first priority. His concern, as much as Menzies', centred on the political implications of disaster. He had not rejected Imperial defence. In fact he wanted a greater effort in the Middle East to minimise the risks of defeat and to ensure that it was held by Britain. His fear was that Britain was not according the region sufficient priority compared with its own defence. He accepted Menzies' assurances that the Middle East was a "crucial theatre" but wanted assurances that Churchill regarded it in the same way. Otherwise, he argued, Australia would be "not only imperilling our men but the Fleet, which was the key to Empire Defence" and that he preferred to "close the Mediterranean with some salvage rather than with none". Although Curtin challenged the British view of the Mediterranean as the "pivotal point of the Empire", he "preferred to fight in the Middle East, and would do so to the extent of taking risks in Australia" if he could be "assured of reasonable chances of success".[45]

The meeting concluded on the note set by Curtin — that Churchill be requested to provide details of the present and prospective British air and tank strength in the Middle East.

This Menzies did, while in an accompanying personal cable he also suggested Churchill provide a message "expressed in your own characteristic way, indicating the significance which you attach to the defence of the Middle East".[46]

Australia certainly was taking risks with its own defence. Despite the realisation that modern fighter aircraft were the key to success in the Mediterranean, Australia had none of its own. Menzies persisted with his long-term plan to produce aircraft in Australia and thereby lay the basis for a post-war, British-owned automobile industry. Though he had not managed to obtain any guarantee of British assistance for his plan, the official report of his efforts in London claimed he had received the backing of Beaverbrook and Sinclair and that "assurances of the fullest possible co-operation from the British Government were given without hesitation". In spite of the steadily worsening defence position, "primary importance" would be given to ensuring that the aircraft factories would be "planned so that they could be effectively used in peace time". Under the proposed program, Australia would produce planes for sale to Britain's Eastern Empire, rather than ones necessarily needed for her own defence. It would be two or three years before it would be in full operation.[47]

Up to that time, Australian aircraft production facilities had been kept going by British orders for training aircraft — Wirraways and Tiger Moths. Although Australia needed operational aircraft, the Government policy of October 1940 stipulated that as the Australian orders for training aircraft were fulfilled the production facilities should not be switched to other aircraft types but used to fill possible export orders. In June 1941, it was planned to transfer Tiger Moth facilities in February 1942 to the production of Beauforts but only after Britain had first declined to order any more Tiger Moths. This policy elevated efficiency and Imperial integration above the need for Australian security.[48]

There were 270 Beauforts on order, the first batch of ninety going to Britain, the next ninety to Australia and the final ninety to Britain. To Menzies' disappointment, Whitehall intended to dispatch the planes Britain had on order to Singapore. Menzies had hoped they would be sent to the Middle East. In July, the Australian Government considered a proposal for the expansion of Beaufort production and, in the more distant future, the commencement of Beaufighter and Lancaster bomber production. These proposals arose from John Storey of the Aircraft Production Commission who had accompanied Menzies to London. Again, they were based more on the prospect of export orders and reasons of efficiency, the Beaufort and Beaufighter having many components in common, than on deciding the best aircraft for Australia's defence. In discussion of the proposals, the Lancaster was dropped for practical reasons while the remainder of the planned program was referred to London for approval. In September, Australia was informed that Britain would purchase any Beauforts produced that were surplus to Australian requirements but that it would not buy any Beaufighters. Accordingly, Australia abandoned its plans for Beaufighter production and expanded the production of Beauforts, most of them being destined for the RAF, despite fears that the Beaufort would be obsolescent before it could be produced in any number.[49]

As for the immediate future, Menzies repeated the opinion of the British Air Ministry that Australia did not require fighter planes on military grounds but, for "psychological" purposes, some squadrons could be formed which would "be valuable as reinforcements for employment elsewhere in the Far East theatre". He then set out the conditional program of plane deliveries that he had received from Beaverbrook and reiterated Britain's "categorical assurance" that, in the case of a Far East war, there would be an "immediate review of air resources".[50] This meant different things in Whitehall than it did to Menzies and his War Cabinet.

In fact, there were already problems with delivery of the 243 Brewster aircraft promised to Menzies by Beaverbrook. Deliveries had been supposed to begin in May 1941 but were progressively put forward to the future. In June, RAAF officers left for the United States to familiarise themselves with the aircraft only to find on their arrival that the aircraft would not even have a test flight before September. Delivery of the first fifty planes was not expected before February 1942 at the earliest. Britain refused to help expedite their production, advising Australia in September to switch their order to another aircraft entirely. An RAAF report concluded that Beaverbrook had been "apparently completely in the dark about the Brewster project and [that] the undertakings given to the Prime Minister

in respect of deliveries were without justification or foundation".
So much for Menzies' success in London.[51]

Following the German attack on Russia, anxious eyes looked
to Tokyo for the Japanese reaction. The attack had effectively
removed Russia as a threat to Japan in the Far East and theoretically freed for use elsewhere some of the Japanese troops
garrisoned in Manchuria. At the beginning of July, the Foreign
Office became convinced that the "beastly Japs" were intent on
consolidating their hold on French Indo-China "as a stepping
stone to other things".[52] In the event of such a move, Eden
recommended to the War Cabinet on 7 July that Britain increase
her defences in Malaya, that Australian troops be sent to Dutch
Timor and Ambon and that Britain renounce her trade treaty
with Tokyo. He also reported on the economic restrictions
that Britain had been progressively introducing against Japan
and the "constant care and vigilance" being taken not to "push
restrictions to the point of provoking Japan to war".[53] While
the stated intention may have been to deter Japan from war,
the effect was to force Japan into making a decision either for
or against entering the war.

In an accompanying memorandum to Eden's, Hugh Dalton
pointed to Japanese complaints and the "threatening attitude
of the Japanese press to the Netherlands East Indies" as providing proof that British policy had "begun to bear fruit". The
Japanese sabre-rattling indicated that Tokyo was being brought
to the point of its fateful decision. Dalton noted with approval
that the Japanese were "finding it more and more difficult to
avoid drawing on their reserves" of strategic raw materials and
that throughout the world they were "meeting with obstruction
ultimately caused either by British or United States action".
He complained that Australia had not played the game and
had, in some instances, "been reluctant to restrict their exports
even to normal quantities".[54]

The War Cabinet could not agree with Eden that "strong
deterrent measures" should be adopted to prevent Japanese
encroachments, deciding instead that Britain "take appropriate
counter-action after each encroachment". At the same time, it
instructed Eden and Dalton to consider "tightening the screw
still further against Japan by means of increased economic restrictions, even in the absence of further provocation".[55] In the
words of the British historian Christopher Thorne, British

policy was directed "above all" towards an "American entry into the war — the current, German war — and if a show-down with Japan would provide that supreme blessing in addition to its direct, Asian benefits, then so much the better".[56]

This was revealed clearly in a War Cabinet discussion two weeks later. The United States had threatened to strengthen the embargo on Japan if it made its expected move in Indo-China. Britain had to decide whether to support America in a firm policy that could lead to war. Eden advised that the "issue with Japan must be faced soon or later and that the risk of the United States not intervening in a war between ourselves and Japan is small". He urged that Britain match any American action while trying to obtain an assurance of their support in the event of war. Though their approaches to the problem diverged, Eden and Churchill were united in not shrinking at the thought of war with Japan, just at the thought of being left on a limb by the United States.[57]

This thought also dominated Menzies' mind when he urged Britain to take the toughest action against Japan, even to the extent of a "complete economic embargo", but subject to Washington being prepared to act concurrently with Britain.[58] Menzies' conditional toughness did not go down well at the Foreign Office which knew that America would resist any such open co-ordination of policies. Cadogan scathingly dismissed the "stupid Dominions" which "get cold feet, and don't want to freeze Japanese assets without an assurance of support from [the] U.S. They *must* know that they can't *get* this."[59] The Foreign Office was prepared to take a chance and talk tough to Tokyo without a prior guarantee of support from Washington. They believed that American political considerations precluded such a guarantee but that Washington would act against Japan in the event of an attack in the Pacific. The following day Roosevelt froze Japanese assets in the United States. Britain did likewise.

While Britain became stronger on actions that could propel Japan into war, it remained much weaker when it came to making provision for such a war. Following the Japanese move into Indo-China, Brooke-Popham wanted to place his staff in Singapore on a "full war footing" and asked for London's sanction to improve matters "while there is yet time".[60] How-ever, he was advised by an Air Ministry colleague that Chur-chill had promised to provide "three months warning of any serious explosion in the Far East".[61] One of Churchill's staff later recalled how Churchill used this promise to overcome opposition to the continued reinforcements for Russia. When proposals were put for reinforcing the Far East, he would simply repeat his promise of three months warning.[62]

In one sense, Britain and Australia were both dependent on American initiatives in the Far East. But Britain's dependence was an act of conscious will that had her primary national interest as the ultimate aim. Australia's dependence was of a different nature. She had never thrown off her colonial mentality and she retained as her primary national interest the security of Britain and the Empire. Australian security remained a subsidiary interest in the belief that, without Britain, there could be no security for Australia.

On 29 July, Menzies informed the Advisory War Council that Australia's policy would "move together with the United Kingdom and the U.S.A.". Despite having appointed a Minister in Tokyo, Menzies admitted that little independent advice was being received from him, that the "position with the Japanese Government was being handled by the British Ambassador and full advice was being received from him through the Dominions Office". When concern was expressed about Britain's naval plans in the event of war with Japan, Menzies outlined them in all their paucity — that a battleship and aircraft carrier would be moved into the Indian Ocean. As some of the council members realised, there was little comfort for Australia in such a move. In Curtin's absence, his deputy, Frank Forde, complained that Australia was being "borne along by the tide of events without any undertaking as to what the U.S.A. would do" and that without them, "we could not keep an enemy out of Australia". He likened Singapore to an "empty garage" and urged Menzies to recall Parliament from its recess to consider the "very grave" position.[63]

Only Jack Beasley, the Labor MP, questioned Australia's continuing commitment to Imperial defence, pressing for the return of Australian forces from the Middle East and arguing that, "in the disposition of Australian troops Australia should be considered first". Despite some apparent sympathy for this position from Spender, the Army Minister rejected a proposal for a full mobilisation. He combined with the other Government members to present the British view of the position and to quash any suggestion that Australian forces be withdrawn from the Middle East which was described as the "gateway for a German advance into Egypt and Asia, and had to be held".[64] Publicly Menzies again called for "sacrifice and a great national effort", exhorting Australians to be "true children of magnificent Britain from where we come".[65]

On 6 August, Curtin was able to attend the Council and joined with Menzies in proposing that Britain should try, by itself if necessary, to "delimit by agreement the expansionist policy of Japan", which he claimed was "still susceptible to a face-saving arrangement". He predicted that any possible American support for Australia would be outweighed by the opposition from Japan. Curtin's argument centred on the need to reach a Pacific agreement in order to continue the concentration of forces against Germany. It was predicated on the mistaken assumption that Japan's entry into the war would cause a dangerous diversion of British resources to meet the threat in the Far East. He also alluded to the domestic political implications if Japanese raids occurred when the AIF was overseas, thereby producing a situation that would be "politically unmanageable". Menzies mentioned the idea of travelling to Tokyo to seek some sort of understanding with the Japanese but admitted that he had recoiled at the similarity with Chamberlain's Munich trip. If this was meant to arouse the interest of the Council, it failed miserably. Both Government and Labor members combined to knock on the head the suggestions of their respective leaders, arguing the importance of remaining in step with the United States.[66]

Instead of proceeding to Tokyo, Menzies set out the following evening on the first stage of a two and a half week tour of Australia designed to lift his stocks with the public. Disgruntled MPs from all parties had been publicly demanding his resignation, while his attempts to return to London had come to nothing. Three days after beginning his tour, he dramatically cancelled it, ostensibly because of reported Japanese concentrations in Indo-China, and returned to Melbourne for meetings of the War Cabinet and Advisory War Council. His intention was to emphasise the gravity of the situation in order to bludgeon his way back to London past the opposition from suspicious MPs on all sides. In London, the British War Cabinet was critical of his "alarmist" public statement on the Far East and ensured that the British press did not "exaggerate the immediate seriousness of the situation". At the time, Churchill was in Newfoundland for his first wartime meeting with Roosevelt. Menzies apparently also feared the implications of this meeting for the Empire and hoped to use the presence in London of two other Dominion Prime Ministers to force his own way into the British War Cabinet.[67]

Although Menzies managed to convince Curtin of his plan to return to London, he failed to achieve the support of other Labor MPs. Moreover, he offended them when he proposed, without first consulting the Advisory War Council, that Britain guarantee the security of Thailand and committed Australia to regard a Japanese seizure of the strategically important Kra Isthmus that bordered on Malaya as a *casus belli*, something that Churchill remained unwilling to do. Menzies and Curtin justified the commitment by claiming that it was in accordance with the previously expressed views of the Council, a claim that was well wide of the mark.[68]

Churchill was in Newfoundland on 7 August when his Defence Committee had also discussed the guarantee for Thailand. Nevertheless, the Committee was aware of his "strong views" on any such guarantee except over something that was "immediate and vital", a view supported by the Admiralty which again advised of its eagerness to avoid war in the Far East for as long as possible. The Committee therefore overruled Eden who was thwarted once more in his attempt to find some territory in the Far East that Britain would be willing to pledge to defend. The Vice Chief of the Imperial General Staff, General Pownall, set out the basis of the military opposition to a Thai guarantee — it was "quite certain that America would *not* go to war for Siam and the last thing in the world we want to do is to have to take on Japan without America".[69]

When the matter came back before the Defence Committee on the following day, opinions were more opposed to Eden than ever. Admiral Phillips argued for a "realistic view" of Britain's ability to effect its will in the Far East. He claimed that Britain had "readjusted" her ideas as to her vital interests and that immediate American intervention could not be relied upon. He also reminded the Committee of Britain's pledge to abandon the Middle East if Australia was facing a "mortal threat", though he also implied that the pledge was worthless since it had been made before Britain had "amassed an Army of 600,000 men in that theatre, a large part of whom were Australians and New Zealanders". Even if Britain refused to honour the pledge and kept her fleet in the Mediterranean, Phillips thought it was doubtful whether she could maintain her "exposed communications with Egypt ... in the face of enterprising Japanese action in the Indian Ocean".[70]

There were two vital questions for Australia in this analysis. What was the current value of Britain's defence assurance towards Australia given the ongoing "readjustment" in Britain's vital interests and the build-up of forces in the Middle East? And, in view of the planned "Germany first" strategy of the Allies, how much assistance could Australia expect even in the event of an Anglo–American stand against Japan? These questions were never put. Menzies' gaze was firmly fixed on his own political advancement in London. On 19 August, he gained the support of his Cabinet for his plan to obtain Dominion representation in the British War Cabinet.[71] He had himself in mind as the occupant of such a War Cabinet seat which was in turn intended to launch him into Downing Street. Churchill, combined with the other Dominions and opposition from the Labor Party, ensured that Menzies' efforts were in vain. On finding his way to London blocked and his support in Australia withering away, Menzies stepped down from the Prime Ministership, apparently in the hope that he could arrive at his London destiny by another route. His long campaign to catapult himself direct from the Lodge to Westminster was at an end.

Menzies' fall was a vital victory for Australia in its efforts to develop some sense of its predicament in the Pacific. However, she still had a long way to go. The scramble for position in Canberra was matched by an equally vigorous scramble for self-advancement in the population at large.

By and large, Australia was doing well out of the war. Though unemployment lingered on into 1941, those in work were able to work overtime and earn good money which they could spend freely on the consumer goods of their choice. Though Curtin supported Menzies' supposedly "unlimited war effort", the Labor leader linked his support to a call for the "workers and the people" to be given "some instalments of the new social order as opportunity offers".[72] To a great extent, the war was seen more as an opportunity than a threat. The government and business leaders saw it as a chance to industrialise the country, while the labour movement saw an opportunity to make good the deprivation suffered during the Depression.

Trade unions resisted the greater involvement of women in the workforce and, despite increasing manpower problems for the Services and the production of munitions, women were refused admission except in their traditional roles such as nurses, cooks and typists. They fared better in the civil economy where the boom in consumer spending allowed them to desert domestic service in droves.[73]

The White Australia policy stayed firmly in place. Despite the nominal wartime friendship with China, restrictions on the admission of Chinese students and businessmen remained. Though the Dominion agreed to allow Britain to transport prisoners of war to Australia, it was careful to stipulate that none of the prisoners should be black. Jewish refugees fleeing from German persecution, including 300 French children, were refused admission to Australia despite eloquent pleas on their behalf. All this was the legacy Menzies bequeathed to his successor.[74]

Menzies was replaced by the ineffectual Fadden who nevertheless was prepared to give greater priority to local defence, as much out of deference to pressure from the Labor Party as to his own inclinations. It still came a poor third behind the needs of Britain and her Empire and the competing needs of the Dominion's civil economy. Menzies' fall also was a victory for Churchill. As a deposed Prime Minister, Menzies presented a lesser threat to Churchill's position and it became a simple matter to prevent his passage to London. Churchill also tore up Menzies' plan for a Dominion Prime Ministers' meeting at which Far Eastern defence could have figured high on the agenda.

Australia remained in a state of political turmoil despite Menzies' resignation. Like Menzies, Fadden's hold on power relied on the continuing support of the two independent MPs. There was no time to waste if Australia was to face the prospect of a Japanese attack, but it still lacked the political leadership able to make the necessary defence preparations.

NOTES

1 For an extended discussion of this, see DAVID DAY, *Menzies and Churchill at War*

2 ADVISORY WAR COUNCIL MINUTES, 8 May 1941, CRS A2682, Vol. 2, Minute 313: AA

3 MORAN DIARY, 10 January 1952, Lord Moran, *Winston Churchill: The Struggle for Survival*, London, 1968, p. 362

4 ADVISORY WAR COUNCIL MINUTES, 8 May 1941, CRS A2682, Vol. 2, Minute 313: AA

5 *IBID.*

6 DALTON DIARY, 29 April 1941, I/24/100−101, Dalton Papers: LSE. See also Letter, Smuts to Wavell, 19 May 1941, in J. Van Der Poel (ed.), *Selections from the Smuts Papers*, iv, Cambridge, 1973, p. 299; R. G. Casey, *Personal Experience*, p. 73

7 POWNALL DIARY, 16 June 1941, in B. Bond (ed.), *Chief of Staff*, ii London, 1974, p. 22

8 SIR R. WINGATE, *Lord Ismay*, London, 1970, p. 58; Pownall Diary, 30 June 1941, in B. Bond (ed.), p. 30

9 LETTER, Dickens to Cunningham, 20 May 1941, ADD. MS. 52569, Cunningham Papers: BL

10 "MY LIFE", Autobiography of Admiral Sir William Davis, p. 256, WDVS 1/3, Davis Papers: CC. Davis was a member of the Plans Division at the Admiralty. He recalled how the Plans Division considered the Middle East and Mediterranean vital for the "whole backbone of our strategy".

11 LETTER, Admiral Ralph Edwards to Captain Grenfell, 25 December [?1951], GREN 2/2, Grenfell Papers: CC

12 CABLE, Fadden to Menzies, 11 May 1941, CRS A5954, Box 630; Cable, Menzies (in Washington) to Fadden, 13 May 1941, CRS CP 290/9, [15] S.C.: AA

13 LETTER, Evatt to Menzies, 24 May 1941, Evatt Collection, "War — ALP Government, Formation of, 1941": FUL

14 C. HAZLEHURST, *Menzies Observed*, Sydney, 1979, p. 230

15 LETTER, Spender to Fadden, 21 April 1941, MS 4875, Box 1, Correspondence 1939−1949, Spender Papers: NLA

16 WAR CABINET MINUTES, 15 May 1941, CRS A2673, Vol. 7, Minute 1073: AA; Letter, Brooke-Popham to Ismay, 16 May 1941, V/1/12, Brooke-Popham Papers: KC

17 See DAVID DAY, chs 13−14

18 ADVISORY WAR COUNCIL MINUTES, 28 May 1941, CRS A2682, Vol. 2, Minute 346: AA

19 WAR CABINET MINUTES, 29 May 1941, CRS A2673, Vol. 7, Minute 1111: AA; Cables No. 2649, No. 347 and No. 363, Menzies to Churchill, 29 May, 6 and 12 June 1941, PREM 3/281/10: PRO

20 See P. HASLUCK, pp. 341−4; D. M. Horner, pp. 108−11

21 WAR CABINET MINUTES, 10 and 11 June 1941, CRS A2673, Vol. 7, Minutes 1138 and 1145: AA

22 WAR CABINET MINUTES, 10 June 1941, CRS A2673, Vol. 7, Minute 1136: AA

23 NOTE BY HUGHES, undated, JWD 5, Durnford Papers: IWM. The note was probably written during a War Cabinet meeting on 24 April 1941, when mines were discussed with Durnford in attendance as Acting Chief of the Naval Staff. See CRS A5954, Box 483: AA

24 See CRS A5954, Box 483: AA

25 IBID.

26 MENZIES DIARY, May 1941.

27 LETTER (COPY), M. Dewar (head of British Tank Mission in United States) to A. Chamberlain (British Purchasing Commission in Washington), 13 May 1941, CRS A5954, Box 619, : AA

28 LETTERS, Lord Sempill to Menzies, 23 April 1941, and Menzies to Sempill, 30 April 1941, CRS A5954, Box 625: AA; *Tatler*, London, 14 May 1941

29 ADVISORY WAR COUNCIL MINUTES, 28 May 1941, CRS A2682, Vol. 2, Minute 346: AA

30 ADVISORY WAR COUNCIL MINUTES, 5 June 1941, CRS A2682, Vol. 2, Minute 356: AA

31 "CO-OPERATION WITH THE NETHERLANDS EAST INDIES", Memorandum by Eden, 5 February 1941, CAB 66/14, W.P. (41)24: PRO

32 DEFENCE COMMITTEE (OPERATIONS) MINUTES, 15 May 1941, CAB 69/2, D.O. (41)30: PRO

33 IBID.

34 CABLE NO. 384, Casey to External Affairs Department, 27 May 1941, and Cable No. 328, Commonwealth Government to Cranborne, 30 May 1941, *DAFP*, iv, Docs 473 and 476

35 See *DAFP*, iv, Docs 485, 490, 512, 517 and 521

36 WAR CABINET CONCLUSIONS/CONFIDENTIAL ANNEX, 21 and 28 July 1941, CAB 65/23, W.M. 72 and 75(41): PRO; See also Cadogan Diary, 21 July 1941, in D. Dilks (ed.), p. 393

37 CABLE NO. 415, Cranborne to Menzies, 14 June 1941, *DAFP*, iv, Doc. 504

38 LETTER, Ismay to General Henry C. Jackson, 18 February 1959, I/14/72, Ismay Papers: KC

39 See DAVID DAY, ch. 13

40 CABLE NO. 2855, Menzies to Bruce, 8 June 1941, *DAFP*, iv, Doc. 493

41 CABLE NO. 409, Churchill to Menzies, 11 June 1941, *DAFP*, iv, Doc. 497

42 See DAVID DAY, "Anzacs on the Run: The View from Whitehall, 1941−2", *Journal of Imperial and Commonwealth History*, May, 1986

43 MENZIES DIARY, 8 and 11 April 1941

44 *Daily Sketch*, London, 6 June 1941

45 ADVISORY WAR COUNCIL MINUTES, 12 June 1941, CRS A2682, Vol. 2, Minute 373: AA

46 IBID.; Cable Gordon 2, Menzies to Churchill, 13 June 1941, PREM 3/281/10: PRO

47 "REPORT BY MR JOHN STOREY, Member, Aircraft Production Commission, on his visit to England and USA with the Right Hon. R. G. Menzies Prime Minister of Australia — January 24th to June 6th 1941", CRS A5954, Box 617: AA

48 WAR CABINET AGENDUM, Supplement No. 1 to Agendum No. 229/1940, by Fadden, 26 March 1941; Cable No. 3065, Clapp to Hyland, 17 June 1941; and Cable, H. 491, Hyland to Clapp, 9 July 1941, all in CRS A5954, Box 223: AA

49 NOTES OF PROCEEDINGS OF CONFERENCE called to discuss Aircraft Manufacturing Development in Australia, 14 July 1941; War Cabinet Minute, 22 July 1941; both in CRS A5954, Box 223: AA; D. Gillison, *Royal Australian Air Force 1939–1942*, Canberra, 1962, pp. 138–40. See also Cable Z88, Burnett to Brooke-Popham, 12 August 1941, V/4/21, Brooke-Popham Papers: KC

50 WAR CABINET MINUTES, 10 June 1941, CRS A2673, Vol. 7, Minute 1139: AA

51 "AIRCRAFT REQUIREMENTS FOR RAAF: SUPPLY POSITION", Report by Air Staff, 12 August 1941, CRS A5954, Box 230: AA; "Vultee and Brewster Bermuda Aircraft" folder, CRS A5954, Box 232: AA

52 LETTER, Sir Horace Seymour to his wife, 4 July 1941, SEYR 2/5, Seymour Papers: CC; Harvey Diary, 6 July 1941, ADD. MS. 56398, Harvey Papers: BL

53 "JAPANESE INTENTIONS IN INDO-CHINA" and "Nature and Extent of our Economic Restrictions Against Japan", Memoranda by Eden, 6 and 7 July 1941, CAB 66/17, W.P. (41)154 and 155: PRO

54 "ECONOMIC RESTRICTIONS AGAINST JAPAN," Memorandum by Dalton, 7 July 1941, CAB 66/17, W.P. (41)155: PRO

55 WAR CABINET CONCLUSIONS, 7 July 1941, CAB 65/19, W.M. 66(41): PRO

56 C. THORNE, *Allies of a Kind*, London, 1978, p. 73

57 "JAPANESE PLANS IN INDO-CHINA", Memorandum by Eden, 20 July 1941, CAB 66/17, W.P. (41)172: PRO

58 WAR CABINET CONCLUSIONS, 21 July 1941, CAB 65/19, W.M. 72 (41): PRO

59 CADOGAN DIARY, 24 July 1941, in D. Dilks, (ed.) p. 394

60 CABLE NO. 111/4, Brooke-Popham to Chiefs of Staff, 26 July 1941, V/4/17, Brooke-Popham Papers: KC

61 LETTER, Air Marshal J. Babington to Brooke-Popham, 1 August 1941, V/11/1, Brooke-Popham Papers: KC

62 LETTER, Sir Ian Jacob to Ismay, 24 January 1959, I/14/69, Ismay Papers: KC

63 ADVISORY WAR COUNCIL MINUTES, 29 July 1941, CRS A2682, Vol. 2, Minute 431: AA

64 *IBID*.

65 *DAILY HERALD*, London, 1 August 1941

66 ADVISORY WAR COUNCIL MINUTES, 6 August 1941, CRS A2682, Vol. 3, Minute 451: AA

67 WAR CABINET CONCLUSIONS, 11 August 1941, CAB 65/19, W.M. 79(41): PRO; See also David Day, ch. 14

68 ADVISORY WAR COUNCIL MINUTES, 14 August 1941, CRS A2682, Vol. 3, Minutes 466 and 467: AA. See also Cable, Menzies to Churchill, 12 August 1941, CAB 66/18, W.P. (41)203: PRO

69 DEFENCE COMMITTEE (OPERATIONS) MINUTES, 7 August 1941, CAB 69/2, D.O. (41)55: PRO; See also Pownall Diary, 8 August 1941, in B. Bond (ed.), p. 35.

70 DEFENCE COMMITTEE (OPERATIONS) MINUTES, 8 August 1941, CAB 69/2, D.O. (41)56: PRO

71 CABINET MINUTES, 19 August 1941, CRS A2697, Vol. 7: AA

72 SPEECH BY CURTIN IN HOUSE OF REPRESENTATIVES, 18 June 1941, CRS A5954, Box 308: AA

73 P. HASLUCK, *The Government and the People*, i, chs 9—10

74 ADVISORY WAR COUNCIL MINUTES, 6 August 1941, CRS A2682, Vol. 3, Minute 542; "Summary of Australian Army War Effort", September 1941, p. 9, CRS A5954, Box 313; Cabinet Minutes, 24 January 1941, CRS A2697, Vol. 5: AA

8

Fadden Takes Charge

29 August to 7 October 1941

When Fadden moved into Australia's Prime Ministerial Lodge, the prospects for peace in the Pacific were precarious. It was becoming a question of when, not if, the Japanese would strike. This prospect was greeted very differently in London and Canberra. The British Government had tried to prevent hostilities so long as it appeared that she would have to face the Japanese single-handed. As the chance of American participation grew more certain, Britain viewed the possibility of a Pacific war in an increasingly positive light. Though Canberra could never embrace the notion of a Pacific war, it did little either to prepare for it or prevent it. Australia had remained tied to the system of Imperial defence for so long that she was unable to loosen the bonds even when her survival might be at stake.

At his shipboard meeting with Roosevelt off the coast of Newfoundland in August, Churchill had been relieved to find that the American President was "obviously determined to come in". Churchill succeeded in stiffening an American message to Tokyo to include a warning that further Japanese encroachment in the south west Pacific would compel the United States to "take counter-measures, even though these might lead to war between the United States and Japan".[1] This would have been one of the reasons why Churchill was described by one observer as being in "very good spirits, and far calmer after his sea trip".[2] According to General Pownall, Vice Chief of the Imperial General Staff, Roosevelt was *all* for coming into the war, and as soon as possible ... but he said that he would never *declare* war, he wishes to provoke it. He wants to create an incident that brings war about, being no doubt sure that he will then be fully supported by the people."[3]

By late 1941, British Ministers generally shared Churchill's optimism and were beginning to welcome the prospect of war with Japan as a means of drawing America back into Europe. Even the arch-Imperialist, Leo Amery, Britain's Secretary of State for India, thought it was "worth making a big effort to keep [Japan] out of the war" but "if her coming into the war brought in the United States the balance of advantage would presently be in our favour". He recognised that Britain "might have to face some bad months in the Indian Ocean and at Singapore" but believed that the "additional fighting power and munition power that would come in if America were really at war and not a spectator would outweigh all that in the end".[4]

Apart from the immediate necessity to have America as an ally against Germany, there was also a growing conviction that the war should be used to cement a permanent Anglo–American alliance to act as the post-war policeman of Europe. This was Churchill's vision and it was also urged on Eden at the Foreign Office. According to his secretary, Oliver Harvey, "The British people will be exhausted after the war and will refuse to police Europe alone. But if it is an Anglo–American operation, then you will get what you want, and I am sure we can manage the Americans. They are children, simple, naif, yet suspicious." Eden riposted that he would not regard Roosevelt as either "simple or naif".[5] Despite his comment, the concept of an English-speaking alliance was in the ascendent and the Empire was being downgraded as a result. In the new scheme of things, the Empire increased Britain's relative strength within the prospective alliance. However, it was also a liability since it was the aspect of Britain that Americans found most offensive. Britain's real strength in any Anglo–American alliance, as would increasingly be obvious, was its strategic position as a virtual aircraft carrier permanently anchored off the shore of Europe. There was little place for Australia in this vision.

Australia was as keen as Churchill to strengthen the Anglo–American bonds, particularly in the economic sphere. It was seen by some as providing an additional market for Australian primary produce, particularly wool and meat.[6] Officials such as Bruce recognised that the pre-war system of imperial preference would lead to post-war economic stagnation for Australia and the withering of her carefully cultivated secondary industries.

He warned Britain that Australia would not support her in any future trade war with America and that the Empire must co-operate with America in generating an expansion of trade in the post-war period rather than fight over the existing amount.[7] With both the economic and strategic rationales of Empire looking increasingly tenuous, the costs of Australia's Imperial attachment were fast outweighing the real and potential benefits. Nevertheless, Australia pushed for closer Anglo–American co-operation on the firm understanding that her own future was tied securely to that of Britain and there was little thought that she might forge an independent existence in the Pacific.

Following Menzies' resignation as Prime Minister on 28 August, the question remained of dispatching a Ministerial representative to London. Menzies had planned to use such a mission to press forward with his own political future in Westminster. With him out of contention for the mission, Australia had an opportunity to use it to try and safeguard its own security. The task would not be easy. Churchill made it clearly understood that an Australian Minister in London would not enjoy the same privileges as a Prime Minister and would not be accorded a seat in the British War Cabinet. Initially, Churchill had tried to kill the whole idea of sending such a Minister but gave way when Fadden's determination to continue with the proposal became plain.[8]

The rank of the Australian representative was not the only impediment to the Dominion's views being heard clearly in London. Australia had undergone a drastic transformation in the affections of British leaders. Menzies' bid for power had put him at odds with Churchill, as well as most of the War Cabinet. The Chancellor of the Exchequer, Sir Kingsley Wood, discussed Menzies' resignation with Bruce, informing the High Commissioner that there were a

> number of people over here who could not feel very sympathetic towards him [Menzies] as he had been very outspoken in his criticisms — the specific instance he gave was that Menzies had said the Prime Minister was surrounded by "Yes" men, and added — naturally many of us do not like a suggestion of this sort.[9]

The personal rivalry for power between the Prime Ministers rubbed at the strained relationship between their countries.

The dispute over Britain's handling of the war in the Mediterranean put salt into the wound.

The successive defeats in Greece and Crete had led to harsh words about Britain in the Australian Parliament and press[10], while the Australian garrison in Tobruk provided the issue for a long-running dispute that seriously damaged the relationship between the two countries and practically destroyed Australia's reputation in the eyes of Britain's political and military leaders for the duration of the war.[11] Even the King was moved to remark on "how different the Australians seemed to be to any of the other Dominions . . . that in Australia they were always being critical".[12] On 31 August, Lord Cranborne wrote bitterly about the "rather hectic time" the Government had been having with the "miserable Australians".[13]

The argument over Tobruk originated with Menzies who had been most apprehensive about the ability of the garrison to withstand a sustained German assault. In Cairo, Blamey became aware of Menzies' concern and played on it for his own purposes to obtain the relief of the trapped 9th Division and the re-constitution of the scattered Australian forces in the Middle East into one unified corps under his command. Latching on to a medical report that cast doubt on the fitness of the Australians in Tobruk, Blamey called for their relief on military grounds in the knowledge that Menzies had political reasons for supporting him.[14] By the time Fadden took over, one brigade of troops had been removed and Blamey pressed for the remainder of the division to be relieved, but not by other Australian soldiers. He justified this stand to Spender with his personal conviction that "the Australian Government would not care to have another Greece and Crete experience". This clinched the matter in Canberra.[15]

Fadden was as politically insecure as Menzies had been. On receipt of Blamey's cable, he immediately requested that Churchill ensure the relief of the remaining Australians and did so in terms that allowed the British Government to recognise the political impetus for the request. Fadden informed Churchill that the Australian Parliament would be meeting in mid-September and that it was his "desire to make a statement when the withdrawal had been completed". In terms not calculated to endear him to Churchill, he warned the British Prime Minister that the relief of Tobruk was a "vital national question here and should any catastrophe occur to the Tobruk garrison ... there would be grave repercussions".[16] Churchill claimed he was prepared to comply so long as it did not hamper the military plans of the newly appointed British Commander in the Middle East, General Auchinleck.[17]

The test came when Auchinleck advised that the relief was not justified and suggested instead that the existing troops in Tobruk be strengthened with a tank brigade. He was supported by the British Minister to the Middle East, Oliver Lyttelton, who claimed that the military arguments were "unanswerable" and that, if they were British troops, "no Commander would consider relief". He perceptively observed that the Australian Government was "anxious to take out a political insurance policy" and argued that the "premium to be paid for it namely, grave risks of splitting the vital operations, seems to me too high".[18]

Armed with this military advice, Churchill informed his War Cabinet that he would send Auchinleck's report to Fadden emphasising the "grave consequences which might ensue, not only to the Australian forces but to our future plans". During discussion, British Ministers made plain that they understood the Australian agitation was motivated by political imperatives. As Cranborne explained, the press had led the Australian public to believe that their troops were "bearing the brunt of the fighting in the Middle East", while the Australian Labor Party was "apt to argue that Australian troops should be kept for the defence of Australian soil". Such notions were dangerous to the British cause and had to be countered.[19] In his cable to Fadden, Churchill warned the Australian Prime Minister to "weigh carefully the immense responsibility which you would assume before history by depriving Australia of the glory of holding Tobruk till victory was won".[20]

Fadden was unimpressed. Point by point, he rejected the arguments of Auchinleck and Churchill and reiterated the Australian request. Churchill accepted this defeat with great regret, informing Auchinleck that he was "grieved" by the Australian attitude, although admitting that he had "long feared the dangerous reactions on Australian and world opinion of our seeming to fight all our battles in the Middle East only with Dominion troops". Auchinleck was infuriated by Fadden's cable and by Churchill's acceptance of it, which he interpreted as a lack of confidence in his military judgement. It was with some difficulty that Lyttelton prevented him from submitting his resignation. Lyttelton was equally annoyed and urged that Churchill request Australia to relieve Blamey whose conduct he described as being "weak and disingenuous".[21]

Churchill shared the anger of Auchinleck and Lyttelton, as did most of Britain's political and military leadership. As one well-placed observer confided, "everybody was furious".[22] But this was carefully concealed from the Australians who still were, after all, important pillars of the Empire in Egypt and the Far East. As Churchill argued when trying to soothe Auchinleck's anger, "great allowances must be made for a Government with a majority of one playing politics with a bitter Opposition, part of whom at least are isolationist". He urged Auchinleck to put aside personal feelings since it was "our duty at all costs to prevent an open dispute with the Australian Government" which might otherwise "injure [the] foundations of Empire and be disastrous to our general position in the war".[23] Churchill also suggested that the British High Commissioner in Canberra be instructed not to discuss Tobruk with the Australian Government and, if the matter was raised, to say that he had "no information and abstain from argument and, above all, reproaches".[24] Although Churchill believed Australia deserved to be reproached, it was not worth the possible risk to the British war effort.

To reassure his own War Cabinet, Churchill ordered the circulation to its members of the Mediterranean casualty statistics broken down by country of origin. These were meant to disprove the allegation from Australia and from German propaganda that Britain would fight to the death of the last Australian in the Middle East. Though the figures showed over half of the casualties to be British, if those declared missing and taken prisoner were excluded, the British proportion was reduced to less than a third. It also made no mention of the other national groups fighting on the British side in the Middle East — such as the Greeks and Poles — that would have reduced the British proportion still further.[25]

The risk of recriminations with Australia was heightened by the personality of the British High Commissioner, Sir Ronald Cross. Cross had been successively Minister for Economic Warfare and Minister for Shipping until his dispatch to Australia in May 1941 and was ill-suited to his new role. Cranborne complained at the end of August that Cross had "taken to lecturing Australian Ministers as if they were small and rather dirty boys".[26] Though Cranborne kept Cross on a short leash to prevent any gratuitous attacks on the Australian Government, it would not be long before Churchill was openly barking his own annoyance at Canberra. All of this boded ill for the success of the proposed ministerial mission to London.

The mission almost became an issue of dispute itself when Fadden attempted unilaterally to elevate the role of the envoy to membership of the British War Cabinet. Churchill had undertaken to welcome the envoy with the "utmost consideration and honour"[27] which Fadden seized upon as implying that Churchill would "welcome the presence of an Australian Minister in the War Cabinet when matters relating to higher policy, operations or other questions which affect the Australian war effort or the Australian forces were being considered".[28] This Churchill certainly did not mean, but the Australians were moving too fast for him to stop. Fadden had already announced that a Minister would go to London and he quickly followed his presumptuous cable to Churchill with another announcing that Sir Earle Page would be the Minister.[29]

Churchill immediately realised that the plain-speaking Australian was deliberately misinterpreting the sense of his deliberately obtuse message. It was a case where Churchill's command of the English language was turned to his disadvantage. However, Churchill was not too concerned. There would be plenty of scope for interpreting the standing of Page's mission once he arrived in London. In the interim, Churchill declined to argue any further and simply signalled that he would confer with Page "freely and fully on all matters concerning Australian interests and the common cause". As he confided to Cranborne, Britain had to "treat these people, who are politically embarrassed but are sending a splendid army into the field, with the utmost consideration".[30] In the event, Page let it be known that he had no expectation of occupying a War Cabinet seat.[31]

The idea of dispatching a representative to London had originated with Menzies on 10 August when he claimed urgent reasons of Far Eastern security as the rationale. However, Page waited for the passage through Parliament of the Federal budget before leaving for London by way of the NEI, Singapore, the Philippines, the United States and Canada. It would not be until 6 November, more than twelve weeks after Menzies had first urgently broached the matter and only four weeks before the Japanese struck at Pearl Harbor, that Page would appear before the British War Cabinet to put Australia's views regarding the urgent need for reinforcements in the Far East.[32]

The tardy manner in which Page planned to proceed to London, duplicating en route many of Menzies' earlier discussions in Singapore, Canada and the United States, raises questions about the rationale of his mission. In originally proposing the mission, Menzies had political ambition high among his priorities. In persisting with the mission following Menzies' fall, Fadden probably was also motivated by political rather than military considerations. There was a popular movement within the press and parliament for such a representative to be sent. As a possible rival for leadership of the Country Party, Page was an ideal choice for the post, at least as far as Fadden was concerned. As far as securing Australia's defence, Page was a strange choice since his political experience had not been in the Service departments but in the Treasury and Commerce departments. Though he was instructed by Fadden to discuss the situation in the Middle East and Far East, he was given no initiative to commit Australia to anything. In fact, he was intructed to refer anything of substance arising from his discussions back to Canberra.[33] In London, he would become a fifth wheel to Bruce's diplomatic coach.

While Australia had been embroiled in political turmoil, her military position continued to deteriorate. In London, Churchill ignored a series of secret German peace feelers in September and "ruled that no contact of any kind be made".[34] He was committed to fighting the war to a finish in fulfilment of the historic role that he obviously believed was his destiny. Though he claimed to have no clear idea as to how total victory against Germany would be achieved, he privately admitted on 23 August that Britain's military position had "vastly improved" and that he could no longer envisage a successful invasion of Britain. Though Tobruk remained surrounded by German and Italian tanks, there was a lull in the Middle East fighting that allowed Auchinleck to prepare plans for a counterattack later in the year. As for the Far East, Churchill predicted that "the Japs would shout and threaten, but would not move".[35]

If the Japanese did move, Australia was ill-prepared to defend itself, and the situation was worsening. One of the main outcomes of Churchill's meeting with Roosevelt was the decision to co-ordinate a vastly increased contribution of war supplies to Stalin. At the end of August, Churchill offered Stalin an extra 200 Hurricanes on top of the forty already being sent and 200 Tomahawk fighter planes promised.[36] Partly as a result of this, Singapore was refused the promised reinforcement of its air strength. In mid-September, the Chiefs of Staff informed Brooke-Popham that their plan to accumulate a force of 336 aircraft under his command by the end of 1941 could no longer be met. They cited the greater priority of Russia and the Middle East and production shortfalls in Britain and America.[37] This force already had been slashed from the recommended level to the bare minimum. Now Singapore and the defending garrison of British, Australian and Indian troops would not even have that.

After two years of war, Fadden took over from Menzies a country with a developing industrial base but with little ability to defend itself from serious attack. The navy was effectively an adjunct of the Royal Navy and much of its limited strength was scattered in the Middle East and Far East. It relied, as it had always done, on the potential power of the Royal Navy to repel any direct naval threat to Australia. The army was similarly scattered on various Imperial missions overseas, with home defence relying on the presence of partly trained and ill-equipped AIF and militia forces. An armoured division was in the process of being formed but its intended destination was the Middle East and only training tanks would be provided for its use within Australia.[38]

In the air, Australia was similarly unprepared to defend itself. Although Menzies had acclaimed the Empire Air Training Scheme as a positive move towards providing Australia with a formidable air force, the reality could not have been more different. Though 1400 aircraft were occupied on the scheme, none were suitable as first-line defence aircraft. Instead, at considerable expense to Australia, thousands of aircrew were trained for use by the RAF in Europe and elsewhere. By September 1941, nearly 12,000 men were either in training or had been dispatched overseas under the terms of the scheme. Under an agreement reached in January 1941, Australia was to provide eighteen squadrons by May 1942 for use overseas in addition to the five squadrons already serving in distant parts. For home defence, it was planned to have thirty-two squadrons with 360 aircraft. By September, twenty squadrons were formed but seven were serving outside Australia. Though there were 227 aircraft within Australia for home defence, most of them were training aircraft flying under the guise of being first-line service planes. In addition, the stocks of aviation fuel were perilously low, being one-fifth of the level deemed necessary to fight a war in the Far East.[39]

During September, a public campaign built up for Australia to acquire fighter aircraft for home defence. To date, Britain had refused to concede the possibility that such aircraft were required by the Dominion, except for psychological purposes. This was based on the opinion that the only dangers Australia faced were cruiser raids on the trade routes. If Britain conceded the necessity for fighter aircraft, she would be admitting the possibility of an invasion. Such an admission would force Australia to concentrate on home defence and reduce its contribution to Imperial defence.

On 16 September, P. G. Taylor, the pioneer Australian aviator, used the pages of the *Sydney Morning Herald* to press his case for fighter aircraft to be included in the strength of the RAAF. In a supporting editorial, the newspaper noted that its readers would be surprised to learn of the Government's tardy effort to obtain fighter aircraft which, it claimed, were "indispensable to our security" and vital if the RAAF was going to "meet an invader at least on equal terms". Presumably, most Australians had been deluded into believing that the hundreds of training aircraft filling the skies had some operational value. The Melbourne newspapers joined in the chorus of outrage, while the Burns Philp company added its voice with a £10,000 donation towards the cost of providing fighter aircraft. McEwen, as Minister for Air, falsely claimed that the expansion of the RAAF along these lines was being pursued with "alacrity and intensity" and that "certain types of these aircraft are being made in Australia". Public disquiet was soothed at some cost to the truth.[40]

Despite the Government protestations, Australia had not

decided on its future plans for aircraft production. Though the Dominion was keen to manufacture twin-engined Beaufighter aircraft, advice from the British Government led them to abandon the plan. Whitehall informed Australia on 16 September that she was not prepared to purchase any Beaufighters that were produced suplus to the Australian requirement but would purchase Beauforts and Wirraways, the latter intended as training aircraft. This cable was finally considered by a government committee in a remarkable meeting on 3 October with Menzies in the chair as Minister for Defence Co-ordination. Although one member expressed concern at the British opposition to local fighter production, the committee was assured by the CAS, Burnett, that it was not worthwhile building Beaufighters unless Australia had a guaranteed export market for them. Anyway, he said, Australia had Beaufighters on order from Britain and the local production was "rated lowest in Air Force priorities". Although McEwen was prepared to accept this argument, he had sufficient sense to recognise the possible political and military risks the Government might incur as a result. Accordingly, he suggested that Britain provide "an assurance in general terms ... that if hostilities extend to Australia, adequate supplies of fighter aircraft will be made available".[41]

The readiness of the committee to comply with the production program suggested by Britain may well be explained by Fadden's fall from power on that same day. With unaccustomed speed, Fadden immediately accepted the recommendations of the committee and dashed off a cable to London acknowledging Australian compliance with the British program and advising that he had already issued instructions that "all work necessary to achieve the proposed programme be put in hand immediately".[42] This incredible and inordinate rush to commit Australia to the British program suggests that the outgoing Fadden Ministry was anxious to prevent their successors from establishing a program on a basis more suited to the defence of Australia rather than to its export earnings. As a result, Australia remained dependent on Britain for the supply of fighter aircraft and continued to clutch at the British assurance that fighters would be sent to Australia in the event of an attack.

Australia's attention remained divided between the Middle East and her own predicament in the Far East, with her trapped division in Tobruk and the dispute over its relief helping to concentrate anxiety in that theatre. In September, American officials had predicted that Germany soon might throw as many as 750,000 troops against Britain's position in the Middle East. The threat was taken very seriously in Australia, especially when Blamey advised of the poor equipment position in Egypt. As Army Minister, it was Spender's role to supply men for the AIF and for home defence. Though the threat of a massive German onslaught might rob Australia of most of her trained troops, Spender could see no alternative than to keep Australia's destiny firmly linked to Britain's. He merely counselled Fadden to plan for possible setbacks while proceeding in the Middle East, "as proceed we must, upon all too slender margins".[43]

In the absence of sufficient aircraft at Singapore, the proposed Far East fleet was resuscitated, albeit in truncated form. Earlier in 1941, Churchill had informed Menzies of British plans to dispatch a battleship and an aircraft carrier to the Indian Ocean on the outbreak of war with Japan. Now that America was adopting a higher naval profile in the Atlantic and removing part of Britain's burden to escort convoys, the Admiralty was able to consider a plan for the gradual build up of its naval strength in the East. This led to considerable dissension within the navy, mainly over whether it was strategically sound to dispatch in piecemeal fashion a fleet that was supposed to deter the formidable naval power of Japan.[44]

At the end of August, while the dispute was still in progress, Churchill informed Fadden that Britain contemplated "placing a force of capital ships, including first class units, in the triangle Aden–Singapore–Simonstown before the end of the year", though he was careful to stipulate that it would be "without prejudice to our control of the Eastern Mediterranean". Again he assured Australia that Britain will "never let you down if real danger comes". Though Australia did not fall within this naval triangle, Fadden was encouraged by the message and responded by confiding to Churchill that the absence of a fleet at Singapore had "aroused a feeling of uneasiness in the minds of many people here, and ... undoubtedly had an adverse effect on recruiting for service overseas".[45] This put Churchill on notice to provide the proposed ships in return for continuing Australian contributions to Britain's war effort. But Churchill had more than this in mind when dispatching the ships.

The naval triangle to be covered by the British force would

provide protection to the Middle East and to India, which was even more important than Australia in supplying troops for Britain and which occupied the central place in Churchill's Imperial cosmos. In the words of Lord Moran, Churchill "looked with pride on the story of our Indian Empire ... His India was the land he knew as a subaltern. He could not conceive of an India without the British."[46] The apex of the triangle, and its most protected point, was the Suez Canal. As another point on the triangle, Singapore was designed to protect against Japanese entry into the Indian Ocean but did little to limit Japan's freedom of movement in the Pacific.

The composition of the proposed Eastern fleet gave a good indication of Churchill's purpose. The navy planned to allocate four elderly *Royal Sovereign* class battleships, the modern battleship *Prince of Wales*, the battle cruiser *Repulse* and the new aircraft carrier *Indomitable*.[47] This fleet, had it ever been formed, was designed primarily for escort duties rather than as a battle group that was capable of tackling the might of the Japanese fleet. Eighteen months earlier, Churchill had judged the four *Royal Sovereign* battleships and the *Repulse* to be unsuitable for use against the Japanese.[48] Even now he described the four "Rs" as "floating coffins" that could only be used for convoy work if there also were "one or two fast heavy units" nearby to prevent attacks on the convoys by individual heavy raiders.[49]

As a result of pressure from Churchill and Eden, the Admiralty reluctantly agreed to include the *Prince of Wales* in the initial group. Admiral Somerville, who later commanded the Eastern fleet, described the dispatch of the *Prince of Wales* as "a great mistake" but "the P.M. and Anthony Eden insisted though what it had to do with the latter I don't know and can't imagine".[50] Churchill's readiness to dispatch ill-suited ships to the East was not foolhardiness on his part nor was it forced upon him by necessity. It was an admission that his intentions were to throw a protective naval mantle over the Indian Ocean and particularly the reinforcement route along the east coast of Africa to the Middle East. Any effect on the Japanese in the Pacific would be solely as a distant and doubtful deterrent. But it was important to steady restive allies: America was keen for Britain to send naval forces to the Far East and Australia wanted signs that its contributions to Imperial defence would be reciprocated. Australia seized on the Eastern fleet as a measure planned for its protection and which appeared to accord with the accepted principles of Imperial defence.[51]

It presumably was more than coincidental that the first echelons of the Eastern fleet were planned to arrive in the Indian Ocean at about the time Churchill anticipated that talks between America and Japan would break down. On 29 August, he very accurately predicted that it was "very likely" that Japan would "negotiate with the United States for at least three months without making any further aggressive move or joining the Axis actively".[52] By his own reckoning, the Eastern fleet was therefore timed to arrive at its station just when Japan might be provoked into war. It therefore would be placed to prevent any interference by Japan with the vital sea routes to the Middle East and India.

On 12 September, Sir Earle Page had met with the Advisory War Council to whom he set out the main aim of his mission as being to obtain strong naval and air forces at Singapore in order to release even more Australian forces from home defence and allow them to rejoin the civilian workforce. He argued that the reinforcement of Singapore would mitigate the "consequent burden on the Budget and manpower that resulted in the calling up for continuous service or long periods of training of a large Home Defence army".[53]

Curtin basically agreed with the priorities of Page. He cited financial reasons for restricting to its present level Australia's contribution to the British war effort and similarly argued that Page should "insist on the location of a strong force of capital ships east of Suez". If he was successful in this, Curtin observed, Page would be in a "better position to discuss the Australian contribution to the common Empire cause".[54] Both men clearly continued to operate under the illusion that Britain had Australian defence as a high priority and that the dispatch of British ships to the Indian Ocean would secure it.

In later discussions with the Australian Chiefs of Staff on 17 September, Page was informed of Britain's intention to gradually build up its naval strength in the Far East. Page seized on this information and urged the immediate dispatch of such ships. He reasoned that such a fleet would prevent Australian forces in the Middle East being isolated while also providing the key to the increasingly vexed problem of Australia's man-power shortage. Instead of the fleet supplementing a policy of self-reliance, Page saw it as an opportunity to reduce Australia's defence burden, releasing as many as 50,000 men from the army into "essential industries and for primary production". He was encouraged in this by the Chiefs of Staff who adopted a rather optimistic view regarding Australia's defence and the security of Singapore. Having regard to their optimism, it is perhaps a matter for wonder why Page saw fit to persist with his mission.[55] But persist he did.

At the end of September, Page arrived in Singapore for talks with Brooke-Popham and other British representatives.[56] After a conference on the defence situation, Brooke-Popham cabled to London with the meeting's "emphatic opinion" that the "only real deterrent to further Japanese aggression would be a British fleet based at Singapore and in the absence of this fleet there is little doubt that Japan will be able to strike at her selected moment". Page asked Fadden to throw his weight behind the request, claiming that a fleet would make Singapore so impregnable that it would not even be challenged. Although Page held out the prospect of a Far East fleet producing a greater Australian contribution to Imperial defence, it is clear that he was primarily concerned with putting soldiers back onto the farms of his rural constituents and into the booming factories of the cities.[57] Whatever his motivation, Fadden was unable to respond. Australia had been plunged into a fresh political upheaval of the type that had plagued the country since 1939.

By throwing Menzies aside just six weeks previously, Fadden had earned the enmity of one of the independent MPs, who soon let it be known that he would switch his parliamentary support to the now united Labor Party. The other independent member also supported Curtin after receiving assurances from the Labor leader about wheat prices for his rural electorate. So, at the most crucial period in its modern history, Australia was given its third Prime Minister in six weeks by the rather quixotic switch of allegiance by one member and a pragmatic personal calculation by another. Meanwhile, the Pacific peace steadily crumbled and Page's cable lay in Canberra unconsidered for two weeks.

NOTES

1 CABLE, TUDOR NO. 15, Churchill to Attlee, 11 August 1941, cited in M. Gilbert, p. 1160

2 LETTER, Cranborne to Emrys-Evans, 31 August 1941, ADD. MS. 58240, Emrys-Evans Papers: BL

3 POWNALL DIARY, 20 August 1941, in B. Bond (ed.), ii, p. 37

4 LETTER, Amery to Lord Hankey, 5 September 1941, HNKY 11/14, Hankey Papers: CC

5 MACKENZIE KING DIARY, 5 September 1941: CUL; Minute, Harvey to Eden, 24 August 1941, ADD. MS. 56402, Harvey Papers: BL

6 See LETTER, J. W Allen, Secretary of Graziers' Federal Council of Australia, to Menzies, 30 June 1941, CRS A1608, D.41/1/5: AA

7 See LETTER, Bruce to Fadden, 25 September 1941, CRS M104, "British Empire — America", Item 9(1); Talk with Sir John Anderson, 29 September 1941, CRS M100, "September 1941"; Cable No. 5779, Bruce to Curtin, 4 October 1941, CRS M100, "October 1941"; Talk with Sir Kingsley Wood, 15 October 1941, CRS M100, "October 1941"; Letter, Bruce to Sumner Welles, 14 November 1941, CRS M103, "1941": AA

8 WAR CABINET CONCLUSIONS, 28 August and 1 September 1941, CAB 65/19, W.M. 87 and 88(41); Cable (draft), Churchill to Fadden, 29 August 1941, PREM 4/50/4A: PRO

9 TALK WITH SIR KINGSLEY WOOD, 15 October 1941, CRS M100, "October 1941": AA; See also fn. 2

10 "THE POLITICAL SITUATION IN THE COMMONWEALTH OF AUSTRALIA", Memorandum by Cranborne, 21 August 1941, CAB 66/18, W.P. (41)198: PRO

11 See DAVID DAY, "Anzacs on the Run: The View from Whitehall"

12 MACKENZIE KING DIARY, 30 August 1941: CUL

13 See fn. 2

14 See DAVID DAY, "Anzacs on the Run: The View from Whitehall"; David Day, Menzies and Churchill at War, ch. 14; For other views see D. M. Horner, pp. 111–17; W. S. Churchill, The Second World War, iii, passim; P. Hasluck, appendix 10

15 LETTER, Blamey to Spender, 8 September 1941, CRS A5954, Box 260: AA; Cable GOC 179, Blamey to Fadden, 4 September 1941, DAFP, v, Doc. 58

16 CABLE NO. 584, Fadden to Cranborne, 5 September 1941, DAFP, v, Doc. 59

17 CABLE T549, Churchill to Auchinleck, 6 September 1941, PREM 3/63/2: PRO

18 CABLE, Auchinleck to Churchill, 10 September 1941, and Cable, Lyttelton to Churchill, 11 September 1941, PREM 3/63/2: PRO

19 WAR CABINET CONCLUSIONS/CONFIDENTIAL ANNEX, 11 September 1941, CAB 65/23, W.M. 92(41): PRO

20 CABLE, Churchill to Fadden, 11 September 1941, PREM 3/63/2: PRO

21 CABLE NO. 590, Fadden to Churchill, (rec'd) 14 September 1941; Cable, Churchill to Fadden, 15 September 1941; Cable, Churchill to Auchinleck, 18 September 1941; Cable, Lyttelton to Churchill, 18 September 1941; PREM 3/63/2: PRO

22 HARVEY DIARY, 15 September 1941, ADD. MS. 56398, Harvey Papers: BL. In the discussion of Fadden's cable by the British War Cabinet, "the view was expressed that the decision was a lamentable one". See War Cabinet Conclusions/Confidential Annex, 16 September 1941, CAB 65/23,

W.M. 93(41): PRO. See also Cazalet Diary, 20 September 1941, in R. R. James (ed.), *Victor Cazalet*, London, 1976, p. 264; Letters, Cunningham to Pound, Pound to Cunningham, both 18 September 1941, ADD. MS. 52561, Cunningham Papers: BL

23 CABLE NO. 094, Churchill to Auchinleck, CAB 65/23, W.M. 94(41): PRO; See also Cable, Churchill to Lyttelton, 18 September 1941, "The Prime Minister's Personal Telegrams 1941", VI/1, Ismay Papers: KC

24 MINUTE M902/1, Churchill to Cranborne, 15 September 1941, PREM 3/63/2: PRO

25 "TOTAL BATTLE CASUALTIES — MIDDLE EAST", 22 September 1941, CAB 66/18, W.P. (41)225: PRO

26 See fn. 2

27 CABLE NO. 607, Cranborne to Fadden, 28 August 1941, *DAFP*, v, Doc. 53

28 CABLE NO. 585, Fadden to Cranborne, 5 September 1941, *DAFP*, v, Doc. 60; See also Letter, Cross to Emrys-Evans Papers: BL

29 CABLE NO. 586, Fadden to Churchill, (rec'd) 6 September 1941, PREM 4/50/5: PRO

30 MINUTE M873/5, Churchill to Cranborne, 6 September 1941, PREM 4/50/5: PRO

31 CABLE NO. 217, Mackenzie King to Churchill, 25 October 1941, PREM 4/50/5: PRO

32 For Page's very subjective account of his mission, see SIR E. PAGE, *Truant Surgeon*, Sydney, 1963

33 LETTER, Fadden to Page, 16 September 1941, CRS A5954, Box 475: AA

34 DALTON DIARY, 7 September 1941, I/25/63, Dalton Papers: LSE

35 KING DIARY, in C. King, *With Malice Toward None*, London, 1970, p. 140

36 CABLE, Churchill to Stalin, 29 August 1941, "The Prime Minister's Personal Telegrams 1941", VI/I, Ismay Papers: KC

37 CABLE NO. 34, Chiefs of Staff to Brooke-Popham, 17 September 1941, V/4/33, Brooke-Popham Papers: KC

38 "SUMMARY OF AUSTRALIAN ARMY WAR EFFORT, SEPTEMBER 1941", CRS A5954, Box 313: AA

39 "SUMMARY OF AUSTRALIAN AIR WAR EFFORT, SEPTEMBER 1941", CRS A5954, Box 313: AA

40 *SYDNEY MORNING HERALD*, 17 September 1941; *Age*, Melbourne, 18 and 24 September 1941; *Argus*, Melbourne, 18 September 1941

41 "PROGRAMME FOR FUTURE AIRCRAFT CONSTRUCTION IN AUSTRALIA", Notes of conference in Canberra, 3 October 1941, CRS A5954, Box 223: AA

42 CABLE NO. 5834, Fadden to Bruce, 3 October 1941, CRS A5954, Box 225: AA

43 LETTER (COPY), Spender to Fadden, 30 September 1941, MS 4875, Box 1 Correspondence 1939–1949, Spender Papers: NLA

44 For details of the dispute, see S. ROSKILL, *The War at Sea 1939–1945*, i, London, 1954, pp. 555–9

45 CABLE NO. 608, Cranborne to Fadden, 31 August 1941, and Cable No. 582, Fadden to Churchill, 4 September 1941, *DAFP*, v, Doc. 54 and fn. 5

46 LORD MORAN, p. 31

47 S. ROSKILL, p. 491
48 "COMPARISON OF BRITISH AND JAPANESE FLEETS", Note by Churchill, 12 March 1940, CAB 66/6, W.P. (40)95: PRO
49 W. S. CHURCHILL, iii, appendix K
50 LETTER, Somerville to Cunningham, 5 October 1941, ADD. MS. 52563, Cunningham Papers: BL
51 Page later wrongly claimed that it was partly due to his efforts that the battleships were dispatched. See SIR E. PAGE, p. 311
52 MINUTE, Churchill to Pound, 29 August 1941, in W.S. Churchill, iii, p. 524
53 ADVISORY WAR COUNCIL MINUTES, 12 September 1941, *DAFP*, v, Doc. 65
54 *IBID.*
55 NOTES OF DISCUSSION between Sir Earle Page and the Chiefs of Staff, Canberra, 17 September 1941, CRS A5954, Box 475: AA
56 LETTER, Brooke-Popham to Ismay, 10 October 1941, V/1/18, Brooke-Popham Papers: KC. Brooke-Popham described Page as a "straight, kindly country gentleman" although a "little inclined to stress the obvious at some length and without any pause ... for interruption".
57 CABLE, Page to Fadden, 1 October 1941, *DAFP*, v, Doc. 75; Page Diary, 29 September 1941, MS. 1633, Folder 2345, Page Papers: NLA; Sir E. Page, p. 311; "Observations by Sir Earle Page on the General Headquarters Situation in the Far East — Singapore, 29/9/41", and Letters, Page to Fadden, 1 and 2 October 1941, CRS A5954, Box 475: AA

9

Approach to Pearl Harbor

4 October to 8 December 1941

With the switch of allegiance by the two MPs, Curtin became Prime Minister but with no greater political security than that of his two predecessors. Like them, he would have to pay attention to his position both within the parliament and within his own party. As Sir Ronald Cross observed, Curtin had two powerful rivals in Beasley and Evatt who had a common aim — "each is determined to stab the other on the steps of the throne".[1] He also had to contend with the endemic Australian apathy towards its own defence. Though the public was anxious about invasion, there was little sense that it was incumbent upon themselves to provide for their own protection. The colonial mentality stipulated that protection would come from the mother country. This presented very real problems to Curtin's new Cabinet as they quickly discovered. After meeting together in Canberra, they tried to depart for Melbourne to take charge of their separate departments only to find that the train was fully booked, mainly by people on their way to Melbourne's spring race meetings.[2]

The new government had a formidable task before it. It took control of a country that had been at war for more than two years but still lacked the basic means for its own defence. Its naval forces were scattered from Singapore to Alexandria while the effort of its army and air force was predominantly directed to providing trained men for use overseas. There were critical shortages of equipment ranging from binoculars for the army to parachutes for the air force. More seriously, there were no modern fighter aircraft, no tanks worth the name and shortages of every type of gun from rifles to anti-aircraft guns and artillery.[3]

The Labor Party had been shouting from the sidelines in the defence debate. Now it had the power to put its policies into practice. It had opposed the original commitment of forces to the Middle East and various Labor members had called during 1941 for the recall of the Australian forces. Once in power the party fell in with Curtin's view and continued with the policy of Fadden and Menzies. The three AIF divisions would remain in the Middle East and be kept up to strength by regular convoys of reinforcements, though there would be no additional infantry divisions dispatched. Though Fadden had refused a British request to raise three more divisions for the Middle East due to the commitment to supply the present force with reinforcements, he did promise that the armoured portion of a division that was being raised in Australia would be available for the Middle East if the situation in the Far East permitted.[4] On Tobruk, Fadden had insisted that the relief of the troops be completed despite fresh appeals from Churchill. Shortly after taking over from Fadden, Curtin was faced with yet another appeal to delay the relief but stuck by the decision of his predecessor.[5]

Churchill previously had blamed the Labor Party for the Australian pressure over Tobruk. It was rather strange that he should request Curtin to reverse Fadden's decision, especially as he admitted to colleagues that there was little prospect of the Australian Government changing its mind. On 11 October, Churchill decided not to make the request to Curtin after all. Then, two days later, he decided he would after hearing that a postponement of the relief would assist Auchinleck in his planned offensive. He put this appeal to Curtin with an assurance that it would not "expose your troops to any undue or invidious risks and would at the same time be taken very kindly as an act of comradeship in the present struggle". There was a clear implication as to how a refusal would be taken. As Churchill put it to Auchinleck, "I should be glad for the sake of Australia and history if they would do this". He addressed his War Cabinet in a similar vein, warning that the "effect on the prestige of the Australian troops would be very great when the full facts and the correspondence became known".[6]

Curtin remained adamant on the withdrawal. When one of the ships was sunk during the evacuation with the loss of British sailors, Churchill felt added vindication for his position and immediately informed Australia of the cost of its stubborn stand. But still Australia would not budge, merely repeating its wish to have all the troops withdrawn at the earliest date. In the event, some still remained when Auchinleck's offensive was launched and the siege of Tobruk was finally lifted. In this instance, Churchill was proved correct.[7]

Tobruk was a dispute marked by a bitterness seldom known in previous relations between Australia and Britain. In Churchill's mind, Australia's action was shameful and unforgivable. It was made worse for him by having to keep his annoyance under check and concealed from public gaze. At the end of November, Churchill reminded Curtin that Australia's insistence on withdrawal had cost Britain "life and ships" but that "no one here . . . outside the circles of Government has the slightest inkling of the distress which we felt".[8] The question remains as to what it was all about.

The Tobruk dispute was begun and sustained by a trio of Australian Prime Ministers who each were motivated more by considerations of political rather than military survival. On the military side, Blamey supported the relief in order to aggregate his scattered forces into a unified corps. Where was Australia's national interest? Once committed to the Middle East and to the defence of Tobruk, it was incumbent on the Australians to see the present battle through to a finish. By not doing so, British antipathy towards Australia was enhanced during a period when British sympathy was required above all else. It may have been possible to justify the cost of the dispute in retrospect if the relieved 9th Division had thereby become available for Australia's defence during the anxious days of 1942, but this did not happen. The Division did not leave the Middle East until January 1943. Neither was the relief part of an attempt by the Labor Government to end the Australian commitment to the Middle East, which now continued on the understanding that a fleet for the Far East was being gradually assembled.

Curtin took up a suggestion by Bruce for the inclusion of a modern battleship in the proposed squadron for the Indian Ocean. On 15 October, the War Cabinet decided to impress upon Churchill the "importance of the proposed re-dispositions for the defence of Empire interests in the Eastern Hemisphere, for the maintenance of communications to the Middle East and for sustaining generally the war efforts of the Dominions in the Pacific and their overseas forces in particular". This was an implicit warning that Australia's commitment to Britain's war effort would depend on the dispatch of this squadron containing one modern battleship.[9] In fact, as we have seen, Churchill had already decided on such a move but faced resistance from the Admiralty. Curtin was letting Churchill off lightly. The ships were not destined for anywhere near Australia's vital eastern seaboard and one modern battleship was hardly sufficient to counter the strength of the Japanese fleet.

Australia not only lacked proper naval protection in the form of ships, but also the elementary protection of naval minefields. Despite two years of effort, Australia had only produced 500 mines and the only mines laid were at Port Moresby. On taking office, the Labor Government ordered an extra 2000 mines to be added to the 1000 then on order. This was still less than the 4000 estimated to be necessary for use in a Far Eastern war and it would be many months before this belated order would become available. At the same time, Australia agreed to send fifteen million rounds of rifle ammunition to China and four anti-aircraft guns to the Middle East. The dispatch of these munitions was predicated on the continuing assumption that British assistance would be forthcoming in the event of a Japanese attack. The ordering of more mines was some insurance against non-fulfilment of the British guarantee. But the mines, even when produced and laid, could only have a limited delaying action against any serious Japanese attack.[10]

On 17 October, Churchill finally reached a compromise agreement with his colleagues and Service advisers over the vexed issue of the Singapore naval squadron. At a meeting of the Defence Committee, Admiral Pound was instructed to plan for the dispatch of one modern battleship and an aircraft carrier to join the *Repulse* at Singapore. There would be an opportunity when the ships arrived at Cape Town to reverse the decision if necessary. So Australia obtained its modern battleship for the Indian Ocean, though it is doubtful whether Dominion opinion played any great part in the decision.[11] It was a decision hotly disputed by Pound who argued that it would be insufficient to deter Japan. But Churchill overruled his tired and aged naval chief with the prediction that Japan would not make war on Britain and the United States, that they would not "attack in force in Malaya" and that the main danger was from cruiser attacks on British trade which needed a fast striking force provided by a modern battleship.[12]

The Foreign Office did not share Churchill's expressed confidence in Japanese passivity. That same day, Eden had informed the War Cabinet that Britain should expect trouble from the Japanese in about three weeks' time, while his Assistant Under-Secretary, Sir Horace Seymour, sagely observed to his wife that "the Japs. move slowly, but I suppose they mean to come in ... each change of Govt. seems to make them more inclined to take the plunge, cautious as they are".[13] Once again, Eden tried to extract a decision from the War Cabinet as to the British reaction to a Japanese attack on either Thailand, Russia or the Burma Road. Churchill still refused any such commitment, while comforting his colleagues with the view that the United States was "nearer to a commitment than they had been in the past" and that Britain ought to regard Washington as "having taken charge in the Far East".[14] Churchill was determined that Britain should not ruin everything by provoking a war with Japan that left the United States on the sidelines.

Meanwhile, Brooke-Popham was visiting Australia again and making contact with its new government. In a generally optimistic report to the Advisory War Council on 16 October, he again claimed that the aircraft at Singapore were superior to those of the Japanese. Although he did admit that Singapore's full allocation of aircraft for 1941 was unlikely to be received, he argued that Japan was preoccupied with launching an attack against Russia and that "for the next three months she would not be able to undertake a large-scale attack in the south". This time, Curtin did not share in the optimism, observing instead that little seemed to have been sent to Singapore since Menzies first raised the problem in April and urging that the needs of the Far East should be "represented strongly to the United Kingdom authorities". Brooke-Popham took umbrage at this implied criticism. He claimed to have "made all representations short of resigning", and argued that the British Chiefs of Staff "were not neglecting the Far East and that probably they have made a fair allocation from the resources available". This seemed to silence Curtin who took solace in various paltry efforts by Britain and America to reinforce respectively Hong Kong and the Philippines.[15]

There was at least one positive measure that Curtin did take that his predecessors had resisted. It was to encourage the American request for aircraft landing rights in Australia, offering such rights for the duration of the war and for twelve months thereafter without preconditions about protecting Britain's economic interests. Britain would be informed but not consulted by Australia.[16] In addition, on 18 October, the War Cabinet considered a formal American request to establish an air route between Hawaii and the Philippines via Australia and to provide air bases at Rabaul, Port Moresby, Rockhampton and Darwin. The Government gave its immediate and blanket permission agreeing to the "urgency of this matter" and offering to "co-operate to the fullest possible degree as regards bases in its territories".[17] But it was too late. The Japanese attacked before the decisions could be implemented.

Even had the Labor Government been so minded, there were considerable impediments preventing the adoption of a more self-reliant defence posture. The decades of dependence on Britain had left Australia with little choice other than to continue in dutiful devotion to its protecting power. Partly due to its own self-induced neglect, Australia lacked the necessary military resources to provide for its own defence. The Labor Government was taking up the ministerial reins after a decade of opposition. Despite their membership of the Advisory War Council, the Labor leaders had not been taken into the full confidence of the previous administrations and now were dependent on the advice of their Service advisers. As Brooke-Popham reported to Whitehall, the Service Chiefs were "all pleased with their new Ministers" who were "fully ready to take the advice of their respective Chiefs of Staff". Despite this, Brooke-Popham acknowledged that the Labor Government was more critical of Britain and more conscious of its predicament in the Pacific. He warned London of the importance of making Australia "feel that we, in England, look upon them as definitely part of one Empire and we must do everything we can to keep them in the Empire and not run any risk of their slipping out of it". He cited the British order for Wirraways which, he claimed, had left the impression in Australia of it being "only given to keep them quiet and not that their Wirraways were essential to the Empire war effort".[18]

Apart from relying on Imperial-minded Service Chiefs for military advice, Curtin's Government inherited a legacy of conservative politicians occupying Australia's diplomatic posts and giving advice that was generally in harmony with British interests.[19] Even Page, who was still in Singapore when Curtin took over, was not recalled but allowed to continue to London on the understanding that he now would pursue Labor policies and ditch the conservative instructions he had taken from Australia.[20] He arrived in London with his two original aims in mind — to secure ships for Singapore and to sell Australian primary produce to Britain.[21] As a Country Party MP and former Minister of Commerce, it was expected that Page should have commercial considerations prominent on his personal agenda. However, it was not necessarily appropriate for Australia at this particular time. At his first War Cabinet meeting on 30 October, Page was welcomed by Churchill and invited to address them the following week. He did not join the War Cabinet, nor was he necessarily invited when matters affecting the higher direction of the war or the Pacific in particular were discussed.

In fact, on 3 November, at the very next meeting of the War Cabinet, Page was not present to hear yet another discussion of the proposal by Eden for a British declaration on the NEI, despite it being a matter of vital significance for Australia. As Page had indicated at a meeting with Eden[22], Australia was keen to send forces to the NEI to pre-empt any moves by Japan in that direction but was hampered by the lack of any defence agreement with the Dutch. Despite this Australian desire, Churchill again countered Eden's proposal, claiming that there was "no evidence of any early intention" by Japan to attack the NEI and that Britain's policy must remain directed towards persuading the United States to cover our "weak position in that area". Although Cranborne warned of the "painful impression" that would be created in Australia if Britain failed to respond to an attack on the NEI, Churchill succeeded in postponing consideration of the issue while he sought to organise a public declaration from America.[23]

On 5 November, Page had his opportunity to put the Australian case before the assembled members of the British War Cabinet. He informed them of the deficiencies he had found at Singapore and pressed for it to be reinforced so that "those forces would constitute an effective deterrent by December or early January at the latest", which might then ensure that the

"Pacific and Indian Oceans remained peaceful for the next few months, so that the Empire could continue to transport the supplies necessary for our war effort". In particular, he stressed the necessity to improve the air strength at Singapore which was deficient by nearly 200 aircraft from its recommended minimum level. His appeal hardly managed to hold the attention of the audience. Cadogan wrote disparagingly in his diary of Page being a "non-stop talker — goes on in an endless, cockney monotone. I asked A. [Eden], who was sitting next to him, whether he couldn't find a handle or something that would switch off the talk."[24]

Churchill was similarly unsympathetic. He pointed to the competing demands on Britain — she was sending 200 aircraft per month to Russia; she had to attain and keep air superiority in the Middle East; and she had to keep Britain safe from invasion. In fact, Churchill privately believed that Britain was secure from invasion.[25] In early October, he had felt sufficiently confident of this to override the opposition of his military advisers and order planning for a British invasion of Norway, a mad plan that was only prevented after strenuous opposition by the Chiefs of Staff.[26] While he could readily contemplate the added burden occasioned by an invasion of Norway, Churchill was not able to contemplate any reinforcement of the Far East.

To pacify Page, he simply repeated Britain's pledge to accept "supreme responsibility" for Australia's defence and, if necessary, to abandon the Middle East.[27] It would not be long before the "responsibility" was put to the test, though Page seems to have been largely convinced by Churchill's account of Britain's difficulties and by news of the *Prince of Wales*. On a train journey with Churchill two days later, Page again tried in vain to put the case for Singapore. In his diary, he admitted that Churchill was "older in the political head even than I am myself and I did not make such wonderful progress".[28] Despite his lack of progress, Page gave Curtin an optimistic assessment of his efforts in London. He reported that Churchill had "made public the dispatch of [a] heavy British fleet to protect British interests in the Pacific and Indian Ocean and has also promised all necessary aid to ensure [the] safety of Australia".[29] Australia was expecting much from Page in his role as special envoy. In the event, she received nothing but a stream of bland assurances that could have been sent equally well by Bruce, or for that matter, Churchill himself.

Meanwhile, Australia was host to another British visitor, Duff Cooper, who had been sent by Churchill on a vague mission to the Far East, the main purpose of which seemed to be to provide a sense of heightened British activity as a way of diverting the pressure for concrete action. One of his first actions was to report adversely on Brooke-Popham. When Churchill then ordered the recall of the hapless Commander-in-Chief, it caused a storm of protest from the Australian Government which had been favourably impressed with him. Curtin immediately telephoned to Duff Cooper in Singapore seeking some explanation. When the British Minister professed ignorance, it led Curtin to conclude that the responsibility was Churchill's. The situation was worsened when the announced replacement for Brooke-Popham was changed within days. Though Australia was providing much of the defence of Singapore, the Dominion was not consulted about the appointments. Even Bruce thought the situation was "intolerable" and claimed to have "left little unsaid" in his comments to the British Government. Again, a matter largely of form succeeded in spurring Bruce into action where matters of greater substance had failed to do so.[30]

To an extent, Churchill was caught in the middle. His fault was his usual one of not consulting Australia on matters of mutual interest. As he complained to Ismay, there had been no consultations over the original appointment of Brooke-Popham. Angrily he denounced the Australian Government as being "out to make the most trouble and give the least help" and instructed Ismay to tidy up the situation, though he observed that there was "no need to answer them in a hurry, as we are in the battle and they are not".[31] In his own attempt to calm the storm, Churchill cabled to Duff Cooper instructing him to "privately explain" to Curtin why he thought the elderly Brooke-Popham was unsuitable.[32] One of the effects of the dispute was to leave Singapore with a "lame duck" commander when the Japanese attacked.

Though Australia was upset by the replacement of Brooke-Popham, who had assuaged much of their fear about British intentions in the Far East, the Government still took comfort from wherever it could. Thus, Duff Cooper was welcomed on arrival in Sydney by a Government representative, Senator Keane, who expressed a hope that Cooper would "clarify any doubts we may have had about the support we may expect in the event of aggression". Duff Cooper duly complied, assuring a meeting of the Advisory War Council on 7 November that Britain would resist a Japanese attack on the NEI despite her reluctance to give a guarantee to this effect. Though Curtin was satisfied by the dispatch of the *Prince of Wales*, feeling that it "altered the whole position", Evatt remained suspicious. He demanded that Duff Cooper set out "the real plans of the United Kingdom Government in relation to Far Eastern and Pacific defence". Duff Cooper replied to this challenge with the familiar claim that Britain would "abandon the Mediterranean altogether if this were necessary in order to hold Singapore".[33] It was the conservative members of the Council who doubted the value of this assurance, although only because they could not countenance a British abandonment of the Mediterranean.

Adopting the pre-war arguments of his opponents, Curtin argued that the basing of a fleet at Singapore was the "core of the whole problem and the essential factor in determining the limits of our action". News of the *Prince of Wales* apparently had convinced him of Britain's good intentions and allowed the Council to advocate the dispatch from Malaya to China of a Buffalo squadron manned with Australian volunteers. They left it to Brooke-Popham to "determine the limit to be placed on numbers of personnel and the consequent reduction in air strength in Malaya which would be entailed".[34] This would have reduced Malaya's air strength to ridiculous levels and probably not produced a commensurate advantage for China. Instead of concentrating their strength to meet an increasingly real threat, Australia continued to dissipate her strength in penny packet contributions at Britain's whim. In this case, the Japanese attacked before effect could be given to the decision.

In London on 12 November, Page made his second appeal to the British War Cabinet for reinforcements for the Far East. Admitting the "paramount importance" of the defence of Britain and the Middle East, Page nevertheless called for an increase in Singapore's air strength "even at the expense of other theatres" and argued against Churchill's policy of following the American lead in the Far East. He held out the prospect of a greater Australian contribution to Imperial defence if Britain

strengthened the defences of Singapore. Churchill thanked Page
for his statement and assured him that it was not within
Japan's power to invade Australia. Anyway, Britain remained
"resolute to help Australia if she were menaced with invasion",
although, Churchill warned, any decision to abandon the Mediterranean was "not one to be taken lightly". Page pronounced
himself "content" that his requests would be considered. In
reporting the meeting to Curtin, Page promised to continue
arguing the Australian case for the immediate air reinforcement
of Singapore and Malaya. But British ears were deaf to his
appeal. Despite Page's failure, Curtin agreed to spread Australia's
defence resources even more thinly by allowing four RAN
destroyers to join Britain's skeletal Far Eastern force.[35]

Britain's reluctance to reinforce the Far East prior to a
Japanese attack was based on the overwhelming priority accorded
to the fight against Germany. Although the downgrading of
the Far East represented a reversal of the inter-war strategy and
left Singapore, Australia and other British eastern interests in a
position of considerable peril, it was justified in Whitehall by
reference to the obvious fact that there was, as yet, no war in
the Pacific. British military and political leaders also had an
over-confident belief in their own racial and military superiority
to the Japanese. Thus, Field Marshal Wavell assured Brooke-
Popham after inspecting Malaya's defences in mid-November
that "you ought easily to be able to deal with any Japanese
attack on Malaya provided that you get the necessary air reinforcements when required. Personally, I should be most doubtful
if the Japs ever tried to make an attack on Malaya, and I am
sure they will get [it] in the neck if they do."[36] Wavell's
reference to air reinforcements was the other justification for
the weakness at Singapore. There was a belief that, even if the
Japanese entered the war, there would be sufficient time to
move aircraft across the world to defend Malaya. It was a
dangerous strategy of bluff by Britain in a game of poker
where her hand was revealed and the Eastern Empire, including
Australia, was very much at stake.

Although Britain was averse to specifying the assistance
Australia could rely upon in case of a Japanese attack, she was
not so backward with Turkey. Churchill and Eden were transfixed by the possibility of winning the numerically strong, but
poorly equipped, Turkish army to the British cause. This had

provided much of the rationale for the disastrous campaign in Greece and it continued to be a top British priority. While Page was in London vainly pressing the cause for Singapore, Eden reminded the War Cabinet of Whitehall's commitment to Turkey and of his anxiety "lest in concentrating on the needs of the Soviet Union the importance of continuing our supplies to Turkey should be overlooked". In the event of a German attack, Britain had offered to provide Turkey with four infantry and two armoured divisions, two tank brigades and twenty-four squadrons of aircraft. In the meantime, Eden suggested that Britain supply Turkey with "non-specialised equipment" and reserve for Turkey one per cent of Britain's allocation of munitions from the United States.[37] As a rather bitter irony, much of the British assistance earmarked for Turkey in the event of a German attack was to be provided by the Australian troops in the Middle East. At the end of November, Australia gave its conditional agreement in principle to such a commitment.[38]

There now came one last opportunity for keeping the peace in the Pacific. America and Japan were holding talks in Washington from which a Pacific settlement could have been reached. Churchill looked to the talks as a breathing space for Britain and a positive indication of greater American willingness to contemplate hostilities with the Axis powers. From the sidelines in London, Bruce urged that, if the talks were seriously intended by America to find a settlement, the British Empire should intervene to influence the nature of the settlement and the economic concessions that would have to be made to Japan to secure it.[39] But Churchill was happy for America to conduct the talks because he did not envisage a settlement being reached and therefore saw no reason to discuss the economic concessions that the Empire might be called upon to provide.[40]

In Canberra, there was increasing suspicion that Britain would look favourably on the outbreak of a Pacific war that also brought America into the conflict as a belligerent. Moreover, there was mounting impatience with Britain's refusal to commit herself to any action in the event of Japan only attacking non-British territories in the Far East. But Australia's legacy of defence weakness and her continued dependence upon Britain only allowed for an outburst of impotent anger. A report by Evatt on 22 November complained of Churchill's refusal to declare various Japanese moves as being sufficient to cause war with Britain. He claimed that Britain "clearly recognised" that a breakdown of the Washington talks could lead to war with Japan and noted that "It seems that the United Kingdom is willing to run the risk for the 'good prospect of active American participation'".[41]

Although Evatt was prepared to countenance a Pacific war with American involvement, he was worried that the war would come before Britain was ready; that is, before the arrival of the naval squadron at Singapore. He urged that Australia should "try very hard to gain time until the arrival of the battleships at Singapore". Japan, he wrote, should be allowed the chance of a "diplomatic retreat without inflicting upon her unnecessary humiliation". He was careful to argue that any concessions would not be "appeasement of Japan, but merely a common-sense expedient of war at a crucial moment in our history". He suggested starting talks with the Japanese Minister to Australia "for the purpose of gaining time" and with the proviso that nothing was done "to suggest that we are acting contrary to the desires of the U.S.A.".[42] However, Australia had no bargaining chips of any consequence. The important concessions, such as the ending of the Anglo–American trade embargo, were not within Australia's power to concede.

Evatt's view produced a flurry of opposition in the Defence Department, with Shedden warning Curtin against any independent initiatives. According to Shedden, Australia had little freedom of action in its relations with Japan. Though he agreed that Australia should try and keep Japan out of the war, Shedden claimed that the initiative must rest with the United States. Like Churchill, he was afraid of venturing out on a limb with Japan without the all-important security of an American safety net. He maintained that there was "no choice but to leave the main initiative to [the] U.S.A., whilst at the same time maintaining contact as to what is happening and expressing opinions where asked for or where it is deemed prudent to suggest a word of advice". He claimed that Britain was leaving a way out for Japan and was equally anxious to play for time.[43] Curtin supported Shedden, preferring to trust in Britain's good faith. On the one hand, he hoped for positive results from the Washington talks, while on the other he was reassured by the developing defence co-operation in the Pacific. Like Evatt, he regarded the British squadron steaming toward Singapore as a "major redistribution of naval forces" but, unlike Evatt, he could "understand the reluctance of the United Kingdom Government to do anything to anticipate the outcome of the [Washington] conversations".[44]

Meanwhile, on 26 November, when the possibility of a limited agreement seemed in sight, Churchill cabled to Washington to stiffen Roosevelt's resolve with the claim that the Japanese were "most unsure of themselves" and a reminder of American responsibility for Chinese interests.[45] That day, the Japanese fleet left on its deadly voyage across the Pacific to Pearl Harbor. Churchill's cable helped to destroy the last chance for recalling them from their mission and preserving peace in the Pacific. On 27 November, Washington sent messages warning of war to its fleet commanders. Though Casey made a last minute effort to act as an honest broker to re-start the Washington talks, his efforts came to nothing.[46]

Right to the end, Australia remained remarkably confident as to the prospects for peace. On 24 November, the Minister for Supply and Development, John Beasley, extolled the benefits of Australian participation in the Eastern Group Supply Council. This Council harnessed Australian secondary industry to the needs of Britain's Eastern Empire. According to Beasley, the Council would allow Australia to "reap a very great advantage during the War period" which "might also be of benefit to Australia in the post-War period". There was no recognition of any overwhelming need for Australia to develop self-reliance as the first priority of its production policy. The material welfare of Beasley's inner-Sydney constituents seemed to take pride of place in his priorities.[47] On 5 December, three days before the Japanese attack on Pearl Harbor, the War Cabinet authorised the return to Qantas Empire Airways of a flying boat requisitioned by the RAAF for reconnaissance work but which Qantas now wanted back to handle the pre-Christmas rush of passengers and mail.[48] It was also proposed to close the Australian information office operating on the United States west coast.[49]

Meanwhile, Australia remained ill-equipped to meet any serious attack. On the ground, she still had only ten light tanks for training purposes. In mid-November, as war with Japan loomed closer, Britain planned to increase this number with the delivery of eighty tanks by March 1942. But these were also designated for training purposes and meant for the armoured division Australia proposed to form for the Middle East. The division would only receive its operational tanks after it arrived in the Middle East. As part of the same allocation discussions that day, the British Defence Committee considered the distribution of some 5000 tanks that were expected to be produced by the following March. Russia was to receive about 1000, nearly 2000 were destined for the Middle East and over 300 for India. Almost 2000 were to be retained in Britain for home defence, so that by June 1942 there would be 3500 tanks deployed in Britain.[50]

The following week, British plans changed but not to Australia's advantage. Instead, India's allocation was to be more than doubled so that it would be able to equip two armoured divisions and one army tank brigade.[51] If risks were to be run with the Japanese, Britain did not want to forfeit the jewel in her Imperial crown. As if to emphasise the point, the following week plans were laid to cut New Zealand's allocation by June 1942 from 110 to just forty-four. This was done on 1 December following the breakdown of the Washington talks and in the full expectation that Japan would soon declare war in the Pacific.[52]

Up to the last minute, Churchill steadfastly refused to make any guarantees in the event of war with Japan except in the case of an attack upon the Empire. He feared the possibility of the American public refusing to defend Britain's Imperial interests in the Far East and pinned his hopes on them reacting "favourably to a war which America has entered in defence of her own interests". Churchill did undertake to declare war on Japan if she attacked a British territory such as Hong Kong but he did not elaborate on the assistance Britain would provide in such an event.[53] The Chief of the Air Staff, Air Vice Marshal Sir Charles Portal, was more forthright. In a conversation with Page on 18 November, he shocked the Australian envoy by admitting that "if Singapore were lost we would pick it up again" and that Britain "might not fight if the Dutch East Indies were invaded". Moreover, Portal acknowledged that Singapore was inadequately defended because of a "political question, not a military one, and that he could, if necessary, get 6 Blenheim Squadrons ... from the Middle East without completely damaging their prospects".[54]

In the final week of peace in the Pacific, Britain held its breath as it waited anxiously for war while Australia just as anxiously sought to preserve the peace. On 1 December, the British War Cabinet refused to respond positively to reports of Japanese troop movements towards the south. The Chiefs of Staff opposed any precipitate action without American support and argued that a Japanese occupation of the Kra Isthmus, which would "only be with the object of attacking Singapore", would not "by itself be an attack on our vital interests". Despite Australian agreement for a pre-emptive British move on the Kra Isthmus, Britain held its hand until it was too late. The Japanese were allowed to occupy it and gain the advantage in their assault on Malaya.[55]

From Canberra on 4 December, Evatt cabled to Australia's overseas representatives in appreciation of their efforts to preserve the peace. Incredibly, he claimed that it was "now obvious that our efforts have not been without some measure of success". He called on them to continue their efforts and reminded them that "Australia will feel [the] first impact of a war against Japan" and "does not wish to become a pawn in the game".[56] For a man who pursued his own interests with almost relentless vigour, Evatt seemed almost oblivious to the very strong interest Britain had in producing a Japanese–American war. The *Prince of Wales* and *Repulse* had steamed into Singapore on 2 December sending up a shower of British propaganda that seemed to have obscured Evatt's vision and misled him as to British motives and intentions.

In London, the discussions continued. Although there were encouraging statements from Roosevelt, Churchill remained steadfast in his desire to "see a Jap–American war start . . . rather than a Jap–British war which the Americans might or might not enter".[57] He strenuously opposed Australian suggestions to seek mutual defence guarantees from Russia in the case of a Japanese attack on either party.[58] Though Russian entry into a Pacific war was a vital Australian interest, it was far from being in Britain's interest. In Churchill's view, anything that diverted Russia from the struggle against Germany was to be deplored rather than welcomed. He was busily assembling a package of promised assistance for Russia that had to be decided before Eden's imminent departure for talks with Stalin.

Two days before the attack on Pearl Harbor, Churchill

regretted that Eden could no longer offer British troops for use in Russia because of the stiffening German resistance in Libya. Instead, he suggested that ten RAF squadrons should be withdrawn from Libya "at the earliest moment when success has been gained" and placed on the southern flank of the Russian armies. At the same time, he reminded Eden of Turkey's claim to British assistance and warned that some of the squadrons destined for Russia might have to be diverted there.[59] Previously, Australian troops had been considered for dispatch to Russia but rejected by Churchill because of the likely opposition from the Australian Government.[60]

In fact, the Australian opposition would not have been as certain as Churchill believed. On 4 December, Australia's Air Minister, A. S. Drakeford, publicly called for all-out aid for Russia, arguing that the "more aid we can give Russia the further will Hitler's dream of embroiling the Pacific in war recede from the realms of possibility". At the same time, he advised the Australian War Cabinet of the prospective delivery dates for the RAAF aircraft on order. According to Drakeford's schedule, Australia would have a fair measure of air defence by the end of 1942. Unfortunately for Australia, Japan was working to a different timetable.[61]

In London, the deteriorating situation in the Far East intruded on Eden's Russian plans. Though it did not diminish the proposals for British assistance to Russia, it did increase the prospects of political disturbances in Westminster. Richard Law, one of Eden's colleagues, urged him to reconsider making the trip in view of the possible developments in the Far East, a possible military setback in Libya and the increasing political criticism in the Commons. Since Eden was a likely successor to Churchill, Law argued that it would be "appalling" for him to be out of reach, particularly in view of the domestic political situation which, he confided, "I don't like the smell of at all".[62] But Eden went ahead with his plans confident that there would be political credits from what promised to be a triumph in Moscow with the British offer of RAF squadrons.

The Japanese also went ahead with their plans after a last minute peace initiative failed. At the Foreign Office, Sir Horace Seymour wondered what the "horrid little Japs" would do next, predicting that it would be "something v[ery] tiresome". Two days later, on 7 December, he thought the Far Eastern situation was "very depressing", though he took comfort from the prospect of it forcing a "final decision" in America.[63] That evening, London time, the Japanese struck at Pearl Harbor and Malaya. Churchill rejoiced at the news, claiming later that "greater good fortune has rarely happened to the British Empire than this event which has revealed our friends and foes in their true light".[64] Australia's reaction was less rapturous. The Dominion's struggle was about to begin and the system of Imperial defence given its ultimate test.

NOTES

1 LETTER, Cross to Cranborne, 20 January 1942, ADD. MS. 58240, Emrys-Evans Papers: BL
2 ARGUS, Melbourne, 11 October 1941
3 See NOTE BY EVATT, 27 July 1943, "War — Matters Relating to — Australia", Evatt Collection: FUL; Cabinet Minutes, 17 October 1941, CRS A2703, Vol I[B]: AA
4 CABLE NO. 653, Fadden to UK Government, 7 October 1941, PREM 3/63/1: PRO
5 CABLE WINCH 1, Churchill to Fadden, 30 September 1941, and Cable Arden 1, Fadden to Churchill, 4 October 1941, DAFP, v, Docs 73 and 77; War Cabinet Minutes, 15 October 1941, CRS A2673, Vol. 8, Minute 1404: AA
6 PREM 3/63/2: PRO; War Cabinet Conclusions/Confidential Annex, 16 October 1941, CAB 65/23, W.M. 103(41): PRO
7 WAR CABINET MINUTES, 30 October 1941, CRS A2673, Vol. 9, Minute 1462: AA; War Cabinet Conclusions/Confidential Annex, 27 October 1941, CAB 65/23, W.M. 106(41): PRO
8 CABLE, Churchill to Curtin, 27 November 1941, VI/1, Ismay Papers: KC
9 WAR CABINET MINUTES, 15 October 1941, CRS A2673, Vol. 8, Minute 1407: AA
10 WAR CABINET AGENDA No. 317/1941, 7 October 1941, CRS A5954, Box 483; War Cabinet Minute No. 1419, 22 October 1941, CRS A5954, Box 495: AA
11 DEFENCE COMMITTEE (OPERATIONS) MINUTES, 17 October 1941, CAB 69/2, D.O. (41)65: PRO
12 DEFENCE COMMITTEE (OPERATIONS) CONFIDENTIAL ANNEX, 20 October 1941, CAB 69/8, D.O. (41)66: PRO; Letter, Admiral R. Edwards to Grenfell, 15 December 1951, GREN 2/2, Grenfell Papers: CC
13 WAR CABINET CONCLUSIONS/CONFIDENTIAL ANNEX, 20 October 1941, CAB 65/23, W.M. 104(41): PRO; Letter, Seymour to his wife, 21 October 1941, SEYR 2/5, Seymour Papers: CC

14 WAR CABINET CONCLUSIONS/CONFIDENTIAL ANNEX, 16 October 1940, CAB 65/23, W.M. 103(41): PRO

15 ADVISORY WAR COUNCIL MINUTES, 16 October 1941, CRS A2682, Vol. 3, Minute 533: AA

16 WAR CABINET MINUTES, 15 October 1941, CRS A2673, Vol. 8, Minute 1412: AA

17 WAR CABINET MINUTES, 18 October 1941, CRS A2673, Vol. 8, Minute 1416: AA; See also War Cabinet Conclusions, 23 and 27 October 1941, CAB 65/19, W.M. 105 and 106(41): PRO

18 LETTER, Brooke-Popham to Sir Arthur Street, Air Ministry, 28 October 1941, V/2/16, Brooke-Popham Papers: KC

19 The diplomats in the various posts were: in London, the former conservative Prime Minister, S. M. Bruce; in Washington, the former UAP Treasurer, R. G. Casey; in Tokyo, the former UAP Deputy Prime Minister, Sir John Latham; in Ottawa, a former conservative Defence Minister, Sir William Glasgow; and in Chungking, the former conservative politician, Sir Frederick Eggleston.

20 CABINET MINUTES, 7 October 1941, CRS A2700, Vol. 1, Minute 2: AA

21 PAGE DIARY, 31 October 1941, MS 1633, Folder 2345, Page Papers: NLA

22 For the meeting with Eden, Bruce and Page had decided to join together to "insist on [the] story of British foreign policy ever since Roosevelt's and Churchill's meeting ... and [to] see how far [the] Foreign Office had receded from its old position of a few months ago [of] being ready to abandon [the] Far East". PAGE DIARY, 31 October 1941, MS 1633, Folder 2345, Page Papers: NLA

23 WAR CABINET CONCLUSIONS/CONFIDENTIAL ANNEX, 3 November 1941, CAB 65/24, W.M. 108(41): PRO

24 CADOGAN DIARY, 5 November 1941, ACAD 1/10, Cadogan Papers: CC; War Cabinet Conclusions/Confidential Annex, 5 November 1941, CAB 65/24, W.M. 109(41): PRO

25 KING DIARY, 3 October 1941, in C. King, p. 142

26 See POWNALL DIARY, 2 October 1941, in B. Bond (ed.), ii, p. 44; Harvey Diary, 3 October 1941, ADD. MS. 56398, Harvey Papers: BL; "Notes on my Life", p. 296, by Lord Alanbrooke, 3/A/iv, Alanbrooke Papers: KC

27 WAR CABINET CONCLUSIONS/CONFIDENTIAL ANNEX, 5 November 1941, CAB 65/24, W.M. 109(41): PRO

28 See SIR E. PAGE, p. 312; Page Diary, 7 November 1941, MS 1633, Folder 2345, Page Papers: NLA

29 CABLE P.I, Page to Curtin, 10 November 1941, CRS CP 290/8, Bundle 1, "Sir E. Page — cables from": AA

30 See CABLE NO. 102, Bruce to Curtin, 19 November 1941, CRS M100, "November 1941": AA; War Cabinet Minutes, 17 November 1941, CRS A2673, Vol. 9, Minute 1500: AA; Minute, Churchill to Ismay, 28 October 1941, PREM 3/52/4: PRO; Letter, Duff Cooper to Brooke-Popham, 3 December 1941, V/5/22, Brooke-Popham Papers: KC

31 MINUTE D300/I, Churchill to Ismay, 24 November 1941, PREM 3/52/4: PRO

32 CABLE, Churchill to Duff Cooper, 26 November 1941, "The Prime Minister's Personal Telegrams 1941", VI/1, Ismay Papers: KC

33 *SUN-HERALD*, Sydney, 6 November 1941; Advisory War Council Minutes, 7 November 1941, CRS A2682, Vol. 3, Minutes 560–3: AA

34 *IBID.*

35 WAR CABINET CONCLUSIONS/CONFIDENTIAL ANNEX, 12 November 1941, CAB 65/24, W.M. 112(41): PRO; Cable P.5, Page to Curtin, 15 November 1941, and Cable, Curtin to Page, 20 November 1941, CRS A5954, Box 475: AA

36 LETTER, Wavell to Brooke-Popham, 13 November 1941, V/5/13, Brooke-Popham Papers: KC

37 "SUPPLIES TO TURKEY", Memorandum by Eden, 10 November 1941, CAB 66/19, W.P. (41)265: PRO

38 WAR CABINET MINUTE, 26 November 1941, CRS A2676, Item 1519: AA

39 CABLE NO. 99, Bruce to Curtin, 15 November 1941, CRS M100, "November 1941": AA

40 See D. CARLTON, *Anthony Eden*, London, 1981, pp. 189–90

41 "MEMORANDUM" by Evatt, 22 November 1941, CRS A5954, Box 475: AA

42 *IBID.*

43 "THE PACIFIC SITUATION", Memorandum by Shedden, 24 November 1941, CRS A5954, Box 475: AA

44 ADVISORY WAR COUNCIL MINUTE NO. 573, *DAFP*, v, Doc. 132; Advisory War Council Minute No. 574, 28 November 1941, CRS A5954, Box 475: AA

45 CABLE, Churchill to Roosevelt, 26 November 1941, VI/1, Ismay Papers: KC

46 R. G. CASEY, *Personal Experience*, pp. 57–8

47 "EASTERN GROUP SUPPLY COUNCIL and Australian Representation Thereon", Memorandum by Beasley, 24 November 1941, CRS A2700, Vol. 1: AA

48 WAR CABINET AGENDUM NO 397/1941, 25 November 1941, CRS A5954, Box 230: AA; The War Cabinet decision was immediately rescinded after the entry of Japan into the war. See Minute, Shedden to Director General of Civil Aviation, 8 December 1941, CRS A5954, Box 230: AA

49 LETTER, Watt to Hodgson, 9 December 1941, MS 3788/1/1, Watt Papers: NLA

50 DEFENCE COMMITTEE (OPERATIONS) COMMITTEE MEMORANDUM, "Production and Allocation of Tanks between Different Theatres", 17 November 1941, CAB 69/3, D.O. (41)27: PRO

51 DEFENCE COMMITTEE (OPERATIONS) COMMITTEE MEMORANDUM, "Production and Allocation of Tanks Between Different Theatres", 23 November 1941, CAB 69/3, D.O. (41)30: PRO

52 MEMORANDUM, 1 December 1941, CAB 69/3, D.O. (41)33: PRO; For London's view of the imminence of war in the Pacific, see Pownall Diary, 15 November 1941, in B. Bond (ed.), pp. 51–2; Weekly Intelligence Report No. 89, 21 November 1941, by the Admiralty, p. 55, DRAX 5/9, Drax Papers: CC; Crace Diary, 28 November 1941, 69/18/1, Crace Papers: IWM.

53 CABLE NO. 112, Bruce to Curtin, 1 December 1941, CRS M100, "December 1941": AA

54 PAGE DIARY, 18 November 1941, MS 1633, Folder 2345, Page Papers: NLA

55 WAR CABINET CONCLUSIONS/CONFIDENTIAL ANNEX, 1 December 1941, CAB 65/24, W.M. 122(41): PRO; See also Harvey Diary, 2 December 1941, ADD. MS. 56398, Harvey Papers: BL; "Far Eastern Policy", Memorandum by Eden, 2 December 1941, CAB 66/20, W.P. (41)296: PRO

56 CABLE NO. 369, Evatt to Bruce, 4 December 1941, CRS M100, "December 1941": AA. See also Cable No. 140, Evatt to Casey, 6 December 1941, CRS A3300, Item 100: AA

57 HARVEY DIARY, 3 December 1941, ADD. MS. 56398, Harvey Papers: BL

58 DEFENCE COMMITTEE (OPERATIONS) MINUTES, 3 December 1941, CAB 69/2, D.O. (41)71: PRO

59 "RUSSIA", Directive, Churchill to Eden, 6 December 1941, CAB 66/20, W.P. (41)298: PRO

60 WAR CABINET CONCLUSIONS/CONFIDENTIAL ANNEX, 27 October 1940, CAB 65/23, W.M. 106(41): PRO

61 "SUPPLIES FOR RUSSIA", speech by A. S. Drakeford at Essendon Town Hall, 4 December 1941, MS 987, 5/191−8, Dedman Papers: NLA; War Cabinet Agendum No. 410/1941, by Drakeford, 6 December 1941, CRS A5954, Box 230: AA

62 MINUTE, Law to Harvey, 5 December 1941, ADD. MS. 56402, Harvey Papers: BL

63 LETTERS, Seymour to his wife, 5 and 7 December 1941, SEYR 2/5, Seymour Papers: CC

64 D. Carlton, p. 190

10

War in the Pacific

7 to 31 December 1941

On 6 December 1941, the Japanese naval task force arrived within striking distance of the Hawaiian islands. The following morning, 360 aircraft from this force struck at the American naval base at Pearl Harbor, effectively crippling the United States Pacific fleet. Less dramatically, but just as efficiently, Japanese forces launched attacks on colonial outposts from Hong Kong to Manila, from Malaya to Singapore. Britain's bluff had been called. British forces were in retreat and there was little standing between Australia and the oncoming Japanese. Churchill's aim had been achieved — the economic embargo had pushed Japan into war with America and drawn Washington back into Europe as a co-belligerent with London. It was time for Australia to call on the system of Imperial defence to work in the Dominion's interest as it had done in Britain's.

On hearing of Pearl Harbor, Churchill was elated, expressing himself "well content with Sunday's developments in the Far East"[1], although he admitted later that he had misjudged the might of Japan and expected "terrible forfeits in the East". Nevertheless, he dismissed these as "merely a passing phase" that was more than compensated for by having America actively at Britain's side "up to the neck and in to the death". As he exulted, Britain now "had won the war. England would live; Britain would live; the Commonwealth of Nations and the Empire would live."[2] Churchill's simple calculation of Allied superiority was correct in its ultimate conclusion. Total victory against Germany was a pipe-dream no longer. However, the intervening struggle would produce Australia's darkest days and sound the death knell of the Empire rather than its salvation.

Churchill's optimism was reflected widely across the spectrum of Britain's political and military leadership. The Foreign

Winston Churchill arrives at Downing Street, "well content" after
the Japanese attack on Pearl Harbor, December 1941
(BBC Hulton Picture Library)

Office had disputed Churchill's methods for drawing the Americans into the war but not his aim. They therefore could regard the result with satisfaction. As Sir Horace Seymour observed with his usual aplomb, the "Japs went off as I expected" and "seem to have started very well". He admitted that "the little beasts are going to be a serious menace" but remarked how "that of course was inevitable". Admiral Somerville, soon to be Commander-in-Chief of the Eastern fleet, had a more down to earth desire to "give the little sods a real kick"[3], although the Admiralty's weekly intelligence report was more sympathetic to the plight of Japan, acknowledging that, "had she not gone to war now, Japan would have seen such a deterioration of her economic situation as to render her ultimately unable to wage war, and to reduce her to the status of a second-rate Power".[4]

Some Australians shared Churchill's relief at the entry of the Americans into the war. At the Australian Legation in Washington, an official claimed that the "main purpose" of their presence had been achieved — Australia had avoided being "drawn into a major war in the Pacific area without the armed support of the United States". However, the sudden and successful strokes by the Japanese left Australia more vulnerable than had been anticipated. It would not be much consolation to be saved in the long run if it meant being lost in the short run.[5] They took comfort from the British battle squadron at Singapore that seemed, by its presence, to fulfil Britain's Far Eastern defence obligations and to block the flow of Japanese forces to the south.

Though Churchill was in the "highest spirits"[6] over the American conflict with Japan, he was aware that Washington might regard the war in the Pacific as her primary task rather than keep to her previous agreement with Britain to fight Germany first. It became his urgent priority to ensure that this did not happen. Within hours of the attack on Pearl Harbor, the British War Cabinet met and declared war on Japan. Eden, who was in Scotland preparing to leave by ship for Russia, was directed to proceed with his mission despite the complications created by the Pacific war. More importantly, Churchill announced his own intention to proceed to Washington so that the world war could be "concerted at the highest level". He was anxious to re-confirm the Anglo–American strategy with

Roosevelt and to prevent an American over-reaction to the humiliation of Pearl Harbor. Churchill informed his colleagues that there were "already indications that the United States Naval authorities proposed to make certain re-dispositions of their Naval forces which would vitally affect us. There was also a risk that they would wish to retain, for their own forces, munitions of war which they had promised to allocate to us."[7] Page, who attended this meeting, apparently made no plea on Australia's behalf, although he did cable to Curtin requesting an increase in status so that he and Bruce could be "kept fully informed and consulted" by Britain.[8]

In deciding on his trip to Washington, Churchill overrode opposition from Eden, some of his other War Cabinet colleagues, the American Ambassador, John Winant, and even Roosevelt himself who preferred to delay the meeting until January. Eden's private secretary, Oliver Harvey, was aghast at the possible political implications if both Eden and Churchill were absent from London at such a critical time. What particularly piqued Harvey was that Eden would not earn the political credits that he could have expected from his Russian trip. The Pacific war would reduce the help he could offer to Stalin and threaten the trip with failure, while Churchill's presence in Washington would upstage anything he might manage to achieve. Two days later, even Harvey was beginning to see the sense of Churchill's mission. Though he still hoped that Churchill would not make an immediate visit, he acknowledged that it was a "poor look-out if the Americans are going to get into a flat spin and concentrate entirely on Japan".[9]

Britain suffered its own naval humiliation with the Japanese sinking of the *Prince of Wales* and *Repulse* on 10 December. Churchill had never intended that the ships should confront the Japanese. His idea was either to withdraw them to a safe distance in the Indian Ocean or to join them to the remnants of the United States Pacific fleet. In either case, the role of the ships would be to exercise from a distance a "vague menace" that would inhibit the Japanese expansion. Events moved too fast for Churchill to control. Apparently without his per-mission or knowledge, the Admiralty allowed the two ships to investigate reports of a Japanese landing party on the Malayan coast. In the process they were both sunk by Japanese torpedo bombers. Churchill reported to the War Cabinet that "the

Admiralty had known that it was intended to use these ships to attack the Japanese forces landing on the coast of Malaya, but they had not intervened to stop the operation". The obvious implication is that Churchill would have intervened had he known of it.[10]

Now there was little in the Pacific to prevent Japan from exercising her power wherever she wished. As Seymour observed, the Japanese navy would have "control of the sea in the E. hemisphere for a long time to come now, which will be very tiresome".[11] Churchill later claimed to have suffered nightmares from the shock of losing these ships that had been sent at his insistence, though he had been forewarned that they were "far more likely to act as a bait than as a deterrent".[12] The Admiralty had regarded their dispatch as a "major strategical blunder fraught with the gravest of risks". Therefore, the sinking of the ships did not come as a surprise at the Admiralty, although the "speed and completeness of their destruction" was unexpected. According to one Admiralty official, the task now was to "build up sufficient forces quickly enough to counter the eventual threat to Australia and New Zealand".[13] But Churchill refused to concede that Australia lay exposed to the Japanese and tried to encourage the Dominion with the thought uppermost in his own mind — that the "accession of [the] United States as [a] full war partner makes amends for all and makes the end certain".[14]

The dramatic loss of the ships did have a beneficial effect for Britain in one respect, namely allowing her to avoid the charge of betraying her interests in the Far East. She could always point to these two ships and claim that she had made a real effort to resist the Japanese. However, with the loss of the ships Britain was still less capable of dispatching a Far Eastern fleet, even had Churchill wanted to form one. Instead, his efforts were directed at stemming the Japanese landward advance towards India, preventing the loss of the "Imperial jewel" and the strategic junction of Japanese and German forces at the Middle Eastern crossroads.

Although Britain found it more than convenient for Japan to make war on America, it was far from convenient for Russia to join in the Pacific war against Japan. This would detract from the Russian effort against Germany which was so important to Britain. From Australia's viewpoint, Russian entry was crucial in order to distract the Japanese from their southward expansion towards Australia. If the Japanese army had had to cope with Russia's Siberian forces as well as the war in China, there would have been little scope for adventures in the south west Pacific. Churchill ensured that Britain would not apply pressure on Stalin to relieve the peril facing Australia.

At a meeting of Britain's War Cabinet on 10 December, the sudden and shocking loss of their two ships was discussed. Churchill announced that Britain could not send more ships to the Far East and would "have to develop a different kind of warfare". Page suggested the use of aircraft and submarines to "keep the Japanese out of the Indian Ocean", that China be provided with more assistance, and that Stalin be requested to declare war on Japan. Churchill refused to countenance the latter request "in view of the enormous service which Russia was giving to us by hammering the German Army".[15] In fact, that same day, the Russian army had launched a large-scale offensive against the Germans along the length of the eastern front. It is doubtful whether Stalin would have threatened his struggle with Hitler by declaring war on Japan. Like Churchill, he recognised that the national interest of his country depended in the first instance on the defeat of Germany rather than Japan.

On 12 December, Churchill informed the War Cabinet that Eden's planned offer to Russia of RAF squadrons had been withdrawn and that Eden had been advised by the Chiefs of Staff that "it would be a great advantage if Russia should declare war on Japan, but that they should not do so until they felt strong enough to take this action without imperilling the maintenance of their European front".[16] To ensure that Eden did not take this advice amiss and on his own initiative press Stalin to join in against Japan, Churchill drove the point home with a series of cables to his far-off Foreign Secretary, reminding him that "victory on the European battlefield must have priority in our minds". Churchill took account of the "evident strong wish of [the] United States, China, and I expect Australia, that Russia should come in against Japan" and cautioned Eden against actively doing anything to discourage Russian involvement while at the same time reminding him not to apply undue pressure in the other direction. Churchill obviously wanted to leave it to Stalin's sense of national preservation, which could be presumed to oppose any action against Japan.[17]

At least some senior officers of the Admiralty seem to have diverged from Churchill's concept of British strategy. The loss of the two battleships off the coast of Malaya was an indication of this conflict. On learning of their loss, the Admiralty's initial reaction was to replace them with the ships from the Mediterranean. Pound sought Admiral Cunningham's agreement to the removal of his battle ships and aircraft carriers from the eastern Mediterranean. Cunningham previously had resisted the formation of a Far East fleet at the expense of the Mediterranean. Even in the after-shock of the *Prince of Wales* sinking, he only accepted the proposal as a "gambler's stake" and only with the "most serious misgivings".[18] He did not have to worry. Churchill would never permit such a diversion.

Although Churchill recalled the loss of the ships as providing the most "direct shock" he ever suffered during the war[19] and acknowledged that it would cause Britain to "suffer considerable inconveniences", he did not alter his strategy. Instead, he took heart from the Russian offensive against Germany, the military success in Libya and, of course, the entry of the Americans. He told his War Cabinet on 10 December that "these developments far outweighed the immediate consequences of the position in the Far East, serious as they were".[20]

Apart from the promised Far East fleet, Australia had been given an assurance during Menzies' London visit that a reallocation of air strength would come into operation if the Japanese attacked. Australia had repeatedly placed its faith in this assurance, which allowed for the commitment to Imperial defence to continue long after it should have ceased. The Dominion now put this assurance to the test. The first-line strength of the RAAF was 179 aircraft, at least on paper. But of the fifty-three Hudsons, twenty were in the NEI. A further fifty-seven aircraft were Wirraways which now were acknowledged by McEwen as training aircraft.[21] As a direct result of Australian compliance with British defence imperatives, there were no aircraft capable of meeting the Japanese fighters on anywhere near equal terms.

After the War Cabinet meeting on 10 December, Page reported to Canberra that he had pressed Churchill to make the "maximum aircraft available from the Libyan fight" to be "flown over to the Burma Road or to Malaya". Australia's envoy did not call for any aircraft to be sent to Australia but requested that the existing Australian production program of

Beaufort bombers be accelerated and that "the machine tools for this programme, if not procurable immediately in America, should be taken out of factories in Britain". It did not seem to occur to Page that, while the dispatch of fighter aircraft by ship might be too late to protect Malaya, their immediate dispatch from Britain could provide a good deal of security for Australia. Instead, he took comfort from the planned transfer of United States battleships to the Pacific and the availability within seven or eight months of three new British battleships, counselling Canberra to "hold fast unfalteringly for the next few months".[22] No one foresaw the speed of the Japanese advance that would soon have enemy forces on Australia's doorstep.

Before receiving Page's cable, the Australian War Cabinet made its own appeal to Britain, reminding Churchill of the assurance given to Menzies and calling for an "immediate review of air resources". It noted that Australia had supplied the RAF with 9000 men, had scattered five squadrons to Britain, the Middle East, Malaya and the NEI and was left with inadequate Wirraway fighter aircraft to form a first-line striking force. Despite her position, Australia did not recall its squadrons from overseas, though it did request from Britain an equivalent number of aircraft.[23] One apparently positive move by the Dominion was the ban on trainee airmen leaving Australia to complete their training in Canada before joining the RAF in Britain. This ban was imposed despite strenuous opposition from the CAS, Burnett, who advised the Government that it would mean "that the crews of ten squadrons will not be forthcoming to [the] U.K. every four weeks". The Government's motivation for the ban was unclear. Certainly there were no suitable operational aircraft for these men to fly in Australia. The main rationale seems to have been a fear that the Japanese naval ascendancy had made the Pacific far too dangerous for the men to be shipped to Canada. After further pressure from Burnett, the ban was eventually lifted in February 1942.[24]

Apart from requesting Britain to make good her assurance regarding the redistribution of air strength, the Australian Government accepted Page's recommendation to boost the local production of aircraft which was now given the "first degree of priority". Unfortunately, the production program was that handed on to Curtin as a last minute legacy by Fadden's outgoing administration. Its principal asset was the Beaufort which had been designed to attack the troop ships of any invasion force. Because of innumerable production delays caused by non-delivery of parts and tools from Britain and America, the Beauforts were far behind schedule. The main aircraft being produced, the Wirraway, had been retained in the production program at Britain's suggestion. Though Australia tried to convert them into fighter aircraft as an urgent stop-gap measure, the effort proved lengthy, costly and ultimately fruitless. By the time they were produced, superior American aircraft were arriving in large numbers.[25] In the interim, Australia was defenceless in the air.

McEwen had been Minister for Air under Fadden and was instrumental in shaping the aircraft production program. He had privately defended the policy of relegating fighter aircraft to the lowest priority in the RAAF while publicly assuring that it was being given a high priority. Now that his Government's policy was revealed as woefully misconceived to say the least, he pressured Curtin to increase the provision for fighter aircraft in the RAAF. He claimed that the previous policy had been based on the assumption that Australia and her allies would have command of the sea but that the situation had now changed with the Japanese naval successes.[26] In fact, the command of the sea had been effectively lost after the fall of France in June 1940. Ever since that time, and with steadily decreasing justification, McEwen and his colleagues had been recklessly banking on the Pacific remaining peaceful while they concentrated on the rapid development of Australian secondary industry under the impetus of the wartime economic boom. Dominion defence was left principally in the hands of Britain. Their policy was now bankrupt and Australia was in dire straits as a result. Over the next few months, Australia would have to face the Japanese attacks almost without being able to fire a shot in her defence.

Churchill's reaction to the Japanese successes in the Pacific held little hope for Australia. As he reminded Curtin, Germany was "still the main enemy".[27] Though Churchill had previously overlaid Singapore with so much Imperial rhetoric, his initial response to its present plight was not to reinforce this distant and largely defenceless bastion but to make a stand on the Indo – Burmese border. On 12 December, he ordered the diversion to Bombay of the British 18th Division, then en route to the Middle East, for "use in stiffening the Indian Divisions now on the Burma frontier. Four squadrons of Fighters, which were now on their way to the Middle East ... would also be diverted to India." To General Auchinleck in Cairo, Churchill justified the diversion of his troops as being "required by [the] grievous need of strengthening long-starved India and enabling a stronger resistance to be made to [the] Japanese advance against Burma and down [the] Malay Peninsula".[28]

The "Germany first" strategy ensured a low priority for the Far East and among the claimants for British assistance in that region, Australia was low on the list. In Churchill's view, the Japanese were aiming to encircle and subdue China and perhaps overrun India as well. He did not consider that they had either the inclination or the capacity to invade Australia. As he later admitted, he was much mistaken in this estimation and was surprised when the Japanese pursued what he described as the "bad strategy" of making "threatening thrusts at Australia".[29]

On 12 December, the same day that Churchill was securing the defence of India, Roosevelt acceded to his request for an immediate meeting in Washington. Churchill informed his War Cabinet that he would leave that night on board the battleship *Duke of York*, and that he would "keep in touch with the War Cabinet by wireless throughout the journey". This would ensure that there would be little opportunity for strategic initiatives by his colleagues during his absence. As for the parliamentary criticism of the disaster in the Far East, Churchill gave instructions that any debate must be in secret session, which would limit its political impact on his public popularity, and that any strong criticism should be "resolutely dealt with".[30] It was interesting that Churchill was unable to dispatch a fleet to the Far East but did feel able to appropriate Britain's most modern battleship for his personal transport to America.

While en route to America, Churchill cabled to Curtin with optimistic news of British plans to organise a fleet of four aircraft carriers with cruisers "for action in the Indian Ocean in a form of novel warfare designed to repair our lack of modern capital ships", with the four elderly "R" battleships being available for convoy escorts. This cable bore little resemblance to the reality of the plans Churchill actually finalised two days later.[31] Ensconced in his cabin in the *Duke of York*, Churchill planned the distribution of his ships, the first priority still being to retain six battleships and two aircraft carriers in European waters to cover the one modern German battleship still in operation. His second priority remained the Middle East where the battleships *Queen Elizabeth* and *Valiant* would be retained by Admiral Cunningham since, according to Churchill, their dispatch to the Far East would "make the victualling of Malta far more difficult, and would exercise a disastrous effect upon Turkey". Churchill even proposed adding another battleship, then under repair, to Cunningham's fleet. He did, of course, wheel out the rather tattered assurance that in a "supreme emergency, or for a great occasion", these three battleships would be available for use in the East.[32]

So, despite the entry of Japan into the war in a far more dramatic and successful manner than had been anticipated, the Far East remained Britain's third priority. Even then, the force proposed for the Far East was really designed to cover the Middle East from attack by the Japanese. The ships for Churchill's Eastern fleet were not destined for the Pacific or even Singapore, but for the Indian Ocean where they would provide a "very powerful deterrent effect upon the movement of Japanese heavy ships into the Indian Ocean or in the waters between Australia and South Africa".[33] In the event, these limited plans were never put into operation. No matter how serious the setback suffered in the Far East, Churchill never felt it sufficiently imperative to send a fleet.

On 18 December, one day after Churchill drew up his grand naval design for the war, Italian frogmen attached limpet mines to Admiral Cunningham's two battleships in Alexandria harbour. The following morning they exploded causing extensive damage which kept the ships out of action for many months. Cunningham held the Mediterranean without them. Had they been released to the Far East following Pearl Harbor, as Cunningham had reluctantly agreed to do in principle, they could have been used in the defence of Britain's Eastern Empire. Churchill now really could claim with some justification to have insufficient ships for a Far East fleet, and it was his own strategy that had produced such a predicament. Australia was not informed until much later of the damage to the two ships, remaining ignorant of the fact that the closest available British battleships were at Gibraltar rather than Alexandria.

Australia had spent over two years of the war relying on a series of British assurances. Despite Churchill's attempt to continue the Dominion's dependence on such assurances, the Australian Government was less willing to co-operate. Even Page seemed to wonder about British sincerity after being fobbed off at successive meetings of the British War Cabinet. On 16 December he advised Canberra that he was "taking every opportunity [to] emphasise [the] Australian point of view" but suggested that a "strong telegram" from Curtin insisting on the "maximum earliest air support in Malaya" may accelerate the efforts Britain was making.[34] At the same time, he urged the Australian newspaper publisher Sir Keith Murdoch to return to Australia and use his influence to "force the pace of Britain's assistance".[35] Nevertheless, he remained willing to accept British plans for the Indian Ocean as being for the defence of Australia. On 18 December, he reported to Curtin that "very substantial naval, air and army reinforcements [were] already on the way or arranged for the Far East".[36]

Even when Page realised that Britain was not taking sufficient measures to retain Singapore, he overcame his anxiety and complied with British needs. At a meeting of the Defence Committee on 19 December, he supported the dispatch to Malaya of an Australian division from Palestine and even suggested that, "if the air support were forthcoming, a division might even be found from Australia herself". Although he pressed for the transfer of aircraft from the Middle East to Singapore, his arguments went largely unheeded and he was left to complain rather resignedly that "it looked as if Australian troops would be required to fight once again without adequate air support".[37] Despite this, he assured the Australian Government that the Defence Committee was anxious to reinforce Singapore to the extent that it was physically practical.[38]

Page wasted his opportunity to direct British strategy away from its single-minded concentration on Germany. With Churchill absent, there was a chance for an able Australian envoy to mobilise dissident political and military opinion in a campaign for a greater British effort in the East. It might have succeeded. Unfortunately, Page was not the man to wage such a campaign. Two days after reporting his anxiety over Singapore and claiming credit for the minor contributions Britain was making to the Far East, Page left London for Belfast on a six-day holiday to spend Christmas with relatives. He noted in his diary that on his return from Belfast on 28 December, "Bruce came at 6:30, v[ery] worried, showed me cables".[39] Leaving his post at such a vital time was an incredible action for Australia's envoy. As the Dominion's military representative in London later reported, Page "created a deplorable impression" while in London and "exerted little influence insofar as Pacific Strategy and Australia's needs were concerned".[40]

Australia's reputation remained low in London, mainly as a result of the Tobruk withdrawal. Her voice in British ears was diminished in line with her reputation. In mid-December, Churchill drafted an angry reply to criticisms by Curtin of the Greek disaster. He asked General Dill whether it should be strengthened even more. In reply, Dill urged moderation despite what he called the opportunity for "rubbing in how the political leaders in Australia have cramped our efforts in the Middle East (Tobruk and our inability to throw Australians into the Western Desert as and when required)".[41]

Despite some wavering, Britain's strategy remained fixed in the simple terms set out by Oliver Harvey — "the Germans are our principal enemy and whatever it means losing elsewhere, we should concentrate on them".[42] Australia's survival depended on this strategy being given a flexible interpretation by Allied planners. The problem was that Australia remained only dimly aware that such a strategy existed.

It seems clear that there was a general assumption in Canberra that the pre-arranged strategy had been tossed into the melting pot by the force and suddenness of the Japanese attack.[43] Evatt certainly acted on this assumption and began a determined campaign to fashion what he believed to be a fluid Allied strategy into a form sufficiently protective of Australian security. On 16 December, he cabled to Casey in Washington with instructions to insist on separate representation for Australia in any Allied conference "even though it may appear unpracticable at first sight". He urged that Australia's "point of view must be continuously stressed or our great needs will be overlooked" and warned that the "views of the United Kingdom representatives will differ from our own both in relation to supplies and forces".[44]

While trying to amplify Australia's voice in Washington, Canberra also tried to strengthen its ties with America. When the Japanese struck at Pearl Harbor, the Pan American air service to Sydney had to be abandoned before it could begin operations. More than ever anxious to develop the link, Canberra responded by unilaterally offering the same landing rights to the United States Government.[45] In addition, Australia agreed to an American request to overturn their long-held objections to a direct radio-telegraph link between the two countries.[46] Despite Australia's new-found readiness to co-operate with Washington, the United States did not suddenly reciprocate and regard Australia as a vital interest. Their colonial and strategic position in the Philippines outranked their interest in Australia.[47] Only when that became militarily untenable through the dominance of the Japanese navy in the surrounding seas would Washington begin to regard the security of Australia with any importance.

Meanwhile, British military leadership remained divided in their reaction to the rush of Japanese successes. General Pownall, on his way to Singapore to relieve Brooke-Popham, watched the pace of the Japanese advance with mounting concern. On 20 December he wrote in his diary that the "Jap war so far looks a long way from being a good show" and worried that the loss of Singapore could "well mean losing Australia, if not New Zealand", not "to the Japanese, but to the Empire, for they will think themselves let down" by Britain. He claimed that General Dill had "regarded the Middle East as less vital than Malaya" but that Churchill "had the priority of these two the other way round".[48] Dill, whom Churchill disparagingly referred to as "Dilly Dally"[49], accompanied Churchill to Washington where he was destined to remain as British military representative. He was replaced as Chief of the Imperial General Staff by General Brooke, a man more in tune with Churchill's "Germany first" strategy. However, Dill was not the only one unable to accept calmly the loss of Imperial outposts in the Far East.

While Churchill was planning to resist any attempt to denude the Mediterranean of battleships, his colleagues in London were moving in the opposite direction, though not primarily out of concern for the Eastern Empire. Following their meeting on 19 December, the Defence Committee dispatched a report to Churchill which included a proposal to build up an Eastern fleet of nine battleships and four aircraft carriers. According to the Admiralty, Britain's sea communications in the Indian Ocean ranked second in priority after the Atlantic because on the security of these communications "rests our ability to supply our armies in North Africa and the Middle East, to supply Russia through Persia, to reinforce Singapore if the local situation permits and to proceed to the assistance of Australia and New Zealand". This ranking revealed that the Defence Committee was not very much out of tune with Churchill on the basic strategy. They did not expect to be able to base a fleet at Singapore in the near future and they envisaged the initial role of the Eastern fleet as being to secure the Imperial triangle that had the Middle East at its apex, and only proceed to Australia's assistance "if a real threat" arises. Still, this was more than Churchill was prepared to do. He only promised to send a fleet *after* Australia had been seriously invaded.[50]

In fact, without capital ships at Singapore and preferably also at Sydney, there was little possibility of any British fleet being able to operate in Australia's defence. Nevertheless, in the absence of definitive orders to the contrary from Churchill, the Admiralty proceeded to dust off its inter-war plans for the Far East. On 27 December, before the Americans stepped in to accept responsibility for the naval defence of eastern Australia, the Admiralty ordered that Sydney and Fremantle be prepared for possible use as eventual bases for a reconstituted Eastern fleet.[51] However, whatever was planned in London by the Admiralty regarding the Eastern fleet, nothing could be decided without reference to Churchill in America. It was on his meeting with Roosevelt that Britain's strategy and Australia's security would depend.

Apart from the strategy, there was also the question of organising the joint Allied control of the war. The War Cabinet advised Churchill on 20 December of "clear indications that the Dominion Governments, especially Australia, will expect to be brought more fully than in the past into any machinery set up for the higher direction of the war" and recommended that co-ordination with the Dominions be retained in London and that measures be introduced to give them a higher level of representation.[52] Though the proposal was an improvement on the current situation, it remained a plan for token representation. This issue would become yet another source of conflict between Australia and Britain before Churchill finally conceded to establish Pacific War Councils in London and Washington.

As for the strategy, the Australian Government acted on the apparent assumption that the Washington meeting would resolve anew on a joint strategy, rather than simply ratify a pre-existing one. In fact, Churchill had spent his trans-Atlantic voyage occupied on the vital task of ensuring the continuation of his favoured strategy. He had to prevent America from diverting most of her military resources over the next few years into a long-term plan to expand the army for an offensive against Japan. Instead, Churchill urged his defence chiefs to encourage American naval concentration on Japan while ensuring that the American army would be primarily directed against Germany. Although he acknowledged that an Allied invasion of Europe was unlikely in 1943, he advised his chiefs to "speak with confidence and decision" to the Americans about just such an invasion and request that they make the forces and equipment available for it. He realised that the "Germany first" strategy would be imperilled if it was widely known that a European offensive was unlikely before 1944, particularly "if all the time Japan is 'running wild' in the East Indies and Northern Australia".[53] Churchill's anxiety was soon put at rest when, at the first joint meeting in Washington on 22 December, the American Chiefs of Staff reiterated their attachment to the "Germany first" strategy despite the events in the Pacific.

On 21 December, Casey cabled to Curtin with news of Churchill's arrival in Washington after his eight-day voyage across the Atlantic. Casey advised of Roosevelt's desire to establish a regional command under American direction and suggested that the Pacific would be the most suitable, that General MacArthur might be the commander and that it would be in Australia's interest to accept the situation gracefully, "even to the extent of making the suggestion ourselves, in the interests of future harmonious working together".[54] Australia seized on this suggestion as a means to press for the urgent reinforcement of Singapore. On 23 December, the Dominion sent messages both to Churchill and Roosevelt forecasting a military disaster in Malaya along similar lines to Greece and Crete and urging them to press for Russian entry into the Pacific war. Australia complained that Britain's planned reinforcements for the Far East, particularly aircraft, were "utterly inadequate" and that Malaya's ability to resist the Japanese would "depend directly on [the] amount of assistance provided by the Governments of the United Kingdom and the United States". In an implicit attack on Churchill, the message claimed that Australian troops would "fight valiantly" but only if they were "adequately supported".[55] Though the message was signed by Curtin, its blunt character suggests that it was composed by Evatt. It only added to Churchill's impatience with his restless Dominion.

Casey immediately passed the Australian message on to Churchill following a meeting between the British Prime Minister and the Dominion representatives in Washington. At this meeting Churchill made a number of general assurances about reinforcements for the Far East and of the "urgent necessity to maintain Singapore even if British forces were slowly driven southwards out of northern Malaya, and of their determination to get naval, land and air reinforcements to Malaya and Singapore by diversion from other theatres".[56] However, he also could not help proclaiming to the Dominion representatives that, "on balance, we could not be dissatisfied with the turn of events".[57] The following day, Christmas Eve, Casey called at the White House where he again argued the Australian case in a meeting with Churchill, Roosevelt, and their officials. He carried with him another cable from Canberra relaying an alarming report from V. G. Bowden, Australia's representative in Singapore.

Bowden had informed Canberra of a deterioration in the defence of Malaya that was assuming "landslide" proportions. He dismissed Britain's planned reinforcement of Singapore with fifty unassembled Hurricane fighters and the limited additions to the troop strength as being useless gestures. He argued for the "immediate dispatch from the Middle East by air of powerful reinforcements, large numbers of the latest fighter aircraft with ample operationally trained personnel".[58] This first-hand and accurate assessment was a considerable embarrassment to Churchill, arriving just as he was trying to divert America's attention from the Pacific war and effectively demolishing his confident assertions about the defence of Singapore. Nevertheless, he did not bend.

In a Christmas Day message to Curtin, Churchill simply denied the truth of Bowden's assessment and repeated Britain's determination to defend Singapore with the "utmost tenacity". Moreover, he stood by his decision not to strip the Middle East of resources for the sake of the Far East until the situation in Libya was secured. He tried to calm the Australian anxiety by holding out the prospect of reinforcements flowing from America through Australia to the Philippines and Singapore and even basing American forces in Australia. He rejected Australian pressure to offer Russia post-war territorial prizes in Europe in return for their involvement in the Pacific war. Curtin had urged Britain to recognise Russian territorial claims over the Baltic states and offer other territorial inducements to encourage Russian action against Japan. He had argued that Britain should indicate to Stalin her support in the post-war peace settlement for "Russian strategical and territorial requirements in the Far East (i.e. Northern Korea, Southern Saghalien and possibly the neutralisation of Manchuria) and also to the long-standing Russian objective of an outlet to the Indian Ocean by way of Iran". After rejecting this suggestion, Churchill set out the reinforcements planned for Singapore including his proposal that Australia withdraw one division from Palestine to go either to India or Singapore.[59]

Curtin's cable may have had some small effect on Churchill, particularly as it was buttressed to some extent by a similar cable from South Africa's Prime Minister Smuts, who argued that unless the Japanese moves were "countered by very large scale action, they may overrun the Pacific ... and the recovery of this vast area would be a most difficult and prolonged affair". Like Curtin, he opposed the idea of sending "small aid in doles of ships or aircraft or troops to Malaya" and suggested that Churchill impress upon Roosevelt the urgent need to "plant the American fighting fleet opposite to that of Japan".[60]

Perhaps in response to this combined pressure, Churchill sent a Christmas Day cable to Auchinleck in Cairo requesting him to dispatch a force of American tanks and four squadrons of Hurricane fighter planes to Singapore and suggesting that he transfer his damaged tanks to India for repair and then use them as a training nucleus for the armoured divisions being formed there. These still were token contributions designed to appease his critics rather than to provide the sort of defence that Singapore needed. The Middle East continued to be a higher priority. Churchill cautioned Auchinleck not to divest himself of anything that would prevent the planned capture of Tripoli.[61]

While Churchill was busy trying to fend off the pressure from Australia, he was faced with another problem concerning his restless Dominion. Oliver Lyttelton, Britain's Minister to the Middle East, had become so tired of Blamey's representation of the Australian interest in Cairo that he recommended that Churchill have Blamey replaced. In a cable to London on 23 December, Lyttelton described Blamey as "little short of being insufferable", that he would not take orders from Auchinleck and that he wanted to be on the Middle East War Council and Defence Committee. Britain's Deputy Prime Minister, Clement Attlee, passed this message on to Churchill in Washington, supporting Lyttelton's request but suggesting that he "persuade Curtin to arrange for Blamey's employment in some other sphere" rather than make "any bleak demands for Blamey's dismissal" that would, "at this juncture, create a first class row". He also noted the "disquieting impression" that had been created by recent "critical and querulous" cables from Australia containing demands and allegations based on "unspecified information and *a priori* assumptions". With this in mind, Attlee cautioned Churchill to boost British consultation with the Dominions, though not to accord them independent representation at international discussions.[62]

Churchill's initial reaction was to support Attlee's suggestion while trying to prevent any adverse effect on the already strained relationship between the two countries. In an initial draft of a cable to Curtin on 27 December, Churchill noted the antagonism between Blamey and Auchinleck and proposed that Blamey be transferred to Australia and that Menzies be appointed as Australian representative on the Middle East War Council. In a second and more imperious draft, Churchill removed the reference to Menzies and claimed it to be a "matter of urgency ... that Blamey should be transferred elsewhere as soon as possible". The regret at raising the issue that had been expressed in the first draft was absent in the second draft. In the event, neither draft was sent. Churchill delayed its dispatch in order to "get the bigger things settled first" and "until other difficulties with Mr. Curtin had been disposed of". Eventually, the Australian Government relieved Churchill of the need to request Blamey's transfer when they made the request themselves after most of the AIF was transferred to the Far East. Churchill was grateful that it had been achieved without any effort on his part, privately noting that Blamey had been a "more ardent politician than soldier".[63] As for Churchill's difficulties with Curtin, these were more fundamental and refused to disappear. Australia was challenging the core of Churchill's strategy.

On 26 December, Evatt sent further fretful cables to both Bruce and Casey dismissing the promised reinforcements for Singapore as being insufficient to restore the situation and again calling for the transfer of aircraft from the Middle East. He informed Australia's representatives that the "stage of gentle suggestion has now passed".[64] Australia was no longer blindly accepting London's lead on foreign and defence policy and intended to boost its pressure independently on both London and Washington for a greater effort in the Pacific. However, she continued to be hampered by having representatives overseas more concerned with pursuing British rather than Australian interests. Casey tried to placate Australian anxiety with assurances that Churchill lacked the means rather than the will to reinforce Singapore.[65] This was not true. The Middle East was continuing to enjoy priority over the Far East in the allocation of equipment. More importantly, Casey, Bruce and Page all neglected to pass on to Canberra the most crucial fact of the continuation of the "Germany first" strategy and the likely implications of this for Australia. Instead of adopting a policy of greater self-reliance in response to the Anglo−American strategy, Australia simply turned more towards America rather than Britain for the wherewithal for her defence and for ultimate victory against Japan.

This was the thrust of a Boxing Day report by Shedden, who had retained his key defence role despite the change of government, and who now advised Curtin of the new situation facing the Australian Government as a result of the Pacific war. He proposed that Australia be involved in the determination of Allied strategy and argued that the allocation of resources and disposition of forces "should have regard to the degrees of the threat in the various theatres in order to provide for equality of defence". This is what Churchill would never concede. Under his plan, there would be no equality of defence; countries in the Far East simply had to accept a greater degree of threat while trusting in their ultimate, rather than immediate salvation from the depredations of the Japanese. Shedden challenged Churchill's central thesis that the Japanese war was an incident in the present war, arguing instead that it was a new war in which Australia had a "very real and vital link" with America.[66]

The following day, 27 December, the Melbourne *Herald* published a New Year message by Curtin along similar lines to Shedden's report. This message has usually been taken as signalling a turning point in Australia's modern history as an Australian Prime Minister looked to America "without any inhibitions of any kind" and "free of any pangs as to our traditional links or kinship with the United Kingdom".[67] Although Curtin tried to placate subsequent domestic criticism of the statement with protestations of loyalty to the Empire, he was not simply turning from Britain to America to "preserve Australia as part of the British Empire".[68] He was striking Churchill at his most vital spot by attempting publicly to alter the agreed Allied strategy at the very time that Churchill was obtaining a renewal of the American commitment to the strategy. Curtin publicly called for Russian entry into the war with Japan, announced Australia's refusal to "accept the dictum that the Pacific struggle must be treated as a subordinate segment of the general conflict" and asked for a "concerted plan evoking the greatest strength at the Democracies' disposal, determined upon hurling Japan back".[69]

Not only did Curtin challenge the "Germany first" strategy, he also threatened to break up the alliance between Churchill and Roosevelt with his claim that the Pacific was "primarily one in which the United States and Australia must have the fullest say in the direction of the democracies' fighting plan".[70] This was dangerous talk, at least for Britain, and perhaps even for Churchill personally given the degree of political dissatisfaction in Westminster. After a rowdy House of Commons

debate on the war on 18 December, the Conservative MP
"Chips" Channon considered that Churchill's Government was
"doomed" in its present form. Similarly, Hugh Dalton was
worried at the "very bad spirtit, pessimism and discontent with
the conduct of the war". Though the opposition to Churchill
lacked a clear leader, Dalton thought that "Malaya now is a
little like Norway in May, 1940" when Chamberlain was pushed
from power.[71]

There was a possibility that Curtin's public championing
of a more vigorous Pacific strategy could mobilise the large
body of opinion in America and, to a lesser extent, in Britain
that questioned the Anglo—American concentration on Germany. On the other hand, to many people in Australia, and
apparently to Roosevelt as well[72], it smacked of panic and
disloyalty and it is on this basis that it was and is often judged.
One Sydney woman wrote to Curtin in outrage claiming that,
since his message, there had been "an increase of vice in every
shape and form, a deliberate indifference to the things of God
and Righteousness, and bitter recriminations against England,
for which you, sir, know yourself to be responsible".[73]

Though it was directed at the Australian public, Curtin's
message reverberated round the world. The conflict now was
very public indeed. Churchill's reaction to Curtin's challenge
was immediate. In a discussion in Ottawa with the War Committee of the Canadian Cabinet, Churchill was "strong and
outspoken" in condemning the Australian statement.[74] He informed his own War Cabinet that he had been "deeply shocked"
on hearing of Curtin's "insulting speech and vexed by his hector-
ing telegrams". He claimed that it had been badly received in
both Washington and Ottawa and warned that Australia must
not be allowed to "impede the good relations" between Britain
and America. What Churchill would have particularly feared
was the stimulus Curtin's statement threatened to provide to
Roosevelt's critics within the United States. Roosevelt had taken a
considerable political risk in supporting the "Germany first"
strategy at a time when the natural inclination of the American
public was to concentrate on hitting back at the Japanese. This
was the danger of Curtin's statement, so far as Churchill was
concerned. Neither Churchill nor his colleagues could conceive
that Curtin might have been expressing a general Australian
view and Churchill threatened to make a radio broadcast to

the Australian people to bring the undisciplined Dominion to heel. In vain, Lord Cranborne tried to placate the antagonism from his colleagues in London by explaining that Curtin's views "represented those of his party only and had already caused strong reactions from other quarters". Nevertheless, Cranborne also cautioned that it would soon be necessary, "if friction was to be avoided, to give the Dominions stronger representation in London in some form or another".[75]

Churchill reacted to the threat from Australia with his characteristic defiance, instructing Cranborne to take a "firm stand against this misbehaviour" and urging that there be "no weakness or pandering to them". In fact, Churchill claimed that Curtin's statement effectively released Britain from her formal obligation to defend the Dominion.[76] As for the deteriorating situation in Malaya, the British Prime Minister remained unrepentant. He informed his colleagues in London that, "If [the] Malay Peninsula has been starved for [the] sake of Libya and Russia, no one is more responsible than I, and I would do exactly the same again."[77]

Curtin's statement threw down the gauntlet to Churchill. The harsh reality of the large-scale Japanese attacks, and the limited opposition that rose to meet them, ate away at the fanciful delusions that had previously provided the touchstone for Australia's defence and increased to fever pitch the Australian anxiety for its own security. The years of Imperial rhetoric were laid bare for a time as Australia lay defenceless before the approaching and fearsome might of the Japanese. It was in these circumstances that Curtin felt impelled to challenge British policy head-on and dared to place Australia's home defence at the top of his Government's agenda. However, it was too late for this switch of priorities to guarantee, by itself, that Australian survival would be ensured. The Dominion had been neglectful of her own defence for so long that she could not make good the glaring deficiencies overnight. While Curtin's statement was a challenge to Churchill, it also was a panic-stricken and general plea for help. It was Churchill's task to ensure that the plea went unanswered.

NOTES

1 CABLE, Churchill to Smuts, 9 December 1941, "Prime Minister's Personal Telegrams 1941", VI/1, Ismay Papers: KC

2 W. S. CHURCHILL, iii, pp. 539–40

3 LETTERS, Seymour to his wife, 8 and 9 December 1941, SEYR 2/5, Seymour Papers: CC. Letter, Somerville to H. MacQuarrie, 8 December 1941, ADD. MS. 50143, Somerville Papers: BL

4 WEEKLY INTELLIGENCE REPORT, NO. 92, 12 December 1942, DRAX 5/10, Drax Papers: CC

5 LETTER, A. Watt to Hodgson, 9 December 1941, MS 3788/1/1, Watt Papers: NLA; R. G. Casey, *Personal Experience*, p. 76

6 HARVEY DIARY, 8 December 1941, ADD. MS. 56398, Harvey Papers: BL

7 WAR CABINET CONCLUSIONS, 8 December 1941, CAB 65/20, W.M. 125(41): PRO

8 CABLE P9, Page to Curtin, 8 December 1941, CRS A1608, H33/1/2: AA

9 HARVEY DIARY, 8 and 10 December 1941, ADD. MS. 56398, Harvey Papers: BL

10 WAR CABINET CONCLUSIONS, 12 December 1941, CAB 65/20, W.M. 127(41): PRO

11 LETTER, Seymour to his wife, 11 December 1941, SEYR 2/5, Seymour Papers: CC

12 LORD MORAN, p. 101; Letter, Admiral Somerville to H. MacQuarrie, 3 January 1943, ADD. MS. 50143, Somerville Papers: BL

13 "MY LIFE", Memoirs of Admiral Sir William Davis, pp. 260–73, WDVS 1/3, Davis Papers: CC

14 CABLE, Churchill to Curtin, 12 December 1941, VI/1, Ismay Papers: KC

15 WAR CABINET CONCLUSIONS/CONFIDENTIAL ANNEX, 10 December 1941, CAB 65/24, W.M. 126(41): PRO

16 WAR CABINET CONCLUSIONS, 12 December 1941, CAB 65/20, W.M. 127(41): PRO

17 CABLES, Churchill to Eden, 12 December 1941, "The Prime Minister's Personal Telegrams 1941", VI/1, Ismay Papers: KC

18 CABLE NO. 842, Pound to Cunningham, 10 December 1942, and Cable, Cunningham to Pound, 11 December 1941, ADD. MS. 52567, Cunningham Papers: BL

19 W. S. CHURCHILL, iii, p. 55

20 WAR CABINET CONCLUSIONS, 10 December 1941, CAB 65/20, W.M. 126(41): PRO

21 ADVISORY WAR COUNCIL MINUTE NO. 586 (EXTRACT), 9 December 1941, CRS A5954, Box 230: AA

22 CABLE P11, Page to Curtin, 11 December 1941, CRS M100, "December 1941": AA

23 WAR CABINET MINUTES, 11 December 1941, CRS A2673, Vol. 9: AA

24 MINUTE, Burnett to Drakeford, 22 December 1941, CRS A5954, Box 236: AA. See Box 236 for other documents covering this issue

25 STATEMENT by Curtin in House of Representatives, 16 December 1941, CRS A5954, Box 313: AA; War Cabinet Minutes, 18 December 1941, CRS A2673, Vol. 9, Minute 1584: AA

26 ADVISORY WAR COUNCIL MINUTE NO. 625, 23 December 1941, CRS A5954, Box 230: AA

27 CABLE NO. 817, Dominions Office to Curtin, 11 December 1941, PREM 4/43B/2: PRO

28 WAR CABINET CONCLUSIONS, 12 December 1941, CAB 65/20, W.M. 127(41): PRO; Cable No. 977, Churchill to Auchinleck, 12 December 1941, "The Prime Minister's Personal Telegrams 1941", VI/1, Ismay Papers: KC. See also Cable No. 978, Churchill to Wavell, 12 December 1941, *ibid.*

29 REPORT OF CHURCHILL'S PRESS CONFERENCE for British correspondents in Washington, enclosed in LETTER, C. Thompson to Beaverbrook, 23 May 1943, BBK D/182, Beaverbrook Papers: HLRO; See also, Mackenzie King Diary, 29 December 1941: CUL

30 WAR CABINET CONCLUSIONS, 12 December 1941, CAB 65/20, W.M. 127 (41): PRO

31 CABLE NO. 1014, Churchill to Curtin, 15 December 1941, "The Prime Minister's Personal Telegrams 1941", VI/1, Ismay Papers: KC

32 "FUTURE CONDUCT OF THE WAR", Memorandum by Churchill, 17 December, CAB 69/4, D.O. (42)12: PRO

33 *IBID.*

34 CABLE P13, Page to Curtin, 16 December 1941, CRS M100, "December 1941": AA; See also Cable P12, Page to Curtin, 16 December 1941, *ibid.*

35 PAGE DIARY, 16 December 1941, MS 1633, Folder 2345, Page Papers: NLA

36 CABLE P14, Page to Curtin, 18 December 1941, CRS M100, "December 1941": AA

37 DEFENCE COMMITTEE (OPERATIONS) MINUTES, 19 December 1941, CAB 69/2, D.O. (41)73: PRO

38 CABLE P16, Page to Curtin, 20 December 1941, *DAFP*, v, Doc. 209

39 PAGE DIARY, 23−28 December 1941, MS 1633, Folder 2345, Page Papers: NLA.

40 NOTE by Shedden, "Mission of Sir Earle Page to the United Kingdom 1941−42", 17 March 1943, CRS A5954, Box 14: AA

41 MINUTE, Dill to Churchill, 17 December 1941, PREM 3/206/2: PRO

42 HARVEY DIARY, 18 December 1941, ADD. MS. 56398, Harvey Papers: BL

43 DAVID DAY, "H. V. Evatt and the 'Beat Hitler First' Strategy: Scheming Politician or an Innocent Abroad?", *Historical Studies*, October 1987

44 CABLE NO. 1079, Evatt to Casey, 16 December 1942, *DAFP*, v, Doc. 196

45 WAR CABINET MINUTES, 11 December 1941, CRS A2673, Vol. 9, Minute 1561: AA

46 CABINET MINUTES, 15 December 1941, CRS A2703, Vol. 1[B], Minute 63: AA

47 R. G. CASEY, *Personal Experience*, p. 79

48 POWNALL DIARY, 20 December 1941, in B. Bond (ed.), pp. 66−7

49 NOTE, Pownall to Churchill, 10 November 1949, II/3/188, Ismay Papers: KC

50 "FAR EAST POLICY", Note by Attlee, 20 December 1941, with attached memoranda, Defence Committee (Operations) Memorandum, CAB 69/3, D.O. (41)40: PRO; See also Cable No. 305, Assistant Chief of Naval Staff (F) to Cunningham, 24 December 1941, ADD. MS. 52567,

Cunningham Papers: BL. The Admiralty informed Cunningham that it was almost certain that his capital ships would have to proceed east after being repaired and asked him to estimate the level of air strength he would need to compensate for the loss of the ships.

51 CABLES, Admiralty to Commander in Chief, Eastern Fleet, 27 and 29 December 1941, in REDW 2/10, Edwards Papers: CC

52 "ALLIED CO-ORDINATION", War Cabinet Memorandum, 20 December 1941, CAB 66/20, W.P. (41)303: PRO; See also War Cabinet Conclusions, 20 December 1941, CAB 65/20, W.M. 132(41): PRO

53 "MOST SECRET", Note by Churchill, 21 December 1941, in M. Gilbert, Road to Victory, London, 1986, pp. 21–2

54 CABLE NO. 1188, Casey to Department of External Affairs, 21 December 1941, CRS A3300, Item 101: AA

55 CABLE NO. 1103, Curtin to Casey, 23 December 1941, CRS A3300, Item 101: AA

56 CABLE NO. 1199, Casey to Department of External Affairs, 23 December 1941, CRS A3300, Item 101: AA

57 WASHINGTON WAR CONFERENCE, 23 December 1941, in M. Gilbert, Road to Victory, p. 25

58 CABLE NO. 1106, Evatt to Casey, 24 December 1941, CRS A3300, Item 101: AA

59 CABLE, Churchill to Curtin, 25 December 1941, CRS A3300, Item 101: AA; Cable No. 819, Curtin to Churchill, 22 December 1941, DAFP, v, Doc. 212

60 WAR CABINET CONCLUSIONS, 24 December 1941, CAB 65/20, W.M. 135(41): PRO

61 CABLE NO. 1071, Churchill to Auchinleck, 25 December 1941, VI/1, Ismay Papers: KC

62 See PREM 3/63/3: PRO

63 CABLE NO. 4038, Lyttelton to Churchill, 23 December 1941; Cable, Attlee to Churchill (no date); Two drafts of a cable, Churchill to Curtin, 27 December 1941; Cable No. 212, Churchill to Attlee, 5 January 1942; Minute, J. M. Martin to Ismay, 19 January 1942; Cable No. 152, Australian Government to Dominions Office, 27 February 1942; Minute, Attlee to Churchill, 28 February 1942; Note by Churchill, 1 March 1942; all in PREM 3/63/3: PRO

64 CABLE NO. 8231, Evatt to Bruce, 26 December 1941, CRS M100, "December 1941"; Cable No. 164, Evatt to Casey, 26 December 1941, CRS A3300, Item 101: AA

65 CABLE NO. 1220, Casey to Evatt, 26 December 1941, CRS A3300, Item 101: AA

66 "THE WAR SITUATION FROM THE AUSTRALIAN VIEWPOINT", Report by Shedden for Curtin, 26 December 1941, CRS A5954, Box 587: AA

67 "THE TASK AHEAD", by Curtin, reprinted in F. K. Crowley (ed.), Modern Australia in Documents, ii, Melbourne, 1973, pp. 49-52; For other views of Curtin's statement, see for example, P. G. Edwards, Prime Ministers and Diplomats, p. 156, and N. Harper, "Australian Foreign Policy", in W. S. Livingston and W. R. Louis (eds), Australia, New Zealand, and the Pacific Islands Since the First World War, Austin, 1979, p. 86

68 ARGUS, Melbourne, 30 December 1941
69 See fn. 67
70 IBID.
71 See CHANNON DIARY, 18 December 1941, in R. R. James, p. 315; Dalton Diary, 19 December 1941, I/25/177, Dalton Papers: LSE
72 M. CASEY, *Tides and Eddies*, London, 1966, p. 83
73 LETTERS, Miss D. Cameron to Curtin, 13 and 30 January 1942, CRS CP 156/1, Bundle 1, Item C: AA
74 MACKENZIE KING DIARY, 29 December 1941: CUL
75 WAR CABINET CONCLUSIONS, 29 December 1941, CAB 65/20, W.M. 137(41): PRO; Draft Cable (not sent), Churchill to Curtin, 29 December 1941, PREM 3/154/3: PRO
76 R. J. BELL, *Unequal Allies*, Melbourne, 1977, p. 48
77 CABLE GREY NO. 172, Churchill to Attlee, 30 December 1941, in M. Gilbert, *Road to Victory*, p. 34

11

The Fall of Singapore

1 January to 15 February 1942

*T*he beginning of 1942 saw Australia's recurrent nightmare turn to reality. The Japanese were sweeping through Europe's colonial outposts as they rushed southward. By 1 January the Japanese had captured Hong Kong, Manila, much of Malaya and were moving into Burma. The Anglo–American naval force that might have impeded the Japanese flow lay on the ocean bottom. Australian forces were scattered throughout the world. Three divisions of the AIF were in the Middle East while many of Australia's best airmen were employed on costly and largely futile bombing raids against Germany. The 8th Division was in Malaya alongside British, Indian and Malayan troops in a hopeless defence of Britain's empty naval "fortress", Singapore.

In Washington, Churchill had secured Roosevelt's renewed commitment to the previously agreed strategy to fight Germany first. Though Australia was vitally concerned with this strategy, it was neither consulted nor informed about its reaffirmation. The Washington meeting also agreed to establish a supreme command in the south west Pacific under the direction of Britain's former army commander in the Middle East, General Wavell. With Brooke-Popham's successor, General Pownall, as his Chief of Staff, Wavell was given the task of halting the Japanese advance in south east Asia. While the task was easy to define, the means were never provided for its accomplishment. It was Roosevelt who had suggested that Wavell be given the command, probably because it was considered to be a hopeless task that should fall on British rather than American shoulders.

Northern Australia fell within the boundary of Wavell's new command. This time Churchill did go through the motions of consulting Australia about the arrangements which, he claimed, were largely for the Dominion's "interest and safety". Though his colleagues in London had serious misgivings about Wavell's command, the British War Cabinet felt compelled to accept it. Ironically, the misgivings voiced in London centred on a fear that the command would attract resources away from the fight against Germany. The Chiefs of Staff acted to forestall such a possibility by pressing for an overall joint body to allocate resources between the various theatres so as to avoid any concentration on the Pacific.[1] Australia felt compelled to agree to Churchill's plan[2], though it did insist on Australian representation in the command and requested details of the forces intended for the south west Pacific. It also continued its ban on the dispatch of Australian airmen for the Empire Air Training Scheme until the "whole question of Australia's present position in relation to manpower requirements" was examined.[3]

Curtin was suspicious of Anglo−American intentions in the Pacific. As his New Year message had indicated, he realised there were strong forces in both London and Washington backing the "Germany first" strategy and that, if left unchallenged, their view would hold sway. Therefore, he called for the formation of an Anglo−American fleet in the Pacific superior to that of the Japanese.[4] This call was buttressed by the Advisory War Council which joined in condemning the Allied plan to have "two inferior fleets, one in the Indian and the other in the Pacific" which "at the best will impose on us a defensive and not an offensive strategy".[5] Although Curtin was not aware of the full extent of American losses at Pearl Harbor or of the damage to the British battleships in the Mediterranean, there was much to commend his plan, even with the naval forces remaining to the Allies. A forceful, combined response might have dealt the Japanese navy such a blow as to cut off its spreading tentacles before they had established their firm grip on the south west Pacific. Instead, Churchill did as Curtin predicted, pitching his inferior naval forces against the Japanese in a pointless exercise of self-annihilation.

Although Australia could acknowledge that Imperial defence was not working in the manner she had envisaged, it was another matter to set it aside and adopt a policy of greater self-reliance. It was much easier simply to shout ever louder for Whitehall's help. It was Churchill, not Curtin, who raised the suggestion of withdrawing Australian troops from the Middle East for the fight against Japan.[6] This sometimes has been depicted as a move by Churchill for Australia's protection. However, Churchill never intended that the Australian troops should return to their homeland. Rather, he suggested that they be sent either to India or Singapore. His idea was to place the Australians athwart the westward thrust of the Japanese towards India. They would do on land what the Eastern fleet was designed to perform in the Indian Ocean. By deterring Japanese progress westward there was the prospect of their forces being deflected southward towards Australia. Churchill made little provision to prevent such an occurrence. In fact, it almost seemed to be his deliberate aim.

Despite the shock of the Japanese advance, the Australian Government had not requested the return of its troops from the Middle East. At the War Cabinet meeting on 30 December, Churchill's proposal to withdraw one of these divisions for use in the Far East was received with some degree of puzzlement. The Australian Chiefs of Staff had recommended that the Middle East forces be maintained at their present level of three divisions along with a reinforcement pool of some 11,000 men. This was approved by the War Cabinet although it now was subject to review in light of Churchill's proposed transfer of one division. While Curtin opposed its dispatch to India, he did not grasp the opportunity to have his troops return home. Instead, the War Cabinet simply requested Bruce to "ascertain definitely what is proposed" and "to submit information as to dates of movement and arrangements for transport and escort".[7] Similarly, the Advisory War Council did not seek to interfere with Churchill's plans except to endorse Curtin's opposition regarding India.[8]

Australia's continuing failure to mobilise her forces in her own defence can be partly explained by the conflicting signals being received in Canberra. Although Churchill was busy ensuring that Australia would not see a British fleet until 1945, the Admiralty was preparing paper plans to meet other eventualities. These included the possibility of basing the proposed Eastern fleet at various Australian ports. On 29 December, the Admiralty requested that Australia agree in principle to make the "necessary arrangements to enable [the] Eastern Fleet or part thereof to be operated from Australian bases". At the same time, the Government was informed by General Bennett, the commander of the 8th Division in Malaya, that Singapore could be defended successfully, provided he was given reinforcements. The Government responded to these comforting signals by approving British arrangements for the Eastern fleet and dispatching a further 1800 men to Singapore.[9] With Imperial defence in tatters and disaster looming, Australia was clutching at straws.

The Dominion was brought back closer to reality on 31 December when Casey advised that Wavell's area of responsibility now was planned to exclude Australia and Papua New Guinea altogether. As well, the United States Pacific fleet would not extend its area of responsibility to the Australian eastern coastline. Australia was to have self-reliance thrust upon her but not the resources to fulfil such a responsibility. As Curtin immediately pointed out to Churchill, the effect was to offer Australia up as a sacrificial offering to the Japanese who were being practically invited to "avoid [the] main allied concentration in South West Pacific Theatre and attack [the] Australian Area which will be weakly held". He threw back in Churchill's face the assurance that Wavell's new command was designed to protect Australian interests and safety and claimed that the Australian Chiefs of Staff were "unable to see anything except [an] endangering of our safety by [the] proposal to exclude [the] Australian mainland and territories from [the] South West Pacific Area".[10] Though this was certainly the trend of Churchill's strategy, he could not afford either to admit it or have it claimed against him.

In a cable quite as strong as Curtin's, Churchill rebutted the claim that Australia was being deliberately endangered. However, as with most of Churchill's cables, it was stronger on rhetoric than information. He claimed to be working night and day to "make the best arrangements possible in your interests and for your safety, having regard to other theatres and other dangers which have to be met from our limited

(*Overleaf*) Describing how it was: the Commander of the 8th Division, Major-General Gordon Bennett, telling war correspondents of the fighting in Malaya
(AUSTRALIAN WAR MEMORIAL)

resources". He justified the exclusion of Australia from Wavell's area because it lay outside the fighting zone and he took
issue with Curtin's claim of a "main allied concentration" being
assembled under Wavell's command. In a denial that should
have heightened rather than reduced the Australian alarm,
Churchill disavowed any intention to make such a concentration.[11] Curtin was not impressed. He repeated his call for
Australia to be included in Wavell's command and for the
United States navy to be responsible for the Australian east
coast.[12]

In a cable to Casey, Evatt tried to disentangle the web of
conflict being constructed between Australia and her Allies. He
warned Casey that there would be a "very hostile" reaction if
Australia was not given a position of responsibility within
Wavell's command and pressed him to present this view with
the "utmost vigour" in order to achieve "true and equal collaboration". Evatt could not comprehend how Australia's needs
could be overlooked by Churchill and Roosevelt. He could not
square their professed intention to defend Australia as a base
against Japan with their tardy response to the Australian appeal
for war resources. He concluded that it must be the Australian
propaganda broadcasts that had "produced the impression that
we are far stronger from a military point of view than is the
actual case" and suggested Casey make "some frank confession
of the true position" to Roosevelt, confiding to the President
that Australian resources had been "devoted to theatres other
than the south-west Pacific".[13] This was in vain. There were no
illusions in London or Washington about Australia's defence
strength.

Churchill, who was spending six days in Florida, rejected
Australia's attempt to be represented on a joint body controlling
the war against Japan. Moreover, he continued to describe
Australia as lying outside the fighting zone and did not budge
from his intention to leave the defence of Australian soil to the
Dominion, though he did suggest that America would be willing to send forty or fifty thousand of its troops to Australia.
He dismissed any suggestion that Australia was in immediate
danger of invasion in force and that, while Australia might
experience Japanese air attacks, the British had had a "good
dose already in England without mortally harmful results". He
requested that Curtin give him a week's grace to formulate a

proper scheme for the direction of the Pacific war while assuring him that he was thinking of Australia's interests "at every moment".[14]

Churchill was exasperated with Australia and his mood was not helped by the humidity of Palm Springs. His cable had to be toned down considerably before it was sent. His medical adviser, Lord Moran, was worried by Churchill's "belligerent mood" and his display of wild, childish temper at the Australians, with Churchill complaining that the situation in Malaya had made Australia "jumpy about invasion". Though Churchill felt Curtin's Government did not truly represent the Australian people, he also allowed his class prejudices to surface, observing that "the Australians came of bad stock".[15] This angry jibe was more than an off-hand comment in a fit of anger. Secure in his own aristocratic background, Churchill could not prevent himself being dismissive of a country established originally as a convict colony and subsequently settled by large numbers of working-class Irishmen. It is more than probable that his feelings were shared widely within Britain's ruling class, if only subconsciously, and that they acted to exacerbate the enmity between the two countries.

By way of contrast to his attitude toward Australia, Churchill was more solicitous of New Zealand's defence. Australia's sister Dominion had been less forthright in requesting assistance and Churchill had responded in kind, observing on 2 January that New Zealand had "behaved so well and deserve[d] every help possible". Accordingly, New Zealand was promised increased supplies of various military items, though not on such a scale as to detract from the Allied concentration against Germany. Churchill thanked the New Zealand Prime Minister for the "splendid courage and loyalty to the Mother Country shown by New Zealand under stress of danger".[16] Unlike Australia, New Zealand's plight had his sympathy and even some limited practical support.

One of the operational measures of great significance for Australia that Churchill now held out to Curtin was the British plan to transfer two of the AIF divisions, rather than one as he had proposed earlier, from the Middle East to the Far East. The Australian War Cabinet agreed accordingly to the withdrawal of the 6th and 7th Divisions to the NEI and asked Blamey to consider joining the remaining 9th Division to the

New Zealand Division to form an Anzac corps for continued use in the Middle East.[17] It really was time for all the AIF to return home, particularly in view of Churchill's refusal to make any proper provision for Australia's defence by other means.

During these dangerous weeks, yet a further source of dispute arose between Britain and Australia. This centred on the Australian movement of troops to garrison Portuguese Timor and so pre-empt a Japanese takeover. Though this had been done at Britain's instigation, London went cold on the project when the Portuguese objected strongly and raised the spectre of them allowing the Germans into the Iberian Peninsula, thereby threatening Gibraltar and the British presence in the Mediterranean. Australia's vital interest rested on keeping the Japanese out of Timor and away from Australia's northern shores but she again complied with British needs and priorities rather than her own, agreeing to withdraw its force on the arrival of Portuguese reinforcements despite them being "unlikely to provide [an] adequate or effective defence". Even at this stage, Australia was willing to put her own vital needs aside to protect those of Britain. As the External Affairs Department explained it to the British representative in Dili, because of the possible Portuguese reaction in Europe, the "matter was really out of our hands".[18]

Meanwhile, the Imperial planners were coming to terms with the Pacific war and allotting it firmly into second priority behind the war against Germany. Admiral Cunningham, who had earlier agreed to the withdrawal of his battleships from the Mediterranean, now argued for their retention. Although he admitted that the Far East needed to be "restored and stabilised", he argued that the war could only be won by beating Germany which would automatically bring in its train the defeat of Japan.[19] The Admiralty swung in behind this view, partly in agreement with Churchill that the Japanese would reach the limit of their expansion before they had over-run Australia. A naval planner recalled that, in early January, the Admiralty expected an "unrelieved succession of disasters" including the loss of Malaya, Singapore, the Philippines, the NEI and New Guinea "as the first stage of a threat to Australia" but that they "guessed contrary to some opinions expressed in Australia that at this stage it was unlikely any attempt would be launched to capture Australia".[20] However, the Admiralty's judgement about the Japanese had not proved too reliable in the past and it was no basis on which to risk Australia's defence.

Britain had spent the first two years of war making increasingly doubtful assurances about Australia's defence position in order to maximise the Dominion's contribution to the British war effort. Now Churchill made similar assurances about the ability of Singapore to withstand a Japanese attack and the inability of the Japanese to push on to Australia. As each domino fell, Churchill would extol the strength of the next one in line. On 14 January, he informed Curtin that the loss of Malaya had been inevitable "once the Japanese obtained command of [the] sea and whilst we are fighting for our lives against Germany and Italy". However, he implied its loss was of little moment since the only vital point was the "Singapore Fortress and its essential hinterland". He rebutted criticism of Britain's effort in the Far East by referring to the "agonising loss of two of our finest ships which we sent to sustain the Far Eastern War". Even in its watery grave, the *Prince of Wales* was proving to be a potent force, though as a defence against Australian criticism rather than Japanese expansion. In this cable, Churchill also had to inform Curtin that America only planned to contribute one cruiser to the defence of Australian waters. But, according to Churchill, the actual strength of their contribution was immaterial, being outweighed by their formal undertaking to accept the naval responsibility for the Australian area.[21]

Despite Churchill's defence of British efforts in the Far East, Curtin remained unimpressed though he still seemed to retain considerable faith in British goodwill and continued to ascribe responsibility for Singapore's deficiencies to British complacency. It begged belief that Britain might abandon Singapore as a deliberate strategy. In his reply to Churchill on 17 January, Curtin was reduced to reciting the litany of Imperial defence principles as established during the 1930s in an attempt to justify Australia's changing concentration from Imperial defence to home defence. The integrity of Singapore and the presence of a Far Eastern fleet were central to the Australian belief and, if these could not be guaranteed, Australia would be forced to concentrate more land and air resources to guard against invasion.[22]

Churchill tried to deflect this latest Australian attack by alluding to the great victories against Germany in Russia and the Middle East and by claiming that the "blame for the frightful risks we have had to run and will have to run rests with all those who, in and out of office, failed to discern the Nazi menace and to crush it while it was weak". This was a direct thrust at Curtin whose Labor Party had opposed rearmament during the 1930s. He also informed Australia of the damage to the Mediterranean battleships that had occurred a month before. Had they not been damaged, Churchill claimed, he would have sent them to the Far East. This was far from the truth but Curtin was not to know it. In place of immediate reinforcements, Churchill offered Australia another dose of rhetoric in which he held out the prospect of being able to turn the balance of sea power against the Japanese. He counselled Curtin not to be "dismayed or get into recrimination" nor to doubt his "loyalty to Australia and New Zealand". He optimistically proclaimed himself "hopeful as never before that we shall emerge safely and also gloriously from the dark valley".[23]

Although Churchill continued to assure Australia about the strength of the Singapore "fortress", he actually had given it up as lost. On 14 January, he confided to Wavell that it had "always seemed to me that the vital need is to prolong the defence of the Island to the last possible minute" though he hoped it would not come to that.[24] By 19 January, Churchill's attention was focusing less on Singapore and more on Burma, the next domino. He informed his War Cabinet that the Singapore garrison must "hold out to the last" and emphasised the "importance of maintaining the Burma Road in operation". Cadogan left the War Cabinet meeting with the impression that Churchill "seems prepared for the worst in Malaya ..." The following day, Churchill set out the scenario he expected for Singapore when he informed Wavell that he expected "every inch of ground to be defended, every scrap of material or defences to be blown to pieces to prevent capture by the enemy and no question of surrender to be entertained until after protracted fighting among the ruins of Singapore City".[25]

Burma was important to Britain for several reasons. It lay on the landward route to India and, as a reinforcement route to China, it was essential to hold the Burma Road in order to keep China in the field against Japan. Roosevelt had emphasised that he would be displeased if Britain lost control of this supply route. Churchill also was motivated by a deep racist fear that the Chinese might negotiate a separate peace with Japan and form part of a pan-Asiatic movement that would expel European influence from that populous continent for ever. During his stay in Washington, Churchill had warned of the possibility of a "Pan-Asiatic movement all over the Far East, including all the brown and yellow races, which might complicate seriously our situation there". Later, he cabled to Wavell urging him to accept Chinese assistance in defending Burma, reminding him that "behind all looms the shadow of Asiatic solidarity, which the numerous disasters and defeats through which we have to plough our way may make more menacing".[26]

This fear of Asiatic solidarity was not confined to Churchill. As a sparsely populated continent on the edge of Asia, Australia shared the fear of such solidarity and the threat of Asian invasion was rooted deep in her psyche. The White Australia Policy of 1901, which excluded non-European immigrants, was a direct expression of this latent insecurity. The Japanese entry into the war brought the Australian fears to the surface and confronted the Dominion with the ironic prospect of being defended, at least partly, by black American troops. Initially, Australia refused to countenance such a prospect for fear of compromising its racist immigration policy. In reply to a query from Casey, the Advisory War Council decided on 12 January that Australia should advise Washington not to include black troops as part of any force that it was planning to dispatch for the Dominion's defence. The Council was concerned at the "probable repercussions of the use of coloured troops on the maintenance of the White Australia policy in the post-war settlement".[27]

After being advised by the United States Legation that such black troops would be used in Darwin on construction work "for which they are peculiarly fitted", Curtin overruled the Advisory War Council and left it to the decision of the United States. The Council reluctantly fell in with this view on the express understanding that the American authorities, "being aware of our views, would have regard to Australian suscepti-bilities in the numbers they decide to dispatch". At the same time, the United States was planning to send 1600 black troops

as part of a larger contingent to New Caledonia. Though
Curtin gave permission for the troops to call at Australian
ports en route to New Caledonia, it was only after instructions
had been given that if the troops were unable to land at New
Caledonia, the "coloured troops are on no account to be
stationed in Australia".[28]

At the same time, the Government was being pressured by
the Malayan authorities to admit up to 5000 Chinese and
Eurasian refugees. Only after strong protests from Malaya did
the Government relent from its initial decision to limit the
number of refugees to just fifty Chinese and fifty Eurasians,
and only on condition that the refugees would be self-
supporting or maintained by the Malayan administration.
Then, on 1 February, the War Cabinet approved a United
States plan to import 25,000 Javanese labourers on a short-term
basis to construct airfields in northern Australia. However,
Java was captured by the Japanese before this plan could be
implemented. Meanwhile, at the end of January, an American
convoy arrived in Melbourne to face the ludicrous situation of
its black troops being refused permission to step ashore by
customs officers zealously enforcing the provisions of the
immigration act. It took yet another decision of the War
Cabinet for this officious ban to be overturned. These War
Cabinet decisions were understood to be temporary expedients
and did not represent an abandonment of the White Australia
Policy. Nevertheless, they provided a graphic illustration of the
desperate straits to which the Dominion was reduced if the
previously sacrosanct White Australia Policy could be waived,
albeit temporarily.[29]

While Australia was reluctantly waiving such traditional
principles as the White Australia Policy, the colonial legacy
continued to have a strong hold on the Dominion. In January
1942, when Australia received an American request to establish
a reinforcement air route across the Indian Ocean to the south
west Pacific, the Dominion referred the request to London.
There it was discussed at a meeting between Bruce, Page and
various Air Ministry officials who jointly decided to approve
the plan on condition that the route was "regarded as supplementary and did not interfere with the existing route from
Britain to Rangoon". Despite this conditional approval, opposition from Qantas officials kept it in abeyance until such time

as the Japanese had made the route untenable. Qantas feared that the American plan would lead to the eventual takeover of Australia's overseas air routes by Pan American Airways to the detriment of the joint Anglo—Australian service in which Qantas had a stake and that it ignored the "needs of the British war effort".[30]

British planners had believed that Japan could not mount a major campaign towards either Australia or Burma until they had first captured Malaya and Singapore. On 20 January, they were proved wrong when Japanese forces moved across the Thai border into Burma in a major thrust towards Rangoon. Britain was in a bind of its own making with one more theatre competing for resources. The day before the attack, the Governor of Burma, Sir Reginald Dorman-Smith, had warned London of the invidious choice that would have to be made between the "competing demands of [the] Mideast, Burma and Singapore". Describing Burma as the "last remaining operational base against the Japs", he maintained that it was "dangerous to think in terms of reinforcing Singapore at the expense of Burma for purposes of prestige".[31] Churchill accepted this view absolutely but, as he discovered, there were Dominion and domestic critics who could not accept it so readily.

On 21 January, the Defence Committee discussed the competing demands of Singapore and Burma in the light of the Japanese attack. Following recent military advice, Churchill now admitted that Singapore was not a fortress and that the battle might well be lost. He then pressed the case for Burma, arguing that "taking the widest view, Burma was more important than Singapore".[32] He complained that Australia had not expressed its view on the possible abandonment of Malaya. In fact, Curtin had cabled to Churchill ten days previously urging that everything possible be done to reinforce Malaya, where Australia's 8th Division was poised to fight the decisive battle for Johore, and warning that a "repetition of the Greek and Crete campaigns would evoke a violent public reaction" in Australia. Page reinforced this point when he now assured Churchill that the Australian Government would "never consent to the desertion of its fighting men".[33]

Churchill reluctantly bowed to the views of his Ministers and Page and delayed the diversion of reinforcements from Singapore to Rangoon. His frustration with Australia was

compounded when the meeting was interrupted to receive
a cable from Curtin rejecting Churchill's plan for allied co-
ordination in the Pacific and calling for a seat in the British
War Cabinet and the formation of an inter-Allied policy-making
body in Washington. At this, Page recalled, "Churchill slammed
the telegram on the table and declared that he had said his last
words — Australia could go to Washington if she wished".[34]

At the same time as Japan was advancing into Burma, a
large force of Japanese planes attacked Rabaul on the island of
New Britain, a vital stepping stone in the Japanese plan to
isolate Australia from America. This was a continuation of the
second prong of the Japanese advance in the south west Pacific
which now could bypass Singapore and strike at points further
south. The attack on Rabaul brought the needs of Burma and
Australia into direct conflict.

Australia remained in the dark as to British intentions. On
21 January, Curtin replied in the affirmative when Churchill
asked whether he considered Australia faced a threat of invasion. He accepted Churchill's suggestion to use American
troops, while stipulating that Australia also needed supplies of
aircraft and military equipment. Curtin extolled the advantages
of the Dominion as a base for reinforcements for offensive
action against the Japanese while observing that it was a "race
against time in Malaya in which the enemy will do everything
possible by air and submarine attacks to prevent our reinforcements getting through".[35] No wonder Curtin was dismayed to
hear from Page, following the Defence Committee meeting,
that Churchill was planning the evacuation of Singapore. As
usual, Page was wrong. The truth, that Churchill planned to
abandon rather than reinforce or even evacuate Singapore,
would be even more dismaying to Australia.

Page's cable arrived on 23 January in time for an emergency
meeting of the Australian War Cabinet, which considered
the deteriorating position in Malaya and instructed that the
strongest representations be made to Churchill. Curtin was not
there to do it, having left on 21 January for his home in Perth,
from where he did not return until 1 February. Though the
Deputy Prime Minister, F. M. Forde, presided in his place, it
probably was Evatt who composed the strong cable to Churchill
in which an evacuation of Singapore was termed "an inexcusable
betrayal". Describing Singapore as a "central fortress in the

system of Empire and local defence", the cable complained rather plaintively that any "diversion of reinforcements should be to the Netherlands East Indies and not Burma", that Australia had "acted and carried out our part of the bargain" and expected Britain "not to frustrate the whole purpose by evacuation".[36]

Apart from pressing Churchill to reinforce Singapore, the War Cabinet discussed the implications of the Japanese attack on Rabaul. One of the most terrible implications was that Australia's first-line fighter strength, the locally produced Wirraway, in its first conflict was confirmed as useless against Japanese aircraft. Australia had lost even the semblance of an air defence force. Of equal importance, the Government was advised by the Chief of the Naval Staff that there was "no prospect of concentrating a battleship force of sufficient strength to defeat the Japanese before May" and that Australia therefore was in danger of invasion, though he did not think the Dominion offered a very attractive target to the Japanese. However, Churchill had ensured that it was an easy target. In the event of such an invasion, the naval chief urged that Australians be told to "remain in their homes and ... keep the roads clear". The Government was so worried that it immediately announced that the forthcoming Australia Day would not be a holiday, albeit only for the munitions industry and war-related government departments.[37]

When Churchill received the Australian cable describing an evacuation of Singapore as an inexcusable betrayal, he immediately rounded on the hapless Page who had unwittingly helped to instigate it, reminding him that Britain was not planning to evacuate Singapore, only to divert its reinforcements to Burma. Poor Page defended his report as being fact mixed with observations and partly intended to serve Britain's purposes by buttressing the arguments to establish the proposed Far Eastern Council in London as Churchill wanted, rather than Washington as Australia wanted. When Page then attempted to put Australia's case for reinforcements, the War Cabinet simply ordered reports setting out their plans for the Far East. Much of this meeting had been taken up with various demands from Canberra — for a seat in the British War Cabinet; for a Pacific War Council in Washington; and for reinforcements for Singapore. Such was the British exasperation with her Dominion at this meeting, ironically held on Australia Day, that one Cabinet member angrily described Australia as being the "most dangerous obstacle in the path of this Gov[ernmen]t", a description one would have thought more apt for Germany or Japan.[38]

From Australia, the British High Commissioner, Sir Ronald Cross, prodded the critics of Australia within the British War Cabinet by claiming that Evatt was behind the hostile material in the Australian newspapers and that Britain should act tough with her Dominion since, he claimed, Australia was "so dependent on our good-will that we can use a big enough stick to get our way".[39] Cross proposed that Britain should respond to the Australian demand for representation in the British War Cabinet by demanding the same for him in Australia and should counter the nationalist trend with an unaccommodating attitude on economic questions.[40]

Cranborne could not endorse his High Commissioner's proposals. Instead, he again urged that the War Cabinet must move urgently to concede Australia's demand for a greater say in Imperial decision-making. He warned that it would be a "great and possibly dangerous mistake" for Britain to underestimate the rising tide of concern in Australia.[41] Cranborne did not have to remind them that the British press was also replete with calls for greater Dominion representation and that there was considerable sympathy for such a move within the Commons by the growing number of MPs critical of Churchill's handling of the war. A *Times* editorial on 19 January had called for greater Dominion participation in the formulation of Imperial policy and the granting of such representation as the Dominions themselves desired.[42] Cranborne warned his colleagues that a "rot which started in Australia might easily spread to other Dominions" and that there were "centrifugal tendencies" in the British Empire that could no longer be ignored. Cranborne's solution was to accord Australia the right of attendance at the War Cabinet whenever questions affecting the war as a whole were discussed on condition that the Australian representative was empowered to commit the Dominion on matters of urgency.[43]

Churchill had refused to consider such a concession ever since Menzies had raised the idea in 1941. On 17 January, he had dismissed it out of hand with the sarcastic comment that before it could be considered, "the Australians ought to lay aside their Party feud and set up a National Government".[44] However, five days later his opposition crumbled and Page was able to attend relevant War Cabinet meetings as the accredited representative of the Australian Government as a matter of right rather than privilege. This concession by Churchill was made both to appease the domestic critics and to remove the detestable Australians from his back.[45] As Ismay privately confessed, Churchill was "having a pretty rough time at the moment with Australia bickering and a few elements in Parliament and the Press (not very important ones) snarling".[46] Also, it was a different matter having Page in the War Cabinet rather than the brilliant, ambitious Menzies.

It was not representation that Australia needed, but reinforcements. Representation could be made into whatever Churchill wanted and would not, of itself, guarantee that Australia's voice would be heard or its needs met. Tanks were essential if Australia was to defend herself against invasion. Menzies had authorised the production of an Australian tank but this program relied on the supply of machine tools and other essential equipment from Britain and America. It proved no easier to extract these than the tanks themselves and the program was eventually ended by Curtin in 1943 after several wasted years of effort and without an operational tank being produced. In January 1942, Australia made a determined effort to obtain the tanks that it had long had on order.

On 21 January, Bruce wrote to Beaverbrook requesting the diversion to Australia of its minimum requirement of 775 cruiser tanks. Meanwhile, Australia learned that America did not plan any deliveries to the Dominion during January, while Britain only intended to dispatch forty. One-third of American production and much of Britain's was going to Russia and Casey urged that Curtin request a temporary diminution in the Russian allocation to provide for Australia's needs. The Government took up Casey's suggestion, advising Bruce that the time needed for delivery and the imminence of the Australian danger justified the "strongest possible pressure being exerted to secure immediate shipments". Britain's intelligence chiefs admitted that Japan had the capability to defeat and invade Australia but they disputed the immediate likelihood of such a move. They reported on 25 January: "Japan will probably be content, at this stage, with trying to isolate Australia and New Zealand without embarking on a major operation to the Southward, except for an attack to capture Port Darwin." The British Government eventually considered the issue on 30 January, nine days after the first letter from Bruce to Beaverbrook.[47]

At the Defence Committee meeting, the Australian requests faced determined opposition from Beaverbrook and Eden. Presumably Churchill would have led the opposition had he been present. Instead it was Attlee who took the chair and provided the single spark of sympathy for Australia. In contrast, Beaverbrook argued that Russia's requirements should not be neglected despite the military situation becoming more favourable and Russia's own tank production being restored. Eden also pressed the case for Russia as well as the Middle East. While there was support for his view, Attlee thought it would be impossible to ignore Australia's claims at the present moment. Accordingly, the Defence Committee approved the dispatch of 125 Kittyhawk fighter aircraft from British sources and undertook to request a similar amount for Australia from American sources.[48] It was a minuscule proportion of the total Allied supply of operational aircraft, of which some nine thousand were produced during the first three months of 1942[49], and was less than one-quarter of the Australian requirement. The Dominion fared little better with regard to tanks.

Under a proposal from the Chief of the Imperial General Staff (CIGS), General Sir Alan Brooke, the tank supply to Russia would be cut by more than half during February and March to allow 321 tanks for Australia, less than half the number requested by Bruce. Brooke advised that the rush of Japanese successes had made the threat to Australia "a very real one". He reported Churchill's view that the home forces should take last priority, although taking last priority still enabled them to receive 602 tanks to add to their stock of 2261. Beaverbrook and Eden attacked Brooke's idea of cutting the supply to Russia, using the rather curious argument that it would be "wrong to approach Russia at the present time just when things were going so well there". On this logic, it would never be the right time to ask Russia to accept less tanks since it could hardly be done if things were going badly. Beaverbrook offered to find a solution that would satisfy both Russian and Australian requirements. This met with general agreement on the understanding that "nothing should detract from the maintenance of the Army in the Middle East which was so vital" and that the needs in the Far East would be met "as far as possible" but without reducing either Russian or Middle East shipments.[50]

This Beaverbrook did with a plan to provide Australia with 325 tanks and with "India, Australia and New Zealand all receiving approximately 50% of their requirements after the arrival of the February and March allocations".[51] When, in mid-March, Beaverbrook discovered tank production was 400 more than anticipated, he immediately asked Churchill to divert all of this unexpected bonus to Russia.[52] So the supplies to Russia went on as much for political reasons as military and at great cost. In July 1942, one convoy to Russia was so heavily attacked by the Germans that ships carrying some 500 tanks and 260 aircraft were sent to the bottom of the Arctic Ocean.[53] As for Australia, Beaverbrook's plan meant that, with delivery times taken into account, the Dominion would have half her minimum requirements by mid-1942, a level of risk that Britain would not have accepted for herself. In fact by the beginning of May most of the tanks still had not arrived. Though Australia had 352 tanks on 9 May 1942, only sixty-three were of British origin, 138 were American, 149 were two-man tanks for training purposes only and the remaining two were Australian-produced prototypes.[54]

Like Menzies in 1941, Page was taken in completely by the wily Beaverbrook who gave the naive envoy the impression he had Australian needs to the fore but who quietly slipped the Dominion requirements to the bottom of the priorities.[55] When Australia successfully sought Roosevelt's support to divert to Australia machine tools originally destined for Britain, Churchill reluctantly agreed on the proviso that no further diversion from British orders would be made.[56] Beaverbrook was dispatched to Washington to put in place a munition assignment system that would prevent any allocation without British concurrence.

There was almost no sympathy for Australia's plight. Eden's Private Secretary, Oliver Harvey, expressed a view prevalent in British Government circles when he seemed to take delight in the Dominion's predicament. On 24 January, as the Japanese consolidated their hold on Rabaul, Harvey wrote in his diary of Australia being "in the greatest possible flap. Almost a panic over [the] Jap approach and our alleged failure to have helped them more and [not to have] prevented it." Describing Curtin as a "wretched second-rate man", Harvey questioned "why Australia hadn't yet got conscription, why in the past she didn't contribute more to the Royal Navy and R.A.F. and so on". He also remarked that the "clamour compares unfavourably with the relative calm of New Zealand". By 1 February, Harvey was relieved to see that Curtin had "calmed down a bit after screaming for help both to Roosevelt and to Chiang Kai Shek" and he reflected with some satisfaction that Australia had lived for a century in a fool's paradise and had now "suddenly woken up to the cold and hard fact that her very existence as a white country depends not on herself but on protection from Gt Britain".[57]

Similar thoughts were going through the mind of Sir Ronald Cross. In a letter to a Conservative colleague on 3 February, he deplored the blunt messages being sent from the Australian Government and criticised Australians as an "inferior people" with poor nerves. Cross urged London to demonstrate that Britain had begun to provide help from "the moment Pearl Harbor was attacked and that our efforts have proceeded ... unaffected by rude squeals". This would not be such an easy matter. Even Cross seemed concerned about Australia's security. He questioned Churchill's judgement in publicly announcing that the Japanese were unlikely to invade Australia, noting that this was, at worst, an invitation to mount such an invasion while, at best, it provided encouragement to complacency in Australia. From his post in Sydney, the Governor of New South Wales, Lord Wakehurst, also took issue with British complacency about Australia's security, observing to a British MP that he did not think there was

> any margin to gamble on. One must face the possibility of Singapore, Java, and New Guinea going. Then what about Darwin, New Caledonia and Fiji? The Japs might be satisfied with cutting our communications with the outside world, but the more significant Australia becomes as a base the more will it be worth their while to destroy whatever strength is gathered here.[58]

Although Australia was likely to be invaded prior to any attack on New Zealand, this diminutive Dominion reacted with uncharacteristic dismay to the British plan to provide Australia with 125 Kittyhawks while allocating only eighteen to New

Zealand. On 4 February, the New Zealand government protested to Churchill that such an allocation would leave the country defenceless. Churchill was taking grave risks with the security of both Dominions but, as before, he responded with greater sympathy to New Zealand's plea. He ordered that, since New Zealand was "so much smaller they should have priority above Australia". In the event, his Air Ministry devised a delivery plan to satisfy New Zealand without detracting from Australia.[59]

On 7 February, Churchill cabled to Roosevelt with news of Singapore where he looked forward to "severe battles", with the Japanese having to "cross a broad moat before attacking a strong fortified and still mobile force". He observed that Tobruk had held out for six months with similar inferiority in air strength. He omitted to note that in Tobruk there was no large civilian population, the troops were not demoralised and they were constantly reinforced with supplies and munitions.[60] The next night, the Japanese crossed the narrow channel from Johore to Singapore island and established a beachhead after ineffective resistance from the Australian defenders. Once the Japanese were ashore, the end was never in doubt. Churchill's hopes were dashed and the myth of the Singapore "fortress" was finished.

The reputation of Australia's troops suffered severely from their role in Singapore's defeat, and not totally without cause.[61] In Singapore's final days, several thousand Australian troops and Britain's 18th Division marched off ships in Singapore harbour in time to join their comrades for the march to Changi prison. After denying Singapore its necessary defence equipment for so long, Churchill instructed its commanders on 10 February to put aside any

> thought of saving the troops or sparing the population. The
> battle must be fought to the bitter end at all costs. The 18th
> Division has a chance to make its name in history. Commanders
> and senior officers should die with their troops. The honour of
> the British Empire and of the British Army is at stake.[62]

Five days later, Britain's General Percival walked down the road to the Japanese lines wearing his long baggy shorts and carrying a white flag to form a tableau that summed up the ignominious defeat. What it did not and could not reveal was the history of British neglect and betrayal that had made that

Surrender in Singapore: General Percival signing the unconditional
surrender of all British forces, February 1942
(AUSTRALIAN WAR MEMORIAL)

lonely march inevitable. It completed a bad fortnight for Britain.
Two German battle cruisers defiantly swept through the English
Channel on a voyage back to Germany from their haven in
France despite the best efforts of the RAF and RN to prevent
them. In the Middle East, Rommel had turned the British
advance on Tripoli into a headlong retreat in the other direction.
The Libyan port of Benghazi changed hands for the fourth
time in twelve months. The political effect in Westminster of
this succession of defeats led to fresh moves for Churchill's
demotion[63], while the strategic implications of Rommel's successes put even more pressure on the limited British effort in
the Far East.

NOTES

1 WAR CABINET CONCLUSIONS, 29 December 1941, CAB 65/20, W.M. 137 and 138(41); "Command in the South West Pacific", Report by the Chiefs of Staff, 29 December 1941, CAB 66/20, W.P. (41)307: PRO

2 Churchill's plan was much less than that mooted to Casey by Dill, which had held out the possibility of Wavell being based in Australia and of an Australian regional commander being responsible for northern Australia. CABLE NO. 1237, Casey to External Affairs Department, 29 December 1941, CRS A3300, Item 101: AA

3 WAR CABINET MINUTES, 30 December 1941, CRS A2673, Vol. 9, Minutes 1631 and 1634: AA

4 CABLE NO. 166, Curtin to Casey, 29 December 1941, CRS A3300, Item 101: AA

5 CABLE NO. 171, Curtin to Casey, 31 December 1941, CRS A3300, Item 101: AA

6 Curtin later helped to create the myth that he had initiated the withdrawal of the troops from the Middle East. In 1944 he informed a meeting of the Empire Parliamentary Association at the House of Commons that "the Australian Government asked for the return of the men who were fighting overseas". ADDRESS by Curtin, 17 May 1944, BEVN 6/21, Bevin Papers: CC

7 WAR CABINET MINUTES, 30 December 1941, CRS A2673, Vol. 9, Minute 1636: AA

8 ADVISORY WAR COUNCIL MINUTES, 31 December 1941, CRS A2682, Vol. 4, Minute 635: AA

9 ADVISORY WAR COUNCIL MINUTES, 31 December 1941, CRS A2682, Vol. 4, Minute 634; War Cabinet Minutes, 30 December 1941, CRS A2673, Vol. 9, Minutes 1631 and 1636: AA

10 CABLE JOHCU 14, Curtin to Churchill, 1 January 1942, *DAFP*, v, Doc. 247

11 CABLE WINCH 2, Churchill to Curtin, 3 January 1942, *DAFP*, v, Doc, 254

12 CABLE JOHCU 15, Curtin to Churchill, 6 January 1942, *DAFP*, v, Doc. 259

13 CABLE NO. 37, Evatt to Casey, 7 January 1942, *DAFP*, v, Doc. 260

14 CABLE WINCH 6, Churchill to Curtin, 8 January 1942, *DAFP*, v, Doc. 262

15 MORAN DIARY, 9 January 1942, in Lord Moran, p. 21

16 See PREM 3/150/1: PRO

17 WAR CABINET MINUTES, 5 January 1942, CRS A2673, Vol. X, Minute 1667: AA

18 RADIO MESSAGE 2, Department of External Affairs to David Ross, 20 January 1942, *DAFP*, v, Doc. 284; See also War Cabinet Conclusions, 1 January 1942, CAB 65/25, W.M. (42)1: PRO

19 LETTER, Cunningham to Vice Admiral Moore, 9 January 1942, ADD. MS. 52561, Cunningham Papers: BL; See also Speech by Lord Croft, Under Secretary of State for War, 15 January 1942, CRFT 2/8, Croft Papers: CC

20 "MY LIFE", Memoirs of Admiral Davis, p. 283, WDVS 1/3, Davis Papers: CC

21 CABLE NO. 50/2, Churchill to Curtin, 14 January 1942, VI/2, Ismay Papers: KC

22 CABLE JOHCU 17, Curtin to Churchill, 17 January 1942, *DAFP*, v, Doc. 278

23 CABLE WINCH 10, Churchill to Curtin, 19 January 1942, *DAFP*, v, Doc. 281

24 CABLE NO. 62/2, Churchill to Wavell, 14 January 1942, VI/2, Ismay Papers: KC

25 WAR CABINET CONCLUSIONS/CONFIDENTIAL ANNEX, 19 January 1942, CAB 65/29, W.M. (42)9: PRO; Cable No. 82/2, Churchill to Wavell, 20 January 1942, VI/2, Ismay Papers: KC; Cadogan Diary, 19 January 1942, in D. Dilks (ed.), p. 428

26 R. SHERWOOD, *The White House Papers of Harry L. Hopkins*, i, London, 1948, p. 478; Cable No. 101/2, Churchill to Wavell, 23 January 1942, VI/2, Ismay Papers: KC; See also Mackenzie King Diary, 19 January 1942: CUL; War Cabinet Conclusions/Confidential Annex, 17 January 1942, CAB 65/29, W.M. (42)8: PRO

27 ADVISORY WAR COUNCIL MINUTES, 12 January 1942, CRS A2682, Vol. 4, Minute 673: AA

28 TELEPRINTER MESSAGE, Hodgson to Secretary, Army Department, 13 January 1942; Notes of discussion with Curtin (extract), by Shedden, 14 January 1942; Cable No. 86, Casey to Commonwealth Government, 16 January 1942; all in CRS A5954, Box 287: AA; Advisory War Council Minutes, 20 January 1942, CRS A2682, Vol. 4, Minute 685: AA

29 WAR CABINET MINUTES, 25 January 1942, CRS A2673, Vol. X, Minute 1759; War Cabinet Agendum No. 11/1942, CRS A2670, 11/1942; War Cabinet Minute No. 1839, 1 February 1942, CRS A5954, Box 287; "Presence of United States Coloured Troops in Australia", CRS A2676, Item 1848; all in AA

30 PAGE DIARY, 12 January 1942, MS 1633, Folder 2345, Page Papers: NLA; H. Fysh, *Qantas at War*, Sydney, 1968, pp. 127−8

31 CABLE NO. 63, Dorman-Smith to Amery, 19 January 1942, "Secret Telegrams of Sir R. Dorman-Smith", Photo. Eur. 11.: India Office Library (hereafter IOL)

32 DEFENCE COMMITTEE (OPERATIONS) MINUTES, 21 January 1942, CAB 69/4, D.O. (42)4: PRO

33 SIR E. PAGE, pp. 326−7; Cable Johcu 16, Curtin to Churchill, 11 January 1942, *DAFP*, v, Doc. 266; See also Dalton Diary, 21 January 1942, I/26/29, Dalton Papers: LSE

34 SIR E. PAGE, pp. 326−7

35 CABLE JOHCU 19, Curtin to Churchill, 21 January 1942, *DAFP*, v, Doc. 287

36 CABLE JOHCU 21, Curtin to Churchill, 23 January 1942, *DAFP*, v, Doc 294; See also War Cabinet Minutes, 23 January 1942, CRS A2673, Vol. X, Minute 1741: AA; Cable Johcu 22, Curtin to Churchill, 27 January 1942, CRS A5954, Box 229: AA. This second cable, drafted in Curtin's absence by Forde and Evatt, buttressed the appeal of the earlier cable and pointedly reminded Churchill of the substantial Australian contribution to the RAF.

37 WAR CABINET MINUTES, 23 January 1942, CRS A2673, Vol. X, Minutes 1742−4: AA

38 WAR CABINET CONCLUSIONS/CONFIDENTIAL ANNEX, 26 January 1942, CAB 65/29, W.M. (42)11; War Cabinet Conclusions, 26 January 1942, CAB 65/25, W.M. (42)11 and 12: PRO; Note, apparently by A. V. Alexander, 26 January 1942, AVAR 5/7/12, Alexander Papers: CC

39 LETTER, Cross to Cranborne, 20 January 1942, ADD. MS. 58240, Emrys-Evans Papers: BL

40 "RELATIONS WITH AUSTRALIA", Minute, Cranborne to Churchill, 22 January 1942, CAB 66/21, W.P. (42)33: PRO

41 "CO-OPERATION WITH THE DOMINION GOVERNMENTS", Memorandum by Cranborne, 21 January 1942, CAB 66/21, W.P. (42)29: PRO

42 TIMES, London, 19 January 1942; See also ARTICLE by Menzies, Times, London, 21 January 1942; For the political situation in Westminster, see, for example, Harvey Diary, 19 January 1942, ADD. MS. 56398, Harvey Papers: BL; and Channon Diary, 20 January 1942, in R. R. James, p. 317

43 "CO-OPERATION WITH THE DOMINION GOVERNMENTS", Memorandum by Cranborne, 21 January 1942, CAB 66/21, W.P. (42)33: PRO

44 WAR CABINET CONCLUSIONS, 17 January 1942, CAB 65/25, W.M. (42)8: PRO

45 WAR CABINET CONCLUSIONS, 22 January 1942, CAB 65/25, W.M. (42)10: PRO

46 LETTER, Ismay to Harry Hopkins, 27 January 1942, IV/Hop/9, Ismay Papers: KC

47 "TANKS FOR AUSTRALIA", Notes by Hollis, 25 and 29 January 1942, Defence Committee (Operations) Memoranda, CAB 69/4, D.O. (42)7 and 8: PRO; See also BBK D/70, Beaverbrook Papers: HLRO; Joint Intelligence Sub-Committee memorandum, 25 January 1942, PREM 3/151/4: PRO

48 DEFENCE COMMITTEE (OPERATIONS) MINUTES, 30 January 1942, CAB 69/4, D.O. (42)5: PRO; See also Cadogan Diary, 30 January 1942, in D. Dilks (ed.), p. 430; "Tank Allocation", Memorandum by Brooke, 26 January 1942, PREM 3/150/4: PRO

49 "MUNITION PRODUCTION, JANUARY – JUNE 1942", Survey by Minister of Production, 3 September 1942, CAB 66/28, W.P. (42)393: PRO

50 See fn. 47

51 "TANK ALLOCATION", Note by Hollis, 31 January 1942, CAB 69/4, D.O. (42)11: PRO

52 MINUTE, Beaverbrook to Churchill, 15 March 1942, BBK D/94, Beaverbrook Papers: HLRO

53 DEFENCE COMMITTEE (OPERATIONS) MINUTES, 13 July 1942, CAB 69/4, D.O. (42)15: PRO

54 WEEKLY PROGRESS REPORT BY CHIEFS OF STAFF, 9 May 1942, CRS A2670, 28/1942: AA

55 See LETTER, Page to Beaverbrook, 4 February 1942, BBK D/408, Beaverbrook Papers: HLRO; Cable P37, Page to Curtin, 9 February 1942, CRS M103, "1942": AA

56 CABLE NO. 23A, Halifax to Foreign Office, 30 January 1942; Cable No. 2020, Foreign Office to Halifax, 6 February 1942; Cable No. 100, Curtin to Churchill, 6 February 1942; Cable No. 202, Churchill to Curtin (but drafted by Beaverbrook), 16 February 1942; all in PREM 3/44: PRO

57 HARVEY DIARY, 24, 25 January and 1 February 1942, ADD. MS. 56398, Harvey Papers: BL

58 LETTER, Cross to Emrys-Evans, 3 February 1942, ADD. MS. 58243, Emrys-Evans Papers: BL; See also Letter, Parker Leighton MP to Emrys-Evans, 10 February 1942; Letter, Lord Wakehurst, Governor of New South Wales to Emrys-Evans, 16 February 1942, ADD. MS. 58263, Emrys-Evans Papers: BL

59 See PREM 3/150/2 and PREM 3/150/6: PRO

60 CABLE NO. 193/2, Churchill to Roosevelt, 7 February 1942, VI/2, Ismay Papers: KC

61 See DAVID DAY, "Anzacs on the Run: The View from Whitehall, 1941–42"

62 CABLE NO. 206/2, Churchill to Wavell, 10 February 1942, VI/2, Ismay Papers: KC

63 HARVEY DIARY, 12, 14 and 15 February 1942, ADD. MS. 56398, Harvey Papers: BL; See also Letter, Harvey to Eden, 13 February 1942, ADD. MS. 56402, Harvey Papers: BL; Letter, Cranborne to Emrys-Evans, 13 February 1942, ADD. MS. 58263, Emrys-Evans Papers: BL

12

From Singapore to Rangoon

Mid-February to Mid-March 1942

*T*he loss of Singapore had important psychological as well
as military effects. The island had been touted in British
propaganda as being a fortress capable of withstanding attack
for many months until it could be relieved by a British fleet.
There was almost complete acceptance of this within Australia
and, in Britain, even Churchill seems to have succumbed to the
popular view of Singapore as a fortress. With its loss, Australia's
recurrent nightmare became a reality — the "Asian hordes" of
the popular literature were beating on the door and proving to
be as formidable as had been widely feared. Australia, which
had hoped to have a good war, now realised that it faced a
question of survival.

On 17 February, after two and a half years of war and more
than two months after Pearl Harbor, the Australian Cabinet
finally put the country on a total war footing. The need was
emphasised for the Dominion to "rely on its own resources as
well as the impracticability of giving substantial aid in countries
outside Australia". The War Cabinet was authorised to "take
immediate steps for the total mobilisation of all resources . . .
in order that the defence of Australia may be provided for".
The authority of the Commonwealth Government was to be
supreme over that of the State governments and the "*whole*
resources of the Commonwealth" were to be "mobilised and
utilised".[1]

Armed with this authority from the full Cabinet, the War
Cabinet set about trying to provide the means for Australia's
defence. Fighter aircraft remained a vital deficiency in the Australian armoury despite promised supplies of Kittyhawks by
Britain. On 18 February, the War Cabinet approved the production of 100 improved Wirraway aircraft as a "reinsurance against

[the] failure of fighter aircraft to arrive in sufficient numbers from overseas". This was despite advice from Burnett that the improved Wirraways could only be justified as a makeshift solution. In fact, the main rationale for the War Cabinet decision was to absorb personnel expected to become idle on completion of the previous Wirraway order.[2] The effort proved to be largely futile but the Government had no alternative. It would take years to plan the production of a new aircraft type, such as a modern fighter, by which time it could be reasonably assumed that the present emergency situation would be long over. The Dominion simply had to press ahead, producing planes it knew were unsuitable. The feeling of desperation was such that the Aircraft Production Minister suggested drafting in criminals for use in the aircraft factories. He claimed that Australia could not be too particular when she was struggling for her life, though he assured trade unions that the criminals would only be used "providing they do not come into competition with organised labor, and are not used to break down awards".[3]

Australia was dependent, as always, on the promises of its protectors being fulfilled. Experience over the previous two and a half years had given her little cause for confidence. Even now, Churchill's promise to provide Kittyhawks was proving to be much less than it appeared. He had undertaken to supply 125 Kittyhawks from British orders in America and to ask Roosevelt for an equal number from America's own allocation. There was still no confirmation that America would comply with the request, while the delivery dates of the British Kittyhawks continued to slip into the future with each cable from Washington. Meanwhile, the Japanese advance continued in the direction of Australia. As the normally unsympathetic British High Commissioner later recalled the position, "the military situation had so worsened that Australia lay open to invasion whilst not possessing the means of effective resistance".[4]

Desperate times called for desperate measures, but Australia was largely powerless to ameliorate its predicament. The years of neglect and misdirection in defence spending could not be put right overnight. Curtin's New Year message had been one attempt to do this. But it misfired, causing anger and resentment both in London and Washington. Now Evatt tried a different course with an appeal to the rising political star in

London, Stafford Cripps. Cripps was a maverick Labour MP who had gained considerable public popularity as British Ambassador to Russia. When he returned to London in the midst of the disasters of early 1942, he was seized upon as a possible panacea for Britain's military ills. Although Churchill had gained some political time with the limited Cabinet changes he made after his return from Washington, the erosion of his political support continued. For the first time, the general public were questioning his leadership. This spurred his parliamentary critics into open rebellion.[5]

Behind the scenes, Churchill's Cabinet colleagues tried to retrieve the situation by suggesting the appointment of a Defence Minister, which would satisfy many of the critics by largely removing Churchill's control over military strategy. On his own initiative, Bruce became involved in these discussions to promote Cripps into the War Cabinet as a restraining influence on Churchill.[6] Meanwhile, Evatt cabled from Canberra with his own support for Cripps in any struggle with Churchill. In this remarkable message, Evatt linked his bitter criticism of Churchill and support for Cripps with an appeal for assistance in securing Australia's urgent defence needs. "It is vital," he wrote, "that someone in England should realise that we must find greater air support from U.S. and U.K.: we are short in everything because we have poured out our resources to help the common cause everywhere in the world." There was much truth in Evatt's plaintive appeal but it was made in vain. Churchill outmanoeuvred his opponents with a more radical change to his War Cabinet that brought Cripps in but left Churchill's hand firmly fixed on the strategic control of the war. It is very likely that he was made aware of the Australian attempts to reduce his power and that it added to his feelings of enmity towards the Dominion.[7]

Increasing the pressure on the Australian Government were calls from Australian servicemen overseas who demanded to be brought back to defend their own homeland.[8] Meanwhile, within Australia, there was increasing resentment directed at Britain for removing the defensive cover under which Australia had sheltered for so long. In the immediate aftermath of Singapore's surrender, the New South Wales Governor, Lord Wakehurst, wrote to London warning of the possible boost to Australian nationalism caused by Britain's failure to defend the Dominion.

He noted that, "deep in the Australian mind is embedded the belief that, come what may, Britain would look after Australia". This had produced a basically bi-partisan approach to the Empire which now was under threat from a "recognisable but not considerable minority that is inclined to say that Australia has been let down". It was compounded by the widespread feeling that, up to that time, Britain had been fighting the war mainly with Dominion forces.[9] Wakehurst's concern was taken up in a leaflet published by the Australian Association of British Manufacturers which tried to refute what it described as "unfair and ill-informed criticism — including the 'England-let-us-down' myth".[10]

As Singapore fell, the Chiefs of Staff had reported to the Defence Committee that the Japanese would continue with their attack in two directions — into Burma and to seal the outer ring of the NEI. After that, they judged that Japan would pause for reorganisation "whether or not a subsequent attack on Australia or India had a place in Japanese plans". They alerted the Committee to the grave situation facing Allied shipping which could not cope with simultaneous movements to the Middle East and Far East and they warned that a choice would have to be made between the two theatres. Since their report was also intended for dispatch to the Dominions, Cranborne urged that the mention of such a choice should be removed from the Dominions' copies.[11]

Churchill immediately bridled at this suggestion that Britain might not be supporting the Dominions to the fullest extent possible. He claimed that Britain already had made a choice and that it was in favour of the Far East. He pointed out that Britain had denuded the Levant–Caspian front in order to protect the Far East and "would have to rely on the Russians if the Germans advanced to the Caucasus in the Spring". In fact, the Chiefs of Staff had reported that there was no risk of a German attack on that front for at least six or seven months by which time reinforcements could be sent. Certainly the choice had been made, though not in the direction Churchill claimed.[12]

Within the Far East theatre, the choices were also being made. The fall of Singapore doomed the NEI to share the same fate. In fact the Japanese had already landed in Sumatra and were quickly exploiting Allied weakness in the region. On 16 February, the Defence Committee immediately stopped all re-inforcements for Java and ordered a fall back to what were termed the "essential bases" — Burma, Ceylon, India and Australia. Among these four bases, Churchill made it clear that Australia would be the last priority. He agreed that it was "clearly urgent to reinforce Burma and Ceylon" but, so far as Australia was concerned there was no mention of urgency, just an acknowledgement that "it would be difficult to refuse the Australians' request that their divisions should return home". The Committee instructed the leading Australian division to proceed to Australia rather than Java and for the 70th British Division to proceed to Burma and Ceylon, if necessary in the shipping designated for the second AIF division preparing to leave the Middle East.[13]

Britain had already transferred most of the responsibility for Australia's naval defence to the Americans and was anxious to transfer the land defence as well. However, Churchill remained ready to use Dominion forces in defence of British interests despite the effect on Australian security. The conflict over Imperial and national interests came to a head in Burma.

On 14 February, Dorman-Smith reported from Rangoon that contingency plans for the evacuation of Rangoon were being completed, although the British forces retained hopes of avoiding such an eventuality and, despite everything, their "tails are wagging hard".[14] Churchill recognised that Australia would resist any diversion of its AIF divisions to Burma but was determined to make the attempt. He blamed Australia for the loss of the British 18th Division which he would have preferred to divert to Burma but which went into Singapore because, according to Churchill, of the Australian accusation of its possible evacuation constituting an "inexcusable betrayal".[15] Diverting an Australian division to Rangoon would compensate for that needless British loss and would assist in what he saw as the all-important defence of Burma.

Churchill had three allies in his campaign to obtain the diversion of the Australian troops. The first was Roosevelt. After the Defence Committee meeting on 16 February, Churchill informed the American President that the Australians "seem inclined to press for the return of their two divisions . . . and probably their third division, now in Palestine, will follow". Churchill confided that he "could not resist them for long" and pointed out that Rangoon and the Burma Road constituted the "most vital point at the moment" and that Wavell had "very rightly already diverted our Armoured Brigade" to Rangoon, implying that Roosevelt should pressure the Australians to do likewise, which he promptly did. In his cable to Canberra, the President proposed to send United States troops to Australia in exchange for two AIF divisions for India or Burma.[16]

Churchill's second ally was Page, who was persuaded to pressure the Australian Government to divert their troops to Burma until they could be relieved by British troops. Page informed Curtin that diverting the troops to Burma would not only keep open the road to China but would "indicate that the Australians were taking the widest co-operative attitude towards the war". He assured Curtin that Britain had promised "very substantial air reinforcements" for Burma that would avoid any repetition of the Greek, Crete and Malayan campaigns. Page's view was supported by Churchill's third ally on this question, Bruce, who also cabled to Curtin using a variety of arguments ranging from moral blackmail to spurious strategic points. He claimed that it would strengthen Australia's position in demanding similar action to meet her necessities and that British recognition of Australia's importance as a base now ensured that the Dominion could "confidently rely on the maximum support it is physically possible to get to us". On the day these cables were sent, Dorman-Smith reported to London that there was "no more than a 50% chance of holding Rangoon".[17]

Fortunately, the Australian Government had no illusions about the prospects for Rangoon. On receipt of Page's cable it immediately instructed him to ensure that the convoy should not be diverted to Burma and advised that the War Cabinet was likely to press for its return to Australia. This the War Cabinet promptly did, despite opposition from the conservative members of the Advisory War Council. It also asked for the early return of the third AIF division and for the diversion to Australia of the British armoured brigade that Wavell had diverted to Burma.[18] The fall of Singapore, even more than the attack on Pearl Harbor, had forced Australia to see through the veils of illusion produced by Imperial defence and to focus more clearly on her own defence requirements.

Despite clear instructions from the Australian Government, Page did not pass on the Dominion's decision regarding the diversion to Rangoon, arguing that Australia should reconsider its decision in view of the offer from Roosevelt.[19] Curtin again insisted that his instructions be carried out. As he explained the position to Blamey, the loss of Malaya, Singapore and the NEI had left Australia "bare" and that, because of the "unsatisfactory strength of our defences in Australia, the destination of the A.I.F. should be Australia".[20] Though Page finally and reluctantly submitted to his Government's view, Churchill appealed and made veiled threats from himself and Roosevelt for Australia to reverse its decision.[21] But Australia now was in the firing line itself.

On 19 February, over 100 Japanese planes descended on Darwin to wreak terrible havoc on Australia's northern capital and destroy its usefulness as a reinforcement base for the East Indies. The attack produced mass panic, both among the population and within the ranks of its uniformed defenders. Looting and desertions were commonplace. The panic was understandable. The town was virtually cut off from reinforcement because of its isolation, while the defenders lacked the necessary aircraft and guns to withstand the force of the Japanese attack and the widely expected follow-up invasion. However, on this occasion, the Japanese intention was limited to protecting the southern flank of its NEI invasion force.

The timing of the Darwin raid, so soon after the fall of Singapore, helped to seal the Dominion's determination to refuse Churchill's request on Burma, despite his accusing Curtin of bearing a heavy share of the responsibility for the loss of the 18th Division in Singapore and threatening that American support for Australia would be withheld if Australia did not submit to the British will. He claimed that the Australian division was the only force available to save the situation and that a "vital war emergency cannot be ignored, and troops en route to other destinations must be ready to turn aside and take part in a battle". Churchill requested an immediate reply since the ships would soon be steaming away from Rangoon and warned that, "for the sake of all interests, and above all your own interests", the Dominion should concede defeat.[22] This was good stirring nineteenth-century stuff, but it was not appropriate to twentieth-century warfare where the supply of equipment and air support was more vital than simply sending in men with rifles.

The Australian Government refused absolutely and did so in terms sure to infuriate Churchill even more. It predicted that the diversion of the 7th Division would probably lead to the diversion of the 6th and 9th Divisions as well and perhaps a "recurrence of the experiences of the Greek and Malayan campaigns". Moreover, the Dominion disputed whether the troops could be landed in Rangoon or removed at a later date in view of the Japanese air and naval superiority in the Bay of Bengal and denied that the diversion was a "reasonable hazard of war, having regard to what has gone before". It also warned of the "gravest consequences on the morale of the Australian people" in the event of another humiliating military defeat for its troops.[23]

On 20 February, the day Churchill dispatched his threatening cable to Australia, he had chaired a meeting of his Chiefs of Staff at which it was assumed that Australia would refuse to back down. Accordingly, arrangements were made to send troops from India, Cyprus and the Middle East. Despite this, Churchill dispatched his final appeal to Curtin at 9.13 pm that night, asking for "an answer immediately, as the leading ships of the convoy will soon be steaming in the opposite direction from Rangoon".[24] In fact, thirteen minutes earlier the Admiralty had ordered the diversion of the convoy to Rangoon. This was despite a Chiefs of Staff decision two days earlier that "orders regarding the diversion of the leading Australian formations to Burma could not be issued until a telegram had been received from Australia agreeing to the proposal". Malice then became mixed with liberal measures of incompetence as Downing Street failed to inform Page of the diversion despite knowing of his assurances to the Australian Government that no diversion had been made. In a note to Churchill, Ismay justified this omission by claiming that, "amidst the exceptional preoccupations of that particular day, the matter did not seem of any great consequence" since it had been "confidently anticipated that the reply of the Australian Government ... would arrive before any complications ensued".[25] The exceptional preoccupations referred to by Ismay were Churchill's changes to his War Cabinet and his preparations for a critical Commons debate on the war situation.

Australia received Churchill's cable on Saturday morning, 21 February, and did not reply until the following day. The delay probably involved a mixture of weekend muddling, incredulity at the tone of Churchill's message and indecision about how to respond. Their indecision was worsened by cables from Roosevelt urging Australia to comply with Churchill's wish and again offering to reinforce the Dominion with American troops. Roosevelt repeated Churchill's claim that the Australian division was the "only force that is available for immediate reinforcement" with the "strength to save what now seems a very dangerous situation". Moreover, the American President denied that Australia's "vital centres" were in "immediate danger". These were strong appeals that also carried the danger of further Anglo–American displeasure with the Dominion in the event of Canberra's non-compliance. But there was never any doubt, even in Churchill's mind, that Australia would refuse this repeated request. By the time the Australian refusal arrived in London, the ships had gone too far from their course to be re-diverted back to Australia without first refuelling. Churchill had overreached himself. As he later recalled, following the decision not to reinforce the NEI, he "now sought only to save Burma and India".[26] He was so desperate to achieve this that he was willing to put Australian security at greater risk and use any methods at his disposal.

On Sunday morning, 22 February, Churchill received word of Australia's predictable and justifiable refusal. Curtin also informed Roosevelt, claiming that, "with a small population in the only white man's territory south of the equator", Australia was "beset grievously" and did not have sufficient means of defence without the returning troops. Curtin's refusal to reinforce Burma was an implicit admission that he lacked faith in the Anglo–American undertakings to secure Australia and that self-reliance was the order of the day for the Dominion.[27] But such appearances were deceptive. Burma was a special case rather than the sign of a new policy.

The Australian decision was based largely on fear of another military disaster along the lines of Greece, Crete and, most potently, Singapore. Like its predecessors, the Labor Government only remained in power through the support of two independent MPs. As Evatt acknowledged in a highly critical cable to Cripps denouncing Churchill's "insolent" request:

> *The defences of this country are in such a state and are known to be such that any decision by our government to permit the A.I.F. to fight in Burma and India would cause upheaval. Rightly or wrongly the people feel that having given all the*

assistance possible to the Allied cause they have been let down badly by Churchill. Indeed his message hardly conceals his own disinclination to help us.[28]

At the same time as the War Cabinet was refusing to reinforce Burma, it was allowing Empire Air Training Scheme men to leave for Canada to complete their training.[29] In addition, of the three AIF divisions left overseas, Australia would leave the 9th Division in the Middle East for another year while, of the two then returning, a large part of the 6th Division would be left in Ceylon at Britain's request.

On hearing of Australia's refusal, Churchill defiantly informed Curtin of his unilateral diversion of the convoy. He claimed that Britain "could not contemplate that you would refuse our request, and that of the President of the United States" and noted that the required refuelling in Ceylon would "give a few days for the situation to develop, and for you to review the position should you wish to do so".[30] Meanwhile, in Rangoon, anarchy prevailed as Dorman-Smith graphically reported:

Fires are raging here and looting has begun on a considerable scale. City is as pathetic as it is smelly. Only 70 police remain and military too few to take real charge though they are now happily shooting looters and convicts which have been prematurely released without orders.[31]

Bruce and Page were aghast at Churchill's actions but counselled Australia to avoid recrimination which would, Page warned, "only do harm to our getting the maximum co-operative effort in the Allied cause".[32] But Australia was not to be calmed over a matter of such vital concern. Curtin's cable angrily denounced Churchill's high-handed treatment of the Dominion and placed on him the responsibility for the convoy's safety.[33] Churchill drafted a defiant and angry riposte which blamed the problem on Curtin's delayed reply. He not only accepted full responsibility for his action, but threatened to defend it in public if it ever became possible. He also claimed that the danger to the convoy was not appreciably increased, a claim that was disputed by Admiral Pound who advised him of the presence of Japanese submarines off Colombo where the convoy now was destined to refuel. Cooler heads than Churchill's prevailed and his draft was much toned down before it was dispatched.[34]

The evacuation of the Burmese capital was ordered by Dorman-Smith on 27 February. Although this was countermanded by Wavell, his resolve to defend Rangoon only delayed its evacuation for a week and nearly resulted in the loss of all the British forces, which barely managed to fight their way past the encircling Japanese and begin their long march to northern Burma and thence into India.[35] Churchill dispatched General Alexander to take charge of Burma's defence, admitting later that never had he "taken the responsibility for sending a general on a more forlorn hope".[36]

Dorman-Smith later absolved the Australians of any responsibility for Rangoon's fall, something that Churchill and Page never did. The Governor admitted that had the Australians arrived, "Lud knows what we'd have done with them. They might have been thrown straight in 'from ship to Jap' — with disastrous results. They'd have died gallantly or would have been rounded up by the Japs, as so many of our own and Indian troops were." In contrast, Page made the serious and unwarranted allegation in his memoirs that Australia's failure to send its troops to Burma effectively condemned the prisoners of war at Singapore to three and a half years of incarceration. In fact, had the Australian Government acted according to his wishes, it would have thrown thousands more Australians into the hands of the Japanese.[37]

Although Churchill accorded Burma a higher priority than Australia within the Far Eastern theatre, his concern for Burma still fell far short of his concern for the struggle against Germany. In fact, at least some of the impetus for his attempt to have the Australians diverted to Burma arose from his desire to buttress China in order to please the Americans and have them leave their commitment to the European struggle undisturbed. During his conflict with Australia over Burma, Churchill revealed his order of priorities quite clearly when his Chiefs of Staff proposed that seventy-two Hurricanes be taken from Russia's allotment and be sent to India and Burma. In support of their proposal, the Chiefs remarked that the Russians did not seem very much to value Britain's monthly deliveries of aircraft. Despite this, on 25 February, Churchill and Eden successfully and strongly opposed any suggestion that the supplies to Russia be interfered with. In fact, on 16 March, Churchill proposed the transfer from the Middle East to Russia of fifteen RAF squadrons after learning that Auchinleck planned to remain on the defensive there for several months.[38]

In his cables to Canberra, Churchill had consistently deprecated the chances of a Japanese invasion of Australia. However, his private view was less sanguine. On 24 February, he had confided to the King that "Burma, Ceylon, Calcutta and Madras in India and part of Australia may fall into enemy hands". That same day, Churchill supported an Admiralty plan for Dutch naval units to be evacuated from Java to Ceylon rather than have them "tucked away in Australia".[39] It was within Japan's capacity to invade the Dominion; Churchill merely thought its strategic priorities would direct Tokyo in other directions, principally towards China. But Australia had to provide for the other contingency.

On 23 February, eight days after the fall of Singapore, Evatt emphasised the Australian peril when he authorised Casey to commandeer shipping space on the American–Australia route to accommodate urgently needed items of war equipment and urged him to purchase supplies regardless of cost. Casey was ordered "not to spare any trouble in securing the equipment without which this country may be almost helpless against attack".[40] Evatt's cables were becoming increasingly hysterical in his attempts to overcome the decade of neglect of Australia's defence. He was convinced that Churchill was motivated by political antipathy towards the Labor Party and that Australia's overseas representatives were conspiring to keep the Dominion defenceless.

After having to fight so hard to prevent Australian troops being wasted in Burma, the Australian Government was requested to leave many of them in Colombo where a Japanese attack was also anticipated. At the same time, Whitehall expected that Darwin and perhaps Perth would be overrun by the Japanese. Though the British Chiefs of Staff admitted that Australia was "insecure", they were prepared to divert part of the returning AIF divisions to protect British territories en route. In their view, the vital south-eastern corner of Australia was not in immediate danger. Australian military opinion was in substantial agreement with this view. On 4 February, the Commander of the Home Forces, Lieutenant General Mackay, urged the Government not to send reinforcements out of the Brisbane—Sydney—Melbourne triangle. This so-called "Brisbane Line" effectively left the bulk of Australia open to Japanese attack while concentrating the Dominion's limited forces on the protection of the country's heartland. It was a sensible response to a desperate situation. As the British Chiefs of Staff later admitted, the Japanese had up to eleven divisions available for a possible attack on Australia. Even with the concentration of her forces, Australia had only five divisions in the Brisbane— Sydney—Melbourne triangle. If their equipment and air support were taken into consideration, the situation was much worse.[41]

It was vital that all available Australian troops be concentrated in the defence of their homeland. The Government's intransigence over Burma had this aim at least partly in mind. Now, while the heat of that dispute was still white-hot, Canberra faced a similar request from London to off-load the returning troops before they reached Australia. Because of Churchill's unilateral diversion of the Australian convoy, the ships had to call at Ceylon for refuelling. This placed the lightly escorted ships in greater peril; moreover, part of the force was requested to remain temporarily in Ceylon to meet the possible danger of a Japanese attack. Incredibly, this suggestion arose from Australia's own representatives.

On 23 February, the British War Cabinet met to consider Curtin's insistence on the return of the AIF. Page expressed his personal regret at the Australian decision and suggested that the Dominion troops be used to garrison Ceylon "for the present". Acknowledging that Churchill might find it difficult to propose such a plan so soon after the Burma dispute, Page offered to propose it himself "provided that the Chiefs of Staff furnished him with an appreciation, which he could quote, setting out the importance of this course". Despite advice from the Chiefs that such a diversion would entail a stay of at least four to six weeks, Page persisted with his offer. The War Cabinet expected a hostile reaction from Canberra and carefully stipulated that Page make the suggestion on his own responsibility.[42]

In recommending the AIF's retention in Ceylon, Page had the full support of Bruce. While Page was meeting with the

War Cabinet, Bruce was busily cabling to Curtin to prepare the ground for Page's proposal. According to the Australian High Commissioner, the security of Burma was "important" but the retention of Ceylon was "vital". He admitted Australia's own defence deficiencies and that the returning AIF provided the most immediate source of reinforcement for the Dominion. However, Bruce argued, self-reliance was not a possible option for Australia. Only with Anglo–American assistance and co-operation could Australia be protected from Japan. He claimed that such assistance would be increased by Australia adopting a compliant attitude on the use of its troops, there being a "vast difference between the help given because of necessity and that afforded out of gratitude and good feeling".[43]

Both Bruce and the Australian Government were well aware that any good feeling Churchill may have had towards Australia had been progressively hardened by the succession of in-creasingly acrimonious disputes during the previous ten months. But Bruce's argument may have had some force with regard to Washington, where Canberra expected a well of sympathy might exist from which it could draw. The Australian Labor politicians felt closer to Roosevelt's New Deal politics than Churchill's conservatism and believed America's strategic interest lay more in the Pacific than the Atlantic. They blamed Churchill for turning American attention towards Europe which they mistakenly believed was against Washington's natural inclination.

On 24 February, Page cabled his own argument for the retention of the 7th Division in Ceylon. Although the Chiefs had stipulated a stay of *at least* four to six weeks, Page suggested to Canberra that it would involve a stay of four to six weeks *at the latest*. He also repeated a list of largely spurious reasons by the Chiefs of Staff why such retention would be in the Australian interest.[44] Curtin was aghast at this further evidence of Page according higher priority to the defence of British colonies than the defence of his own homeland. As he scathingly com-mented, "there are numerous geographical centres where an A.I.F. or any other Division would be useful" but, from Australia's viewpoint, "there is none east of Suez of greater importance than Australia". Curtin informed Page that he had received the impression that "we are going to have difficulty in getting the A.I.F. back to Australia" which is why he was stressing the importance of its return for the Dominion's defence and the importance of Australia's security as a base for a future offensive against Japan. Vainly, he instructed Page to "press this most strenuously".[45]

Evatt adopted a similar tone in a corresponding cable to Bruce, although he felt Bruce's guilt was mitigated by his long absence from Australia and his consequent ignorance of the Australian defence position. As for Page, Evatt confided to Bruce that he "seems to have acted in (direct) opposition to his instructions and matters can hardly continue in this way". Evatt must have realised that both of Australia's representatives were culpable but perhaps intended to drive a wedge between them in the hope that Bruce, at least, would pay heed to his instructions and not add to Australia's problems.[46] However, Bruce was unrepentant.

Rather than retreating on the question of retaining the AIF, Bruce simply approached the British Government in an attempt to apply more pressure on Canberra. Realising that Churchill's word no longer carried much weight in Canberra, Bruce appealed to Attlee and Cripps to help convince Australia that there was a "real appreciation [in London] of the defence of Australia as a great base in the Pacific". According to Bruce, Britain needed to set out a "definite plan for the reinforcement of Australia" which would allay Australia's anxiety and allow for its continued commitment to Imperial defence.[47] Although no such plan was forthcoming, Bruce still went ahead to argue for the retention of Australian troops in Ceylon. Citing the opinion of Cripps, he cabled to Curtin on 27 February with the tenuous proposition that Ceylon was "not only essential to our whole position but was of the utmost importance in relation to the defence of Australia". Cripps asked for the 7th Division to remain in Ceylon for thirty days, claiming that Australia would create thereby "an atmosphere of goodwill towards her that would have a very real value in overcoming in the United States the difficulties in the way of sending adequate assistance to Australia in men and equipment". In fact, according to General Wavell, Britain's Commander in Chief in India, Ceylon could not be secured by additional troops but only by naval and air units. In his view, pouring in more troops "to provide against large scale invasion would involve locking up troops which could be better used in offensive operations elsewhere". Wavell was probably right but Australia never heard his opinion.[48]

After all the defiant talk of previous cables, Australia suddenly relented on 2 March and agreed to Australian troops helping to garrison Ceylon. However, it would not be the troops of the 7th Division, some of whom were then in Ceylon, but two brigades of the 6th Division that were about to board ship in the Middle East for their return to Australia. The Dominion's about-turn remains a puzzle. Perhaps the combined pressure of London and Washington simply became too much to bear. Canberra had already alienated Churchill and was anxious not to upset Cripps in a similar manner, particularly since Cripps' political path was being widely seen as ending in Downing Street. The Dominion was also intent on nurturing its relationship with Washington and feared the apparent influence that Churchill had over Roosevelt. By agreeing to the brigades of the 6th Division, Australia at least was assured that she would obtain the use of the 7th Division and the other brigade of the 6th Division. It should also have reduced the total time the troops would be in Ceylon before the arrival of the British reinforcements. Canberra also made its agreement conditional on the two brigades being "escorted to Australia as soon as possible after their relief" and for the 9th Division being returned from the Middle East "under proper escort as soon as possible". In fact, as soon as Australian agreement was cabled to London, Churchill instructed his Chiefs of Staff to ensure that the two brigades stay in Ceylon for seven or eight weeks and that "the shipping should be handled so as to make this convenient and almost inevitable". The Chiefs did even better than this, ensuring that the two brigades of the 6th Division did not leave Ceylon until mid-July in a convoy of eleven ships escorted by just one British cruiser and an armed merchant cruiser, an inadequate level of protection for such an important convoy.[49]

The Australian Chiefs of Staff had advised Curtin that the temporary retention of the troops in Ceylon would not expose Australia to undue risk since, to invade Australia, Japan first had to secure possession of New Guinea and New Caledonia.[50] This advice was tendered on the assumption that the troops would be in Ceylon for four to six weeks, as promised by Page and Churchill, until the British 70th Division arrived to take their place. In fact, it took the Australian troops six weeks just to unload the equipment from their ships in Colombo's harbour, which had been deserted by its normal labour force. Also, as soon as Churchill had secured the commitment of the troops, he cabled to Wavell offering two of the three brigades of the 70th Division for use in India or Burma.[51] The stay of the Australian troops was thereby extended for the duration of the threat to Ceylon. They did not arrive back in Australia until August 1942, too late to be used in the crucial battle to save Port Moresby; moreover, their absence had increased the Australian dependence on United States forces. The wisdom of their use in Ceylon was also disputed by Wavell and Somerville. The Australians were meant to defend the British naval bases at Colombo and Trincomalee but, as Wavell again advised on 7 March, the real defence of the bases could only be provided by adequate air and naval forces, both of which were lacking in Ceylon. In fact, on 18 March, the Admiralty instructed the Eastern Fleet commander not to engage his scratch force with any superior Japanese fleet that might care to attack Ceylon. Instead, he was to "accept [the] possible loss of Ceylon with [the] object of preserving [the] fleet in order to defend our communications to [the] Middle East and India".[52]

While Britain and Australia were locked in their cabled combat, the real war was proceeding at an alarming pace. By the end of February, the Japanese thrust into Burma had reached Rangoon and would soon push British forces on a long march northwards until they were finally expelled across the border into India. With Singapore in Japanese hands, the southerly thrust of the Japanese moved on to capture Java and the rest of the NEI. On 18 February the Pacific War Council in London recommended that no more reinforcements be sent to the NEI and that the mixed garrison of Dutch, British and Australian troops stay and fight it out with the Japanese.[53] The Australian Government stoutly opposed this plan, preferring to rescue their troops in an orderly evacuation rather than mount a futile defence against impossible odds. This produced another conflict between London and Canberra.

The decision not to reinforce Java also meant the end for Wavell's short-lived command of that region. His staff quickly packed up their equipment to make a timely withdrawal.

Wavell's Chief of Staff, General Pownall, blasted the Australian Government for their "damnable attitude" in demanding a similar withdrawal for some 3000 men of the AIF who had arrived by fast ship ahead of their other comrades from the Middle East. Despite orders that the AIF was not to be sent to Java, Wavell ordered their disembarkation. When the Australian Government tried unsuccessfully to have their troops evacuated, Pownall complained in his diary of the Australians having been

> *shown up in their true colours. Not so much the troops and commanders themselves . . . as their Government, actuated presumably by a mixture of public opinion in Australia and common funk. Winston had little enough use for them before, especially after they demanded to be relieved at Tobruk, to everyone's great inconvenience. He'll be madder still now . . . If the Australians weren't so damn well pleased with themselves all the time, and so highly critical of everyone else, it would be a bit better. But they are the most egotistical conceited people imaginable.*[54]

In the event, the troops remained in Java where they were captured by the Japanese after the surrender on 12 March.

Australia had hoped to use the island chain of the NEI as a means of fencing off the Japanese advance and preventing the feared yellow man from gaining a foothold in Australia. From London, Darwin was seen as an untenable Allied base once the Japanese began moving through the NEI. But, from Canberra, it was proclaimed as being essential to Australian security. This doubtful strategic claim was presumably motivated by the over-whelming desire to keep the Australian continent inviolate, no matter how distant the outpost. The 1930s had seen punitive expeditions against the black owners of northern Australia. It was unthinkable that a territory so recently robbed from the black man should now fall to the yellow man. As Curtin had inaccurately claimed to Roosevelt, it was seen as being the only white man's country in the southern hemisphere.

The Japanese were not the only threat to Australia's warped vision of racial purity. The Dominion was also faced with the predicament of harbouring 580 Chinese miners, evacuated from Nauru and Ocean Islands where they had been employed in the extraction of phosphate for the ultimate benefit of Australian farmers. On 2 March, the Australian Government decided to send them all to mine tungsten in the harsh conditions of central Australia. Isolated by hundreds of kilometres of desert from the populated east coast, these luckless evacuees might have done better being captured by the Japanese. Their Australian rescuers forced them to work for £2 per month, segregated from white miners in order to "avoid any suggestion of exploitation of cheap labour for private interests".[55]

By early March, after just three months of war with Japan, the invasion of Australia was being freely predicted. Some observers, mostly from a London vantage point, contended that the Japanese invasion would be limited to the north and possibly the west of Australia. Closer to the island continent, the view was rather different. On 8 March, the commander of Britain's Eastern fleet, Admiral Somerville, was advised by his deputy, Vice Admiral Willis, that an attempted Japanese invasion of Australia "must be expected" once the NEI and New Guinea had been mopped up. Willis expected the total occupation of the Dominion would be a gradual affair depending on the speed with which Japan could consolidate any initial invasion and build up sufficient forces to complete the occupation. He complained of the "very leisurely" rate at which the Eastern theatre was being reinforced. Like some other British officers, Willis had trouble reconciling the wartime neglect of the Far East with the pre-war priority it had been accorded, at least on paper. As for Ceylon, where Willis was based, an invasion of that island was seen as unlikely since the Japanese would have difficulty supplying any invasion force while Britain retained control of the nearby Indian mainland.[56] This accurate view of the threat from Japan was shared by the Australian Chiefs of Staff who set out the likely Japanese timetable as being to attack Port Moresby in mid-March, Darwin in early April, followed closely by New Caledonia and, some time in May, an attack upon the east coast of Australia.[57]

This was a timetable to which Churchill gave no credence. Both his political position and strategic priorities depended on a more limited view of Japanese capabilities. When his own Chiefs of Staff put together a gloomy view of British propects against Japan, Churchill unsuccessfully tried to prevent it being shown to the Dominions. It held out little hope of immediate relief in the Pacific and admitted that Australia was "insecure" and dependent on America for reinforcements. It was important to Churchill that the Dominions be kept in the dark on the present pessimistic position in the hope that a "very different picture and mood may be with us in a couple of months". His own view of the situation was probably best summed up in a cable to Roosevelt on 5 March when he confided that it was "not easy to assign limits to the Japanese aggression. All can be retrieved in 1943 or 1944, but meanwhile there are very hard forfeits to pay."[58] Meanwhile, Churchill steadfastly resisted suggestions that Russia relieve the pressure in the Pacific by attacking the Japanese flank.[59] Churchill had led the Empire onto thin ice and watched as each of its territories sank through the cracks produced by his "Germany first" strategy. Australia saw the cracks and tried to skate around them but remained only dimly aware of the cause.

Under the new strategic plan for the Pacific following the demise of Wavell's command, Australia was to be put largely in the care of the United States. At the same time, Australia was expected to communicate with Washington through the medium of the Pacific War Council in London. It was not good enough, and the Dominion was determined to create a proper Allied council in Washington that would circumvent the influence of Churchill and provide direct access to Roosevelt. This, together with the urgent need to accelerate the flow of reinforcements of men and supplies, impelled the Australian Government to dispatch Evatt on a desperate mission to Washington and London. The decision to send Evatt was hastened by the despair felt in Canberra at the performance of their representatives in the two Allied capitals. In advising Churchill of the mission, Curtin explained that Evatt was being sent "so that there can be direct Ministerial representation of the Government by a Minister who is fully familiar with its present problems and views thereon".[60]

In varying degrees, Bruce, Casey and Page all accepted the dictates of the "Germany first" strategy and played down the urgency of Australia's position. Page had ignored the Dominion's request for the return of the 9th Division, suggesting to Churchill that it be retained in the Middle East while its place in Australia was taken by American troops untested in battle. Churchill willingly grasped this suggestion and thrust it upon Curtin.[61] At the same time, Page opposed the plan for Australia to become the responsibility of America. In his memoirs he recalled how the aim of Curtin and Evatt had been to obtain "immediate help without regard for the future consequence of co-operation" while, in stark contrast, he was "prepared to stake everything to keep the Empire intact".[62] There was apparently no recognition by Page that the interests of Australia and the Empire might clash.

As the strategic control of the war against Japan gradually shifted to Washington, Casey's post as Australian Minister to the United States remained crucial. On 12 March, the eve of Evatt's departure for the United States, Churchill dropped a bombshell on Canberra with his proposal to remove Casey from Washington and appoint him as British Minister in the Middle East. The origins of this incredible plan lay in the political turmoil in Westminster where there was a persistent demand for greater involvement by the Dominions in Imperial decision-making. Despite the Cabinet changes of February, Churchill was still being hard pressed by political critics who used the demand for Imperial involvement as a means of diluting his power over policy.[63]

By offering the Cairo appointment to Casey, Churchill managed to neutralise the demand of his critics within Westminster, as well as Canberra's call for an Australian to be made a permanent member of the War Cabinet. The side benefits were also considerable. It opened up an Australian post in Washington which Churchill suggested that Menzies should fill. Menzies had kept a high public profile despite being deposed as Prime Minister and had continued his attempts to transfer his political talents to Westminster.[64] Removing Casey might also divert Menzies from his primary political ambition. There was the additional advantage to Churchill that Australia would lose an able representative with a wide circle of contacts at the very time that the Dominion was desperate for friends in Washington. Although Casey, like Bruce and Page, supported the "Germany first" strategy, he was more concerned than his colleagues in London with the security of Australia. He was critical of the planned reinforcement for the Far East and had exchanged harsh words with Churchill in Washington. On every point, Casey was perfect for Churchill's purposes and the British Prime Minister was determined to have him despite attempts by Curtin to prevent the appointment. Before long, this dispute would cause all the bitterness built up over the previous months to burst upon the public stage.[65]

It was ironic that Australia's first major battle after the loss of Singapore should have been a battle of words with Britain over Burma. By their resolute determination to resist the diversion of their troops to Rangoon, the Australian Government had struck a blow for self-reliance. But the troops were not all home. The 6th and 7th Divisions were strung out across the Indian Ocean in poorly protected convoys from Suez to Fremantle, while the 9th remained in Palestine. Two brigades of the 6th Division were destined to be off-loaded in Ceylon when they would have been better employed defending their homeland. The first American division had still not arrived in Australia and the supply of aircraft and munitions had not increased in line with the mounting threat of invasion. The Japanese attack on Darwin and their capture of Rabaul revealed that Japan could soon be in a position to spring an invasion on the still defenceless Dominion.

Notes

1 CABINET MINUTES, 17 February 1942, CRS A2703, Vol. 1[C]: AA
2 "AIRCRAFT PRODUCTION POLICY: Proposal to build Wirraway-Interceptors", 13 February 1942; "Wirraway Interceptors", Report by Burnett, 16 February 1942; War Cabinet Minute No. 1908, 18 February 1942; all in CRS A5954, Box 216: AA
3 HERALD, Melbourne, 18 February 1942
4 LETTER, Cross to Cranborne, 13 April 1944, RC/4/23, Cross Papers: IWM; See also CRS A5954, Box 229: AA
5 KING DIARY, 16 February 1942, in C. King, p. 158; See also David Day, "An Undiplomatic Incident: S. M. Bruce and the Moves to Curb Churchill, February 1942", Journal of Australian Studies, November 1986
6 TALK WITH CRIPPS, 16 February 1942, CRS M100, "February 1942": AA
7 CABLE (DRAFT), Evatt to Cripps, 16 February 1942, DAFP, v, Doc. 335
8 See CRS A1608, A.C. 45/1/1: AA
9 LETTER, Wakehurst to Emrys-Evans, 16 February 1942, ADD. MS. 58243, Emrys-Evans Papers: BL
10 "THIS RIDDLE, THIS PARADOX, THIS ENGLAND!", four-page leaflet by Australian Association of British Manufacturers, RC/1/56, Cross Papers: IWM
11 "THE SHIPPING SITUATION", Memorandum by Chiefs of Staff, 13 February 1942, CAB 69/4, D.O. (42)16: PRO
12 DEFENCE COMMITTEE (OPERATIONS) MINUTES, 16 February 1942, CAB 69/4, D.O. (42)6: PRO
13 IBID.

14 CABLE NO. 160, Dorman-Smith to Amery, 14 February 1942, "Secret Telegrams of Sir R. Dorman-Smith", Photo. Eur. 11: IOL

15 WAR CABINET CONCLUSIONS, 16 February 1942, CAB 65/25, W.M. (42)21: PRO

16 CABLE NO. 241/2, Churchill to Roosevelt, 16 February 1942, VI/2, Ismay Papers: KC; Cable No. 299, Casey to External Affairs Department, 17 February 1942, *DAFP*, v, Doc. 340

17 CABLE P44, Page to Curtin, 18 February 1942, CRS M103, "1942": AA; Sir E. Page, p. 332; Cable No. 31, Bruce to Curtin, 18 February 1942, *DAFP*, v, Doc. 344; Cables No. 177, No. 180 and one unnumbered, Dorman-Smith to Amery, 18 and 19 February 1942, "Secret Telegrams of Sir R. Dorman-Smith", Photo. Eur. 11: IOL

18 CABLES NO. 27 AND NO. 28, Curtin to Page, 18 and 19 February 1942, *DAFP*, v. Docs 343 and 345; War Cabinet Minutes, 18 and 19 February 1942, CRS A2673, Vol. X, Minutes 1896 and 1914: AA

19 CABLE NO. 228, Cranborne to Curtin, 19 February 1942, and Cable P47, Page to Curtin, 19 February 1942, *DAFP*, v, Docs 346–7

20 CABLE NO. 30, Curtin to Page, 20 February 1942, and Cable No. 8, Curtin to Blamey, 20 February 1942, *DAFP*, v, Docs 348–9

21 See *DAFP*, v, Docs 352–6

22 CABLE NO. 233, Churchill to Curtin, 20 February 1942, *DAFP*, v, Doc. 352

23 CABLE NO. 136, Curtin to Churchill, 22 February 1942, *DAFP*, v, Doc. 357; Though this cable was signed by Curtin, it may have been composed by Evatt. On 21 February, Cross informed London that although Curtin agreed with the Australian decision, he was not involved in it because of illness. Cross suggested that Churchill should try again to change the decision. Cable No. 160, Cross to Dominions Office, 21 February 1942, PREM 3/63/4: PRO

24 See fn. 22

25 NOTE, Ismay to Churchill, 23 February 1942; Letter, Page to Churchill, 22 February 1942, PREM 3/63/4: PRO; Chiefs of Staff Committee Minutes, 18 February 1942, PREM 3/154/3: PRO

26 *DAFP*, v, Docs 353–6; W. S. Churchill, iv, p. 128

27 *DAFP*, v, Docs 357–9

28 CABLE, Evatt to Cripps, 22 February 1942, *DAFP*, v, Doc. 360

29 See CRS A5954, Box 236: AA

30 CABLE NO. 241, Churchill to Curtin, 22 February 1942, *DAFP*, v, Doc. 362

31 CABLE, Dorman-Smith to Amery, 22 February 1942, "Secret Telegrams of Sir R. Dorman-Smith," Photo. Eur. 11: IOL

32 CABLE NO. 1613, Page to Curtin, 22 February 1942, and Cable No. 33A, Bruce to Curtin, 23 February 1942, *DAFP*, v, Docs 364–5

33 CABLE NO. 139, Curtin to Churchill, 23 February 1942, *DAFP*, v, Doc. 366

34 DRAFT AND FINAL COPY OF CABLE, Churchill to Curtin, 23 February 1942, PREM 3/63/4: AA

35 CABLES NO. 104 AND NO. 105, Dorman-Smith to Amery, 27 February 1942, "Secret Telegrams of Dorman-Smith," Photo. Eur. 11: IOL

36 W. S. CHURCHILL, iv, p. 146

37 "AUSTRALIAN WAR HISTORY", undated note by Dorman-Smith, MSS. Eur. E.215/1, Dorman-Smith Papers: IOL; For Churchill's view, see W. S. Churchill, iv, pp. 136−48; For Page's view, see Sir E. Page, pp. 341−2

38 WAR CABINET CONCLUSIONS/CONFIDENTIAL ANNEX, 25 February 1942, CAB 65/29, W.M. (42)24: PRO; M. Gilbert, *Road to Victory*, p. 76; Cable No. 66094, Churchill to Wavell, 23 January 1942, PREM 3/154/1: PRO

39 KING GEORGE VI DIARY, 24 February 1942, cited in M. Gilbert, *Road to Victory*, pp. 66−7; Minute, Pound to Churchill 24 February 1942, PREM 3/163/8: PRO

40 CABLE NO. 227, Evatt to Casey, 23 February 1942; Cable No. 349, Casey to Evatt, 24 February 1942; Cable No. 240 (extract), Evatt to Casey, 25 February 1942; all in CRS A5954, Box 229: AA

41 "FAR EAST APPRECIATION", Report by the Chiefs of Staff, 21 February 1942, CAB 66/22, W.P. (42)94: PRO; War Cabinet Agendum No. 96/1942, CRS A2670, 96/1942: AA

42 WAR CABINET CONCLUSIONS/CONFIDENTIAL ANNEX, 23 February 1942, CAB 65/29, W.M. (42)23: PRO

43 CABLE NO 34A, Bruce to Curtin, 23 February 1942, *DAFP*, v, Doc. 369

44 CABLE P50, Page to Curtin, 24 February 1942, *DAFP*, v, Doc. 372

45 CABLE NO. 33, Curtin to Page, 25 February 1942, *DAFP*, v, Doc. 374

46 CABLE SL1, Evatt to Bruce, [rec'd] 25 February 1942, *DAFP*, v, Doc. 375

47 TALK WITH ATTLEE, 26 February 1942, *DAFP*, v, Doc. 377

48 CABLE NO. 36A, Bruce to Curtin, 27 February 1942, *DAFP*, v, Doc. 382; Cable No. 4231/G, Wavell to Chiefs of Staff, 28 February 1942, PREM 3/154/2: PRO

49 CABLE NO. 160, Curtin to Churchill, 2 March 1942, *DAFP*, v, Doc. 385; G. H. Gill, *Royal Australian Navy 1939−1945*, ii, p. 185; Minute D. 44/2, Churchill to Ismay, 4 March 1942, PREM 3/154/2: PRO

50 "DEFENCE OF CEYLON", Report by the Chiefs of Staff, 28 February 1942, CRS A2670, 106/1942: AA

51 CABLE INDIA NO. 10577/C, Wavell to Brooke, 30 April 1942, CAB 66/24, W.P. (42)184: PRO; Cable No. 320/6, Churchill to Wavell, 4 March 1942, VI/2, Ismay Papers: KC

52 G. H. GILL, ii, pp. 12−13; S. Roskill, *The War at Sea 1939−1945*, ii, p. 22; Cable No. 0228A, Admiralty to S.O. Force "V", 18 March 1942, PREM 3/233/1−4: PRO

53 CABLE P43, Page to Curtin, 18 February 1942, *DAFP*, v, Doc. 341

54 POWNALL DIARY, 25 February 1942, in B. Bond (ed.), ii, pp. 90−1; For a detailed discussion of the Java episode, see D. M. Horner, pp. 162−7

55 See CRS A2670, 126/1942: AA

56 "POLICY AND STRATEGY IN THE EASTERN THEATRE", by Willis, 8 March 1942, WLLS 5/5, Willis Papers: CC

57 CRS A2670, 143/1942: AA

58 MINUTE M.71/2, Churchill to Attlee, 4 March 1942, PREM 4/43B/2: PRO; Cable No. 323/2, Churchill to Roosevelt, 5 March 1942, VI/2, Ismay Papers: KC; Cable No. Z31, UK Dominions Office to Cross, 2 March 1942, *DAFP*, v, Doc. 386

59 CADOGAN DIARY, 1 March 1942, in D. Dilks (ed.), p. 438
60 LETTER, Curtin to Evatt, 11 March 1942, and Cable Johcu 24, Curtin to Churchill, 13 March 1942, CRS A5954, Box 474: AA
61 TALK WITH CRIPPS, 5 March 1942, and Cable SL 4, Evatt to Bruce, 8 March 1942, CRS M100, "March 1942": AA; War Cabinet Conclusions/ Confidential Annex, 9 March 1942, CAB 65/29, W.M. (42)32: PRO; Cable No. 359/2, Churchill to Curtin, 10 March 1942, VI/2, Ismay Papers: KC
62 SIR E. PAGE, p. 356
63 CABLE WINCH 11, Churchill to Curtin, 12 March 1942, *DAFP*, v, Doc. 406; Cadogan Diary, 5 March 1942, in D. Dilks (ed.), p. 440; David Day, *Menzies and Churchill at War*, ch. 15; David Day, "An Undiplomatic Incident: S. M. Bruce and the Moves to Curb Churchill, February 1942"; Channon Diary, 20 February 1942, in R. R. James, p. 322; King Diary, 25 February 1942, in C. King, p. 160; Harvey Diary, 27 February 1942, ADD. MS. 56398, Harvey Papers: BL; Dalton Diary, 5 March 1942, I/26/93, Dalton Papers: LSE
64 See PREM 4/50/15: PRO
65 CASEY DIARY, 4, 6 and 18 January 1942, in R. G. Casey, *Personal Experience*, pp. 83, 86; Letter, Casey to Evatt, 17 January 1942, CRS A1608, D.41/1/5: AA; Cable Johcu 25, Curtin to Churchill, (rec'd) 13 March 1942, *DAFP*, v, Doc. 409

The Struggle over Strategy

13 March to 30 April 1942

*F*rom January to June 1942, Japanese naval power held sway in the Pacific. Australia's defence was its distance and its size. Although weakly defended, it was separated from Japan by 6000 kilometres of Pacific Ocean, while the size of the country ensured that a major invasion force would be necessary to subdue and hold it. Though an invasion of Australia had not been an initial Japanese aim, their sequence of easy victories culminating in the fall of Singapore caused them to include among their next objectives the isolation of Australia from America, with the eventual possibility of a total occupation. Meanwhile, the Allied strategy remained one of concentrating on the defeat of Germany. This had serious implications for Australia in the circumstances of March 1942.

Although America had plunged into the war alongside Britain, it would be many months before she could provide much support for Britain's floundering Empire. Meanwhile, everything seemed to be going wrong. The crucial battle of the Atlantic, on which ultimate success against Germany depended, had turned against the Allies after the German U-boats changed their codes and thereby ended for a time Britain's ability to intercept their messages and anticipate their moves. Attacks on Allied shipping increased immediately and dramatically. In Russia, the prospect of a massive German summer offensive led Churchill to fear the possibility of Stalin making a separate peace with Hitler. In the Middle East, Auchinleck's offensive at the end of 1941 had been repelled by Rommel with both armies retiring behind defensive lines to build up their strength for a decisive battle.

With the Russians facing an imminent German offensive, Churchill found the idea of a four-month lull in the Middle East intolerable, particularly as the Axis air attacks on the

British island of Malta increased to such a level as to threaten its existence. Malta was a thorn that Rommel was eager to extract from his flank. With its capture, his supplies and re-inforcements could flow to the Middle East uninterrupted. Churchill was desperate to retain Malta and push Auchinleck into resuming offensive action against Rommel. These were his dominant military concerns during March 1942. Meanwhile, Australia remained at risk so long as Japan maintained sufficient naval power to mount an invasion. It was Australia's urgent task to impress upon Allied leaders the importance of the Dominion's survival. With all the strategic areas competing for attention and with the overriding Allied commitment to defeat Germany first, this was a difficult task and one that was made almost impossible by the vitriol flowing freely between Canberra and London. Nevertheless, it was Evatt's primary aim when he left Sydney for Washington and London on 13 March.

Although Evatt was keen to elevate Australia's priority in the strategic plans of Britain and America, he remained unaware of the actual Anglo−American agreement to defeat Germany before taking the offensive against Japan. This agreement had been reached at the series of meetings in Washington between Churchill and Roosevelt in the aftermath of the attack on Pearl Harbor and was enshrined in a top secret document coded as "W.W.I." and by which it was subsequently known. Although it is clear that the Australian Government had an understanding of the general outline of the "Germany first" policy, it also appears clear that the Government presumed that the force and suddenness of the Japanese attack had thrown the accepted Allied strategy into the melting pot.[1]

Churchill's conference in Washington with Roosevelt, code-named Arcadia, confirmed the strategic priorities reached at the tentative Anglo−American staff conversations of early 1941. It is clear that the terms of "W.W.I." were never trans-mitted to the Australian Government in early 1942, that Canberra was unaware that formal agreement had been reached on a joint strategy and that Australia's urgent pleas for im-mediate assistance would be answered in accordance with the terms of the agreement. As late as May 1942, the Australian Minister to China reported that he had learned of the "Ger-many first" policy from an old newspaper article and com-plained of the lack of any information on it from the External Affairs Department in Canberra.[2] Nevertheless, it seems clear

that Curtin and Evatt were aware that the weight of official
Allied opinion favoured such a policy and that Australia would
have to exert a supreme effort to ensure an adequate level of
men and supplies to deal with the fast approaching Japanese.[3]
They did not appreciate that Australia's urgent calls for reinforcements would bounce back automatically upon hitting the
brick wall of "W.W.I." Despite the Japanese attacks, Britain
and America were going to continue taking risks with Australia
in order to concentrate their power against Germany.[4]

Though Churchill and Roosevelt did not cable the terms of
"W.W.I." to Australia, there were enough indications that the
"Germany first" policy was guiding the strategic decisions of
the Allies. From Washington on Christmas Day 1941, Churchill
had informed Curtin that the defeats of the German army
were the "dominant military factor in the world war at this
moment"[5], while Curtin freely acknowledged in his reply that
British naval priorities gave precedence to the Atlantic over the
Indian Ocean.[6] At the same time, the world press was reporting the "Germany first" policy as an accepted fact, though
not in terms of a formal agreement. In Sydney the *Daily
Telegraph* reported that the "British War Office still believe
that conflict in the Pacific is a minor segment of the main
conflict in Europe", while in London the *Times* reviewed
Churchill's trip to Washington with the observation that the
Allies had not been diverted by the "crucial distractions of the
Japanese war", that "victory means first and foremost the defeat of Germany" and that "in Washington, London, and
Moscow there is complete unity of view upon the fundamental
aim".[7]

On 21 January, Churchill had informed the Defence Committee, with Page in attendance, that "the Americans were
completely in agreement with ourselves that the main enemy
was Germany". Page may not have been behaving deviously
when he failed to report this basic strategy to the Australian
Government; he may have overlooked its important implications after being strenuously assured by Churchill as to the
reinforcements earmarked for the Pacific war and that the basic
strategy would "not mean that the war in the South West
Pacific would be allowed to languish".[8]

Though Page did not inform Australia of the Arcadia decisions, a statement by the United States Navy Secretary, Frank

Knox, that Hitler must be defeated first should have alerted Australia to the outline of the Allied strategy. However, it seems that Curtin and Evatt saw it as a broadside in a continuing war between Allied planners, that the policy was not fixed and that Australia still could modify decisions relating to the south west Pacific. Casey helped to create this impression in Canberra when he relayed an assurance from Knox that "there would be no slackening of American effort in relation to [the] war against Japan".[9] It was on the assumption of there being a continuing strategic debate that Evatt left Sydney for Washington and London to argue the Australian case.

Evatt left in the midst of the most traumatic days in Australia's modern history and just four days before the secret arrival of General Douglas MacArthur. The British base at Singapore had fallen, much of the Royal Australian Navy had been sunk in the seas around Singapore and the Netherlands East Indies, and Australia's northern towns were being devastated by Japanese bombing raids. On 9 March, the Australian War Cabinet was informed by its military advisers that the expected Japanese invasion timetable would include attacks on Port Moresby, Darwin and New Caledonia during March and April, culminating in attacks on the Australian east coast during May. Although Churchill would not have conceded such a possibility, his naval chiefs in the Indian Ocean did share the Australian view.[10] Time was therefore at a premium in reinforcing the Dominion's defences.

Although Australia had successfully resisted Churchill's attempt to divert her troops to the hopeless defence of Burma, the Dominion had agreed to dispatch two brigades to Ceylon. By so doing, Australia made a serious sacrifice of its own defence position in order to acknowledge her continuing allegiance to Imperial defence and in the expectation that it would earn military credit in London. Evatt's trip was an attempt to draw upon this credit. His urgent message for Britain and America was for the maximum assistance necessary to prevent a Japanese invasion.

The fact that Evatt was prepared to fly across the world and back was some indication of his concern for Australia's safety. Like Curtin, he was desperately afraid of flying, a fear not uncommon at that time. The Australian businessman, W. S. Robinson, who accompanied Evatt, described how the nervous

Minister reacted to turbulent weather on one section of the journey by not only donning his lifejacket but inflating it and, during a visit to the toilet, "found himself wedged in the door — it took the steward and I to release him". Evatt surmounted his fear on the understanding that his long and arduous trip could influence the application of the agreed Allied strategy.[11]

By his personal intervention, Evatt hoped to persuade Allied leaders of Australia's argument for immediate reinforcements. But the portents for success were not good. In fact, on the day of Evatt's departure, Churchill had received an intelligence report of Japanese troop movements which, according to Churchill's interpretation, indicated that an "immediate full scale invasion of Australia" was "very unlikely".[12] Although the British Chiefs of Staff seemed to share this optimism for the immediate future, they did admit that the evidence on which it was based was "scanty and in some cases lacks confirmation". For good reason, the view in the south west Pacific was less sanguine and an imminent invasion continued to be widely expected. Even General MacArthur, who considered that such an invasion would be a strategic "blunder", had to admit that the Japanese "might try to overrun Australia in order to demonstrate their superiority over the white races".[13] Whatever the conflicting views and the value of the evidence on which they were based, there was no prospect of Britain increasing the priority for the war against Japan, particularly in view of the imminent renewal of the German offensive against Russia.

Now that America had joined the fight against Germany, it was essential to Churchill that Russia be kept fighting for the many months that it would take America to gather and deliver her overwhelming might against Germany. This meant that the supply of war materials to the Soviet Union had to proceed without interruption and that there remain no question of enticing her into the war against Japan. Previously, Australia had suggested that the Allies should offer to secretly recognise Russia's 1941 borders as a means of bringing her into the Pacific war. Invoking the moral principles of the Atlantic Charter, Churchill had stoutly resisted such suggestions that would have threatened his grand strategy. However, with a major German offensive in the offing, Churchill now feared that Stalin's war effort might falter and that he might even conclude a separate peace with Hitler.

In these circumstances, Churchill cabled to Roosevelt on 7 March arguing that the "principles of the Atlantic Charter ought not to be construed so as to deny Russia the frontiers she occupied when Germany attacked her". What had been morally unthinkable as a means of drawing Russia into the war against Japan, now became a sensible expedient in the war against Germany. Although Roosevelt demurred at Churchill's suggestion, the British Prime Minister did ensure that Stalin received other encouragement in the form of uninterrupted war supplies and the resumption of the British air offensive against Germany. Both of these moves would severely limit the amount of assistance that was theoretically available for the war against Japan.[14]

Although Japanese intentions remained unclear, Britain made little concession to the Australian belief that the Dominion lay well within the range of Tokyo's ambition and ability. It was not because Britain had firm evidence to the contrary. Rather, it was a combination of slim evidence, a persistent inclination to regard Australia as not worth invading and an underlying feeling within Whitehall that Australia did not deserve being made secure against invasion. Australia's reputation had been practically destroyed in the minds of Britain's military and political leadership after the defeat of Australian troops in Greece and Crete and the drawn-out dispute over the relief of the Australians in Tobruk. Following Pearl Harbor, the Australian calls for reinforcements exacerbated the feeling in Whitehall that the Dominion had become an unreliable ally — that her assistance for the common cause had become too qualified with conditions and had been outweighed by her own calls for assistance. The fall of Singapore confirmed the worst fears of Britain's military and political leadership.[15]

Singapore had fallen after Japanese troops managed to cross to the part of the island defended by troops of the Australian 8th Division. This inevitably focused criticism on the Australians when explanations were needed for the failure to defend the island against underwhelming odds. There were also reports of discreditable behaviour by Australian troops. These reports gradually filtered back to London over the following months and added to the existing bitterness felt towards Australia.

Churchill also blamed Curtin for insisting on the reinforcement of Singapore and thereby indirectly causing the capture of the British 18th Division. The situation was made even worse by the questionable behaviour of Australia's commander in Singapore, Major General Bennett, who fled his captured troops to make a hazardous escape back to Australia. Though Australian opinion was divided on the correctness of Bennett's action, it was viewed most critically in London where it was seen as a serious transgression of proper military behaviour. His action was aggravated in British eyes by his public criticism on his return to Australia of the quality of British military leadership.[16]

Long after the event, the circumstances of Singapore's fall continued to be an underlying source of grievance against Australia. For reasons of wartime solidarity and, in the postwar period, to protect the Anglo–Australian relationship, the full depth of the British anger towards Australia has never previously been revealed. Churchill ensured that there would be no inquiry into the causes of the disaster, for which he knew himself to be the ultimate cause. The British Government acted to prevent the publication by the press of Bennett's critical comments and, when his official report of the Malayan campaign was sent to London, Churchill pronounced it unfit for publication. Presumably, this was because of Bennett's criticism of the Indian troops and of the British military leadership. Ironically, it also contained implicit admissions of wholesale desertions by Australian troops.[17]

Privately, Churchill described Singapore's fall as the "most shameful moment of his life" but singled out the Australians as being primarily responsible.[18] Such was the effect of its fall that, two months afterwards, one observer in Westminster described the events going "round and round in the head like some horrible obsession".[19] It all contributed to British impatience with Australian requests for reinforcements. As Oliver Harvey noted on 21 March from his post at the Foreign Office, the Dominion was "soft and narrow" and had "screamed for help from the Americans, making it quite clear that they think us broken reeds".[20] It did not augur well for the success of Evatt's mission.

The day before Evatt's departure, Churchill made his rather outrageous suggestion to pluck Casey from Washington. The

Casey appointment was a means of stopping the continuing suggestions for greater Dominion participation in Imperial decision-making. These suggestions had provided a convenient cover for Churchill's political opponents in their attempts to dilute his power over policy. Casey's appointment blunted the thrust of their criticisms. In addition, Churchill appointed Attlee as Deputy Prime Minister and Dominions Secretary thereby bringing the latter post within the ranks of the War Cabinet. Imperial decision-making was given a new gloss although, beneath it all, Churchill's control remained untrammelled.[21]

Curtin's initial reaction was to refuse permission for Churchill to approach Casey with the British offer, asking that he not make the request "at this juncture" in view of the value to Australia of Casey's contacts in Washington and the difficulty of finding a suitable replacement.[22] But Churchill had been trying to fill this post for nearly four weeks and he remained under great political pressure in Westminster. More importantly, his standing within the country had slipped for the first time since he had taken office as Prime Minister and the press were becoming openly critical of his leadership. As he later shamefully admitted, the Ministerial reconstruction was a "concession or rather submission to Press criticism and public opinion". Looking back with regret, Churchill described his submission as "certainly not my Finest Hour" and claimed that he actually had been "strong enough to spit in all their faces".[23]

Despite this retrospective bravado, the political pressure was real enough and had to be appeased. So, immediately rejecting Curtin's objections, Churchill pressed his case even harder. Citing the support of his colleagues, the Chiefs of Staff and Casey's own desire for a change of post, Churchill suggested that Menzies could fill the gap caused by Casey's departure for an appointment which "strikes the note of bringing Statesmen from all over the Empire to the highest direction of affairs". Curtin was taken aback by the disclosure of Casey's wish to leave his Australian post in Washington and submitted to Churchill's repeated request, asking only that Casey remain long enough to meet Evatt and brief him on the American situation.[24]

As soon as he received Curtin's permission to proceed on 14 March, Churchill made his approach to Casey, offering him the Cairo post and informing him that Curtin was "very sorry to lose your services" but "interposes no bar".[25] This was technically correct. Curtin would not instruct Casey to remain against his will, but this did not imply agreement with Churchill's action. Curtin did not want to lose Casey but he would leave it to Casey's better instincts to refuse the offer and not place the Australian Government in the predicament of having to find a replacement. Casey's reaction was to consult with President Roosevelt, the British Ambassador, Lord Halifax, and other leading Americans of his acquaintance. In a cable to Curtin, he claimed that they unanimously urged him to accept the appointment and that, subject to Curtin's concurrence, he would do so. He assured Curtin that while the opinions of the others were of "great interest to me your judgement, as an Australian, is of greater moment to me in what is for me a decision of great importance".[26] If Casey retained hopes of one day resuming his political career in Australia, it was important that he should not be accused of deserting his Australian post during such a vital time for the Dominion.

Casey's obvious desire to obtain Curtin's support was not fulfilled. If Casey was so desperate for advancement, Curtin would not make it any easier for him. Far from giving his concurrence, Curtin set out the "great difficulty and embarrassment" Casey would cause to Australia if he accepted Churchill's offer. Not only would it be difficult to find a replacement, but Australia would be put at a "serious disadvantage" if it lost the many contacts Casey had made in the United States and the "familiarity which you have acquired as Minister with the many urgent and weighty matters now current in our relationship with the United States". Although Curtin again left the final decision to Casey, he obviously hoped that his arguments would cause Casey to reconsider.[27]

Unlike Curtin, Evatt was not sorry to see Casey leave Washington. He felt that Casey had not pushed Australia's views sufficiently and that the appointment of MacArthur to Australia would reduce the importance of the Washington post. Therefore, on meeting with Casey, he helped to overcome any reluctance that might have been created in Casey's mind by the tone of Curtin's cable. On 19 March, Casey informed Curtin that Evatt supported his acceptance of the appointment. He denied that Australia's interests would suffer because of his decision, claiming that the "Australian cause is now so bound up with the American cause ... that our interests are their interests and MacArthur's representations as to our Australian needs will be a much stronger voice in all matters of importance". With everything considered, he proposed to accept.[28] So much for the weight he promised to place on Curtin's judgement.

Casey's decision, however regrettable from Australia's point of view, should have been the end of the matter. But the question had been dragging on for six days and Churchill was anxious to announce the appointment to his critics in the House of Commons. This he did as soon as he heard that Casey proposed to accept but before the proper formality of Casey's resignation from Australia's service had been concluded. Then, to compound the insult, the Australian public heard the announcement from a BBC news bulletin broadcast on 19 March, hours before Curtin had even received Casey's cable. Curtin was furious and was only just persuaded not to publicly blast the British Government over the incident. However, he did reveal his Government's opposition to the appointment.[29]

This was sufficient to ignite a chain reaction of explosive cables that blew up the issue into a very public dispute between Curtin and Churchill, both of whom rightly felt aggrieved. Churchill believed that he had Curtin's agreement to the appointment, however reluctant it may have been. On the other hand, Curtin obviously harboured hopes of retaining Casey's services but now found his hopes dashed by Churchill's rather precipitate announcement. Casey joined in the fray on Churchill's side, supplying London with copies of the cables passing between Canberra and Washington. Then Curtin and Churchill published their versions of the dispute along with the transcripts of the cables passing between the Allied capitals. Roosevelt became embroiled after it became public that he had advised Casey to accept the British post. The dispute exacerbated the task facing Evatt in his desperate mission. In London, official opinion was firmly against Curtin, believing he was "behaving deplorably" and engaging in a "childish fit of temper".[30]

Churchill seized upon the dispute to try and neutralise Evatt's mission in Washington. In a cable to Roosevelt on 23 March, he blamed the bickering on "Australian party politics, which proceed with much bitterness and jealousy, regardless of national danger". Churchill singled out Evatt as an Australian politician who had made his way in politics by "showing hostility to Great Britain" and he asked for Roosevelt's "personal impressions of Evatt and how you get on with him".[31] The irony was that Evatt had made strenuous efforts to support Casey's appointment to Cairo and had earned Casey's thanks for the "friendliness and personal help" extended during the time prior to the latter's departure for London. In return, Casey undertook to "prepare the ground for you [Evatt] with Churchill and the others".[32]

Evatt spent some six weeks in Washington while Churchill watched his activities from London. It was vitally important to Churchill that the results of the Arcadia conference not be undone by the pleas of a vociferous Australian. Churchill advised his Ambassador in Washington, Lord Halifax, to keep in close touch with Evatt and warned him that the Australian was "reputed to be one of the least friendly of the Australian Ministers, and most eager to throw himself into the arms of the United States".[33] Throughout Evatt's stay, Churchill was kept informed of the Australian's pronouncements and activities, while his own advice to Halifax and Roosevelt probably helped to undercut Evatt's arguments.[34]

Churchill regarded Evatt as a prime cause of the various disputes that had erupted between London and Canberra. The "Germany first" policy was a struggle vital to both of them. Evatt quickly staked out his position with a cable to Bruce on 23 March warning of the effect on Imperial solidarity produced by the "continuous rowing over unfortunate things and attempt to hector over more important things". He urged that Britain should make a gesture towards Australia that would recover the previous warmth of their relationship. Specifically, Evatt asked Bruce to request the immediate delivery to Australia of six weeks of Britain's allocation of American war production which, he claimed, would make Churchill the "saviour of Australia". He also asked that Australia's 9th Division, her only troops remaining in the Middle East, be permitted to proceed to Australia as previously agreed. However, Churchill had already made a strong move to retain the 9th Division.[35]

In a cable to Canberra on 11 March, Churchill had suggested that Australia accept an extra American division in exchange for leaving the 9th Division in the Middle East. Citing support from Roosevelt, he argued that it would economise on shipping since it would require just one shipping movement rather than two. With the increased sinkings by U-boats and the pressure on shipping from the United States entry into the war, Churchill was hard pressed to provide for all Allied shipping needs. Retention of the 9th Division seemed to provide some relief from this pressure and would also, as Churchill argued, increase the United States stake in Australia and thereby "emphasize to the United States the importance of protecting that area by its main sea power and also of accelerating the equipment of existing Australian forces". There was some sense in these arguments but they paid no heed to Australian sensitivities and ignored Canberra's loss of faith in Britain's good intentions. In addition, it was not a simple swap of divisions — the 9th Division was much more valuable to Australia, being fully-trained and battle-hardened and, if returned to Australia, it would be fighting for its homeland. Also, if left in the Middle East, the Division would continue draining Australia of troops because of the need for constant reinforcements to replace losses.[36]

In agreeing to the temporary retention in Ceylon of the two brigades from the 6th Division, Australia had tried to establish a clear understanding with Churchill that such retention would be conditional on the prompt return of the 9th Division. Now Churchill not only pressed for the retention of the 9th, but also implied that a refusal from Canberra would lengthen the stay of the brigades in Ceylon. Australia once again felt betrayed, and not without cause. However, Churchill's cable was closely followed by the secret arrival in Australia of General MacArthur, who was promptly nominated by Curtin as Supreme Commander of the South West Pacific Area (SWPA). This provided Australia with the prospect of achieving influence commensurate with its contribution and importance to the Allied war effort and removed any immediate need to bow to Churchill's pressure on the retention of the 9th Division.

Evatt was quick to seize on MacArthur's appointment to provide himself with extra leverage in Washington. He realised the latent support by the American public for greater action against Japan and, on 22 March, urged Curtin to ensure that MacArthur made the strongest possible appeals for reinforcements. As Evatt confided, "the [American] public would condemn the United States Government unless MacArthur is sufficiently supported".[37] His hand was strengthened even more when Roosevelt made it clear that the commitment of United States troops to Australia was not conditional on the retention of the 9th Division in the Middle East as Churchill had claimed. Armed with this information, Evatt immediately suggested that Churchill withdraw his request for the Division's retention.[38] On the following day, 24 March, Evatt seemed to have a change of heart and tried to use the 9th as a bargaining counter, offering to leave it in the Middle East in return for an armoured division, either British or American, being sent to Australia.[39] When this apparently failed, he recommended to Canberra that the 9th Division be returned to Australia. Although Evatt's recommendation received the support of Blamey, MacArthur and the Advisory War Council, Churchill refused to withdraw his request for the Division's retention.[40]

Apart from trying to extract the 9th Division from Britain's grasp, Evatt also renewed his call for Britain to stimulate the flow of munitions to Australia. In a cable to Bruce on 26 March, he held out the spectre of a full-scale Japanese invasion and pleaded for Churchill to make "some immediate sacrifice ... to protect two of His Majesty's Dominions from violation by the enemy". He also introduced a new argument — that a moderate contribution from Britain prior to an invasion could prevent the invasion altogether and negate the possible need for a much heavier contribution in the case of an invasion occurring. He also asked Bruce to approach any other British Ministers who might be in a position to further the Australian case.[41]

Bruce was not the best advocate for Evatt's arguments. Though he was considerably concerned at the rift between Australia and Britain, he was not convinced that Australia faced invasion by Japan nor that Australia warranted a large diversion of resources from the European theatre. In fact, on 8 April Bruce privately canvassed with Eden the idea that Britain should abandon the Indian Ocean to the Japanese and instead open a second front against Hitler in Europe.[42] Such a second front in 1942 would have consumed such a large proportion of Allied resources that the Pacific War would have been ceded almost by default to the Japanese.

So, when Bruce met with Churchill on 31 March, his priorities were not those of Evatt. He had already sent Evatt's cables on to Churchill, not merely the gist of them as Evatt had requested, and he now used them to urge Churchill to improve the atmosphere of Anglo–Australian relations. He did not raise Evatt's request for six weeks' allocation of Britain's supplies from America nor did he ask for British fighter planes. Instead, Bruce merely suggested that Churchill seize Evatt's proffered hand of friendship and put an end to the ceaseless disputes. Bruce admitted that some of the Australian cables had been "somewhat ill-advised and certainly irritating" but asked him to make allowances for the inexperience of the Labor Ministers and the situation in which they found themselves. Disinterring Churchill's promise of August 1940 to defend Australia if she was seriously invaded, Bruce suggested that Churchill resuscitate this commitment with an undertaking to divert British divisions en route to the Middle East and India if Australia was invaded on a large scale.[43] Bruce composed such a conciliatory telegram to Evatt from himself, sending a copy to Churchill, apparently as a guide for Churchill's own reply to Evatt.[44]

Rather than pressing vigorously for Evatt's requests, Bruce had joined in a campaign to support the "Germany first" policy and divert Evatt from his course with fairly meaningless platitudes. After all, if Australia was seriously invaded by the Japanese, the dispatch of two divisions of British troops would hardly be sufficient to expel them, nor would they be likely to be able to break through the Japanese naval supremacy that such an invasion would entail. It was another worthless promise made to secure continued Australian contributions to Imperial defence. In fact, Churchill had already made such a promise to Curtin on 17 March in response to the appointment of MacArthur. At that time he had re-stated the British Government's

> determination and duty to come to your aid to the best of their ability, and if you are actually invaded in force ... we shall do our utmost to divert British troops and British ships rounding the Cape, or already in the Indian Ocean, to your succour, albeit at the expense of India and the Middle East.[45]

Now he seized upon Bruce's suggestion with alacrity and proceeded to invest his previous promise with more precision in an effort to placate Evatt and limit the possibility of the promise being called upon.

Churchill informed Evatt that he would divert the two

British divisions then rounding the Cape of Good Hope if
Australia was invaded by at least eight Japanese divisions, three
more than the Japanese had used to capture Malaya and Singapore and two more than British intelligence chiefs considered
likely for a Japanese invasion of Australia. He also advised
that removing the 9th Division would be a "mistake" and that
Australia could not have six weeks' production of munitions as
Evatt had requested. Churchill claimed to have "already left
the Mediterranean denuded of all heavy ships and carriers in
order to build up a naval force in the Indian Ocean, which
is already respectable". Moreover, he claimed Britain had
Australia's interests at heart, and that "not a day passes when
we do not think of Australia".[46] This was certainly true, but
not in the sense Churchill was trying to convey. As for the
much-vaunted Eastern fleet, it looked much better on paper
than in reality.

Although the Eastern fleet had the responsibility for defending the west coast of Australia, it did not have the means
to do so, nor could it even provide adequate escorts for convoys.
Churchill was much more honest with Roosevelt about the size
of this fleet, informing him that Britain was building up a
respectable naval force, rather than claiming to have already
achieved one, while also admitting that the fleet was "to a great
extent [composed] of old ships with short-range guns" — these
being the four "R" class battleships that Churchill had earlier
described as floating coffins. The main weapon in the armoury
of this antiquated fleet was deception, both of the Japanese
and the Australians, as to its strength. In the words of Vice
Admiral Willis, the Eastern fleet had to practise "strategical
evasion with the object of preventing the enemy knowing
precisely where it is for any length of time".[47]

The Japanese did not wait long before calling the British
bluff. On 4 April, a large Japanese fleet steamed towards Ceylon
seeking to destroy the remnants of British power in the Far
East. Fortunately for Britain, the two fleets never met. Instead,
the Japanese managed to find and sink various ships isolated
from the main British force — two cruisers, one small aircraft
carrier and two destroyers. Discretion then became the better
part of valour as the Admiralty ordered most of the fleet to
withdraw to the east African coast where it sheltered in
Mombasa harbour. As one of the naval officers wrote at the

time, the Japanese fleet could "polish us off in a matter of minutes".[48] On 13 April, Vice Admiral Willis noted the consequences of the strategic withdrawal — "it concedes control of the Bay of Bengal to the enemy, uncovers Ceylon and increases the threat to India".[49] Japan now ruled the waves of both the Indian and Pacific oceans.

In the wake of the Japanese naval thrust, the British Chiefs of Staff reversed previous undertakings to supply Australia with aircraft. The promised delivery of 125 Kittyhawks had been increased to 205 aircraft, of which none had yet been delivered. The extra eighty planes were now deleted from the commitment and diverted to the Middle East. At the same time, the Chiefs of Staff decided that India had "prior claim" to British Vengeance dive-bombers requested by Australia and awaiting shipment from US factories. By their decision, India was to receive three quarters of the production with the remainder going to Australia. Churchill concurred, noting advice from General Ismay that the Australian reaction was "likely to be violent".[50]

At sea, Britain responded to the humiliation of its Eastern fleet by seeking United States naval assistance to ease the pressure from the Japanese in the Indian Ocean. But the Far East still remained low on the list of British priorities. It was mainly the shipping routes of the west Indian Ocean that Churchill was concerned to preserve. These routes were vital for supplying British forces in the Middle East and India, for the shipping of oil from the Arabian Gulf and for supplying munitions to Russia via Iran.[51] The Eastern fleet was allowed to remain weak, with India, Ceylon and Western Australia all exposed to Japanese attack. From Delhi, Wavell was as frantic as the Australian Government about the situation. He was advised by Admiral Somerville that he could not expect any naval assistance to resist a Japanese attack before June 1942 at the earliest. Somerville continued his strategy of subterfuge, intending to "remain at sea as much as possible and use unfrequented anchorages in order to make the Japanese uncertain of my movements" and thereby "deter them from attempting any interference with our Middle East and Indian communications, except with a heavy Fleet concentration".[52]

Just as Britain was faced with demands to reinforce the Eastern fleet, a competing demand arose that left no doubt about the place of the Far East in British priorities. The island of Malta was under heavy air attack and desperately needed supplies to avert disaster. Churchill's planned solution was to send a fast, heavily protected convoy through the Suez Canal and across the hazardous waters of the Eastern Mediterranean to Britain's embattled fortress. On 22 April, the Defence Committee approved this plan, intending to use much of Admiral Somerville's Eastern fleet for the task in the knowledge that it could well involve "paying forfeits" in the Indian Ocean. Although the plan was never actually implemented, it was, as Britain's official naval historian later noted, "important historically" for revealing the "lengths to which the British Government was prepared to go to save Malta" and, by way of contrast, the risks it was still prepared to run in the Far East despite the rush of Japanese successes.[53]

The Malta plan caused dismay in Delhi, with Wavell warning the British War Cabinet of the "very grave risks" being taken with the defence of Ceylon and India. Like Australia, India had sent her best troops to fight for Britain in the Middle East and now clamoured for their return. Wavell confided that he had "so far been able to resist this and to do something to maintain [the] sinking Indian morale by assurances that H.M.G. are determined to give every possible assistance to [the] defence of India". He warned that he could not "honourably continue to give these assurances if reinforcements for India are constantly diverted or deferred like this".[54] Even without the diversion of naval forces to Malta, the situation remained grave. As one officer with the Eastern fleet noted at the end of April, the "whole of the Indian Ocean [was] open to attack if the Japanese should move strong forces this way and India and Ceylon are completely and absolutely undefended".[55]

Churchill ensured that it would remain in that state when he refused Wavell's request for naval assistance, claiming as justification the need to retain sufficient naval forces in British home waters and noting, in an accompanying report by the Admiral of the Home Fleet, the maxim that the "first duty of any Government is to its own country".[56] If India could be left undefended at sea, it was not surprising to find that successive Australian requests for British naval assistance during March and April were similarly refused by Churchill.[57]

At the beginning of April, Evatt had received with "great

satisfaction" the confirmation by Churchill of his previous pledge to defend Australia in the event of a serious invasion. At the same time, Evatt was getting encouragement from a different direction. Following MacArthur's appointment as Supreme Commander in the south-west Pacific, a directive had been issued to him with Evatt's concurrence by the United States Chiefs of Staff. This directive set out MacArthur's objectives as being to "hold the key military regions of Australia as bases for future offensive action against Japan" and to "prepare to take the offensive". This directive was determined by the overriding Allied priority to concentrate against Germany, though nowhere was this priority specifically spelt out.[58]

Evatt seems hardly to have noticed the implication that the war in the Pacific would be a holding war for the immediate future. Instead, he seized on the apparent United States commitment to defend Australia's key military regions and the commitment to take the offensive against Japan, not realising that any offensive would be in the distant future. With his legal background, Evatt seems to have judged the directive as being akin to a contract and he set about ensuring that its provisions were enforced. In a memorandum to Roosevelt on 5 April, Evatt called for munitions to be allocated on a theatre rather than a government basis and claimed that the relative importance of the Pacific theatre had not yet been assessed. Evatt was taking the directive at face value, demanding that MacArthur be provided with the men and matériel to fulfil its objectives.[59]

The following day, Evatt warned Curtin of an impending visit by the United States Army Chief, General George Marshall, to London to discuss the prospects for a second front in Europe. This idea of a second front in 1942 had originally been raised in Washington by Churchill as a ploy to retain the United States commitment to Europe and prevent back-sliding by American military chiefs anxious to take the offensive after the humiliation of Pearl Harbor. Evatt correctly recognised Marshall's visit as a threat to his own attempts to boost Allied activity in the Pacific. But it was still in terms of a continuing debate in which, Evatt urged, Curtin should make his views known to Churchill before a commitment was made.[60]

Marshall's meeting with British leaders in London occurred against the background of naval disaster in the Indian Ocean.

The proposal to invade Europe in 1942 was scrapped and replaced by the more realisable objective of capturing North Africa. At a Defence Committee meeting on 14 April, Churchill reported with satisfaction their agreed conclusion to mount the North African operation which would continue their "concentration against the main enemy". Though it would ensure that no major diversion of force was possible for the war against Japan, he did stipulate that India and the Middle East must be safeguarded and that Australia must not be completely captured or isolated from America. However, the United States representatives made it clear that while they would discharge their obligations to Australia, their "whole heart would be fully engaged" in the struggle against Germany. Marshall assured Churchill that he had made "careful calculations" of Australia's requirements and would provide them but he "did not want to divert further forces to these places".[61] The "Germany first" strategy remained in place.

On the same day as the Defence Committee was meeting in London, Curtin finally buckled under the British pressure and offered to allow the 9th Division to remain in the Middle East for the time being. He made a rather half-hearted attempt to make his agreement conditional on the provision by Britain of naval and air reinforcements for Australia and made it clear that the Division could not be left in the Middle East indefinitely. Curtin also claimed, contrary to Churchill's earlier cable, that Roosevelt did not dispute the right of Australia to determine the destination of her own troops. Curtin's change of mind was produced by a combination of factors. There was the persistence of Churchill's demand, the fact that MacArthur expressed a more optimistic view of the Dominion's security and, perhaps of most importance, the Japanese naval ascendancy in the Indian Ocean had made the immediate withdrawal of the 9th Division a much more hazardous operation.[62] If there were conditions attached to Curtin's agreement, Churchill tried not to notice them. At Bruce's suggestion, he simply thanked Curtin for the decision, claiming impudently that Australia had "always been and will be perfectly free to decide the movement of all your troops".[63] In fact, through circumstance and design, the "Germany first" strategy continued to keep Australia in its grip despite the Dominion's efforts to fight itself free.

Evatt made a public contribution to the imaginary strategic

debate during a brief visit to Canada when he announced on 9
April that the dramatic Japanese gains in the Pacific had "transformed the entire stategy of the war". In blithe ignorance of
"W.W.I.", he weighed in with his view of the "interdependence
of all of the theatres of the war", arguing that "You can't 'beat
Hitler first', or 'beat Japan first'. You've got to beat them both
together."[64] So sure was Evatt that his various efforts had
successfully modified the Allied strategy that he reported to
Curtin on 17 April that his purpose in the United States had
been substantially achieved and that he would proceed to Britain
on 22 April where he was hopeful of obtaining "a number of
high performance modern fighters".[65] Again, on the following
day, Evatt claimed to Curtin that the "accepted position" in
Washington accorded Australia a "major place in the general
strategic scheme" and that he had ensured that the allocation
of equipment to Australia would "accord with the strategical
necessity so clearly shown in the Directive" and that "this
broad line of approach has been acceptable both to the President
and to the military and naval chiefs".[66]

On 20 April, two days after he had taken control of Allied
forces in the south west Pacific, MacArthur met with Curtin to
discuss Evatt's achievements in Washington. MacArthur noted
the instruction contained in his directive to prepare to take the
offensive against Japan and questioned how this could be done
with the forces then on hand or promised. Rather than accepting
Evatt's optimistic assessment of Australia's position in the general strategic scheme, MacArthur arranged a meeting with the
Australian Chiefs of Staff to compile a list of requirements for
the south west Pacific that would enable him to give effect to
his directive. With the backing of MacArthur, Blamey and the
War Cabinet, Curtin asked Evatt to remain in Washington
until he had received this military shopping list and had obtained
from United States authorities a definite program for its fulfilment. It was with the utmost reluctance that Evatt agreed to
postpone his departure.[67]

On 23 April, MacArthur and Blamey met with Australia's
State Premiers in Melbourne to report on the progress of the
Dominion's defence effort. MacArthur reiterated his opinion
that the Japanese were unlikely to invade Australia, though
such an event was not impossible. If it happened, Australia
remained in a poor position to mount a successful resistance.

Blamey acknowledged that the army was "by no means ready to fight. The infantry was not much more than 50% equipped, we were very short of motor transport and had practically no tanks, though these were arriving. There was no non-divisional artillery and we were deficient in engineering and similar units."[68] The experience at Darwin did not bode well for the fortitude likely to be shown by Australian servicemen or civilians in the case of a major attack. Reinforcements of men and supplies were imperative if Australia was to be assured of remaining inviolate.

With Casey gone from Washington, Evatt was well placed to press Australia's needs onto United States officials. But he remained loath to do so. His motives remain unclear but it is likely that he was misled into believing that the terms of MacArthur's directive would dictate the level of supplies being sent to Australia. In his view, the only problems were organisational and these were best left to officials. As he informed Curtin on 23 April, any attempt to argue Australia's needs at meetings of the Pacific War Council only produced a free-for-all with each delegate competing to press the needs of his particular country. According to Evatt, it had become a matter for the military and supply officials to resolve along the lines of the overriding directive. He therefore asked to be released from the instruction to remain in Washington, claiming to have "driven myself and my colleagues almost to a standstill in order to get the results we have obtained. MacArthur at your end and our officers here can now exploit these results."[69]

In order that the Australian public should also learn of his supposed achievements, Evatt briefed an Australian reporter with this version of his visit. The correspondent, George Warnecke, cabled to the Melbourne *Herald* on 28 April, claiming that Evatt had ensured that "Australia's strategic importance and political consequence have been realised", this recognition being embodied in MacArthur's directive. Openly acknowledging the resolve of the Arcadia conference to "rate Hitler still as [the] chief enemy", Warnecke argued that the "Evatt Roosevelt parleys have resulted in drastic revision" of the Allied strategy with America now "binding herself to direct cooperation with Australia and other Pacific countries in an offensive policy against Japan". Warnecke apparently submitted a draft of his cable to Evatt. The draft had described the appointment of MacArthur and the terms of his directive as creating a "formal bond between America and Australia". In place of "formal bond" was inserted, apparently by Evatt, the words "binding formal agreement", which was a reflection of his legalistic interpretation of MacArthur's directive. He regarded it as a virtual contract between the Australian and American governments that effectively superseded the "Germany first" strategy. If, as it seems, this report was inspired and vetted by Evatt, it reveals him as a naive actor on the international stage who soon would have his illusions shattered.[70]

The signs already were there to indicate the hollowness of Evatt's achievement. Despite Evatt's optimistic interpretation, MacArthur's directive was in accordance with the secret Anglo–American strategy and both Bruce and Curtin sent signals to Evatt which should have indicated to him that the "Germany first" strategy held firm. On 24 April, Bruce had advised Evatt of his failure to obtain greater priority for Australia in the allocation of munitions from Britain. At a sub-committee meeting of the Munitions Assignment Board in London, Bruce's request had been rejected and then, after a protest by Bruce, passed to the British Chiefs of Staff for a decision on strategical grounds. The Chiefs promptly rejected it. Bruce informed Evatt that this decision "cannot be altered save by the intervention of the Prime Minister and the President" and that, in the present instance, he doubted whether Australia's case was strong enough to warrant such intervention.[71] This cable should have indicated to Evatt that, despite the perilous situation in the south west Pacific and the terms of MacArthur's directive, Australia actually remained a low priority and the Allies would be slow to give much practical effect to MacArthur's instructions.

The second signal to Evatt came from Curtin. It must have hit Evatt like a bombshell since it reached Washington on 28 April, the same day that Warnecke cabled to Australia with his overblown account of Evatt's achievements. In complete contradiction to Warnecke, Curtin reported that MacArthur had absolutely rejected Evatt's achievements in Washington as providing adequate men and matériel for the fulfilment of his directive. He advised that MacArthur was "bitterly disappointed with the meagre assistance", which was not only "entirely inadequate to carry [out] the directive given him but [would] leave Australia as a base for operations in such a weak state that any major attack will gravely threaten the security of the Commonwealth". Curtin ordered Evatt to remain in Washington until answers were provided on the adequate supply of forces for MacArthur and requested Evatt to seek an appreciation from the Combined Chiefs of Staff so that Australia could learn of the "general strategic basis governing [the] allotment [of] forces and equipment to various theatres".[72] It is clear that Curtin was still oblivious of "W.W.I.", though he seemed to suspect some such agreement in the light of the resources allotted to MacArthur.

Despite Curtin's order to remain in Washington, it does not seem to have delayed Evatt's travel plans, although he did approach Roosevelt's adviser, Harry Hopkins, enclosing copies of Curtin's cable and asking that Roosevelt intervene to speed up the flow of supplies to Australia. As he confidently asserted to Hopkins, the "strategy for the area is absolutely fixed by the directive" and the "question is merely one of assessing what is required to carry out this agreed strategy".[73] It seems that Evatt did not even wait for a reply to his letter and, ignoring Curtin's order to remain in Washington, flew on to London where he arrived on 2 May.

Evatt had spent six weeks in Washington at a most crucial time in Australian history when the possibility of a successful Japanese invasion was very real. His attempts to ensure Australian security and obtain a greater share of Allied resources had been in vain. The Pacific War Council had been established by Roosevelt but it had no executive powers and quickly degenerated into a forum for rather idle discussion rather than decision. Evatt had apparently helped to convince Casey of the wisdom of the Cairo appointment. Although there remains some question about Casey's proper fulfilment of his Government's instructions and whether he adequately discerned the distinction between British and Australian interests, there is little doubt that his appointment to Cairo represented a net loss to Australia. Evatt should have prevailed upon him to remain at his post, at least for the duration of those critical months in 1942. But Evatt's greatest failure in Washington was his apparent ignorance of the "Germany first" strategy as embodied in "W.W.I.". Linked with this was his persistent reading of MacArthur's directive in a legalistic light. His refusal to ensure personally that its terms were fulfilled and his abrupt departure from Washington were actions not calculated to serve Australia's interests.

Curtin's cable to Evatt ordering him to remain in the American capital was sent in the context of a deteriorating security situation for Australia. A message from Churchill had acknowledged the loss of British naval control in the Indian Ocean and had held out little prospect of it being regained in the near future. There was also no sign of the air and naval reinforcements requested from Britain in return for the retention of the 9th Division. Although American reinforcements were beginning to arrive, the equipment position remained poor. Of the 494 American aircraft in Australia on 26 April, only 237 were in a serviceable condition. Moreover, MacArthur advised that the US air force units in Australia required four months of intensive training before they could even be considered as "effective first-line units". Of the 210 tanks held by the Australian army, eighty were light two-man tanks diverted from delivery to the Dutch forces in the NEI. In these circumstances, and with nearly two divisions of the AIF still in British hands, Curtin requested that Churchill divert two British divisions shortly due to round the Cape of Good Hope en route to India. Churchill had promised to divert them in the event of Australia being seriously invaded but, as Curtin had informed him, in such an event there was little chance of reinforcement convoys being able to reach Australia.[74]

In London's view, Australia was overreacting. Although some British officials recognised that an invasion of the Dominion figured among the various options open to the Japanese[75], the more common feeling was much less sympathetic, based on a refusal to admit the possibility of Australia falling within the ambit of Japanese territorial ambitions. Thus, the Japanese thrust through the Solomon Islands and New Guinea, which was designed to cut the American—Australian reinforcement route, was seen in London as a diversionary thrust. As such, Curtin's appeals for assistance were dismissed as frightened "squeals".[76] Cranborne, now the Colonial Secretary, privately berated the Australians for assuming that Britain "could protect them under all circumstances", an assumption he had been instrumental in helping to foster. He regarded with considerable equanimity the consequent Australian anger at Britain's betrayal of her defence pledge. He acknowledged that Australians "have suddenly to face unpleasant facts, and the process is very painful. But perhaps, taking a long view, it is better that our relationship [should] be put on a realistic basis."[77] With the Japanese assembling in Rabaul for attacks on Port Moresby and the Solomons, it was rather late in the day for Britain to spell out the small print on her defence guarantee for Australia.

As for Curtin's request for two British divisions, this was immediately and forthrightly rejected by Churchill. He argued that the threat to India was greater than that to Australia and that Britain would "certainly be judged to have acted wrongly if we sent to an uninvaded Australia troops needed for an invaded India".[78] Curtin had made his appeal on the basis of recommendations from MacArthur. This boost to Australia's voice alarmed Churchill, who correctly saw it as a threat to the "Germany first" strategy and quickly moved to silence it. In a message to Roosevelt on 29 April, Churchill set out the details of MacArthur's recommendations and asked whether the Supreme Commander had "any authority from the United States for taking such a line". Britain, he wrote, was "quite unable to meet these new demands, which are none the less a cause of concern when put forward on General MacArthur's authority".[79] This message had the effect Churchill desired, producing a strong rebuke from Washington for MacArthur and helping to mute Australia's voice once again.

On the day of Churchill's message to Roosevelt, the British Defence Committee reaffirmed its commitment to the "Germany first" policy and the resulting overriding priority for Russia in the allocation of aircraft. Although Churchill expressed regret at the cost to British commitments elsewhere, he successfully argued that "it was in our own vital interests to do so, as the Russians would shortly be engaged in mortal combat with our main enemy".[80] Three days later, Evatt arrived in London with the proclaimed aim of obtaining aircraft for Australia. Meanwhile, Australia's main enemy completed its preparations for the capture of Port Moresby. The next few weeks would be the most crucial in the modern history of the Dominion.

NOTES

1 JOHN ROBERTSON, "Australia and the 'Beat Hitler First' Strategy, 1941—42: A Problem in Wartime Consultation", *Journal of Imperial and Commonwealth History*, May 1983, p. 310

2 LETTER, Eggleston to Evatt, 4 May 1942, "Eggleston, F.W. (a)" Folder, Evatt Collection: FUL

3 CABLE NO. 1079, Evatt to Casey, 16 December 1941, CRS A3300, Item 100: AA

4 CABLE NO. 323/2, Churchill to Roosevelt, 5 March 1942, VI/2, Ismay Papers: KC

5 CABLE, Churchill to Curtin, 25 December 1941, CRS A3300, Item 101: AA

6 CABLE NO. 166, Curtin to Casey, 29 December 1941, to be passed on to Churchill in Washington, CRS A3300, Item 101: AA

7 CABLE NO. 402, Curtin to Bruce, 16 January 1942, CRS M100, "January 1942": AA; *Times*, London, 19 January 1942

8 DEFENCE COMMITTEE (OPERATIONS) MINUTES, 21 January 1942, CAB 69/4, D.O. (42)4: PRO

9 CABLE NO. 119, Casey to External Affairs Department, 20 January 1942, CRS A3300, Item 219: AA. See also Cable No. 11, Evatt to Casey, 25 January 1942, CRS A3300 Item 219: AA

10 WAR CABINET AGENDUM NO. 143/1942, CRS A2670, 143/1942: AA; "Policy and Strategy in the Eastern Theatre", Report by Vice Admiral Willis, 8 March 1942, WLLS 5/5, Willis Papers: CC

11 LETTER, W. S. Robinson to L. B. Robinson, 1 November 1950, "L. B. Robinson 1946—1956, (Personal and General)" Folder, W. S. Robinson Papers: UMA. See also Letter, Evatt to his wife, undated but probably 1942 or 1943, "Evatt — Family Correspondence, M. A. S. Evatt to Evatt" Folder, Evatt Collection: FUL

12 M. GILBERT, *Road to Victory*, p. 74

13 JOINT INTELLIGENCE COMMITTEE APPRECIATION, 14 March 1942, REDW 2/8/22 and 29, Edwards Papers: CC; Advisory War Council Minutes, 26 March 1942, CRS A2682, Vol. 4, Minute 869: AA; See also "Appreciation of the Defence of New Zealand 25th March, 1942", 71/19/4, Parry Papers: IWM; Memoirs of Lord Wakehurst, ch. 18, pp. 6—7, Wakehurst Papers: HLRO; Letter, Wakehurst to Emrys-Evans, 6 April 1942, ADD. MS. 58263, and Letter, Cross to Emrys-Evans, 26 April 1942, ADD. MS. 58243, Emrys-Evans Papers: BL

14 M. GILBERT, *Road to Victory*, pp. 73—7

15 See DAVID DAY, "Anzacs on the Run: The View from Whitehall, 1941—2"

16 WAR CABINET MINUTE NO. 1931, 2 March 1942, CRS A5954, Box 264: AA; Cable SC1, Evatt to Eggleston, 26 February 1942, "External Affairs — Far East — Cables — 1942—45", Evatt Papers: FUL; Nicolson Diary, 24 and 27 February 1942, in Sir H. Nicolson, *Diaries and Letters*, ii, London, 1967, pp. 213—14; Edwards Diary, 5 March 1942, REDW 1/4/40, Edwards Papers: CC; Letter, Rear Admiral Boyd to Admiral Cunningham, 14 March 1942, ADD. MS. 52570, Cunningham Papers: BL

17 WAR CABINET CONCLUSIONS, 16, 18 and 30 March, 6 April 1942, CAB 65/25, W.M. (42)34, 35 and 38 and CAB 65/26, W.M. (42)42: PRO; See also CRS A5954, Box 264: AA

18 "NOTES FOR HISTORY. Talk with Air Marshal Richard Peck, 21 March 1942", by Liddell Hart, 11/1942/20, Liddell Hart Papers: KC; King Diary, 23 March 1942, in C. King, p. 170; Nicolson Diary, 26 March 1942, in Sir H. Nicolson, p. 221

19 SIR H. NICOLSON DIARY, 10 April 1942, in Sir H. Nicolson, p. 221

20 HARVEY DIARY, 21 March 1942, see also Harvey Diary, 16 April 1942, ADD. MS. 56398, Harvey Papers: BL

21 See DAVID DAY, *Menzies and Churchill at War*, ch. 15

22 CABLE JOHCU 25, Curtin to Churchill, (rec'd) 13 March 1942, *DAFP*, v, Doc. 409

23 TALK WITH EDEN, 19 March 1942, CRS M100, "March 1942": AA; Harvey Diary, 16 and 20 February, 3, 9 and 14 March 1942, ADD. MS. 56398, Harvey Papers: BL; "Notes 1942", Paper by Churchill, 12 July 1949, II/2/165, Ismay Papers: KC

24 See *DAFP*, v, Docs 412−13

25 CABLE, Churchill to Casey, 14 March 1942, VI/2, Ismay Papers: KC

26 CABLE S10, Casey to Curtin, 15 March 1942, *DAFP*, v, Doc. 414

27 CABLE SW16, Curtin to Casey, 17 March 1942, *DAFP*, v, Doc. 416

28 CABLE S16, Casey to Curtin, 19 March 1942, *DAFP*, v, Doc. 423

29 See *DAFP*, v, Docs 426−7

30 HARVEY DIARY, 21 March 1942, ADD. MS. 56398, Harvey Papers: BL; R. G. Casey, *Personal Experience*, pp. 94−6; Cables No. 436/2 and No. 461/2, Churchill to Curtin, 21 and 23 March 1942, VI/2, Ismay Papers: KC; Cadogan Diary, 23 March 1942, in D. Dilks (ed.), p. 442; War Cabinet Conclusions, 23 March 1942, CAB 65/25, W.M. (42)36: PRO; Cabinet Minutes, 24 March 1942, CRS A2703, Vol. 1[C]: AA; *DAFP*, v, Docs 431, 433, 435, 437 and 449

31 CABLE NO. 458/2, Churchill to Roosevelt, 23 March 1942, VI/2, Ismay Papers: KC

32 LETTER, Casey to Evatt, 2 April 1942, "Evatt — Overseas Trip — 1942 — Correspondence", Evatt Papers: FUL; Dalton Diary, 22 April 1942, I/26/145, Dalton Papers: LSE

33 CABLE NO. 437/2, Churchill to Halifax, 21 March 1942, VI/2, Ismay Papers: KC

34 JOHN ROBERTSON, p. 312

35 CABLE NO. 39, Evatt to Bruce, 23 March 1942, CRS M100, "March 1942": AA

36 CABLE PM3, Curtin to Evatt, 20 March 1942, *DAFP*, v, Doc. 428

37 CABLE PM2, Evatt to Curtin, 22 March 1942, CRS A5954, Box 474: AA

38 CABLE NO. 39, Evatt to Bruce, 23 March 1942, CRS M100, "March 1942": AA

39 "AIDE MEMOIRE for discussion with Hon. Harry Hopkins", by Evatt, 24 March 1942, CRS A3300, Folder 233: AA

40 CABLE, Evatt to Curtin, 28 March 1942, CRS A3300, Folder 233; Advisory War Council Minutes, 8 April 1942, CRS A2682, Vol. 5, Minute 894; Cable PM14, Evatt to Curtin, 29 March 1942, CRS A5954, Box 474;

Cable 16, Curtin to Evatt, 1 April 1942, CRS A5954, Box 474; Minutes of Prime Minister's War Conference, 8 April 1942, CRS A5954, Box 1: all in AA; Cable No. 508/2, Churchill to Evatt, 1 April 1942, VI/2, Ismay Papers: KC

41 CABLE NO. 44, Evatt to Bruce, 26 March 1942, CRS M100, "March 1942": AA

42 TALK WITH EDEN, 8 April 1942, CRS M100, "April 1942": AA

43 TALK WITH CHURCHILL, 31 March 1942, CRS M100, "March 1942": AA

44 LETTER, Churchill to Bruce, 3 April 1942, CRS M100, "April 1942": AA; See also PREM 3/151/2: PRO

45 CABLE NO. 401/2, Churchill to Curtin, 17 March 1942, VI/2, Ismay Papers: KC

46 CABLE NO. 520, Evatt to Curtin, 2 April 1942, CRS A5954, Box 474: AA; Joint Intelligence Sub-Committee Memorandum, 25 January 1942, PREM 3/151/4: PRO

47 CABLE NO. 400/2, Churchill to Roosevelt, 17 March 1942, VI/2, Ismay Papers: KC; "Policy and Strategy in the Eastern Theatre", Paper by Vice Admiral Willis, 8 March 1942, WLLS 5/5, Willis Papers: CC; S. Roskill, *The War at Sea*, ii, p. 23; G. H. Gill, ii, p. 4

48 S. ROSKILL, p. 32; Edwards Diary, 6 – 10 April 1942, REDW 2/7, Edwards Papers: CC; "General Remarks", by Willis, undated, WLLS 5/5: CC

49 LETTER, Willis to Moore, 13 April 1942, WLLS 5/5, Willis Papers: CC; See also "The Naval Situation in the Indian Ocean", Memorandum by Rear Admiral Tennant, 12 April 1942, TEN 25, Tennant Papers: NMM; Harvey Diary, 9 April 1942, ADD. MS. 56398, Harvey Papers: BL

50 MINUTE, Chief of Air Staff to Churchill, 9 April 1942; Minute, Ismay to Churchill, 9 April 1942, PREM 3/150/9: PRO

51 CABLES NO. 570/2 AND NO. 591/2, Churchill to Roosevelt, 15 and 19 April 1942, VI/2, Ismay Papers: KC; See also PREM 3/163/8: PRO

52 MEMORANDUM, Somerville to Wavell, 21 April 1942, SMVL 8/7, Somerville Papers: CC; See also PREM 3/142/2: PRO

53 S. ROSKILL, *The War at Sea*, ii, p. 60; See also Cable No. 618/2, Churchill to Roosevelt, 24 April 1942, VI/2, Ismay Papers: KC

54 "THE DEFENCE OF INDIA", Note by Bridges for War Cabinet, 1 May 1942, CAB 66/24, W.P. (42)184: PRO

55 EDWARDS DIARY, 28–29 April 1942, REDW 2/7, Edwards Papers: CC

56 CABLES NO. 660/2 AND NO. 661/2, Churchill to Wavell, 30 April 1942, VI/2, Ismay Papers: KC

57 CABLES NO. 428/2, NO. 546/2 AND NO. 658/2, Churchill to Curtin, 20 March, 5 and 30 April 1942, VI/2, Ismay Papers: KC

58 CABLE 520, Evatt to Curtin, 2 April 1942, CRS A5954, Box 474: AA; Cable, Evatt to Curtin, 3 April 1942, CRS A3300, Item 233: AA

59 MEMORANDUM, Evatt to Roosevelt, 5 April 1942, CRS A3300, Item 233: AA

60 CABLE, Evatt to Curtin, 6 April 1942, CRS A3300, Item 233: AA

61 DEFENCE COMMITTEE (OPERATIONS) MINUTES, 14 April 1942, CAB 69/4, D.O. (42)10: PRO

62 CABLE NO. 245, Curtin to Churchill, 14 April 1942, CRS A5954, Box 474: AA

63 CABLE NO. 571/2, Churchill to Curtin, 15 April 1942, VI/2, Ismay Papers: KC; Note, Attlee to Churchill, 15 April 1942, PREM 3/63/10: PRO

64 "SPEECH FOR CANADIAN CLUB LUNCHEON, Chateau Laurier, Thursday, April 9th, 1 pm", "War — Statements and Articles", Folder, Evatt Collection: FUL

65 CABLE, Evatt to Curtin, 17 April 1942, CRS A3300, Item 233: AA

66 CABLE ES9, Evatt to Curtin, 18 April 1942, CRS A3300, Item 233: AA

67 MINUTES OF PRIME MINISTER'S WAR CONFERENCE, 20 April 1942, CRS A5954, Box 1; Cables No. 49 and No. 50, Curtin to Evatt, 21 and 20 April 1942; Cable ES12, Evatt to Curtin, 20 April 1942, CRS A5954, Box 474: AA; See also *DAFP*, v, Docs 468–70

68 MINUTES OF PRIME MINISTER'S WAR CONFERENCE, 23 April 1942, CRS A5954, Box 1: AA

69 CABLE ES17 PART I, Evatt to Curtin, 23 April 1942, CRS A5954, Box 229; Cable ES17 Part 2, Evatt to Curtin, 23 April 1942, CRS A5954, Box 474: AA; Australia's senior diplomat in Washington, Alan Watt, noted the effect of Evatt's temperamental presence, with all senior officials being "*trodden on, discarded, not used*" by the mercurial Minister. Although Watt admitted the need to shake up Australia's supply organisation in the United States, he complained that "other things have occurred which I can scarcely put on paper". Letter, Watt to Hood, 16 April 1942, MS 3788/1/1, Watt Papers: NLA

70 CABLE (COPY), Warnecke to *Herald*, 28 April 1942, "Evatt — Overseas Trip — 1942", Evatt Collection: FUL

71 CABLE NO. 48, Bruce to Evatt, 24 April 1942, CRS A3300, Item 233: AA

72 CABLE SW34, Curtin to Evatt, 28 April 1942, CRS A3300, Item 233: AA

73 LETTER, Evatt to Hopkins, 29 April 1942, CRS A3300, Item 233: AA

74 ADVISORY WAR COUNCIL MINUTE NO. 914 (EXTRACT), 28 April 1942, CRS A5954, Box 229: AA; War Cabinet Agendum No. 275/1942, CRS A2670, 275/1942: AA; Advisory War Council Minutes, 28 April 1942, CRS A5954, Box 537: AA; Cable No. 252, Curtin to Churchill, 17 April 1942, *DAFP*, v, Doc. 467 and note 5, p. 720; Minute, Shedden to Curtin, 2 May 1942, CRS A5954, Box 3: AA

75 "THE PROBLEM OF ALLIED STRATEGY for the Defeat of Japan", Paper by Captain French, undated, pp. 4, 11, GDFR 2/3, French Papers: CC

76 HARVEY DIARY, 30 April 1942, ADD. MS. 56398, Harvey Papers: BL

77 LETTER, Cranborne to Emrys-Evans, 25 April 1942, ADD. MS. 58243, Emrys-Evans Papers: BL

78 CABLE NO. 658/2, Churchill to Curtin, 30 April 1942, VI/2, Ismay Papers: KC

79 CABLE NO. 653/2, Churchill to Roosevelt, 29 April 1942, VI/2, Ismay Papers: KC

80 DEFENCE COMMITTEE (OPERATIONS) MINUTES, 29 April 1942, CAB 69/4, D.O. (42)13: PRO

14

The Battle for Australia

May to June 1942

On 2 May, Evatt flew into Britain with the clear aim of securing Australia from invasion and occupation by the Japanese. Even as he arrived, the Japanese forces were moving steadily south along the chain of Solomon Islands in their bid to cut the sea and air route between Australia and America. At the same time, a Japanese armada with its convoy of troop ships was preparing for an assault on Port Moresby. Although the Americans knew of the impending attacks and were preparing to resist them, their naval strength in the Pacific was insufficient to give them a preponderance of power over the Japanese — quite the reverse. On Australia's western flank, much of the British Eastern fleet was hugging the coast of Africa for fear of discovery by the Japanese. The Indian Ocean, which had been a British "lake" for so long, was now effectively in the hands of the Japanese. The Allies' trump card was the very extent of the Japanese conquests, which had outrun her power to hold them.

Meanwhile, Australia had an army in the Turkish style — numerically strong but poorly trained and equipped. Of her four battle-hardened divisions, the 8th Division, minus its commanding officer, was imprisoned in Singapore's Changi gaol while the 9th Division remained stranded in Palestine, prevented from returning by the determined opposition of Churchill. Two brigades of the 6th Division were virtually trapped in Ceylon by the combined power of the Japanese navy and Churchill's refusal to relieve them as promised. The remaining brigade of the 6th Division, together with the 7th Division, had safely returned to Australia where they were being deployed in defence of the Dominion's south eastern seaboard. However, air and naval support were almost totally lacking. The RAAF's main role continued to be as a training organisation for the Empire Air Training Scheme by which Australian airmen were expended in Churchill's strategically doubtful air offensive against Germany. American combat aircraft were starting to arrive in Australia but they were equipping the United States forces rather than the RAAF and were still far from constituting an adequate front-line air defence force. The seas surrounding Australia were almost empty of Allied warships. About half of Australia's navy had been destroyed in the previous twelve months, mainly in the hopeless defence of the East Indies. Acting on Admiralty advice, Australia was busily preparing her harbours to berth the ships of an Allied fleet. But her anxious eyes could only see on the horizon the smoke stacks of the Japanese fleet.

Across the world in London, Evatt was anxious more than ever that Australia be provided with a sufficient level of reinforcements to ensure its security but was increasingly conscious of the difficulty of making Australia's voice heard in the capitals of her Great Power allies. As he complained to Curtin following his arrival in Britain, "Australia has had very little if any share in the formulation and direction of the general policy of the war".[1] And it would be some days before Evatt would even discover what constituted the general policy.

As in Washington, Evatt revealed his belief that the Allied strategic direction of the war was still at least a partially open question that could be susceptible to Australian pressure. He was determined to do what he could to boost the importance of the Pacific theatre in the minds of Allied planners. In an initial discussion between Evatt and Bruce on 3 May, Bruce was surprised to find Evatt ignorant of Allied strategy and "too inclined to think in terms of Australia only".[2] Given the situation of Australia at that time and MacArthur's low opinion of its defence capability, it was perfectly understandable as well as appropriate that Evatt should have the security of Australia in the forefront of his mind. The surprising thing is that Bruce did not feel it incumbent upon him as Australian High Commissioner to mirror Evatt's concern. In fact, his primary concern was to smooth over the recent rough patches in Anglo–Australian relations and preserve the Dominion as a loyal Imperial partner. Bruce had already approached the British

Cabinet Secretary, Sir Edward Bridges, to argue the importance of Churchill avoiding any row with Evatt. Bridges was sympathetic but warned of possible difficulties due to the "peculiarities of the Prime Minister".[3]

After his meeting with Bruce, Evatt travelled to Chequers for his first meeting with Churchill where he apparently pushed the Australian case quite hard, although Bruce noted the following day that he did not seem to have got very far. It was apparent to Bruce that Evatt had "not got the whole picture too clearly in his head" and they agreed to "have a serious couple of hours conversation on these strategic problems before he made any move with regard to them".[4] However, before Bruce was able to enlighten Evatt on the facts of Imperial life, his ignorance of "W.W.I." had brought him into sharp dispute with the Munitions Assignment Board, composed of equal numbers of British and American Service representatives and chaired by Britain's Minister of Production, Oliver Lyttelton.

Despite having Bruce and four Australian Service advisers with him at this meeting, Evatt launched an attack on the amount of supplies reaching Australia and argued that greater priority be accorded to the Pacific in the Allied strategic plan. He admitted that he "did not even know whether there was any strategic plan" but argued that he "did not see how strategy could be considered separately from supply". In front of the Board members and the Australian advisers, Bruce pointed out to Evatt that strategy was not within the purview of this meeting which could only allocate resources according to a master strategy decided by the Combined Chiefs of Staff. He then tried to divert Evatt's argument into the sidetrack of deciding where the Australian demands should be put — London or Washington. Evatt strenuously ploughed on, dismissing Bruce's argument as "a matter of detail" and complaining instead that there "seemed to be a gap between strategy and allocation". Then, realising that he was not making any headway against this blank refusal to consider wider questions of strategy, Evatt abruptly quit the gathering leaving Bruce to settle the minor matters before the meeting.[5]

In a report on the meeting to Churchill, Lyttelton warned that Evatt was "considerably aggrieved" after having spent six weeks in Washington without being able to "discover how the strategy of the war ... was conducted". Despite this, Lyttelton assured Churchill that he "did not, of course enter into any discussions on the purely strategical points".[6]

Evatt went straight from the meeting of the Munitions Assignment Board to a meeting of the British War Cabinet where he tried to resurrect his arguments, requesting a "reassessment of the general strategical situation" which might provide "good grounds for strengthening the forces available for the defence of Australia" and pleading for aircraft with which to beat off, or even deter, a Japanese attack. In reply, Churchill merely assured him of Britain's continuing commitment to "do all in our power to defend our kith and kin in Australia" and suggested that Evatt meet with the relevant officials to assure himself on the flow of supplies. At no point did he enlighten Evatt about "W.W.I." or the priority accorded by the Allies to the Pacific theatre.[7] As one British observer at the meeting noted, "Evatt wasted a lot of our time".[8] According to Bruce, one of Evatt's aims at this time was to secure a Privy Councillorship for himself and he was bitter at Curtin for not pushing the case hard enough with Churchill. In fact, it was Churchill who would not countenance such a recent Minister of the Crown as Evatt being elevated to the Privy Council.[9]

On 5 May, his fourth day in London, Evatt attended a press conference at the Ministry of Information where he was closely questioned about his attitude to Allied war strategy. When asked whether he objected to "the theory that the Pacific is a side show", Evatt pounced on this chance to argue his case, claiming that "Nobody openly supports the theory any longer, but they rather assume it by other suggestions which really bring that into the case". He blissfully assured the press that the Allied strategy does "not contemplate concentration on one enemy" and there was "great danger to the common cause in talking along the line, 'Let us beat Hitler first'". Pointing to MacArthur's directive, Evatt repeated his argument that it "has been laid down, must be carried into effect, and will be carried into effect by providing him with the necessary supplies to carry out his mission".[10]

Hosting Evatt's press conference was Brendan Bracken, Britain's Minister for Information and a close associate of Churchill. Bracken's reaction to the conference is not recorded but he seems to have been sufficiently alarmed to mount a determined effort to turn Evatt aside from his crusade to safeguard Australia. Describing Evatt as "a dreadful fellow" who "drinks a good deal too much", Bracken later claimed to have "dined with him at least 20 times to get him better educated on viewing the War from the point of view of the world and not the fruitless parochial angle of one Dominion alone". Churchill was also heavily involved in this systematic attempt to soften Evatt's nationalistic attitudes, though he also found this duty an onerous one. On one occasion at Chequers, Churchill reportedly appealed to Bracken to take the Australian Minister away as, he said, "I simply can't *bear* this fellow". Despite their distaste, their efforts were successful. As one observer judged, Churchill and Bracken did "a great deal to educate and mellow this parochial, restless, rude, ambitious, indefatigable and by no means unintelligent creature whose brain and energy one cannot help respecting and to some extent liking, in spite of his drab appearance, dreary droning voice with its nazal [sic] whine, and his unattractive personality."[11]

While Evatt was confidently proclaiming the Allied commitment embodied in MacArthur's directive, the American General continued to complain about the lack of forces provided to fulfil the terms of his instructions. At a meeting with Shedden on 2 May, MacArthur had been informed of Churchill's refusal to divert British ships and troops to Australia's defence. MacArthur had been rebuked by General Marshall for openly supporting the Australian request. He now concluded from the paucity of the forces being committed to his charge that Churchill and Roosevelt must have come to an agreement to defeat Germany first and that Evatt would be unable to change it. Whatever the rhetorical promises from London and Washington, MacArthur was convinced that

> little assistance was to be afforded the Southwest Pacific Area. He considered the President and General Marshall were under the influence of Mr. Churchill's strategy. An officer who had recently arrived from America had reported that General Marshall, in referring to assistance to Australia, had said that if

(*Overleaf*) H. V. Evatt, Australian Minister for External Affairs, and Winston Churchill
(Sport and General Press Agency, London)

*the Japanese overran the Commonwealth "it would be just too
bad. He could help the Australians no more than he could help
MacArthur in the Philippines."*[12]

MacArthur informed Shedden that he had now asked
Marshall to specify the offensive action envisaged for the south
west Pacific and with what forces it was to be accomplished.
MacArthur had also informed Marshall that the United States
forces arriving in Australia needed several months' training
before they would be ready to face the Japanese. Even though
there were over 400,000 Allied troops in Australia, the level of
training, equipment and air and naval support left them incapable of withstanding a major attack. In view of this and of
Churchill's refusal to send British reinforcements, MacArthur
urged that Australia demand the recall of the 9th Division. This
opinion was backed up by Blamey who also "emphasized the
number of enquiries that are being received from relatives
regarding the return of these troops".[13]

On 6 May, Curtin put the opinions of Blamey and MacArthur
before a meeting of the Advisory War Council. It seemed a
strange way to run a war, waiting four days to decide on such
an important communication while a Japanese invasion force
was steaming into the Coral Sea towards Port Moresby and
other Japanese forces were tightening their hold on the Solomon
Islands, within bombing distance of the Queensland coast.
Again, this was probably a reflection of the political situation
in Canberra where two independent MPs continued to hold
the balance of power, keeping Curtin in office on sufferance.
With this weakest of mandates, discussion rather than decision
was often the order of the day. In this case, the Council
accepted the prediction that Australia would not be supplied
with sufficient forces to mount offensive operations against the
Japanese and that the Dominion's "predominant concern is the
security of Australia". After thirty-two months of war, six of
them against Japan, this was a fundamental change in thinking.[14]

Armed with the unanimous view of his military advisers
and political opponents, Curtin had the curious task of en-
lightening Evatt about the situation in the Allied capitals the
External Affairs Minister was then visiting. He informed Evatt
of MacArthur's scepticism about "the degree of assistance that
will be extended to the South West Pacific area" and about

how "it would be very difficult to get the President or Mr. Churchill to deviate from the view that all efforts have to be concentrated on knocking out Germany first". In view of this apparent policy of her allies, Australia's "predominant consideration and objective" had to be its own security "whether or not it is to be used as a base for offensive action". Evatt was to be advised of the forces necessary to achieve this more limited objective and was warned by Curtin of imminent naval action by Japan that might hinder the further reinforcement of the Dominion.[15]

It was ironic that Curtin and MacArthur in the comparative isolation of Australia had a better appreciation of Allied strategy than Evatt who was at the heart of Allied decision-making. Even with Curtin's cable, Evatt continued to believe the constant assurances from Washington and London and to pin his faith on the words of MacArthur's directive. Though he agreed to press for the return of the 9th Division, he refused to scale down his demand that the Allies find the means to carry out the directive in full. Far from reflecting the pessimism emanating from Australia, Evatt was positively optimistic, claiming that the position had improved and urging MacArthur to continue pressing for "those forces which will not only (a) successfully defend Australia but also (b) be able to operate offensively within a reasonable time". Evatt advised Curtin that he would be meeting with Churchill and the Chiefs of Staff within a few days to discuss the "general strategy of war including any relevant written appreciations".[16] The veils of illusion surrounding the pugnacious External Affairs Minister would then be suddenly lifted.

In the meantime, from 5 to 8 May, American and Australian naval forces in the Coral Sea prevented a Japanese invasion force landing at Port Moresby. Forewarned by its deciphering of Japanese communications, the United States was able to dispatch sufficient forces to the largely undefended seas of the south west Pacific to pre-empt the Japanese stroke. In a new type of naval warfare in which the two fleets never came within sight of each other, carrier aircraft searched the tropical seas for the opposing ships and attacked on sight. In this game of hide and seek, luck was a major factor. Although the two fleets were evenly matched, the Allies' major loss was a fleet carrier compared to the loss of a light carrier by the Japanese. In fact, the Japanese believed they had sunk two American carriers. The Japanese troop convoy escaped unscathed back to Rabaul.

Despite this apparent overall victory for their forces, the loss of the light carrier had caused Japan to postpone their seaborne attack on Port Moresby. Subsequent events caused its cancellation altogether and, instead, an ill-fated landward attack against Port Moresby was launched later across the jungle-covered heights of the Owen Stanley mountains. In hindsight, the battle of the Coral Sea represented a strategic defeat for Japan. However, in Australia, the Japanese thrust seemed to confirm its worst fears, which in turn were heightened by the Allied losses. At best, the battle of the Coral Sea was seen as providing a breathing space for the Dominion. As such, the pressure increased on Evatt to secure urgent reinforcements from the Allies.

While naval forces were fighting off-shore, the working men of Townsville in north Queensland had another worry — the possible use of black American labour units on work formerly done by Australian workmen and the reported importation of Javanese coolie labour for the same purpose. Though there were no Javanese coolies in Australia, there were over 5000 black American labourers within the American forces, nearly 2000 of them being based at Townsville enlarging the aerodrome from which United States bombers had flown in the battle of the Coral Sea. The Townsville Trades and Labour Council had requested that a Government statement be made about the use of this black labour to "allay any doubts which might exist in the minds of the workers as to the future of their hard won Trade Union conditions". However, as Shedden advised Curtin at the end of May, it would be inexpedient to make such a declaration since the Government had agreed to the admission of the black construction units into Australia and "any public statement on the subject might only serve to emphasise this fact and to draw attention to [their] presence". Curtin agreed, refusing to make any public declaration but assuring the Council that black labourers were part of the United States forces and that therefore "their presence in Australia in the present emergency" would not offer "any threat to Trade Union conditions".[17]

One week after the Coral Sea battle, the War Cabinet was faced with another threat to the comfortable assumptions of white Australia — the use of a Sydney sports oval as a camp for black US construction workers. After protests from Beasley, the local MP for Glebe where the oval was situated, the Government proposed alternative sites — next to a power station and a railway marshalling yard.[18] Australia was not alone in its racism. Britain was similarly upset at the influx of black American troops and even asked for advice from Australia on ways to restrict the numbers of blacks without upsetting American sensitivities.[19] But Australian racism was much more overt than Britain's, and for good reason. Australians enjoyed the bounty of a continent stolen from its original inhabitants, the bounty being that much richer and more coveted for being shared among such a small population. Now it was threatened by a fresh wave of invasion. As W. S. Robinson the Australian mining magnate wrote while accompanying Evatt to London,

> We must not forget that the East, with all its cruelties, lies at our door ... Australia and New Zealand have a total population of about 9,000,000 whites. Their neighbours are 1,000,000,000 of the coloured races — only a few hours away by air ... Australia and New Zealand are in the uncomfortable position of having most to lose and the greatest chance of losing it.[20]

The battle of the Coral Sea did not increase Australia's confidence in being able to preserve the sanctity of this white society in the South Pacific. On 11 May, MacArthur warned Curtin that the Dominion had to be ready to repulse further attacks and that the Coral Sea victory had been achieved by United States aircraft carriers which had since left Australian waters, leaving just two cruisers to provide naval protection. To face a further attack, MacArthur argued that Australia desperately needed aircraft, both sea-borne and land-based, since no amount of troops would be sufficient "if the enemy has superior naval and air power".[21] From Washington, Roosevelt also warned that Australia faced the possibility of further Japanese attacks as part of its campaign to isolate the Dominion from American assistance.[22] But Churchill remained determined to resist calls to secure Australia from such attacks which, he claimed, were designed to force the Allies to "lock up as many troops as possible in Australia". Rather than reinforcement, the build up of the Eastern fleet was delayed even further. Australia remained ignorant of the fleet's weakened state.[23]

As the Japanese and Allied fleets were taking their places

for the Coral Sea battle, Evatt informed Curtin of the initial British response to his mission. The External Affairs Minister remained puzzled about Britain's reluctance to reinforce her Imperial partner but suspected the worst. He suggested that Britain had effectively wiped her hands of Australia with the transfer to Washington of strategic responsibility in the Pacific. Evatt claimed that the defence of India had become Britain's "primary interest" and that there was "reason to believe that one of the objectives of the concentration of aircraft carriers in the Indian Ocean is to force the Japanese to operate on the Pacific side of Singapore" which "immediately adds to the danger of Australia". Evatt was correct in claiming that India counted for more than Australia in British calculations but he still seemed not to realise the extent of the risk that Churchill was prepared to run even with India. Instead, he took comfort from the re-statement by Churchill of his promise to divert the two British divisions rounding the Cape if Australia was "heavily invaded" and to "throw everything possible into the defence of Australia preferring it to the defence of India". According to Evatt, there was a real possibility that Britain could be prevailed upon to supply Australia with additional aircraft and accord the Dominion a greater priority in the allocation of munitions.[24]

The following day, 8 May, Evatt reiterated his rather naive optimism in a further message to Curtin which rejected the Australian demand for reinforcements for its own security only and proclaimed that MacArthur must refuse to accept "anything short of those forces which will not only (a) successfully defend Australia but also (b) be able to operate offensively within a reasonable time. This is his present mandate and it is binding upon all the Governments concerned." Evatt complained of "continual propaganda and persuasion" being needed in London to prevent the "Pacific front from being regarded as a side show". He explained the relegation of the Pacific by referring to Anglo–American authorities who "grossly under-estimated Japan's strength" and who now found it difficult to accept their blunder and "face up to the true position".[25] Certainly there was a blunder, but, as General Pownall confided in his diary in February 1942, "With all our other commitments I don't believe that, however highly we had rated the Japs as fighters, we would have been caused thereby to improve the condition of our Services in the Far East."[26]

On 12 May, Evatt met with Bruce prior to a meeting with the British Chiefs of Staff. Bruce had been forewarned by the Australian Service adviser in London, Brigadier Wardell, that the Chiefs had prepared briefing papers for the meeting which explicitly referred to the "Germany first" policy. Bruce well realised that Evatt was opposed to this strategy but deliberately omitted to advise him of it. Following Evatt's meeting with the Chiefs of Staff, he was relieved to learn that Evatt had not sighted the briefing papers and had allowed himself to be fobbed off by Britain's defence chiefs. However, this relief was short-lived when Wardell confided to Bruce later in the evening that one of the papers had been shown to Evatt who had "reacted very violently".[27]

It is unclear who was responsible for bringing "W.W.I." to Evatt's attention. It may well have been revealed by his unofficial adviser, W. S. Robinson, who enjoyed a friendship with Oliver Lyttelton. Then again, it may have been one of Australia's Service advisers in London in an act of conscientiousness or by simple inadvertence. A further possibility is that it may have been revealed by one of Evatt's British Labour Party counterparts with whom he dined on 12 May.[28]

Anyway, whoever revealed the strategy is largely irrelevant compared with the crucial question of identifying those who deliberately concealed it for so long from Evatt. And here Australia's firm allies, Britain and the United States, must take much of the responsibility. There was a careful campaign orchestrated by Churchill and connived at by Roosevelt to conceal the reality of Allied strategy. Australia's representatives in London and Washington did a grave disservice to their duty when they became involved in this campaign and withheld vital information from their political masters. Earle Page, S. M. Bruce and Richard Casey were all either past or present conservative members of the Australian Parliament and were ill-suited to serve the needs of a more nationalistic Labor Government. Bruce provided an interesting insight into his patrician attitudes when he calmly recorded for posterity his deliberate deceit of Evatt.

The following morning, 13 May, Evatt requested from the Chiefs of Staff, and was finally given, a copy of "W.W.I.". It is clear that it came as a shock to him and that he was not feigning surprise as has been suggested by one historian.[29] But neither was it a total surprise. Evatt had adequate warning of

the strong pressure in London and Washington to concentrate
Allied attention on the defeat of Germany. In fact the whole
tenor of his trip was pitched to counter this pressure. His
surprise was caused by his misplaced confidence in having
achieved a modification of the strategy as supposedly exemplified
by MacArthur's directive. The discovery of "W.W.I." revealed
to Evatt the rigidity of a strategy that he had believed was
fluid. The limitation of MacArthur's directive was now painfully
apparent as was the failure of Evatt's prolonged trip to achieve
a substantial improvement in Australia's defence capability.

Evatt's reaction to his discovery of "W.W.I." is interesting.
Despite the vital implications of this document for Australia's
defence strategy, Evatt did not cable its full contents to Curtin
or discuss it with Bruce until 28 May, fifteen days after he first
sighted it.[30] He only raised the matter with Bruce after Bruce
acknowledged that he already knew of "W.W.I.".[31] Evatt's failure
to confirm the details of "W.W.I." to Curtin was the reaction
of a politician concerned to paint his trip in the colours of
success. He had proclaimed a great personal victory at the end
of his stay in Washington, a victory that would prove to be
hollow with the announcement of "W.W.I.". So he delayed
cabling the contents of "W.W.I.", except in the most general
terms, until he could first offset this embarrassing failure with a
dramatic and visible success for Australia.

Evatt had already held out the hope to Curtin of achieving
an allocation of fighter planes from Britain. He now set about
fulfilling this objective and paid less attention to pressing the
issues raised by Curtin, including the return of the 9th Division.
Although "W.W.I." made the return of Australian troops
even more vital, Evatt appears to have realised that the strategy
also made these issues more difficult to achieve and he was
unwilling to force Churchill to a showdown over them.
Churchill's efforts in assiduously cultivating his favour began
to pay dividends as Evatt moderated his stance to protect the
special relationship that he mistakenly believed he had developed
with the British Prime Minister.

On the same day that Evatt was discovering the terms of
"W.W.I.", Australia's Advisory War Council met to discuss
the results of the Coral Sea battle. Far from seeing it as a
decisive victory, the Council claimed it to be "rather disappointing" and a missed opportunity, that with all the advance

Taking the reins: the Supreme Commander in the south-west
Pacific, General MacArthur, addresses the Australian Advisory War
Council. Listening on his left are Prime Minister John Curtin,
Country Party leader "Artie" Fadden and Treasurer Ben Chifley
(AUSTRALIAN WAR MEMORIAL)

information available of the Japanese intentions, the Allies
"should have been able to concentrate the superior strength
necessary to have ensured a complete victory".[32] Backed with
this opinion and the support of MacArthur, Curtin again pressed
Britain to make a commitment of reinforcements prior to a
Japanese invasion of Australia and, perhaps by doing so, forestall an invasion altogether.

In a cable to Evatt, Curtin acknowledged that any captured
Australian territory would probably be recovered in the long
term but by then the "country may have been ravished and the
people largely decimated". He predicted that the judgement of
history would "gravely indict such a happening to a nation
which sacrificed 60,000 of its men on overseas bettlefields in
the last war and at its peril has sent its Naval, Military and Air

Forces to fight overseas in this one." Curtin claimed that, from the Japanese viewpoint, Australia was more attractive as an immediate objective than India and concluded his message with a desperate plea for the Dominion's defence deficiencies to be made good — they "must come from elsewhere and come quickly".[33]

Evatt received this message on 14 May and immediately passed it on to Churchill who in turn referred it to the War Cabinet. That night, Evatt left with Churchill on a two-day tour of Yorkshire and Durham. This proved to be a turning point in Evatt's advocacy of the Australian case. Armed with his newfound knowledge of the "Germany first" strategy, Evatt might have been expected to take Churchill to task for not informing Australia of such a vital Allied strategy and for placing the Dominion in consequent peril. There is little evidence that he did so.

Instead, Evatt's public tour with Churchill through northern England impressed upon him the strong hold that the British Prime Minister had on the affections of his national constituency. Earlier in 1942, Evatt had entertained hopes of Churchill being replaced by a leader more sympathetic to Australia's plight. Now he realised these hopes were forlorn, that Churchill had "popular backing everywhere outside Parliament".[34] Evatt was faced with a leader with a national following, a phenomenon practically unknown in Australia and woefully missing in wartime. Australia would have to deal with Churchill's presence for the foreseeable future and this obviously worried Evatt sufficiently for him to limit the pressure he was willing to apply on the Dominion's behalf. It also seems that Evatt was captivated by Churchill's personality and by the strenuous effort being made to woo him from his pursuit of the primary Australian national interest — its security.

Evatt returned from his tour on 17 May and immediately cabled to Curtin, confirming the reality of the Allied strategy but noting how difficult it was to press for reinforcements "without being importunate". He was beginning to accept the arguments of Churchill and expressed to Curtin his fear that a strong demand might "adversely affect the relationship [with Churchill] which has built up during my fortnight here and thereby injure Australia". Evatt claimed that Churchill was "impressed" with Australia's argument and was anxious to do more for the Dominion but was "perplexed as to the source from which it should come". Evatt did not draw the obvious implication from Churchill's dilemma — that Australia was outranked in priority by almost every other claimant on British resources.[35]

Evatt also found on his return a letter from W. S. Robinson strongly advising him that his strident attitude was no longer appropriate and could be dangerous to the Australian cause. He reminded Evatt of the "generous hospitality" and the "tremendous reception" he had received in Britain. Coupled with Churchill's promises of help, Robinson urged that the time had arrived to moderate his rough approach and become

> *warmly appreciative of all that has been done in the past for Australia — all that has been promised and you hope Britain can do today. I know you will not carry in your mind the slightest suspicion that promises are now being made to you that cannot or will not be fulfilled or that there is the least desire to neglect Australia and Australians or that the utmost Britain can do herself and can influence the United States to do will not be done.*[36]

It seems that Evatt had already reached this conclusion himself. His discovery of "W.W.I." and his appreciation of Churchill's entrenched political position had made him realise that a confrontation over Australia's defence would be futile and could even prove harmful to the limited assistance already offered. In fact, on the day he discovered the terms of "W.W.I.", Evatt apparently decided instead to make a strong stand on wool prices, informing Bruce that he would demand a 3d increase rather than the 2d previously contemplated. He was determined to have at least one popular victory from his mission.[37]

On 18 May, the day Robinson was counselling moderation, Evatt was already assuring Bruce that because of Churchill's grip on the British public "it would be a bad thing for us to have a quarrel with Winston [on the issue of Australian representation in the War Cabinet] as it might hurt Australia's interests in obtaining reinforcements and supplies we need if we antagonise him". Bruce was amazed at this change from Evatt's previous "blood and thunder" attitude and he was forced to try and steel Evatt to take a stronger line. He tried to downplay the importance of the public demonstrations of support for Churchill, arguing that the "people's favour was notoriously a somewhat uncertain quantity". But Evatt would not budge and the High Commissioner was left to remark on how Churchill had obviously "exercised his charm and unquestionable astuteness upon Evatt".[38]

Though Evatt's ruffled nationalist feathers were being smoothed down by Churchill's beguiling touch, the Australian remained desperate to obtain a commitment of fighter aircraft from Britain. He had held out to Curtin the prospect of such an achievement even before he left Washington and, on 18 May, Robinson had signalled to Curtin that most of the problems facing Evatt in London would soon be solved, that the "results of his firm and persistent pressure" would "give great satisfaction to your Government and the Australian people".[39] MacArthur had provided Evatt with arguments to use in his appeal, noting that Britain had only supplied 316 of the 2087 aircraft requested from her for the RAAF. In fact, between January and August 1942, Britain supplied just seventy-seven combat aircraft for the RAAF from her own production, although there were a further 366 training aircraft supplied. These combat aircraft had been ordered by Australia prior to Pearl Harbor.[40]

On 20 May, Evatt achieved his objective, at least in the political sense. Churchill finally relented and agreed to support the dispatch of three Spitfire squadrons to Australia, two of them to be drawn from RAAF units based in Britain. Mrs Churchill was instrumental in Evatt's success when she intervened over lunch in an argument between himself and Churchill. Evatt thanked her for her comments, noting that afterwards "the Prime Minister was most helpful". In fact, Churchill was anxious to make a token contribution to Australia's defence. Just three days before his lunch with Evatt, Churchill observed that Britain had to consider her "permanent relationship with Australia, and it seems very detrimental to the future of the Empire for us not to be represented in any way in their defence."[41] On 21 May the Spitfire proposal came before the British War Cabinet for approval. Evatt was in attendance for what he then believed was to be his last meeting before departing for Australia; his departure was subsequently delayed for a week.

In assessing the proposal, the Air Ministry was less concerned with solving Evatt's political problems than in deciding the most efficient distribution of Allied resources. The Chief of the Air Staff (CAS) therefore suggested that Australia accept Kittyhawk fighters from America and use the abundant personnel within Australia to crew them rather than the slower and less economic plan to dispatch whole squadrons of Spitfires complete with aircrew and ground staff. On purely military considerations, there was much to recommend the arguments of the CAS. His alternative would probably have been in the interests of all the Allies, including Australia. However, it was not in Evatt's interest, and Churchill intervened to countermand the Air Ministry argument in accordance with his agreement with Evatt and to do so in a way that allowed Evatt to squeeze the maximum personal political benefit from the decision. Churchill asked the CAS to draw up a plan for the dispatch of the squadrons which "should form a basis for a communication to be made by Dr. Evatt to the Australian Government. No communication should be sent in the meantime by the United Kingdom authorities on the matter."[42]

To ensure that the plan did not go awry, Evatt extracted a promise from Churchill that the dispatch of the two Australian squadrons would not be publicly portrayed as being done at Australia's behest and, most importantly, that the commitment of the three squadrons from Britain would not detract from the commitment of planes already promised from America.[43] As an added precaution, Evatt was provided with a written statement by Downing Street listing the various undertakings by the British Government to provide for Australia's defence. Apart from the Spitfire squadrons and the accelerated delivery of certain military supplies, the other undertakings were re-statements of previous pledges, the value of which could only be tested in the event of Australia being invaded.[44]

At this same War Cabinet meeting on 21 May, Curtin's cable of the previous week was discussed. As Evatt now advised the meeting, this cable had been dispatched from Canberra before Curtin knew the grand strategy of the war. In fact, Curtin still only knew this strategy in the most general terms since Evatt had not yet sent him the contents of "W.W.I.". Although Evatt argued Curtin's case for reinforcements, there was little heat in the discussion. Churchill merely trotted out the previous assurances regarding the possible diversion of

British troops in the event of a large-scale invasion. He also claimed that, notwithstanding Australia's appeal for help from the United States and the Dominion's subsequent allocation to the American strategic sphere in the Pacific, Britain did not regard her traditional obligation to help Australia "as being lessened in any way". However, Churchill refused to commit British forces prior to an actual invasion of Australia, although he was doing so in the case of India. In Australia's case, the immediate assistance was limited to the dispatch of the Spitfire squadrons. Although Evatt also raised the need for naval forces in Australian waters, his words were not heeded. After successfully extracting his Spitfires, the meeting concluded with an expression by Evatt of his "gratitude to all the War Cabinet for the help which they had given him".[45]

The extent of the help and the value of the commitment were illusory. Despite Evatt's shouting and stamping, nothing had changed. On 30 May, General Ismay made this very clear in a note to Churchill in which he questioned the commitment to Australia, asking whether it would affect the order of British priorities whereby "the Middle East is regarded as having priority over Australia, India and Ceylon in the matter of the allocation of resources". Churchill readily confirmed that these priorities remained unchanged, that the promise to abandon the Mediterranean in the event of a serious invasion of Australia was an "undertaking related only to a contingency ... regarded as highly improbable, and that it was not intended to have any bearing on the immediate problem of allocation of resources". Churchill's own view was revealed by the changes he made to the draft commitment drawn up for Evatt. He sliced out the reference to Australia's "unswerving" support and also scrawled his pen through Britain's promise to "cut her losses in the Mediterranean".[46]

On 28 May, Evatt finally cabled to Curtin with the full terms of "W.W.I.". He blamed Page and Casey for not informing Australia of the agreement and claimed that Wardell, but not Bruce, knew the substance of "W.W.I.". Once back in Canberra, Evatt succeeded in having Wardell removed from his London posting.[47] So Bruce largely escaped Evatt's wrath. Anyway, his wrath was tempered now by a belief that even "W.W.I." could be made to help the Dominion since it called for the security of Australia as a base against Japan. Evatt's emphasis, therefore, shifted from his previous stance of opposition to the "Germany first" policy to one of grudging acceptance provided that its clause relating to Australian security was applied to the letter. In fact, he went on at great length in his cable to put Australian demands in the context of a global conflict, much in the way that Churchill must have argued during Evatt's visits to Chequers.[48]

Apart from reporting on "W.W.I.", Evatt repeated the promises given by Churchill for the diversion to Australia of British land forces, then en route to India and the Middle East, if Australia was heavily invaded. Australian troops temporarily garrisoning Ceylon would be returned to Australia "at the very earliest possible moment". Instead of pressing for the return of the 9th Division from the Middle East as instructed by Curtin, Evatt passed the matter back to Canberra on the dubious pretext that it was "a matter of the highest Government policy". It is difficult to escape the conclusion that Evatt came to an understanding with Churchill whereby the Spitfires would be traded for the retention of the 9th Division. As for the accelerated delivery of military supplies from Britain, Evatt admitted that they "fall short of full requests" but reassured Curtin with the fanciful British claim that "the Australian army will very shortly be the best equipped in the world".[49] According to Wardell, any additional assignments of munitions gained by Evatt were subsequently subtracted after his departure from London, thereby leaving Australia with no improvement in her nett position.[50]

To compensate for the disappointments, Evatt announced with a flourish his great victory with regard to the promised delivery of three Spitfire squadrons leaving Britain by the end of June as an additional allocation of air strength to Australia. He described them as "two crack R.A.A.F. squadrons" and "a first class R.A.F. squadron" with planes of the "most modern character" which together comprised a "small air expeditionary force".[51] This description of the rather minuscule force of forty-eight secondhand aircraft served its purpose and allowed Evatt to claim a victory from his trip that would fudge the harsh reality of "W.W.I.". Although Curtin expressed his gratification at the news of the Spitfires, he also suggested that Evatt use the continuation of Australia's participation in the Empire Air Training Scheme as a bargaining counter to ensure the provision from Britain of aircraft for the RAAF. This suggestion came too late and was not sufficiently explicit for Evatt to act upon. Moreover, given Evatt's change of heart, it is doubtful whether he would have agreed to the use of Australian contributions to Imperial defence as a means to force Britain to fulfil her obligations to the Dominion's defence.[52]

Whitehall celebrated Evatt's departure from London. British officials had regarded the arrival of the rough colonial politician with trepidation and, rushing to count the nation's stock of military hardware on his departure, were relieved to find him leaving the Imperial capital with such light baggage. Churchill, who had warned Roosevelt to be on guard against Evatt, now informed the President that Evatt had "shown himself most friendly, especially to me personally, and I think you will find that he will help in every way".[53] This was confirmed by a well-placed observer in London who reported that Evatt had been "entirely captured by Winston" and departed "much better disposed and less anti-British after getting his wool prices and the Spitfires".[54] The New South Wales Governor, Lord Wakehurst, later reported to London that, on his return, Evatt was "full of Winston and genuinely impressed by the war effort in England. His trouble is that although he has brains he has neither courage nor integrity. One should make use of his ability without putting too much strain on his reliability."[55]

Evatt's three-month trip had added little to Australia's security. Certainly there are limits to which a small power can coerce Great Power allies into ensuring its protection. But there is little evidence that Evatt made any serious attempt at arm-twisting in London or Washington. As a lawyer, he was accustomed to words having a precise meaning. This ill-served him in his new role as a politician where words had shades of meaning, mean different things to different people and are open to sudden reinterpretation. Although, like Alice, he sensed that things were not quite as they seemed, the Dominion's historic dependence on Britain curbed his independent inclinations.[56] Ultimately, Australia had more to lose than Britain from any open breach in their relations. So Evatt returned with a semblance of achievement and in the apparently genuine belief that Churchill had Australia's interests at heart.

Although Evatt was able publicly to proclaim his mission a triumph[57], there were few such illusions in Canberra. Throughout Evatt's trip, Shedden had been keeping track, presumably at Curtin's request, of Evatt's claimed achievements and comparing them with confirmed improvements in the supply of men and equipment from Britain and America. The trend of these reports generally disparaged his efforts and concluded that Evatt's trip had done little to improve Australia's security position. Similarly, General MacArthur informed Curtin that, based on information from Evatt's own cables, the External Affairs Minister had "no doubt evoked a sympathetic hearing from Mr. Churchill and other Ministers, but from the practical military point of view little had been achieved".[58]

Evatt's Spitfires finally arrived in Australia nearly six months late after the original consignment was diverted to the Middle East. Then the United States simply subtracted an equivalent number of aircraft from their allocation to Australia. Despite his assurance that this would not occur, Churchill refused to intercede on Australia's behalf. Once in operation, the aircraft were found to be second-hand and some of the pilots second-rate. On balance, Australian security was probably worsened as a result of Evatt's single major "success" in London.[59]

Evatt's trip highlighted several problems that continued to dog Australia. The first concerned the lack of consultation by Great Power allies on matters of vital concern to Australian security. There was not only a lack of consultation on "W.W.I." but a more or less deliberate attempt to conceal from Australia the terms of an agreement that vitally affected its security. Australia was led to believe that her interests were being safeguarded by the benevolence of her two protecting powers — Britain and America. It was only by chance that she learned of "W.W.I.". In this she was ill-served by her officials in London and Washington. Most of them seem to have fallen in with the Allied policy despite the possible ramifications for Australia. They became conduits of misinformation, misleading their Government in Canberra and putting their country at potential risk. For five perilous months the Australian Government prepared its defences while being kept largely in ignorance of the basic strategic policy of its allies.

If Australia's officials were culpable for misleading their masters, how much more so was Evatt? After spending two months in Washington and London knocking on doors in the confident belief that he was re-shaping Allied strategy, Evatt realised that all the doors he had been through were of the revolving type. He had played the part of the rough colonial but was really an innocent abroad in the care of his worldly wise cousins from the metropolis. Like innumerable Australian politicians before and since, Evatt then became pre-occupied with making a display of personal achievement rather than in promoting national interests. By the end of his stay in London, he had become a virtual apologist for the "Germany first" policy. There is little in Evatt's trip to London in 1942 to sustain the concept of him being the father of a distinctive Australian foreign policy. The reverse could well be argued — that his visit reconciled him to the reality of Australia's dependence on powerful and distant allies and that any distinctiveness in the Australian foreign policy would lie in its details rather than its substance.

While Evatt had been concluding his stay in London, the Japanese navy was assembling a massive assault force of 200 ships scheduled to capture the Pacific island of Midway during the first week of June. In the process, Tokyo intended to destroy the remaining vestiges of American naval power in the Pacific. If this operation was successful, the expanded Japanese Empire might be virtually invulnerable for several years, by which time war weariness might have set in and a compromise peace achieved whereby the Japanese would be permitted to retain their conquests. Australia took no part in this decisive battle, during which its fate hung in the balance. The sense of Australian impotence was heightened by having the scales weighted heavily against the Allies. Although, as in the battle of the Coral Sea, Allied intelligence had alerted the United States navy to the Japanese intentions, it could not make up for the huge imbalance of forces, with the United States managing to assemble just seventy-six ships as against the 200 of the Japanese.

Australian leaders waited anxiously for the decisive battle to begin. In a meeting with MacArthur on 1 June, Curtin informed the American Supreme Commander of the results of Evatt's mission. After looking over the various cables from Evatt, MacArthur blasted the "distressing" results of his trip and bitterly criticised Britain's failure to provide for Australia's security. He noted that since his arrival in the Dominion, Australia had not received from Britain "an additional ship, soldier or squadron". Although MacArthur admitted that America had also been niggardly with its reinforcements, he noted that, unlike Britain, America had "no sovereign interest in the integrity of Australia" and were only sending forces to the Dominion because of its "utility as a base from which to hit Japan". He also argued that by promising reinforcements in the case of an invasion, Britain was now making an implicit admission that the forces within Australia were insufficient to withstand a serious attack. MacArthur rightly described such a promise of reinforcements as "an extremely weak reed on which to rely" and he berated Britain for not returning in kind the "assistance Australia had rendered overseas with naval, military and air forces". MacArthur contrasted Britain's recent 1000 bomber raid against Cologne with the forty bombers given to his command, most of them now unserviceable.[60]

MacArthur advised Curtin that Australia's fate would depend on the forthcoming naval battle. If it resulted in a Japanese victory, the Dominion's isolation would quickly follow. Although Australia could not influence the outcome of that battle, the Dominion could act to protect itself in the event of an adverse result. Accordingly, MacArthur recommended that Australia insist on the return of the 9th Division from the Middle East and obtain Britain's support for the supply of aircraft to the RAAF. He observed that, "in Australia's hour of peril she was entitled at least to the use of all the forces she could raise herself". Those forces that could not be returned should be replaced with equivalent British forces. These were matters that Evatt's mission should have tried to achieve but did not. MacArthur was particularly derisive about Evatt's principal achievement — three Spitfire squadrons — noting that "Churchill was only giving back to Australia part of her forces and one R.A.F. squadron as a gesture". He criticised Evatt for regarding them as a "favour and a concession" when, in MacArthur's view, "they and more should be forthcoming as a right".[61]

The following day, Blamey backed up MacArthur's opinion, urging the return of the 9th Division as an essential move for Australia's security in the absence of sufficient naval and air forces.[62] On 3 June, as the opposing fleets were positioned for battle across the disputed expanses of the central Pacific, Australia's Advisory War Council met to consider the Dominion's position in the wake of Evatt's failure in London and Washington. Although they supported the view of Curtin and MacArthur, the sound of battle around Midway stopped them giving effect to their view. Instead of its remaining aircraft carriers being destroyed, the United States navy, largely by a stroke of luck, sank four of the Japanese carriers and forced the Japanese onto the defensive for the remainder of the war. When the decisive nature of the victory had been appreciated, it was obvious that the Dominion's struggle was no longer one of survival. As MacArthur advised on 11 June, "it would now be interpreted as a timid cry for help, if we were to persist in demands for assistance for the defence of Australia".[63] The struggle now was to obtain sufficient forces to take the offensive and expel Japan from her Pacific conquests and restore the "prestige of the white races".[64]

Though Evatt had not counted among his successes in London his discovery of the Allied strategy, it was a positive achievement of some sort for Australia to be stripped of its illusions about the protective instincts of her Allies. The Dominion's initial reaction, encouraged by MacArthur, was to concentrate on local defence and adopt a policy of greater self-reliance. However, this salutary lesson slipped from the Australian consciousness before it could be assimilated. Three days after the battle of Midway, the Australian Cabinet effectively acknowledged its fortuitous rescue by establishing a committee to examine the problems of demobilisation. Three weeks later, the War Cabinet approved a reduction in Australia's army by one or two divisions.[65] Ultimate victory against Japan was far from imminent but defeat for Australia was no longer a real possibility.[66] Confident in her new-found security, the Dominion gradually released her short-lived attachment to self-reliance and slid back into the habit of entrusting her security to others, forgetting the dictum that the first duty of a government is the protection of its people.

NOTES

1 CABLE, Evatt to Curtin, 7 May 1942, CRS A3300, Item 234: AA
2 TALK WITH EVATT, 3 May 1942, CRS M100, "May 1942": AA
3 TALK WITH BRIDGES, 2 May 1942, CRS M100, "May 1942": AA
4 TALK WITH EVATT, 4 May 1942, CRS M100, "May 1942": AA

5 LONDON MUNITIONS ASSIGNMENT BOARD, MINUTES 4 May 1942, PREM 3/44: PRO

6 NOTE, Lyttelton to Churchill, 6 May 1942, *ibid.*

7 WAR CABINET CONCLUSIONS, 4 May 1942, CAB 65/26, W.M. (42)56: PRO

8 CADOGAN DIARY, 4 May 1942, ACAD 1/11, Cadogan Papers: CC

9 TALK WITH EVATT, 4 May 1942, CRS M100, "May 1942": AA

10 TRANSCRIPT OF EVATT'S PRESS CONFERENCE, 5 May 1942, "War — Matters Relating to — Australia", Evatt Collection: FUL

11 WAR JOURNAL OF GERALD WILKINSON, 15 April 1943, WILK 1/2, Wilkinson Papers: CC

12 "NOTES of Discussion with General MacArthur, Commander-in-Chief, Southwest Pacific Area, 2-5-42", Minute, Shedden to Curtin, 2 May 1942, CRS A5954, Box 3: AA

13 *IBID.*; "Notes of Discussion with General Sir Thomas Blamey, Commander, Allied Land Forces — Monday, 4th May, 1942", by Shedden, 4 May 1942, CRS A5954, Box 4: AA

14 ADVISORY WAR COUNCIL MINUTES, 6 May 1942, CRS A2682, Vol. 5, Minute 932: AA

15 CABLE PM57, Curtin to Evatt, 6 May 1942, CRS M100, "May 1942": AA

16 CABLE E4, Evatt to Curtin, 8 May 1942, CRS M100, "May 1942": AA

17 See CRS A5954, Box 287: AA

18 "CAMP FOR U.S. COLOURED TROOPS at Jubilee Oval, Glebe, — New South Wales", CRS A5954, Box 290: AA

19 WAR CABINET CONCLUSIONS, 10 and 31 August 1942, CAB 65/27, W.M. (42)109 and 119: PRO

20 MEMORANDUM, by Robinson, 16 April 1943, but written from notes made during May and June 1942, "Wars", Folder, W. S. Robinson Papers: University of Melbourne Archives (UMA)

21 MINUTES OF PRIME MINISTER'S WAR CONFERENCE, 11 May 1942, CRS A5954, Box 1: AA; "Weekly Resumé", 28 May – 4 June 1942, CAB 66/25, W.P. (42)237: PRO

22 CABLE NO. 135, Smith to Curtin, 20 May 1942, CRS A3300, Item 229: AA

23 CABLE NO. 691/2, Churchill to Auchinleck, 5 May 1942, and Cable No. 687/2, Churchill to Wavell, 5 May 1942, VI/2, Ismay Papers: KC; G. H. Gill, ii, pp. 185–6

24 CABLE E3, Evatt to Curtin, 6 May 1942, *DAFP*, v, Doc. 484

25 CABLE E4, Evatt to Curtin, 8 May 1942, *DAFP*, v, Doc. 486

26 POWNALL DIARY, 25 February 1942, in B. Bond (ed.), ii, p. 92

27 TALK WITH EVATT, 12 May 1942, CRS M100, "May 1942": AA

28 See DALTON DIARY, 12 May 1942, I/26/183, Dalton Papers: LSE

29 CARL BRIDGE, "R. G. Casey, Australia's First Washington Legation and the Origins of the Pacific War, 1940–42", *Australian Journal of Politics and History*, 1982, 28/2

30 CABLE ET30, Evatt to Curtin, 28 May 1942, CRS A3300, Item 228: AA

31 TALK WITH EVATT, 28 May 1942, CRS M100, "May 1942": AA

32 ADVISORY WAR COUNCIL MINUTES, 13 May 1942, CRS A2682, Vol. 5, Minute 938: AA

33 CABLE PM62, Curtin to Evatt, 13 May 1942, *DAFP*, v, Doc. 487; See also "Defence of Australia", Note by Bridges, 18 May 1942, CAB 66/24, W.P. (42)210: PRO

34 CABLE NO. 4501, Evatt to Curtin, 17 May 1942, *DAFP*, v, Doc. 490

35 *IBID.*

36 LETTER, W. S. Robinson to Evatt, 18 May 1942, "Robinson, W. S., 1942–45(a)" Folder, Evatt Collection: FUL

37 TALK WITH EVATT, 13 May 1942, CRS M100, "May 1942": AA

38 TALK WITH EVATT, 18 May 1942, CRS M100, "May 1942": AA

39 CABLE NO. 4503, Robinson to Curtin, 18 May 1942, CRS A5954, Box 474: AA

40 LETTER, MacArthur to Curtin, 16 May 1942, CRS A5954, Box 229: AA; Teleprinter message, Polglaze to Shedden, 1 October 1942, CRS A5954, Box 229: AA

41 LETTER, Evatt to Mrs Churchill, 20 May 1942, "Evatt — Overseas Trips — 1942 — Correspondence", Evatt Collection: FUL; Minute, Churchill to Alexander and Pound, 17 May 1942, PREM 3/151/4: PRO

42 WAR CABINET CONCLUSIONS/CONFIDENTIAL ANNEX, 21 May 1942, CAB 65/30, W.M. (42)65: PRO

43 *IBID.*

44 CABLE NO. 46, Evatt to Smith (Washington), repeated as ET33 to Curtin, 28 May 1942, CRS A3300, Item 228: AA

45 WAR CABINET CONCLUSIONS/CONFIDENTIAL ANNEX, 21 May 1942, CAB 65/30, W.M. (42)65: PRO

46 Note, Ismay to Churchill, 30 May 1942; Draft note, Ismay to Evatt, 26 May 1942, PREM 3/151/4: PRO

47 See CRS A5954, Box 461: AA

48 CABLE ET30, Evatt to Curtin, 28 May 1942, CRS A3300, Item 228: AA

49 *IBID.*

50 "MISSION ABROAD OF DR EVATT ...", Report of Talk between Shedden and Wardell, 17 March 1943, CRS A5954, Box 14: AA

51 CABLE ET30, Evatt to Curtin, 28 May 1942, CRS A3300, Item 228: AA

52 Curtin duly cabled back with his "warmest congratulations", assuring Evatt that the news of the squadrons was "very gratifying". CABLE PM76, Curtin to Evatt, 29 May 1942, CRS A3300, Item 228: AA

53 CABLE NO. 785/2, Churchill to Roosevelt, 30 May 1942, VI/2, Ismay Papers: KC

54 LETTER, Emrys-Evans to Lord Wakehurst, 23 July 1942, ADD. MS. 58243, Emrys-Evans Papers: BL; See also War Journal of Gerald Wilkinson, 30 March 1943, WILK 1/2, Wilkinson Papers: CC; Cable, R. D. Elliott to Beaverbrook, 23 December 1942, BBK C/131, Beaverbrook Papers: HLRO

55 LETTER, Lord Wakehurst to Emrys-Evans, 30 September 1942, ADD. MS. 58243, Emrys-Evans Papers: BL

56 See TALK WITH EVATT, 28 May 1942, CRS M100, "May 1942": AA

57 See ADVISORY WAR COUNCIL MINUTES, 1 July 1942, CRS A2682, Vol. 5, Minute 978: AA; Statement by Evatt in House of Representatives, 3 September 1942, CRS A5954, Box 474: AA; Text of radio broadcast by Evatt, 7 March 1943, "War — Speeches by Evatt '43(a)", Evatt Collection: FUL

58 See CRS A5954, Box 474: AA

59 See DAVID DAY, "H. V. Evatt and the 'Beat Hitler First Strategy'"

60 PRIME MINISTER'S WAR CONFERENCE, MINUTE 23, 1 June, 1942, *DAFP*, v, Doc. 510

61 *IBID.*

62 PRIME MINISTER'S WAR CONFERENCE, MINUTE 24, 2 June 1942, CRS A5954, Box 231: AA

63 PRIME MINISTER'S WAR CONFERENCE MINUTES, 11 June 1942, CRS A5954, Box 1: AA

64 ADVISORY WAR COUNCIL MINUTES, 17 June 1942, CRS A2682, Vol. 5, Minute 967: AA

65 On 11 June, Curtin informed the Advisory War Council that MacArthur considered "the defensive position of Australia was now assured". Two days earlier, the Cabinet had appointed a demobilisation committee. ADVISORY WAR COUNCIL MINUTES, 11 June 1942, CRS A2682, Vol. 5, Minute 960; Cabinet Minutes, 9 June 1942, CRS A2703, Vol. 1[c]: AA; Letter, Blamey to Curtin, 29 June 1942, and War Cabinet Minute No. 2224, 30 June 1942, CRS A5954, Box 261: AA

66 See "WAR SITUATION FROM THE AUSTRALIAN VIEWPOINT. A Review at 1st July 1942", Report by Shedden for Curtin, 10 July 1942, CRS A5954, Box 587: AA

15

Summary and Conclusions

SUMMARY

*T*he Anglo–Australian relationship went through its greatest crisis during the Second World War. By 1942 both countries were fighting against powerful enemies on opposite sides of the globe. It was a situation that the pre-war Imperial planners had preferred not to contemplate. It spotlighted the declining power of Britain to defend the scattered outposts of her Empire and forced her to adopt a system of priorities that relegated parts of the Empire to possible annihilation. Australia had lived in blithe confidence that the mother country gave her far-off Dominion's security high priority and she held tight to her Imperial bonds, concentrating on her domestic prosperity rather than face the hard decisions entailed by a policy of greater defence self-reliance.

Australia's refusal to confront the harsh reality of her defence position during the pre-war period was partly a result of deliberately misleading British assurances. It was not in Britain's interest that Australia should be self-reliant and concentrate her defence resources on the security of her huge continent. Instead, Australia was beguiled into believing that her fate hung on that of Britain and that the Middle East provided the front door to Australia. On this assumption, British interests and priorities in that region became Australian interests and priorities.

Although Britain was aware that her promises to Australia might turn out to be empty, Whitehall took comfort from the confident and far from unjustified belief that the worst would not happen. Certainly, in 1939, a direct threat to Australia looked unlikely and an invasion seemed inconceivable. The United States Pacific fleet provided a powerful argument against any distant naval thrust by Japan. British planners correctly believed that the Japanese navy would be unwilling to leave their home islands uncovered in order to attack Singapore while the United States fleet remained as a potential threat on their flank. The pre-emptive strike on Pearl Harbor was the obvious but totally unexpected solution to the Japanese predicament.

Britain also took comfort from the fact that she did not stand alone in the Far East. Apart from the United States, there were two other friendly naval powers in the Pacific. French, Dutch and British naval forces were a potentially powerful naval combination and all had adjacent colonial interests to protect. In Whitehall's confident calculation, the Japanese fleet could not attack Singapore without first sailing past American forces in the Philippines and French forces in Indo-China. Even if this were possible, Singapore was meant to be able to withstand an attack for many months and thereby allow the dispatch of a British fleet from the Mediterranean which would make short work of the "inferior" Japanese navy. The quick collapse of France and the neutralisation of its fleet were not contemplated. The entry of Italy into the war finally invalidated British strategic assumptions, leaving it alone in Europe and practically defenceless in the Far East.

Australia's willingness to believe British assurances cannot be laid totally at the door of Downing Street. Despite the experience of the Great War, Australia still exhibited many of the characteristics of a colony. Unlike most former colonies, there had been no clear and clean break between colonial status and independence. Instead, the six Australian colonies had simply been joined together into a larger body that was accorded little power. Much control of domestic policy remained in the hands of the former colonial administrations while external policy remained, in effect, largely the prerogative of Whitehall. In many respects, the Commonwealth Government was simply a co-ordinating body for channelling the opinion of the separate colonies and strengthening their case in London. Significantly, all the colonies retained their own representation in the Imperial capital, a colonial anachronism that has continued to this day.

The Statute of Westminster, which would have formally acknowledged Australia's independent existence as a sovereign state, was left unratified in Canberra until 1942. Even then, it was justified by Evatt merely as being necessary for practical

reasons and was not portrayed as a step towards Australian
independence from Britain. He informed the Cabinet that the
"adoption by Australia of certain clauses of [the] Statute of
Westminster will be necessary to remove threats of invalidity
which now hang over important Commonwealth laws and
regulations". In a letter to the Opposition leader, W. M.
Hughes, Evatt maintained that the adoption of the Statute was
"not an occasion for raising any issue such as Australia v.
Britain". He pleaded with Hughes to "avoid the slightest unnecessary controversy over these matters" which are "technical
in character and do not involve any general declaration of
status at all". As a former judge, Evatt presumably knew better
but, despite the events of 1942, still felt constrained not to
introduce the Statute as a step towards greater Australian
independence.[1]

Though several factors combined to ensure continued
Australian dependence upon Britain, the Dominion was not an
uncritical, client state of the mother country. Towards the end
of the 1930s, Australia made increasing efforts to establish the
nucleus of a defence industry that would provide her with
greater independence. As John McCarthy revealed, in order to
protect their commercial advantage in the Dominion, Britain
strenuously resisted Australian attempts to develop an aircraft
industry with American participation. However, Australia's
persistent attempts in the face of this opposition provided a
sign of growing impatience with the dictates of Whitehall.[2] In
addition, the attempt to establish such things as an Australian
aircraft industry was made within the context of Australian
economic development in which the defence component was
seen as a logical step in the country's gradual industrialisation.
To some Australian imperialists with grandiose ideas, the development of the Dominion was seen in evolutionary terms,
with the distant and sturdy son in the south seas supplanting
the elderly and declining parent as the Imperial leader. Casey
put these thoughts on paper in 1949 when he called for a

> centrifugal movement from Britain to the outer reaches of the
> Commonwealth and Empire, of people, industries and capital,
> which would lessen the pressure of existence on the people of
> Britain and at the same time build up the Dominions and
> Colonies. It may well be that a considerable part of the future of
> the British race will lie in Australia.[3]

So it was as an increasingly critical but nevertheless keen Imperial dependency that Australia rushed to the colours in September 1939, just as she had done in the past. Despite the rush to Britain's side, Menzies and Bruce retained their commitment to a peaceful settlement, with their attachment to appeasement lasting far longer than has previously been acknowledged. This was partly out of concern for Australia's position in the Pacific, but it also reflected a calculated and pessimistic assessment of British chances in a knock-down fight with Germany.

The fall of France and the entry of Italy into the war in June 1940 caused alarm bells to ring throughout the Empire. It only needed Japan to become a belligerent for Australia's worst fears to be realised. Under the impact of these shock-waves, Menzies appealed to the United States to provide assistance for Britain. The defeat of Britain stared Menzies in the face and his efforts became bent towards staving off such a disaster. Australia provided more men and equipment for Britain at the expense of its own defence and despite the worsening of its own security situation. The competing priorities of the Middle East and Far East became compelling. Britain chose to take risks with the security of her possessions in the Far East, including Australia, in order to protect her interests in the Middle East. But it was not simply protection of her interests that Britain had in mind. With no prospect of an early return in force to Europe, the essentially side-show war in the Middle East and the largely useless and wasteful strategic air offensive over Germany were necessary to sustain the British will for war until sufficient allies could be found for British feet to march once more on European soil.

From mid-1940 there was little prospect of a British fleet being able to go to the Far East. British assurances regarding Australian security were made with even less concern for the possibility of them being implemented. Japanese forces entered Indo-China and prepared the bases for their next move southward. Australia's only substantial defence against the threat was that of distance — the sheer effort of moving sufficient Japanese troops to subdue Australia became the most potent force in the Australian armoury. There was little else to deter a Japanese attack. Australia had the men but not the equipment with which to mount a proper defence. There were no tanks, no modern operational aircraft of any description, few anti-aircraft guns and few mines with which to protect Australian shipping lanes and ports. Only with the successful conclusion of the Battle of Britain did Australia make any serious effort to remedy these deficiencies. It was partly in pursuit of this effort that Menzies planned his trip to London in January 1941. Even then, the Dominion's faith in the theory of Imperial defence was little diminished despite the increasing criticism of it in practice.

Though Menzies ostensibly went to obtain defence equipment for Singapore, once in London he was faced with the choice of running risks in the Far East or of placing the British position in the Middle East under threat. Whitehall had made its decision already and Menzies was quick to give it his imprimatur. Anything else would have placed the troops of the second AIF under threat and possibly led to their defeat. Withdrawal of the troops to the defence of their homeland did not appear on Menzies' agenda. Instead, he committed them further to Churchill's Mediterranean strategy with his agreement to the strategically unsound expedition to Greece. This negated all the previous victories in the Middle East, tied the Australian troops more firmly to the region and dealt the Royal Navy such serious blows that a Far East fleet almost became a practical impossibility even if it was approved in principle. At the same time, Menzies was enticed into a movement to topple Churchill. His personal and political ambitions coincided in this plan to insert himself into the British War Cabinet with a view to the possible eventual replacement of its Prime Minister. Menzies entertained hopes of occupying Downing Street and of replacing Churchill's policy of total victory with one of compromise towards the Axis Powers.

While Menzies sought a compromise solution to the war, Churchill sought the means to achieve his aim of total victory, an aim that appeared all but impossible after the defeat of France and the entry of Italy. Churchill pinned his faith on the Americans whom he assiduously courted and encouraged in their slow slide towards belligerency. He recognised their strong resistance to involvement in another European war and their greater willingness to contemplate war in the Pacific. With this in mind, Britain did much to stiffen the American resolve to resist further Japanese encroachments in south east Asia. At the same time, British economic restrictions on Japan pushed that country into the further encroachments designed to upset the Americans. Pearl Harbor was the culmination of the Anglo–American policy. To Churchill, it meant that his aim of total victory in Europe became capable of achievement.

While trying to create war in the Pacific, Churchill did not retract his assurances to Australia regarding their protection, nor did he encourage the Dominion to look to its own moat. This cavalier attitude towards Australia's defence was not one that Churchill held with regard to Britain's defence. Nevertheless, it seems that Churchill genuinely believed that the strength of the Singapore "fortress" and the weakness of the Japanese would combine to provide effective protection for Australia. In addition, he had difficulty conceiving of Australia as a prize worth capturing. In his view it was India and China that were most at risk from the Japanese.

Menzies' resignation from the Prime Ministership in August 1941 effectively removed him as a serious challenge to Churchill and ended the attempts to resurrect the pre-war model of Empire in which the Dominions would be accorded a voice in British policy formulation. Menzies' efforts, while seriously intended, were probably doomed from the beginning. Not only did he have scant support in Australia for his activities but he was opposed by all the other Dominions who preferred not to interfere with Churchill's control over Imperial policy and war strategy. Menzies' activities, together with those of Bruce, simply embittered Churchill towards Australia at a time when the Dominion needed all the sympathy it could muster.

Contrary to the usual impression of Australians being sturdy sons of Mother Britain willing and impressively able to do her bidding and her fighting, Australians came to be regarded in Whitehall during 1941 as timid allies over-anxious for their own security, both military and political. Though the arguments over the evacuation of Greece and Crete caused considerable rancour in London, they were issues on which Churchill was on weak ground. The dispute over the relief of Tobruk was different. There was unanimity among British political and military leaders that Australia's action in repeatedly insisting on the relief of their troops was shabby and discreditable. There was much force in this British criticism, with Menzies having begun the process primarily out of concern for his shaky political position in the event of Tobruk being overrun.

Curtin inherited this issue when he came to power in October 1941. He had supported the actions of his predecessors and did not waver under pressure from Churchill. This confirmed Churchill's prejudices against the Labor Party, which he had blamed for much of Menzies' actions. Despite Churchill's view, Curtin did little to change his predecessor's commitment to the defence of British interests. He made no attempt to bring the AIF back to defend Australia, despite suggestions he made to that effect while in Opposition. Nor was there any substantial evidence of a greater war effort under Curtin prior to Pearl Harbor. Like his predecessors, Curtin pinned his hopes on an accommodation with Japan and made little effort to prepare for its failure. In addition, by retaining his predecessors' political appointments to diplomatic posts, Curtin ensured there would be a built-in force against any change in Australian policy.

The Japanese attack on Pearl Harbor was as climactic for Australia as the fall of France had been for Britain in 1940. However, whereas the fall of France had caused Australia to intensify its efforts to support Britain, the attack on Pearl Harbor was greeted with relief in London because of its probable effect on the British effort against Germany. At the same time, rather than rushing to assist Australia to meet the very real threat from Japan, Churchill ensured that the Pacific war remained relegated to second place behind the war against Germany. Though this strategic decision had crucial implications for Australia's security, its confirmation by Churchill and Roosevelt in December 1941 was made without consulting Australia and was not even communicated to the Australian Government.

In addition, the limited British effort to hold the Japanese advance was concentrated in the triangle, Cape Town—Aden—Singapore. When Singapore fell and the Japanese advance split between an attack on Burma and the Netherlands East Indies, Britain channelled all its resources into Burma and India while continuing to play down the chances of Australia being overrun by the Japanese. In a callous disregard for the defence of the Dominion, Churchill high-handedly attempted to divert to Burma Australia's only battle-hardened troops who had been destined to defend their homeland. Had he been successful in diverting them, the troops either would have been captured by the

Japanese or forced to join the arduous retreat through Burma into India. They would have been lost to Australia's defence and unable to partake in the successful defeat of the Japanese landward assault on Port Moresby.

Curtin has rightly earned kudos for resisting Churchill's attempt to weaken Australia further. However, his agreement to the diversion to Ceylon of part of the AIF force must be set against this. Churchill's deliberate and lengthy detention of these troops in Ceylon made them unavailable for the defence of New Guinea until 1943, thereby increasing the difficulties of its defence and Australia's consequent dependence on American manpower. Curtin's agreement to the garrisoning of Ceylon was an indication of the continuing strength of the Imperial bonds that still extracted valuable contributions from Australia for Imperial defence despite the pressing imperatives of its own defence.

The Australian Government claimed that Britain's threatened decision in January 1942 not to reinforce Singapore would be classed as an "inexcusable betrayal". Churchill relented on that occasion and sent a British division which was uselessly added to the prisoners of war captured by the Japanese. Though the Australians accused Britain of betrayal over Singapore, there were no such open accusations over Britain's refusal to implement its long-promised assurances regarding Australian defence. Ironically, it was left to MacArthur to make the allegation of a British betrayal of the Dominion. Australians were unwilling or unable to understand that Britain faced a number of harsh choices in 1942 and that, in the event, she chose, firstly, to concentrate her resources in Europe on arguably useless strategies in North Africa and in the bombing offensive over Germany, and, secondly, to concentrate the remainder of her resources in protecting the Imperial "jewel", India.

Though the fall of Singapore and the absence of British forces protecting Australia both acted to shake Australian confidence in the Empire, the stark reality of being a distant European outpost devoid of great power protection seems to have been too much for the Australian consciousness to assimilate. Instead, the sunken *Prince of Wales* was cited as a token of continuing British protectiveness, while the appointment of General MacArthur was seized upon as a token of the new-found and supplementary American protectiveness.

If Britain had a realistic recognition of its own national

interest and pursued it with some success, Australia showed little recognition of an independent national interest. The consistent failure of both Menzies and Curtin to develop an alternative air route across the Pacific provided a vivid example of Australia's willingness to favour the interests of its supposedly protecting power, be it Britain or America, over its own. Similarly, the Empire Air Training Scheme (EATS) was a magnificent machine for producing aircrew for the RAF but only incidentally served Australian interests. Instead of developing the RAAF into an operational force capable of defending Australia, EATS ensured that the Dominion's air effort would be directed largely towards satisfying Britain's insatiable hunger for aircrew, that were then swiftly digested in the air war over Europe. Despite the war in the Pacific, Australia retained its commitment to EATS, which continued to drain off valuable men for the war in Europe. Although more RAAF men were lost in Europe than in the Pacific, Australia earned little credit from Britain for its effort. They would have been more usefully employed in the Australian theatre repelling the Japanese.

Australian forces were not essential for the fight against Japan and they played little or no part in the decisive battles that ensured the Dominion's security. However, they were important in the battle for New Guinea and, had the Midway battle not favoured the Allies, the Dominion forces might have had to provide the principal defence against the encirclement and invasion of Australia. Even in a coalition war, the first responsibility of a nation's forces must be the preservation of its own territory. This maxim went without saying in London and Washington. Had Australia assembled all its scattered forces in 1942, there would have been more sense of self-reliance and independence and less sense of continued reliance on Great Power protection. By leaving airmen in Europe, the 9th Division in the Middle East and part of the 6th Division in Ceylon, Curtin made Australia unnecessarily more reliant on the United States than it needed to be and perpetuated the colonial propensity to leave the Dominion's defence largely to the benevolence of others.

CONCLUSIONS

What stands out immediately from the story of these events is the persistence of Australia's colonial mentality. Nothing could have highlighted this more dramatically than the Dominion's remarkable readiness to place the interests of her protecting power above that of her own. Whether it was sending troops to Timor or establishing aerial links across the Pacific, Australia's security was usually not the prime determinant during the formulation of the Dominion's decision.

Australia's predicament was not unique nor was it just an extension of its colonial past. Stripped of the colonial trappings, it is the problem faced to some degree by all dependent, client states in their relationship with their Great Power protectors. This is particularly true in time of war when dependence upon the protection is heightened and when the minor partners in a coalition struggle become expendable assets in the hands of the Great Power. Ironically, it has since become a problem familiar to Britain in her own subordinate relationship to the United States. In Australia's case, the problem was exacerbated by her British heritage and the consequent difficulty in disentangling distinctive Australian interests. By generally failing to make the distinction and to extinguish her colonial mentality, the Dominion carried this outlook among her baggage when entering upon the new Australian–American relationship.

What then of Australian nationalism? Without a clear sense of national interest separate from that of Britain, there could be no developed sense of national identity. Australian leaders were unable to delineate in their own minds where their own "Britishness" ended and their "Australianness" began. Menzies felt remarkably free to consider a political future in Westminster while Casey had no compunction about leaving his vital post in Washington for a British post in Cairo. Once in Cairo, Casey took umbrage at any suggestion that British and Australian troops in the region should be separated statistically. In Casey's view they were all British.[4] As for Bruce, he played a crucial role in convincing Australia that Britain had her Dominion's security high among her priorities. Page was also involved in this, but was perhaps less culpable for being less capable. Page reached the height of his folly and revealed the depth of his attachment to Empire when he took the initiative in proposing that Australia should send troops to Rangoon.

The Labor Government was ill-served by the performance of these conservative politician/diplomats. The fact that they were allowed to remain in their posts was an indication that although nationalism was more pronounced on the Labor side of Australian politics it remained muted, there being a basic and persistent bi-partisan attachment to Britain and the Empire. Australian troops were withdrawn from the Middle East at the suggestion of Churchill not Curtin. And it was Curtin who agreed to leave many of these troops in Ceylon when they were desperately needed in Australia.

As for foreign policy, it is difficult to sustain the reputation of Evatt as the father of a distinctive Australian foreign policy. Though he stamped his restless personality on Australia's overseas image, he was less successful in developing a foreign policy that would have as its first criterion the pursuit of Australian rather than British, American or overall Allied interests. His experience during his first overseas trips as External Affairs Minister seems to have been crucial in impressing upon him the limitations of a small, dependent power exerting influence within the context of a coalition war. As was noted above, these limitations were partly self-imposed. Australia could have exerted more influence had she retained close control of her scattered forces. Instead, her dependence was exacerbated by the unnecessary extent to which she had to rely on American forces for her defence, while her own forces were dissipated in the wider Imperial interest and, in consequence, diminished Australia's voice everywhere. Moreover, Australia did not benefit from sacrificing her interests to those of Britain or the United States. Her real salvation proved to be her distance from Japan and the size of the country. She was simply not worth the considerable trouble of invading, at least in the short term.

Britain's abandonment of Australia is usually ascribed to a lack of resources and, therefore, a lack of choices. Certainly there was a lack of British resources, but not a lack of choices. The entry into the war of Japan simply added a fresh choice for Britain as to where her limited resources would be applied — in the Atlantic, in the Middle East, Russia, the Far East or the so-called Imperial triangle in the Indian Ocean. There was no compulsion on her virtually to ignore the Japanese challenge and leave Australia to her fate. That she did so was a dramatic illustration of the fact that great powers will usually pursue their national interests regardless of treaties and understandings and, in the Anglo–Australian case, despite the closest Imperial ties with their racial, historical, economic and political aspects.

Complicating Australia's plight were the twin factors of cowards and convicts. The relief of the Australian troops from Tobruk had sent a wave of revulsion through Whitehall, the ripples of which continued to be felt right through the war. Military planners who had spent the inter-war years doing annual, theoretical exercises at the Imperial Defence College for the dispatch of a Far East fleet quietly dropped their plans when the eventuality arose. They made little objection to Churchill's "Germany first" strategy and the consequent abandonment of their distant Dominion. Their bitterness was compounded by the ignominious defeat of the British Imperial forces in Singapore. The Australian component of this force was the butt of much British comment; and friction of this kind brought to the surface deeper British prejudices regarding Australians, based on their convict legacy and the strong Irish component in the population. This was revealed in Churchill's unguarded comment about Australians coming from "bad stock" and the jibe by Cross about Australians being "inferior people".

Both these factors help to explain why Australia was criticised more than any other Dominion. South Africa contributed much less to the British war effort and placed more stringent conditions on their contribution. Yet she was criticised hardly at all and her Prime Minister, General Smuts, was acclaimed more than any other by British political leaders. Similarly, the Canadian contribution was limited by the need to appease the minority French segment of the population and the Canadian Government was not averse to driving a hard bargain for the contribution that it did make. Yet the Canadians were warmly regarded in Whitehall and their political problems met with much understanding from Churchill, who refrained from pressuring the Canadian Prime Minister, Mackenzie King, on the contentious Canadian issue of conscription.

As for New Zealand, its opposition to the dictates of Downing Street was much more sporadic than Australia's and its reputation in British eyes was that much better as a consequence. In April 1943, following the withdrawal of the 9th

Division, Australia's last remaining troops in the Middle East, the question arose of using the New Zealand division in the capture of Sicily. Churchill was in favour, denying that it would be "trading on New Zealand loyalty" to make such a request. On the contrary, he claimed that it would be a "great opportunity for them to win honour, and the fact that Australia has failed us makes it all the more necessary". In the case of New Zealand refusing, Churchill wrote, "there is nothing more to be said. They will then place themselves on the same level as Australia. But I do not think they will refuse." Churchill was correct. Despite pressure from Canberra to bring their troops back to the Pacific, New Zealand left its troops in the European struggle.[5]

If the Great Powers were following their national interests at Australia's possible expense, so too were their leaders pursuing personal interests. If the business of war is too important to be entrusted to generals, it is perhaps doubly true with respect to politicians. The eventual Allied victory has tended to vindicate Churchill's war leadership and overlook the many lamentable strategic decisions of which he was the author. Greece, Crete and Singapore were just three of Churchill's blunders that cost Australia dearly. As for Menzies, he was entrusted with the security of the Dominion but, instead, went off in a vain quest for power on a grander stage. Neither should Curtin escape from this criticism, with his refusal to countenance a national government in Canberra during the first two years of war. Had Australia been united behind such a government, her voice would have been stronger during those years and she would have been better prepared to meet the emergency of 1942. Instead, until Labor's electoral victory in 1943, the Dominion was saddled with three successive governments that had political security at least as high on their agenda as military security.

If Australia's reputation slipped in British eyes, so too did the Empire slip in the scale of British priorities. Though this study has not been able to do much more than allude to this apparent change, some tentative conclusions about Britain's changing attitude to the Empire can be drawn from her wartime relationship with Australia.

First though, it is necessary to make the point that when Britain and Australia considered the Empire, they were really considering two different entities. To Britain, the Empire was a possession that, in the last resort and however reluctantly, could be added to or subtracted from as necessary in accordance with British national interests. To Australia, the Empire was seen as an entity independent of any one of its parts. Given these different views, conflict was inevitable when the defence of its far-flung reaches was being considered. Seeing them as her possessions, it was natural for Britain to accord defence priority to the various parts of the Empire roughly in line with their distance from Britain and their relative importance to her own survival. Australia's priority ranked low on both counts. Her distance from Britain made her both more expensive to defend and less important for the economic and military sustenance of Britain.

This attitude to the Empire, together with the risks that Britain was prepared to run in its defence, suggest a weakening of the will to retain it as the central feature of British external life. Her preference for defending her largely informal Empire in the Middle East, rather than the formal Empire in the Far East, point towards a largely implicit re-ordering of national priorities. As had been indicated elsewhere, there was a gradual switch in British military thinking during the inter-war period away from naval defence based on the Empire to a continental commitment utilising the army and air force. There was a similar shift in the economic sphere during the second half of the 1930s away from the Imperial economy that had reached its high point at Ottawa in 1932. The Anglo–American trade agreement of 1938 exemplified this switch in British thinking. It was subsequently confirmed in the Atlantic Charter agreed between Churchill and Roosevelt in 1941.[6] This study has tended to confirm these accounts of the Empire being gradually displaced from its prominent pre-war position in the priorities of Britain.

The "Germany first" strategy was the most dramatic example of this. Despite the economic importance of Malaya, the humiliating defeat at Singapore and the feared growth of a pan-Asiatic movement spelling doom for European imperialism, there was little attempt by Britain to prevent Japan enjoying the fruits of its military victory. Almost everything was concentrated on the total defeat of Germany. Only after that had been achieved, so it was claimed, could resources be switched to the Pacific war. However, while unconditional victory was the war-cry in

Europe, Churchill was prepared to compromise in the Pacific and, in the event, failed to fulfil his promise to bring the full weight of British power to bear on Japan.[7] Abandoned beyond the shrinking periphery of British power, Australia's wartime experience provided stark evidence of the realignment of British priorities.

The inter-war period also saw an increase in the importance of the Middle East to Britain. Before the Great War, the Middle East was largely seen as the axis of Britain's Eastern Empire. The Suez Canal was one of the Empire's "choke-points" through which passed the voluminous trade with India and the galaxy of British possessions arrayed around her. Increasing discoveries of oil helped to invest the Middle East with a different focus of importance. In addition, it had a strategic importance for any struggle in Europe, providing a possible springboard from which to launch British forces into the Balkans and thence into contested areas of eastern Europe, Germany's soft underbelly as Churchill called it. The dramatic rise in importance of the Middle East to Britain was confirmed after the fall of France when it siphoned off mountains of men and matériel at the expense of the Far East. The ignominious loss of Singapore was the inevitable and, one suspects, acceptable price that Britain had to pay. By the end of the war, she had begun the retreat from Empire in relatively good order and had carved out a new position in Europe that was more within her capacity to defend.

Curtin's New Year message of December 1941, in which he turned to the United States without inhibitions, combined with the passage of the Statute of Westminster in 1942, have stood as the symbolic signposts to a realignment of Australia's position in the world. In fact, the realignment came much later under the impact of economic and social changes as much as military ones. In 1942, there was a common assumption that the Imperial relationship could be resuscitated to provide the basis for Australian defence in the post-war period.

In Canberra, America was seen simply as a transient protector, providing defence guarantees supplementary to the supposed British protection and on the understanding that Australia remained a British country. The Dominion refused to acknowledge the fact of her abandonment by the mother country, preferring to believe that Britain had had the will but not the immediate means to provide protection against the Japanese. Australia simply scrambled with undue and undignified haste for the temporary protective cover of the United States, thereby eventually replacing one dependency with another.

NOTES

1 CABINET AGENDA NO. 335, 22 September 1942, CRS A2700, Vol. 4: AA; Letter, Evatt to Hughes, 29 September 1942, "Hughes, W. M." Folder, Evatt Collection: FUL
2 J. MCCARTHY, ch. 5
3 R. G. CASEY, *Double or Quit*, Melbourne, 1949, p. 10
4 R. G. CASEY, *Personal Experience*, p. 122
5 MINUTE, Churchill to Attlee, 8 April 1943, PREM 3/63/5: PRO
6 See M. HOWARD, *The Continental Commitment*, London, 1972; B. Bond, *British Military Policy Between the Two World Wars*, Oxford, 1980; R. F. Holland, *Britain and the Commonwealth Alliance 1918−1939*
7 See DAVID DAY, "Promise and Performance: Britain's Pacific Pledge, 1943−45", *War and Society*, September 1986

Bibliography

I Unpublished Material

(a) Official Documents — Australian Archives, Canberra

CRS CP 156/1, General Correspondence of the Rt Hon. John Curtin, October 1941–December 1944

CRS CP 290/7, Cables from the Prime Minister of Great Britain and the Secretary of State for Dominion Affairs 1939–1943

CRS CP 290/8, Cables to and from Sir Earle Page during his visit to London 1941 (25 September–29 December)

CRS CP 290/9, Cables to and from Rt Hon. Menzies and party during his visit to London, 21 January–26 May 1941

CRS CP 290/16, Papers relating to Wartime Policy 1940–45

CRS M100, S. M. Bruce, Monthly War Files

CRS M103, S. M. Bruce, Supplementary War Files

CRS M104, S. M. Bruce, Folders of Annual Correspondence

CRS M113, S. M. Bruce, Travel and Appointment Diaries

AA 1970/559, S. M. Bruce, Miscellaneous Papers, 1939–45

CRS A461, Prime Minister's Department, Correspondence Files, Multiple Number Series (Third System), 1934–50

CRS A1608, Prime Minister's Department, Correspondence Files, Secret and Confidential War Series (Fourth System) 1939–45

CRS A2031, Defence Committee Minutes 1939–45

CRS A2670, War Cabinet Agenda, 1939–46

CRS A2673, War Cabinet Minutes, 1939–46

CRS A2676, War Cabinet Minutes without Agenda Files, 1939–46

CRS A2679, Advisory War Council Agenda, 1940–45

CRS A2682, Advisory War Council Minutes, 1940–45

CRS A2697, Cabinet Secretariat, Menzies and Fadden Ministries, minutes and submissions, 1939–41

CRS A2700, Cabinet Secretariat, Curtin, Forde and Chifley Ministries, Cabinet Agenda 1941–49

CRS A2703, Cabinet Secretariat, Curtin, Forde and Chifley Ministries, Cabinet Minutes 1941–49

CRS A3300, Australian Legation to USA, Correspondence Files, 1939–48

CRS A5954, Sir Frederick Shedden, Papers

(b) Official Documents — Public Record Office, London

CAB 65, War Cabinet Conclusions and Confidential Annexes

CAB 66, War Cabinet Memoranda

CAB 69, War Cabinet Defence Committee (Operations), Minutes and Memoranda

PREM 1, 3, 4, 7, AND 10, Prime Minister's Papers

(c) Private Papers — Australia

FLINDERS UNIVERSITY LIBRARY
Dr H. V. Evatt, Papers

NATIONAL LIBRARY OF AUSTRALIA
Lord Casey, Diary
J. J. Dedman, Papers
Sir Frederick Eggleston, Papers
Henry B. S. Gullett, Papers
R. V. Keane, Papers
Sir John Latham, Papers
Norman Makin, Papers
E. A. Mann, Papers
Sir Robert Menzies, Papers
Sir Keith Murdoch, Papers
Sir Keith Officer, Papers
Sir Earle Page, Papers
F. T. Smith, Transcripts of Curtin's press conferences
Sir Percy Spender, Papers
P. G. Taylor, Papers
Sir Alan Watt, Papers

UNIVERSITY OF MELBOURNE ARCHIVES
W. S. Robinson, Papers

(d) Private Papers — Great Britain

BRITISH LIBRARY
Lord Cecil, Papers
Admiral Sir A. B. Cunningham, Papers
P. Emrys-Evans, Papers
Oliver Harvey, Papers
Admiral Sir James Somerville, Papers

CAMBRIDGE UNIVERSITY LIBRARY
Viscount Templewood, Papers
W. Mackenzie King, Diary (microfiche)

CHURCHILL COLLEGE ARCHIVES
A. V. Alexander, Papers
Earl Attlee, Papers
Rear Admiral T. P. H. Beamish, Papers
Ernest Bevin, Papers
J. B. Bickersteth, Papers
General Sir Charles Bonham-Carter, Papers
L. F. Burgis, Memoirs
Sir Alexander Cadogan, Papers
Lord Caldecote, Diary extracts
Lord Chandos, Papers
Major-General J. S. Crawford, Papers
Sir Walter Crocker, Memoirs
Lord Croft, Papers
Admiral Sir A. B. Cunningham, Papers
Admiral Sir William Davis, Memoirs
Admiral Sir Reginald Drax, Papers
Admiral Sir John H. Edelsten, Papers
Admiral Sir Ralph Edwards, Diaries and Papers
Air Marshal Sir Thomas W. Elmhirst, Memoirs and Papers
Captain Godfrey French, Papers
Admiral J. H. Godfrey, Memoirs
Captain Russell Grenfell, Papers
Sir Percy James Grigg, Papers
Lord Halifax, Papers (microfilm)
Lord Hankey, Papers
Sir H. M. Knatchbull-Hugessen, Diaries and
Correspondence
Sir Eric Phipps, Papers
Cecil Roberts, Papers
Sir Horace Seymour, Papers
General Sir Edward Spears, Papers
Lord Swinton, Papers
Viscount Weir, Papers
Gerald Wilkinson, Diary
Admiral Sir Algernon Willis, Papers

HOUSE OF LORDS RECORD OFFICE
Lord Beaverbrook, Papers
David Lloyd George, Papers
Lord Wakehurst, Papers

IMPERIAL WAR MUSEUM
Admiral Sir John Crace, Papers
Sir Ronald Cross, Papers (microfilm)
Vice Admiral J. W. Durnford, Papers
John Hughes, Papers
Admiral Sir Edward Parry, Papers

INDIA OFFICE LIBRARY
Sir Reginald Dorman-Smith, Papers

KING'S COLLEGE, LONDON
Lord Alanbrooke, Papers
Air Chief Marshal Sir Robert Brooke-Popham, Papers
Lord Ismay, Papers
Captain Liddell Hart, Papers
Major-General W. R. C. Penney, Papers

LONDON SCHOOL OF ECONOMICS
Hugh Dalton, Papers

NATIONAL MARITIME MUSEUM
Lord Chatfield, Papers
Admiral Kelly, Papers
Admiral Sir William Tennant, Papers

READING UNIVERSITY LIBRARY
Waldorf Astor, Papers
Nancy Astor, Papers

SCOTTISH RECORD OFFICE, EDINBURGH
Lord Lothian, Papers

II PUBLISHED OFFICIAL DOCUMENTS

MURRAY, D. R. (ED.), *Documents on Canadian External Relations*, volumes 7–8, Ottawa, 1974, 1976

NEALE, R. G. ET AL. (EDS), *Documents on Australian Foreign Policy 1937–49*, volumes 1–6, Canberra, 1975–83

Official Year Book of the Commonwealth of Australia: No. 32, 1939, Canberra, 1940

III MEMOIRS, COLLECTED LETTERS, PUBLISHED DIARIES, ETC.

(a) General

MANSERGH, N. (ED.). *Documents and Speeches on British Commonwealth Affairs 1931–1952*, volume 1, London, 1953

(b) Australia

BLAINEY, G. (ED.), *The Memoirs of W. S. Robinson, 1876–1963*, Melbourne, 1968

CALWELL, A. A., *Be Just and Fear Not*, Melbourne, 1972

CASEY, M., *Tides and Eddies*, London, 1966

CASEY, R. G., *Personal Experience 1939–46*, London, 1962

COLLINS, VICE ADMIRAL SIR JOHN, *As Luck Would Have It: The Reminiscences of an Australian Sailor*, Sydney, 1965

CROWLEY, F. K. (ED.), *Modern Australia in Documents*, ii, Melbourne, 1973

FADDEN, A., *They Called Me Artie: The Memoirs of Sir Arthur Fadden*, Melbourne, 1969

FYSH, H., *Qantas at War*, Sydney, 1968

HOLT, E., *Politics is People: The Men of the Menzies Era*, Sydney, 1969

LYONS, (DAME) ENID, *So We Take Comfort*, London, 1965

MENZIES, (SIR) R. G., *Afternoon Light*, London, 1965
  The Measure of the Years, London, 1970
  To the People of Britain at War, London, 1941
  Speech is of Time: Selected Speeches and Writings, London, 1958

PAGE, E., *Truant Surgeon*, Sydney, 1963

TAYLOR, P. G., *The Sky Beyond*, Melbourne, 1963

WATT, (SIR) A., *Australian Diplomat*, Sydney, 1972

WELLER, P. (ED.), *Caucus Minutes 1901–1949*, Melbourne, 1975

(c) Canada

MASSEY, V., *What's Past is Prologue*, Toronto, 1963

PICKERSGILL, J. W. (ED.), *The Mackenzie King Record*, volumes I and II, Toronto, 1960 and 1968

(d) Great Britain

ATTLEE, C., *As It Happened*, London, 1954

AVON, EARL OF, *The Eden Memoirs*, volume 2: *The Reckoning*, London, 1965

BOND, B. (ED.), *Chief of Staff*, ii, London, 1974

BRYANT, A., *The Turn of the Tide: 1939–1943*, London, 1957

BUTLER, LORD, *The Art of the Possible*, London 1971

CHANDOS, LORD, *The Memoirs of Lord Chandos*, London, 1962

CHATFIELD, LORD, *It Might Happen Again*, London, 1947

COLVILLE, J., *The Churchillians*, London, 1981
Footprints in Time, London, 1976
The Fringes of Power: Downing Street Diaries 1939–1955, London, 1985

COOPER, A. D., *Old Men Forget*, London, 1953

CROSS, C. (ED.), *Life with Lloyd George: The Diary of A. J. Sylvester 1931–45*, London, 1975

DILKS, D. (ED.), *The Diaries of Sir Alexander Cadogan O.M. 1938–1945*, London, 1971

HALIFAX, LORD, *Fulness of Days*, London, 1957

JAMES, R. R., *Victor Cazalet: A Portrait*, London, 1976
(ED.), *Chips: The Diaries of Henry Channon*, London, 1967
(ED.), *Winston Churchill: His Complete Speeches 1897–1963*, volume 6, New York, 1974

JONES, T., *A Diary with Letters 1931–1950*, London, 1954

KENNEDY, MAJOR-GENERAL SIR J., *The Business of War*, London, 1957

KING, C., *With Malice Toward None: A War Diary*, London, 1970

LONGMORE, SIR A., *From Sea to Sky*, London, 1946

MARTIN, K., *Editor*, London, 1968

MORAN, LORD, *Winston Churchill: The Struggle for Survival 1940–1965*, London, 1968

NICOLSON, SIR H., *Diaries and Letters*, volume 2, London, 1967

REITH, J. C. W., *Into the Wind*, London, 1949

ROLPH, C., *The Life, Letters and Diaries of Kingsley Martin*, London, 1973

TAYLOR, A. J. P. (ED.), *My Darling Pussy: The Letters of Lloyd George and Frances Stevenson 1913–41*, London 1975

YOUNG, K. (ED.), *The Diaries of Sir Robert Bruce Lockhart*, volume 2, London, 1980

(e) United States

EDWARDS, P. G. (ED.), *Australia Through American Eyes 1935–1945*, Brisbane, 1979

HARRIMAN, W. AVERELL AND ABEL, E., *Special Envoy to Churchill and Stalin 1941–1946*, New York, 1975

HULL, CORDELL, *The Memoirs of Cordell Hull*, volume 1, New York, 1948

SHERWOOD, R., *The White House Papers of Harry L. Hopkins*, volume 1, London, 1948

WELLES, S., *The Time for Decision*, London, 1944

WINANT, J. G., *A Letter from Grosvenor Square*, London, 1947

(f) South Africa

VAN DER POEL, J. (ED.), *Selections from the Smuts Papers*, volume 6, Cambridge, 1973

IV Secondary Works

AMERY, L. S., *The Forward View*, London, 1935

ANDREWS, E. M., *Isolationism and Appeasement in Australia: Reactions to the European Crises*, Canberra, 1970

AUSTRALIAN INSTITUTE OF INTERNATIONAL AFFAIRS, *Australia and the Pacific*, Princeton, 1944

BARKER, E., *Churchill and Eden at War*, London, 1978

BELL, R. J., *Unequal Allies: Australian–American Relations and the Pacific War*, Melbourne, 1977

BOND, B., *British Military Policy Between the Two World Wars*, Oxford, 1980

BUTLIN, S. J., *War Economy 1939–1942*, Canberra, 1955

CALLAHAN, R. A., *Churchill: Retreat from Empire*, Delaware, 1984

CARLTON, D., *Anthony Eden*, London, 1981

CASEY, R. G., *Double or Quit: Some Views on Australian Development and Relations*, Melbourne, 1949

CHURCHILL, W. S., *The Second World War*, volumes I–IV, London, 1948–51

COLLIER, R., *Armageddon*, London, 1982

CROWLEY, F. (ED.), *A New History of Australia*, Melbourne, 1974

DARWIN, J., *Britain, Egypt and the Middle East*, London, 1981

DAY, D. A., *Menzies and Churchill at War*, Sydney, 1986

DILKS, D. (ED.), *Retreat from Power*, volume 2: *After 1939*, London, 1981

DRUMMOND, I. M., *British Economic Policy and the Empire 1919–1939*, London, 1972

DUNN, M., *Australia and the Empire: From 1788 to the Present*, Sydney, 1984

EDWARDS, C., *Bruce of Melbourne: Man of Two Worlds*, London, 1965

EDWARDS, P. G., *Prime Ministers and Diplomats: The Making of Australian Foreign Policy, 1901–1949*, Melbourne, 1983

ESTHUS, R. A., *From Enmity to Alliance: US–Australian Relations, 1931–41*, Seattle, 1964

FITZHARDINGE, L. F., *William Morris Hughes: A Political Biography*, volume 2: *The Little Digger 1914–1952*, Sydney, 1979

FULLER, J. F. C., *Empire Unity and Defence*, London, 1934

GILBERT, M., *Finest Hour: Winston S. Churchill 1939–1941*, London, 1983
    Road to Victory: Winston S. Churchill 1941–1945, London, 1986

GILL, G. H., *Royal Australian Navy 1939–1945*, 2 volumes, Canberra, 1957 and 1958

GILLISON, D., *Royal Australian Air Force 1939–1942*, Canberra, 1962

GRANATSTEIN, J. L., *Canada's War: The Politics of the Mackenzie King Government, 1939–1945*, Toronto, 1975

GRENFELL, R., *Main Fleet to Singapore*, London, 1951

HAGGIE, P., *Britannia at Bay*, Oxford, 1981

HAMILL, I., *The Strategic Illusion*, Singapore, 1981

HAMMOND, R. J., *Food*, History of the Second World War, United Kingdom Civil Series, volume 3, London, 1962

HANCOCK, W. K., *Smuts: The Fields of Force, 1919–50*, volume 2, Cambridge, 1968
    Survey of British Commonwealth Affairs: Problems of Economic Policy 1918–1939, London, 1940

HARPER, N. (ED.), *Australia and the United States*, Melbourne, 1971

HASLUCK, P., *The Government and the People 1939–41*, Canberra, 1952

HAZLEHURST, C., *Menzies Observed*, Sydney, 1979
    (ED.), *Australian Conservatism*, Canberra, 1979

HINSLEY, F. H., *British Intelligence in the Second World War*, volume 1, London, 1979

HOLLAND, R. F., *Britain and the Commonwealth Alliance 1918–1939*, London, 1981

HORNER, D., *High Command: Australia and Allied Strategy 1939–1945*, Sydney, 1982
  (ED.), *The Commanders: Australian Military Leadership in the Twentieth Century*, Sydney, 1984

HOWARD, M., *The Continental Commitment*, London, 1972

HUDSON, W. (ED.), *Towards a Foreign Policy, 1914–1941*, Melbourne, 1967
  Casey, Melbourne, 1986

JAMES, R. R., *Churchill: A Study in Failure 1900–1939*, London, 1970

JOSKE, P., *Sir Robert Menzies, 1894–1978*, Sydney, 1978

LEE, J. M., *The Churchill Coalition 1940–1945*, London, 1980

LEVI, W., *American–Australian Relations*, Minneapolis, 1947

LEWIN, R., *Slim: The Standardbearer*, London, 1976

LIDDELL HART, B., *History of the Second World War*, London, 1973

LIVINGSTON, W. S. AND LOUIS, W. R. (EDS), *Australia, New Zealand, and the Pacific Islands since the First World War*, Austin, 1979

LONG, G., *Greece, Crete and Syria*, Canberra, 1953

LOUIS, W. R., *British Strategy in the Far East, 1919–1939*, Oxford, 1971
  Imperialism at Bay: The United States and the Decolonization of the British Empire, 1941–1945, Oxford, 1977

LOWE, P., *Britain in the Far East: A Survey from 1819 to the Present*, London, 1981
  Great Britain and the Origins of the Pacific War, Oxford, 1977

MCCARTHY, J., *Australia and Imperial Defence 1918–39: A Study in Air and Sea Power*, Brisbane, 1976

MACINTYRE, CAPTAIN D., *The Battle for the Pacific*, London, 1966
  Fighting Admiral: The Life of Admiral of the Fleet Sir J. Somerville, London, 1961

MADDEN, A. F. AND MORRIS-JONES, W. H. (EDS.), *Australia and Britain: Studies in a Changing Relationship*, London, 1980

MANSERGH, N., *The Commonwealth Experience*, volume 2: *From British to Multiracial Commonwealth*, 2nd edition, London, 1982
  Survey of British Commonwealth Affairs: Problems of Wartime Co-operation and Post-War Change, 1939–52, London, 1958

MARDER, A. J., *Old Friends, New Enemies: The Royal Navy and the Imperial Japanese Navy: Strategic Illusions, 1936—1941*, Oxford, 1981

MEANEY, N., *The Search for Security in the Pacific, 1901—14*, Sydney, 1976

MILLAR, T. B., *Australia in Peace and War: External Relations 1788—1977*, London, 1978

MILLER, J. D. B., *Britain and the Old Dominions*, London, 1966

NEIDPATH, J., *The Singapore Naval Base and the Defence of Britain's Eastern Empire, 1919—1941*, Oxford, 1981

OSMOND, W. G., *Frederic Eggleston: An Intellectual in Australian Politics*, Sydney, 1985

OVENDALE, R., *Appeasement and the English Speaking World*, Cardiff, 1975

OWEN, F., *Tempestuous Journey*, London, 1954

PAWLE, G., *The War and Colonel Warden*, London, 1963

PELLING, H., *Winston Churchill*, London, 1974

PERKINS, K., *Menzies: The Last of the Queen's Men*, London, 1968

REESE, T. R., *Australia, New Zealand and the United States*, London, 1969

REYNOLDS, D., *The Creation of the Anglo—American Alliance 1937—41: A Study in Competitive Co-operation*, London, 1981

ROBERTSON, J., *J. H. Scullin*, Perth, 1974
          Australia at War 1939—1945, Melbourne, 1981

ROSKILL, S., *Hankey, Man of Secrets*, volume 3, London, 1974
          Churchill and the Admirals, London, 1977
          The War at Sea 1939—1945, 2 volumes, London, 1954
          and 1956

ROSS, L., *John Curtin*, Melbourne, 1977

SAYERS, S., *Ned Herring*, Melbourne, 1980

STIRLING, A., *Lord Bruce*, Melbourne, 1974

TAYLOR, A. J. P., *Beaverbrook*, London, 1972
          (ET AL.), *Churchill: Four Faces and the Man*,
          London, 1969
          (ED.), *Lloyd George: Twelve Essays*, London, 1966

TENNANT, K., *Evatt*, Sydney, 1970

THOMPSON, L., *1940 — Year of Legend, Year of History*, London, 1966

THORNE, C., *Allies of a Kind: The United States, Britain and the War Against Japan, 1941–1945*, London, 1978
The Issue of War: States, Societies, and the Far Eastern Conflict of 1941–1945, London, 1985

WARNER, P., *Auchinleck: The Lonely Soldier*, London, 1981

WATT, (SIR) A., *The Evolution of Australian Foreign Policy 1938–1965*, Cambridge, 1967

WINGATE, SIR R., *Lord Ismay*, London, 1970

WRENCH, J. E., *Geoffrey Dawson and Our Times*, London, 1955

WRINCH, P. M., *The Military Strategy of Winston Churchill*, Boston, 1961

YOUNG, K., *Churchill and Beaverbrook*, London, 1966

V Articles

ANDREWS, E. M., "The Australian Government and Appeasement", *Australian Journal of Politics and History*, April 1967

BAILEY, K. H., "Australia in the Empire", *The Australian Quarterly*, March 1942

BALL, D. J., "Allied Intelligence Cooperation Involving Australia During World War II", *Australian Outlook*, December 1978

DAY, D. A., "Anzacs on the Run: The View from Whitehall, 1941–42", *Journal of Imperial and Commonwealth History*, May 1986
"H. V. Evatt and the 'Beat Hitler First' Strategy: Scheming Politician or an Innocent Abroad?", *Historical Studies*, October 1987
"P. G. Taylor and the Alternative Pacific Air Route, 1939–45", *Australian Journal of Politics and History*, volume 32, number 1 (1986)
"Promise and Performance: Britain's Pacific Pledge, 1943–45", *War and Society*, September 1986
"An Undiplomatic Incident: S. M. Bruce and the Moves to Curb Churchill, February 1942", *Journal of Australian Studies*, November 1986

DEDMAN, J. J., "The Brisbane Line", *Australian Outlook*, August 1968
"The Return of the AIF from the Middle East", *Australian Outlook*, August 1967

D'CRUZ, V., "Menzies' Foreign Policy, 1939–41", *Australian Quarterly*, September 1967

EDWARDS, P. G., "R. G. Menzies's Appeals to the United States, May–June, 1940", *Australian Outlook*, April, 1974 "S. M. Bruce, R. G. Menzies and Australia's War Aims and Peace Aims, 1939–40", *Historical Studies*, April 1976

FADDEN, (SIR) A., "Forty Days and Forty Nights: Memoir of a War-Time Prime Minister", *Australian Outlook*, April 1973

HAMILL, I., "An Expeditionary Force Mentality?: The Despatch of Australian Troops to the Middle East, 1939–1940", *Australian Outlook*, August 1977

IRVINE, P. F., "The Implications of Australian War Aims", *Australian Quarterly*, December 1939

MCCARTHY, J., "Australia: A View from Whitehall 1939–45", *Australian Outlook*, December 1974

MEANEY, N. K., "Australia's Foreign Policy: History and Myth", *Australian Outlook*, August 1969

MILLAR, T. B., "A Rejoinder", *Australian Outlook*, August 1969

ROBERTSON, J., "Australian War Policy 1939–1945", *Historical Studies*, October 1977 "Australia and the 'Beat Hitler First' Strategy, 1941-42: A Problem in Wartime Consultation", *Journal of Imperial and Commonwealth History*, May 1983

SIMINGTON, M., "Australia and the New Caledonian Coup D'Etat of 1940", *Australian Outlook*, April 1976

TAMCHINA, R., "In Search of Common Causes: The Imperial Conference of 1937", *Journal of Imperial and Commonwealth History*, volume 1, 1972–3

TROTTER, A, "The Dominions and Imperial Defence: Hankey's Tour in 1934", *Journal of Imperial and Commonwealth History*, volume 2, 1973–4

WOOD, F. L. W., "Dominion Status, 1942", *Australian Quarterly*, June 1942

VI Unpublished Papers

HEMMINGS, W. J., "Australia and Britain's Far Eastern Defence Policy, 1937–42", B. Litt. thesis, Oxford, 1972

PRIMROSE, B., "Australian Naval Policy 1919–1942: A Case Study in Empire Relations", Ph.D. thesis, ANU, 1974

WARD, M., "Sir Keith Murdoch: The Flinders Street Broker", B.Litt. thesis, ANU, 1981

WOODWARD, D. F., "Australian Diplomacy in the Second World War — Relations with Britain and the US 1939—41 under the Menzies and Fadden Governments", B.A.(Hons) thesis, Flinders University, 1973

WRIGHT, P., "Great Britain, Australia and the Pacific Crisis, 1939—1941", M.A. thesis, Manchester University, 1974

INDEX

Numbers in italics indicate pages with illustrations. In cross references, *infra* and *supra* are used to refer to other subentries within the same main entry.